Aztecs,

Moors,

and

Christians

T0385876

Max Harris

Aztecs, Moors, and Christians

Festivals of Reconquest in Mexico and Spain

UNIVERSITY OF TEXAS PRESS

AUSTIN

Portions of this book have been abbreviated or otherwise adapted from articles
which previously appeared in the following publications:

"The Arrival of the Europeans: Folk Dramatizations of Conquest and Conversion in New Mexico,"
Comparative Drama 28 (1994): 141–165;
"A Catalan Corpus Christi Play: The Martyrdom of Saint Sebastian with the Hobby Horses and the
Turks," *Comparative Drama* 31 (1997): 224–247;
"Fireworks, Turks, and Long-Necked Mules: Pyrotechnic Theatre in Germany and Catalonia,"
Comparative Drama 32 (1998): 362–388. Reprinted with permission of
Medieval Institute Publications, Western Michigan University.

"Muhammed and the Virgin: Folk Dramatizations of Battles Between Moors and Christians in
Modern Spain," *The Drama Review* 38, no. 1 (1994): 45–61. Reprinted with permission of
New York University and MIT Press.

"The Dramatic Testimony of Antonio de Ciudad Real: Indigenous Theatre in Sixteenth-Century
New Spain," *Colonial Latin American Review* 5 (1996): 237–251. Reprinted with permission of
Carfax Publishing Limited, P.O. Box 25, Abingdon, Oxfordshire, United Kingdom.

Library of Congress Cataloging-in-Publication Data

Harris, Max, 1949–
    Aztecs, Moors, and Christians : festivals of reconquest in Mexico and Spain / Max
Harris.— 1st ed.
        p.   cm.
    Includes bibliographical references and index.
    ISBN 0-292-73131-0 (alk. paper)—ISBN 0-292-73132-9 (pbk. : alk. paper)
    1. Moros y Cristianos Festival—Mexico.   2. Moros y Cristianos Festival—Spain.   I.
Title.
GT4014.A2 H37 2000
394.26946—dc21   99-057705

Design by José Clemente Orozco

To Richard Axton and Bob Potter,
wise teachers and good friends

CONTENTS

LIST OF ILLUSTRATIONS

Photographs by Max Harris.

ACKNOWLEDGMENTS

WERE I to thank by name all those who have helped me with this book, I would not only end up with a list too long for all but the most determined to read, but I would almost certainly fail to recall someone to whom I am deeply indebted. Even more troubling to my conscience, I would privilege scholars and friends whose names I know over the innumerable local actors and dancers whose names I do not know but without whose devotion to their craft this book really could never have been written. So, I have tried to acknowledge specific personal contributions in the notes, and I offer here a general thanks to all who, by their art, friendship, or scholarship, have made this book so much better than it would otherwise have been. Thank you.

PART ONE
PROLOGUE

I

Beheading the Moor (Zacatecas, 1996)

EACH year in late August several thousand Moors and Christians invade Zacatecas. Dressed in brightly colored uniforms and armed with swords, scimitars, and arquebuses, warriors from European history clog the streets of a city that was once the silver-mining capital of colonial Mexico. Music from a dozen well-drilled drum and bugle corps orchestrates the invasion. In 1996, scurrying to and fro along side streets that intersected the main path of the parade, I saw the Twelve Peers of France battle their eighth-century Turkish counterparts in a massed sword fight that moved slowly across the sloped square of Santo Domingo. And I saw Moorish infantry from the naval battle of Lepanto (1571) fire arquebuses into the air as they passed the exuberantly detailed facade of Zacatecas's baroque cathedral. Above the caption "They'd said they wouldn't burn powder in the city center but in the end they did," a newspaper photograph the next day displayed the evidence: a crowd of Moors, raised arquebuses, and clouds of smoke.[1]

The soldiers are members of the confraternity of Saint John the Baptist, whose unifying mission is the annual staging of an extraordinary theatrical spectacle known as the Morismas de Bracho. Officially, the mock battles, religious processions, secular parades, fireworks displays, and saint plays tell three interwoven stories: the martyrdom of John the Baptist, commemorated by the church each year on 29 August; a legendary crusade of Charlemagne and the Twelve Peers of France, said to have taken place in 770 and to have had as "its sole purpose the rescue of holy relics" captured by the Turks;[2] and the historical battle of Lepanto (1571), in which a Christian fleet under the command of John of Austria decisively defeated the Ottoman navy at the entrance to the Gulf of Corinth. The tradition of *morismas,* which has its roots in late medieval Spain, is believed to have arrived in the region of Zacatecas in the early seventeenth century.[3]

At the physical heart of the *morismas* of Bracho is a small chapel, dedicated to John the Baptist and set in a scrubby basin of the hills of Bracho a couple of miles northeast of town. Behind the chapel, to the west, is a dusty parade ground or plaza, well over a hundred yards long and forty wide. From its center rises a single tree, at whose foot the climactic execution of the Moorish king takes place. On the western slope overlooking the square stands the stone facade of a castle. To the north of the chapel is an open area, joined to the parade ground by a small stone bridge over a dry stream bed ("We used to have a little water for the battle of Lepanto," one of the actors joked). Below the chapel, to the east, is a second parade ground, equally dusty but shorter than its companion. To the south, during the fiesta, is a makeshift market of food stalls and fairground booths. The chapel itself boasts a paved fore-court, enclosed on two sides by covered arcades. The hills rise most sharply, after a brief drop into a wooded valley, to the east. The action of the *morismas* spreads out from the several acres of open space around the chapel to the high peak of the east-ern hill a mile away and two or three miles along the road into the center of the city. It is perhaps the largest "stage" I have ever seen.

When I first arrived at Bracho, merchants were erecting stalls, workmen mak-ing final repairs to the castle facade, and custodians cleaning the chapel. Inside the chapel were two statues of the Baptist, one above the altar and the other on a pedestal against the south wall. The latter's feet and calves were worn from the kisses of pilgrims. Hanging on the opposite wall was a carving of the crucified Christ, painted blood running down his pale limbs. Dominating a poster advertising the *morismas* was a picture of the martyred John the Baptist's head being presented to King Herod on a platter. Sacrifice and decapitation were to be the central motifs of the fiesta.

The fiesta began, late on Thursday afternoon, with the "washing of John the Baptist." The statues of the Baptist were placed in front of the altar, where two couples lovingly cleansed every inch of the images with cotton balls and hand cream. Then the congregation filed up to kneel before the saint, kiss his foot or the hem of his freshly laundered loin cloth, wipe him with scented cotton, and place a coin on an offering tray. Making change was permitted. Afterward, in the vestry, an old man introduced himself to me as Philip II. Proudly he showed me his con-fraternity membership card, identifying him by his role in the *morismas* as King Philip II of Spain. Outside the chapel, the confraternity's priest told a national tele-vision crew the biblical story of the saint's beheading.

I am not sure why the saint was so carefully cleaned. It may have prepared him for sacrifice or it may have been nothing more than a wash and a change of clothes be-fore the visit of the Virgin Mary. A few minutes later, the Virgen de la Preladita arrived, encased in a transparent plastic shrine, her feet surrounded by flowers, and a spray of tall silver foil prongs representing rays of light fanning out behind her. Placed beside an altar overlooking the lower parade ground, she presided over the first mass of the *morismas*. A light rain fell and a rainbow spread across the sky above the eastern hills. It struck me that, because of his association with water, John the Baptist is often linked with Tlaloc, the Aztec god of rain. After the mass, Mary was carried into the chapel. At eight o'clock an audience gathered for the first of two annual performances of a *coloquio* (play) entitled *The Beheading of Saint John the Baptist*. But by then, having spent the previous night on a flight from Chicago, I had walked back to my hotel and fallen asleep.

On Friday morning, I arrived in time to see Moors and Christians take com-

1. *Barbones*. Zacatecas, 1996.

munion together. Afterward, with much noise of drums and bugles, the several companies of soldiers formed up on both parade grounds. They had been practicing every Sunday since the beginning of May. Around midmorning, the troops marched off to town. Leading the parade were the *barbones* (bearded ones), Christian soldiers with long, false beards, black leather aprons, arquebuses, and huge wooden axes (Fig. 1). One of the *barbones* told me that the beards identified them as Spaniards. Another said that they were a kind of "disguise" so that no one could see their faces. According to a written source, the aprons and axes marked the *barbones* as sappers in the service of Charles V,[4] but by Sunday it had become clear that they also signified the key role of the *barbones* in the final butchering of the Moorish king. Next came three Christian battalions, in the uniforms of late-nineteenth-century Mexican or Spanish infantry, followed by Charlemagne and the Twelve Peers of France. The latter wore costumes that ranged from stylized medieval tunics and crowns to the short skirt, breastplate, and plumed helmet of a Roman centurion. Then came the Moors, in baggy, red cotton trousers, white shirts, blue cummerbunds, and a kind of loose, red turban that hung down over their shoulders. They, too, were armed with arquebuses. In their midst were the Turkish counterparts of the Twelve Peers of France and, on horseback, the Moorish king, Argel Ozmán, and his ambassador, Captain Granados.

The armies marched on this first day only to the edge of town, climbing, on their return journey, a series of rough footpaths up to a road that intersects the eastern hill and then descending through the wooded valley that divides the hill from the chapel and parade grounds. Like most movements of the *morismas*, it was counterclockwise, the direction of the sun in Aztec cosmology and the sacred direction of Mesoamerican indigenous ritual and dance.⁵ The midday sun was sweltering. The confraternity had mustered some 450 Moors and Christians for its first outing.

Back at the large plaza, the first of the dramatic narratives began to unfold. Fierabras, son of Admiral Balam, the king of the Turks, issued a challenge to Charlemagne. One of the Twelve Peers of France, Oliveros, took up the challenge on behalf of his emperor. After a series of sword fights, punctuated by declamatory speeches by both knights (who carried their scripts in small notepads concealed behind their shields), the defeated Fierabras was led to Charlemagne and there converted to Christianity. This was the signal for the first massed battle, eighth-century knights clashing swords in the center of the parade ground and sixteenth-century arquebusiers firing from either side, drums and bugles playing loudly all the while. The morning ended with the Moors in control of the castle.

After lunch, the Virgin left. A wind arose, the air turned cold, and the heavens let loose with a display of thunder and lightning and a mighty downpour of rain and hail. The parade grounds turned to mud. "If this is a rain dance," I wrote in my notebook, "it works!" Later, the procession returned without the Virgin, who was on her way back to her convent, and without the Christians, who had formed up across the valley ready to attack. John of Austria made a brief speech on horseback in front of the chapel before riding to the large parade ground, where he challenged Argel Ozmán. Both cantered up and down as they harangued one another. Then, amidst the firing of arquebuses and the shrill music of drums and bugles, the Moors vacated the parade ground, marching counterclockwise around the single, central tree and retreating in good order to the lower parade ground, while the Christians advanced from the far side of the valley, marched counterclockwise around the plaza, and were left in charge of the castle. In like manner, Aztec warriors and priests celebrating military victory used to move around the sacrificial altar at the heart of Tenochtitlan, strengthening the stone's magical properties in preparation for the sacrifice of captives.⁶

The pattern on Saturday was much the same, but the numbers were greater: some 2,100 Moors and Christians marched toward town. The parade was led by an image of John the Baptist, supported by an enlarged group of Carolingian knights. The numbers of Moors and Christians were more or less equal, but the *barbones* outnumbered all the other Christians by a ratio of three to one. Philip II and his half brother, John of Austria, rode in the midst of the Christian battalions, and each army had added a contingent of heavy artillery. Sweating soldiers pushed wheeled cannon over rutted, paved, and cobbled streets.

In addition, most of the Moors carried trussed provisions on their backs: a long loaf of French bread; grapes, lettuce, radishes, peppers, corn, and other fruits and vegetables; a bottle of wine; and a miniature bottle of brandy or rum. By doing so, they signaled that they also represented Zouaves, members of a French light-infantry corps that had taken part in the unsuccessful French attack on Puebla (5 May 1862) celebrated by Mexicans each year on the national holiday of Cinco de Mayo. Together with the Christian soldiers who wore nineteenth-century Mexican uniforms, the Zouaves added the national victory over the French at Puebla to the morismas' official repertoire of more distant historical and legendary referents. Moreover, since the unit was named after its original recruits—members of the warlike Zouaouah tribe who had been pressed into service after the French colonization of Algeria in 1830—the Zouaves were arguably both French and Moors.[7] Moorish costumes in the French colors of red, white, and blue embraced both identities. Folk theater is typically rich in this kind of multiple reference.

Today, the parade advanced to within a half mile of the city center. Along the way, I spoke to an ambulance driver, who said that the heat was a greater danger than the guns, but another spectator told me that a few years back a boy had been killed when his carbine exploded and a metal shard entered his brain through his eye. I also noted the absence of alcohol, surprising for a Mexican fiesta, and was told that the leaders of the confraternity had some years ago banned the sale and consumption of alcohol during the morismas. Now the fiesta was much more "orderly" and fewer participants dropped out. "Why, then," I asked, "are there so many police?" "Because," a friend told me, "we get lots of outsiders who don't know the rules." Once back at Bracho, Charlemagne's knights returned the Baptist to the chapel and joined the other members of the confraternity as they filed through the courtyard to cast their ballots for the new president of the confraternity.

The dramatic narrative for the day began with an embassy of Christian knights sent by Charlemagne to inform Admiral Balam of the capture and conversion of his son, Fierabras, and to demand the release of the holy relics. En route, the knights met fifteen "Turkish kings," whom they fought and beheaded to the sound of widespread gunfire and martial music. As they approached the castle, the Christian ambassadors were captured. Balam dispatched his own embassy, suggesting the exchange of Fierabras for the captured knights, but these Turks, too, were killed. On the intercession of Floripes, the daughter of Balam, three of the Christian prisoners were released, but one, Guy of Bourgogne, was recaptured and sentenced to death by hanging. As the Turks strung him up on a gallows below the castle walls, a contingent of Christian knights came to his rescue. Freed, he joined the other knights in a massed sword fight in the large plaza, while the surrounding gunfire and the noise of drums and bugles filled the air with smoke and music. Once again, the

Moors beat an orderly retreat, marching counterclockwise around the square and down to the lower parade ground, while the Christians took possession of the battlefield.

In performance, the midday plot was more confusing than this summary suggests. The action was spread out over a hundred yards or more, from the castle, across the large parade ground, over the stone bridge, and beyond the open area to the north of the chapel, to a small canopied stage at the far end representing Charlemagne's camp. Moreover, it was impossible to hear the speeches from anything but very close range. I have had to piece together the narrative from printed materials, explanations over lunch, and my own video footage. I did find myself at the foot of the gallows as Guy de Bourgogne was strung up, but I missed the beheading of the Turkish kings. I can now glimpse it in the distance on the videotape. The local audience, of course, knows the story well and is, in any case, less interested in the particular details of the plot than in the visual and aural spectacle and in the climax of the dramatic ritual that was still to unfold in full force and clear view on Sunday.

After another procession, outdoor mass, and late-afternoon rain, the Moorish ambassador, flying a white flag of truce, rode a zig-zag trail down the lower slopes of the eastern hill, across the wooded valley, and up to the larger parade ground, where he delivered a challenge to his Christian counterpart. A thousand Christian soldiers lined the square and the castle walls. When the embassy was rejected, the Moors charged. From the road that intersected the eastern hill, a thousand warriors ran down the trail and through the scrub, pausing only to fire their arquebuses before running on. Where I was standing, near the castle, the defending Christians filled the air with explosions, smoke, and martial music. Three battles followed, represented by massed Carolingian sword fights and by an endless flow of Moors marching repeatedly (and counterclockwise) between the two parade grounds, passing through the Christian forces en route. An account of the *morismas* written in 1925 reports that, on the second day, "the Moors cut off the head of St. John the Baptist, which they carry bleeding on the point of a lance . . . to the Sultan."[8] If this happened in 1996, I missed it. It may be that the evening *coloquio* is now considered sufficient representation of the martyrdom. As night fell, it was John of Austria rather than John the Baptist who was captured and led, bound but not beheaded, around the lower parade ground. For the first time, the day ended with the Moors in charge of the castle.

Shortly after nine thirty, the second performance of the *coloquio* began behind Charlemagne's camp. Billed as a "literary composition," it was decidedly less lively than the mock battles. Endlessly creative in the staging of rituals and spectacles that depend on visual and kinetic effects, folk actors share the weaknesses of other amateurs when it comes to the performance of literary texts. A small audience huddled on bleachers or stood against the fence that enclosed the playing area. A light rain was falling and it was growing cold. After about fifteen minutes, a rival attraction burst into sudden life a few yards away. Afraid that the rain would render his creation impotent, the pyrotechnician had ignited his "castle of fireworks," a bamboo tower some thirty feet high wrapped with a tangle of linked firecrackers, roman candles, Catherine wheels, and rockets that hissed, sparkled, exploded, and fired missiles into the air for the next ten minutes. The actors in the *coloquio* pressed on, but the younger members of the audience abandoned literature for fireworks. Some time after ten o'clock, cold and wet, I set off back to my hotel. The *coloquio* was still mired in John the Baptist's childhood, and his martyrdom looked as if it would be a long time coming.

The numbers in Sunday morning's parade had more than doubled from the previous day. I counted 2,550 Moors, 1,630 *barbones,* and 520 other Christians, making a total of almost 5,000 marchers. Men, women, and children took part, some of the younger children fully costumed but still in a parent's arms. Crowds lined the streets. At one point the front of the parade, having wound its way counterclockwise through the city center, met the rear of the parade still advancing on Zacatecas.

The Moors, who had ended Saturday in charge of the plaza, led the parade. Some, despite a promise of restraint, fired their arquebuses repeatedly. The ostensibly festive penetration of the city by a large army, led at once by the traditional enemies of Spanish Catholicism (Moors) and Mexican nationalism (French), suggested a number of symbolic challenges to authority that I was not yet able to identify. That most of the "Christians" who followed were dressed as ax-wielding butchers and concealed their personal identities behind thick, false beards, did nothing to defuse the implicit threat of the army's march through the city center. At some level, we were seeing a climactic show of force by a burgeoning army of "wild men," who had camped at the city margins, advancing each day closer to the urban heart of civilization. Now, for a few hours, they claimed the streets as their own before retreating to leave the city to its own devices, shaken but unharmed. The action was both threatening and innocuous, hinting at a present danger but sanctified by its devotion to a Christian saint.

When the parade returned to Bracho, the chapel forecourt throbbed with the rhythm of *matachines* dancers. Several troupes danced simultaneously. Some wore tall, plumed headdresses; others, a kind of horizontal, feathered disk, thirty inches in diameter, from which a fringe of bamboo hung down over their eyes. The members of a group from the neighboring state of Aguascalientes had images of an Aztec princess and a jaguar warrior sewn into the white scarves that covered their shoulders. Others incorporated mirrors, sequins, tassels, and several rows of rustling bamboo fringes. Each group had its own drummer, and each dancer carried a gourd rattle and a percussive bow and arrow. The stamping of the dancers' feet further accentuated the rhythm. The basic choreography was simple: each line of dancers traced an oval, passing together up the middle of the two rows and back down the outside to return to its original formation. Within this framework there was room for smaller circular movements and reversals and for intricate footwork.

Each troupe also had one or two "clowns" or "*viejos* [old men or ancestors]," who improvised their own steps, at times caricaturing those of the other dancers, in the spaces between and on the margins of the lines. Unlike the other dancers, the *viejos* wore masks. One wore a wooden tiger mask; two had store-bought werewolf masks. One of the latter had "El wicho y sus fieles" emblazoned on the back of his jacket. Since the clowns also described themselves to me as "*brujos* [pagan priests, healers, or male witches]," this was probably a mixture of Spanish and Hispanicized English: "the witch and his faithful followers." Most of the clowns carried whips, made of lengths of rope, and rag dolls.

A troupe from Visitador, about six miles southwest of Zacatecas, had the most inventive *viejos*. Both wore painted, papier-mâché masks. One was white, with red, yellow, and black markings on the eyes and nose. Framed by a wide-brimmed straw sombrero and a long, white beard, the mask made its wearer look like a kind of bizarre Mexican Santa Claus in a daringly multicolored, padded suit (Fig. 2). The other was a pale, flesh-colored mask, with a wrinkled forehead, an exaggerated nose and chin, and a permanent grimace. Both *viejos* carried rag dolls, about three feet tall, with which they danced from time to time, holding the dolls by the hands and letting their feet skim across the ground. Each *viejo* wore a smaller mask on his chest and had a collection of tiny dolls, each no more than an inch long, pinned to his hat. Later, I was able to talk to the two *viejos* as, unmasked, they sipped soft drinks. "Our dance represents sacrifice," they told me cheerfully. "The dolls depict those who will be sacrificed, mostly *chicas* [young women], but this one [pointing to one of the dolls] is a male. We are *brujos,* tribal chiefs. The whip is to make those who are unwilling take part in the sacrifice. The victims are sacrificed by beheading. The masks on our chests represent the heads of those already sacrificed, and the little dolls on our hats represent other sacrifices."

With this conversation, the unofficial subtext of the *morismas* began to come into clearer focus for me. The fiestas were devoted to John the Baptist precisely because he was beheaded. References to his martyrdom served to license the staging of the *morismas* in a Catholic context. But, together with the *matachines* dances, the execution of the Turkish knights, and the climactic beheading of the Moor, the martyrdom also recalled the pre-Christian, indigenous sacrifice of prisoners of war. Andrés Pérez de Ribas, who served as father provincial of the Jesuit order in Mex-

2. *Viejo* of the Visitador *matachines*. Zacatecas, 1996.

ico in the early seventeenth century, described such sacrifices in Sinaloa, to the west of Zacatecas: "Drunken orgies were held especially when they were assembling for war or in celebration of victory. The beheading of an enemy was motive for a general dance, with much drinking. At such dances, the beating of their war drums could be heard three miles away. Women entered into these dances also. The head or scalp, or perhaps the limb of a victim, would be hoisted on a pole in the central plaza and the dance would be celebrated around it. There would be much barbarous clamor, including insults to the dead enemy, and there would be songs of victory."[9] Moreover, in the Aztec ritual calendar, the sacrifices of the late-August festival of Ochpaniztli were distinguished from all others "by the fact that the victim was not executed by having her chest opened and her heart torn out, but by

3. Human cross. Zacatecas, 1996.

decapitation."[10] When I asked the viejo of the Aguascalientes *matachines* about the significance of his dance, he said simply, "We are Aztecs."

While I watched the *matachines,* the midday battles were taking place in the space between Charlemagne's camp and the castle. I was aware of their clamor, but could not follow the action in detail. I gather that Charlemagne set out in search of his captured knights, that the beautiful Floripes contrived to free the prisoners and to flee with them, that Floripes was reunited with her brother Fierabras and baptized, and that Admiral Balam was killed by Charlemagne. He was not the only casualty. According to Monday's newspaper, a seventeen-year-old suffered second degree burns on both legs when his gun malfunctioned.[11]

For the first time in four days, there was no religious procession or outdoor mass during the afternoon. A brochure published by the confraternity describes the *morismas* as "these pagan and religious festivals." For three days, the symbols of Catholic religion had dominated, but, after the early-morning mass on the fourth day, the officials of the church had retreated and the balance was now more even.

Late on Sunday afternoon, the final series of battles began. The Moors were in control of the castle and the upper plaza. Few Christians could be seen. Then, magnificently, the Christian vanguard appeared over the crest of the eastern hill, a mile away, marching in disciplined formation. For the next twenty minutes, three hundred Christians walked slowly down the face of the hill in the form of a huge human cross (Fig. 3), while an audience of several thousand watched from below. At the paved road that crosses the hillside, the Christians broke ranks and started running down the zig-zag trails toward the chapel. Moorish arquebuses fired in the plaza and Christian cannon sent clouds of smoke billowing across the hillside. Hundreds of other Christians burst over the brow of the hill and joined the race to the plaza, appearing first as an ominous line of dark silhouettes against the pale sky and then scattering into a jumble of red-and-white specks pouring pell-mell down the sere hillside. Astonishingly, when the first Christian soldiers reached the square, hundreds more were still swarming over the hilltop a mile away. In ever-thickening ranks, the *barbones* surrounded the Moors who flanked the upper plaza, while the other Christian battalions formed up with Philip II in the lower plaza. In the chapel forecourt, the *matachines* were still dancing.

For the next hour, boisterous battles alternated with horseback harangues. Carolingian nobles fought Turkish lords, gunfire and smoke swirled around the full length of the plaza (Fig. 4), drums beat, and bugles shrilled. The Christian battalions swept around both sides of the chapel to join the assault on the castle. Philip II rode through the Moorish ranks swinging his sword, the wounded Moorish king had blood on his shirt, John of Austria was liberated, and the castle went up in flames. From where I stood, near the tree in the center of the square, I saw flames leaping up from a combustible frame set behind the stone facade and fading to smoke against the background of the setting sun.

Until now, arquebusiers had been kept to the edge of the square, and spectators had been prevented from coming too close to the gunfire. Now, gun-toting soldiers filled the plaza, the audience was unrestrained, and the performance verged on disorder. Within a few feet of me, on all sides, *barbones* were firing at will. Some were celebrating victory by blowing holes in their own hats, placing them over the end of a gun barrel and firing, sending the hats flying, tattered, into the air. One youngster, right next to me, fired his gun, flung it down, and clutched his eyes. For a moment, which seemed to last forever, I was sure that he had blinded himself and that I was the only witness. Then, Red Cross workers and older soldiers rushed to his

4. Moorish arquebusiers. Zacatecas, 1996.

aid and it was soon clear that he was unharmed. He walked away, blinking and sobered.

Meanwhile, a crowd of *barbones* had gathered at the foot of the tree. One told me to stay close: something important was about to happen. Troops lined up on either side of a corridor between the tree and the castle. The captured Moorish king, Argel Ozmán, was brought into view. Some kind of exchange took place in the crowd at the foot of the tree involving Ozmán and a *barbón* with an enormous ax. The poster had said that Ozmán would convert to Christianity, but I saw neither profession of faith nor baptism. In any case, the Moorish king emerged alive and was taken up the hill to another gathering beneath the castle walls. An axe was raised. Ozmán escaped, running frantically to and fro down the corridor of troops to the plaza, where he was recaptured and led once more to the tree. I never saw him again after he disappeared into the crowd of *barbones*. As the sun set, the axe rose and fell. Two white doves were released into the air. Moments later a lifelike model of Ozmán's head, mounted on a tall pole, was held high above the crowd. The gruesome trophy was handed to John of Austria, who, flanked by Philip II and the Christian ambassador, rode counterclockwise around the upper square, proudly displaying the Moor's head. *Barbones* and other Christian infantry followed. The Aztecs believed that a force emanated from the sacrificial stone, strengthening those who walked in ritual procession around it.[12]

Among the *barbones* were Moorish captives, some walking and others carried, as

14

if dead, on the shoulders of friends. Their shirts were torn and bloodied, and animal entrails protruded, in grisly imitation of severe wounds, from their mouths, eyes, and stomachs. One lay on his back on the ground, his eyes closed and face scarred, a knife visibly sticking into his belly (Fig. 5). In my photographs, he looks quite dead, but, after he had posed, he grinned and rejoined the parade. The gore may have been intended to suggest no more than battle wounds, but I suspect it was also meant to link the captive Moors to their executed king, for it was Aztec practice to sacrifice many captives of war and not just a single leader. By now, the references to European Catholic triumph over Moors and Turks formed a very thin veil over potent signs of native sacrifice.

The gory victory parade circled the plaza three or four times before heading down, past the chapel, to the lower parade ground. As the Moor's head disappeared

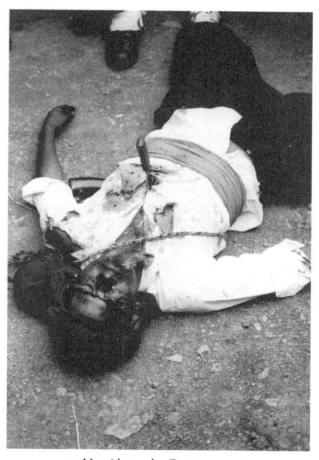

5. Moorish casualty. Zacatecas, 1996.

from view, a falcon was released. For a while, I lingered under the central tree. What I had at first seen only as a good vantage point for photography and a place of safety in the midst of battle, I now recognized as an *axis mundi*, a ritual link between heaven and earth, rising from the place of sacrifice at the meeting point of the four cardinal directions. I joined a throng of soldiers that inched its way into the chapel to kiss the statue of the Baptist one last time. Four *barbones* stood in front of the altar singing "San Juan Bautista is our god." At least, that's what I wrote down. The official hymn of praise, printed in the confraternity's brochure, has a line in praise "of San Juan Bautista/ and of our God." Perhaps I misheard.

There is no doubt in my mind that the last day of the *morismas* of Bracho enacts in barely veiled form a pre-Hispanic ritual of human sacrifice. Unlike the Aztec rites, however, the *morismas* of Bracho retain the critical distinction between mimesis and reality. No human blood is intentionally shed, and the Red Cross is on hand to care for any real wounds. After all, the Catholic mass is also a reenactment of human sacrifice, whose prototype Christians believe to have been ordained by God, and the *morismas* are no more a real human sacrifice than is the mass. (I leave aside the vexed question of transubstantiation.) Do the *morismas*, then, bear a similar relationship to pre-Hispanic human sacrifice as the Catholic mass is said to bear to Calvary? Are they both believed to perpetuate, without the actual shedding of blood, the effectiveness of a distant blood sacrifice? I think not. Nor do I believe that the *morismas* bespeak some kind of hankering after a reintroduction of indigenous religion. The members of the confraternity are devout Catholics. Thousands turned out when Pope John Paul II visited Bracho in May 1990.

Rather, I think that the *morismas* have a political significance. In a colonial or postcolonial situation, indigenous practices suppressed by the colonial power take on a new meaning. What was once dominant becomes subversive. Such practices can therefore be used, without any necessary adherence to the cultural and religious values that they once expressed, as potent symbols of resistance to present subjugation. Those in Mexico who now feel marginalized by the national government, by the rapid process of urbanization, and by market forces that seem to benefit only the wealthy might well identify with indigenous predecessors who were conquered by forces they neither invited nor understood. To join a confraternity, elect your own president, create your own world, subdue (albeit in raucous play) the nearest urban center of government, and finally enact a sacrifice long forbidden by colonial and ecclesiastical authority is to enjoy a moment in which the balance of power seems to have shifted in your favor. Unless I am much mistaken, the *morismas* of Bracho do not express any nostalgia for Aztec religion. Rather, the members of the Catholic confraternity draw, consciously or unconsciously, on a mixed lexicon of Aztec calendar ritual, Catholic devotional practices, and European mythic history to enact a powerful challenge to the dominant structures of the world in which they live. To play at being Aztecs is not to renounce Catholicism but to recall an imagined time of freedom from control by outside forces.[13] The result, in the case of the *morismas* of Bracho, is one of the world's most powerful theatrical events.

2

Reading the Mask (Cuetzalan, 1988)

THE *morismas* of Bracho are part of a tradition of mock battles between Moors and Christians that is long-standing, widespread, and formally diverse. It draws on both European and indigenous sources, and, despite its apparent focus on past heroics, it is equally concerned with present power structures.

The tradition may have begun in Spain as early as 1150 and is arguably more popular there today than at any time in the past eight centuries. Along a broad swath of Spain's Mediterranean coast, stretching from Catalonia in the north to Andalusia in the south and from the Balearic Islands offshore to the mountains and central plateau inland, *fiestas* (festivals) and *danzas* (dances) of Moors and Christians make up a large part of the annual festive calendar. Scattered examples can be found in Galicia, in neighboring Portugal, across the Pyrenees in southern France, and in parts of Italy once ruled by Spain.

The tradition's European roots were transplanted to Asia and the Americas by sixteenth-century conquistadors, missionaries, and traders. Its offshoots can be found as far afield as Mexico, Guatemala, El Salvador, Colombia, Peru, Bolivia, Ecuador, Paraguay, Chile, Brazil, New Mexico, Puerto Rico, the Philippines, and south India. In some cases, the historical referent remains European: Moors and Christians, the Twelve Peers of France, or Santiago Matamoros (Saint James, patron saint of Spain and killer of Moors). In other cases, it has been transposed into a local key: the conquest of Mexico, Pizarro and the Incas, or Spanish settlers and Comanche raiders. Many scholars assume that the *danza de los matachines* is another variant of the same tradition.

Formally, too, the tradition covers a wide range. Some performances are on a large scale. In Spain, the *fiestas de moros y cristianos* in Alcoy (Alicante) dwarf even the *morismas* of Bracho. As many as twelve thousand lavishly costumed participants, armed with arquebuses and detonating several tons of gunpowder, struggle for control of a strategic castle erected annually in the town's main square. *Kāralmān Charitam,* a traditional south Indian musical dramatization of the story of Kāralmān (Charlemagne) and the Twelve Peers of France, "formerly required . . . one hundred performers and fifteen days to perform."[1] Now it is divided into four separate plays. On a smaller scale, the two dozen Moors and Christians who fight on horseback in the field behind the parish church of Chimayo (New Mexico) use swords rather than guns, as do the four Moors and four Christians who stage bombastic tirades and comic interludes in a narrow street in the high mountain village of Trevelez (Granada). Dances may be as long as the eight-hour *danza de la pluma* that tells the epic story of Cortés and Motecuzoma during the first week of July in Teotitlan del Valle (Oaxaca), or as brief as the ten-minute circle dance of Turks and hobby horses that opens the Corpus Christi festivities in the Catalan town of Berga (Barcelona). The tradition, in other words, is united less by formal boundaries than by its common theme of the conquest of Moors, Turks, and Native Americans by European Christians.

The tradition draws on both European and indigenous sources. The Aztec calendar was packed with religious festivals that incorporated dances, mock battles, gladiatorial combat, long-distance runs, and human sacrifices. Activity spread not only through all the public and much of the private space of the capital city of Tenochtitlan but also into the surrounding mountains. These and other indigenous practices have profoundly influenced the tradition of *moros y cristianos* in the Americas. They may also have helped, in less obvious ways, to shape the tradition in Spain. In 1522, two years before the first notice of a *moros y cristianos* in the Americas, Mexican dancers performed in Seville.

As theatrical works rather than historical reenactments, the performances represent the past in order to comment on the present, often interrogating it in startling ways. In the *morismas* of Bracho, the sanctioned narrative of Catholic triumph masks a subtext that invokes the world of the Aztecs in order to challenge current power structures. While such a dissenting voice is not always present in festivals and dances of Moors and Christians, it is common enough in Mexico and in folk performances in Spain to warrant careful attention. The capacity of the tradition to embrace such dissent is one reason it has survived so long in so many different settings.

Rather than cover all possible terrain, I have concentrated on the formative years of the tradition in the two regions where it has the deepest roots and the most secure hold on the popular imagination: Spain and Mexico. An account of the tradition worldwide has yet to be written. My book has four parts. The first deals with the Spanish origins of the tradition in courtly tournaments and Corpus Christi processions before 1521. The second explores the extraordinary array of mock battles embedded in Aztec calendar festivals before the arrival of the Spaniards. The third addresses the confluence of the two traditions in Mexico in the aftermath of the conquest, paying particular attention to the way in which the performances became occasions for discreet indigenous commentary on Spanish pretensions to empire. The fourth focuses on the development of the tradition in Spain and its European dominions after 1521, as the courtly tradition reached its luxuriant apogee and New World influences began to filter into Spanish folk performances. By 1600, the worlds of Europe and America had met, the key elements of the tradition were in place, the aristocracy was tiring of the practice, and mock battles between Moors and Christians were well on their way to becoming a regular feature of the folk calendar.

I will also weave into my story of the tradition's early years accounts of performances I have seen over the last decade. As I began with a description of the

6. *Santiago* and *santiago caballero*. Cuetzalan, 1988.

morismas of Bracho, so I will end with a first-person account of New Mexico's *danza de los matachines* and Oaxaca's *danza de la pluma*. Along the way, I will tell of Turks, hobby horses, and fire-breathing mules in Catalonia; the mockery of Spanish settlers and subsequent Anglo "invaders" in native New Mexico; dramatizations of the Morisco Revolt in Andalusia; and deafening, smoke-shrouded battles between supporters of Muhammed and the Virgin in the Spanish province of Alicante. This will also afford an opportunity to comment on the tradition's interim development in each location.

In the rest of this chapter, I want to take a closer look at the notion of dissenting voices in festivals of reconquest, for such spectacles have often been dismissed as nothing more than orchestrated manifestations of power, aimed at persuading conquered groups of the inevitability and justice of their subordination. In an influential essay published in 1984, Richard Trexler argued that mock battles between Moors and Christians in colonial Mexico constituted a "military theatre of humiliation," in which the indigenous performers, linked emblematically to the Moors, "exhibited their [own] defeat."[2] I will make the case that this was no more true of colonial performances than it is of the *morismas* of Bracho. For now, I want simply to introduce the vocabulary of the case. A brief discussion of a dance that I saw in Cuetzalan (Puebla) in 1988 will illustrate the interpretive principle of "reading the mask" and lead us into James Scott's helpful distinction between "public" and "hidden transcripts." These terms will prove useful descriptive tools.

Cuetzalan is a picturesque colonial town of red-tiled roofs and winding cobbled streets, terraced into the steep mountainside of a subtropical valley in Mexico's Sierra de Puebla. It was there that I saw the *danza de los santiagos.*[3] There were eight dancers in the troupe. *El señor santiago caballero* (Sir Saint James the Knight) wore a miniature white wooden horse strapped to his waist. The five *santiagos* (soldiers of Saint James) wore lightweight carved wooden masks, painted bright red, with golden eyes, eyebrows, mustache, and chin. The masks were pushed back over the forehead, facing upward (Fig. 6). The *pilatos,* named after Pontius Pilate in the Easter drama, were the clowns and villains of the troupe. They fought the *santiagos,* engaged in comic mimicry, and demanded money from photographers in the crowd. The *pilatos* wore pink masks on which were painted a black beard, red cheeks, and a red nose tip. Unlike the *santiagos,* they wore their masks over their face (Fig. 7). The dance ended, late in the afternoon of the second day, with the death of *el rey pilato* (King Pilate) at the hands of *el señor santiago caballero.* The dance is said to recall the legendary appearances of Santiago, charging into battle on his white horse to lead Spanish forces to miraculous victory over Moors and Aztecs. Frances Toor describes it as "the dance of St. James, fighting the heathen on his white horse, . . . the Christians winning and making the heathen ruler accept Christianity."[4]

But Pablo Huerta Ramir, who carves and paints the masks for many of the troupes in the area, told me that the *santiagos* represent the sun.[5] This is why, he explained, the face of the mask is red, its eyes and chin display golden sun emblems, and the dancers wear the masks on their foreheads. "They are," he said, "looking at the sun." Some *santiagos* carry a small wooden shield on which a red face, surrounded by golden rays, beams from a sky-blue background.[6] A dancer with such a shield told me simply that the *santiagos* "are the sun." At the end of the dance, the mask maker added, Santiago Caballero, whom he also called "*el rey sol* [the Sun King]," kills "*el rey pilato.*" Who then, I asked, are the *pilatos?* Huerta was

7. *Pilato*. Cuetzalan, 1988.

evasive. The sun, he said, is challenged by "a less powerful sun," represented by a pink or white mask. The *pilatos* are this less powerful force. Watching the dancers later, it dawned on me that the pale faces, rosy cheeks, and dark beards of the *pilatos'* masks were intended to represent the features of the Spanish conquistadors. My suspicion was confirmed by a spectator who volunteered the observation that the *pilatos* "are the Spaniards."

The *danza de los santiagos* that I saw in Cuetzalan was evidently susceptible to two readings. The Catholic reading, which permitted the dance to be performed at a church festival, accorded victory to Santiago, the militant patron saint of Spain. According to this reading, the masked *santiagos* were Christian soldiers overcoming the infidel *pilatos*. But the indigenous reading, revealed only by the masks, pitted the sun and his warriors against the "weaker" invading force of Spanish conquista-

22

dors. According to this reading, it was the conquistadors who were defeated when King Pilate was killed.

Masks, which are ordinarily thought to conceal, in this instance reveal resistance. Since my experience in Cuetzalan, I have begun to use the phrase "reading the mask" to describe my approach to a wide variety of performances and texts in which, as James Scott would put it, a "hidden transcript" of resistance has been "insinuated" into the "public transcript" of subordination. In the present context, reading the mask embraces two interpretive acts. First, and more narrowly, there is the process of identifying and decoding those particular details of a traditional performance that reveal a reading at odds with the explanation usually offered to clergy, government agents, anthropologists, and other outsiders. These details may be, as in the case of the *danza de los santiagos,* actual masks, or they may be other elements, such as costumes, gestures, or movements, that challenge the official discourse of the performance. Such elements are often easier to identify than they are to decode. Second, reading the mask signifies the broader interpretive task of reading a whole performance and its festive context so as to discern the hidden transcript that the event contains and to which it gives discreet public expression. All this is tricky enough when watching an actual performance. It is considerably more difficult (and necessarily speculative) when working with historical records that may omit, from ignorance or political interest, the crucial details that form the "mask." But, it is not impossible.

I have been much helped in this endeavor by the distinction drawn, in Scott's book *Domination and the Arts of Resistance,* between "public" and "hidden transcripts." Scott writes about unbalanced power relationships, such as those between colonizers and colonized, masters and slaves, or totalitarian governments and disenfranchised people, but the insights he offers hold true for other less polarized but still conflicted relationships. Scott argues persuasively that "every subordinate group creates, out of its ordeal, a 'hidden transcript' that represents a critique of power spoken behind the back of the dominant. The powerful, for their part, also develop a hidden transcript representing the practices and claims of their rule that cannot be openly avowed. A comparison of the hidden transcript of the weak with that of the powerful and of *both* hidden transcripts to the public transcript of power relations offers a substantially new way of understanding resistance to domination."[7]

There are, then, in Scott's model, three transcripts that we must learn to read if we are to understand any given political relationship of dominance and subordination. First there is the public transcript. This is the record of all that takes place openly "between subordinates and those who dominate." It attests only to what those in power want outsiders and subordinates to believe about the nature of social and political relationships within their realm of influence and about the ideology that justifies those relationships. With varying degrees of coercion, it proclaims order and conceals dissent among both the rulers and the ruled. "The public transcript," Scott comments, "where it is not positively misleading, is unlikely to tell the whole story about power relations." For example, he observes, "any analysis based exclusively on the public transcript is likely to conclude that subordinate groups endorse the terms of their subordination and are willing, even enthusiastic, partners in that subordination."[8] White testimonies to the contentment of black slaves are a graphic case in point.

Second are the hidden transcripts, which are more difficult to retrieve but vital to an understanding of political relationships. There is first the hidden transcript of the powerful. "The attempt by dominant elites," Scott remarks, "to sequester an offstage social site where they are no longer on display and can let their hair down is ubiquitous."[9] In such sites, contempt for the ruled may replace a public rhetoric of concern for the well-being of "the people"; private discord may be at odds with public unity; insecurity may appear beneath the brash mask of public confidence. Once made public, the hidden transcript can discredit or even topple a ruling party or regime. The cynicism of the taped Oval Office conversations in the Nixon White House is an example of a hidden transcript made public to devastating effect.

Most difficult to read, because most carefully concealed, are the hidden transcripts of the powerless. Private conversations among trusted friends, hushed whispers in the slave quarters at night, or plans drawn up in furtive gatherings of proscribed societies bespeak a view of things very much at odds with both the public transcript and the hidden transcript of the powerful. The records of such conversations are not readily available to scholars and outside observers. We are saved, however, from throwing up our hands in frustration "by the fact that the hidden transcript is typically expressed openly—albeit in disguised form." Popular festivals, "rumors, gossip, folktales, songs, gestures, [and] jokes" are all, according to Scott, avenues through which the powerless "insinuate a critique of power" into the public forum "while hiding behind anonymity or behind innocuous understandings of their conduct." From U.S. history, Scott cites the slaves' appropriation of their masters' biblical text in the antebellum South: Christian hymns about the promised land were sung by the slaves in anticipation not only of heaven but also of freedom in the North. The condition of the hidden transcript's public expression "is that it be sufficiently indirect and garbled that it is capable of two readings, one of which is innocuous."[10] Such is the case with the *morismas* of Bracho and the Cuetzalan *danza de los santiagos*.

The various ways in which subordinate peoples insinuate their resistance into the public transcript are testimony not merely to human creativity under difficult conditions but to the "tremendous desire and will" of such groups to express publicly, despite the risk of punishment by those in power, the message of the hidden transcript. To speak the truth in the face of the powerful grants a sense of necessary dignity to the powerless, but, as long as the truth remains disguised, that dignity is qualified. The next step, therefore, is to publish the hidden transcript in a way that may claim innocence and yet be clearly understood by those in power as an act of defiance. Supporters of Solidarity, in the Polish city of Lodz in 1983, "decided that in order to demonstrate their disdain for the lies propagated by the official government television news, they would all take a daily promenade timed to coincide exactly with the broadcast, wearing their hats backward. Soon, much of the town had joined them. Officials of the regime knew, of course, the purpose of this mass promenade . . . [and therefore] shifted the hours of the Lodz curfew so that a promenade at that hour became illegal. In response, for some time, many Lodz residents took their televisions to the window at precisely the time the newscast began and beamed them out at full volume into empty courtyards and streets." [11]

The veil of innocence covering the intent of the residents of Lodz may have been transparent, but it was still in place. Finally, there is the moment when the veil is removed and "the dissent of the hidden transcript crosses the threshold to open resistance." In 1988, a normally cautious member of Chile's opposition party looked into the camera during a live television interview and openly charged General Pinochet with "torture, assassination and the violation of human rights." Refusing to be interrupted by the panic-stricken interviewer, he justified his outburst with the words, "I speak for fifteen years of silence." Such moments are charged with political electricity and almost always accompanied by a "sense of personal release, satisfaction, pride, and elation." [12]

Of the several relationships between public and hidden transcripts, the student of traditional theater will be most interested in "the manifold strategies by which subordinate groups manage to insinuate their resistance, in disguised forms, into the public transcript." [13] An outsider's appreciation of the complex and often very sophisticated sign systems of traditional theater often depends on the ability to penetrate such disguises. Success, I suspect, is fundamentally a matter of paying attention to just those elements, like the masks in Cuetzalan or the *brujos'* dolls in Zacatecas, that are at odds with the public transcript and therefore likely to be overlooked or to be regarded as "garbled," "confusing," or "irrelevant."

In many cases, the hidden transcript is consciously insinuated into the public transcript. The dancers in Cuetzalan knew that their masks challenged the dance's public transcript of Catholic triumph, and antebellum slaves knew that their songs of "crossing Jordan's River" anticipated emancipation rather than (or as well as) death and entry into heaven. But it may not always be the case that such insinuation is a matter of conscious intent. Sometimes the unconscious may be at work, and one may be able to read the mask as a window onto conflicts that remain hidden, in some measure, even from the one who wears the mask. Such may have been the case with the concluding moments of the *danza de los santiagos*. After his death inside the church, *el rey pilato* lay motionless at the foot of the steps leading up to the altar. The second *pilato* knelt beside the corpse, moaning in quiet desperation. The *caballero,* his white horse still strapped to his waist, stepped slowly back and forth across the corpse, tears streaming down his face. To a single, slowly repeated drumbeat, the flute played a haunting dirge. There were few spectators. An elderly man took flowers from near the altar and placed them on the dead *pilato's* chest. Then he put a lighted candle at the corpse's head. Finally, the *santiagos* lifted the corpse of King Pilate and bore him at shoulder height down the central aisle to the last row of pews before the church door. There the play was over. The pallbearers set the *pilato* on his feet and all filed back, no longer in character, to the altar, where they knelt and prayed. The actor who had played the *caballero* was still weeping.

It was a denouement of unexpected poignancy. The public transcript had led me to expect a Christian victory and the hidden transcript had presaged a triumph of the sun. Instead, the victory of the *santiagos* was, it seemed, an occasion for grief. The nature of the conflict to which the dance bore witness was not, after all, a matter of simple opposition between Spanish and indigenous peoples. As Mercedes Díaz Roig points out, such "dances of the conquest" dramatize the ambivalence felt by their indigenous Catholic performers toward the conquest that brought them both a Catholicism they have adopted and a foreign domination they have resisted. The encounter between two worlds dramatized by these dances, she writes, is not "external to [the performer], but internal: his *indigenismo* and his *catolicidad;* neither one nor the other can be conquered."[14] The triumphs signaled by both the public and hidden transcripts of the *danza de los santiagos,* in other words, also simultaneously signal the irreparable loss of one or the other of the conflicting heritages still valued by the performers. Hence they weep. It is not, I suspect, an ambivalence to which the dancers could give articulate voice apart from the dance nor of which they are fully conscious. Nathan Wachtel is right to insist that "the trauma of the conquest remains deeply imprinted on present mental structures" in Mexico.[15] The dances offer a window onto those scars, conscious and unconscious, in all their complexity.

We may, therefore, have to modify Scott's suggestion that there are just three transcripts to which we must pay attention if we are to understand any given power relationship or human conflict. For, in addition to the public transcript and what we may now have to call the conscious hidden transcripts of the powerful and the weak, there are also the unconscious hidden transcripts of both parties. The interplay between them takes various forms. In the *danza de los santiagos,* there is both a conscious hidden transcript of resistance to Spanish domination (revealed in the masks) and an unconscious hidden transcript of grief (revealed in the tears) over the impossibility of overcoming the trauma of the conquest without a loss of either the Catholic or the indigenous heritage. To understand the conflict being represented requires that we be alert to the possibility of both conscious and unconscious hidden transcripts being "masked" within the public transcript.

With this modification, we now have in place at least a rudimentary set of lenses through which to discern something other than a "military theatre of humiliation" in colonial mock battles between Moors and Christians. So long as the tradition remains a courtly one, in medieval Europe, such lenses will not reveal much in the way of hidden transcripts. But in Mexico, both before and after the conquest, and in Spain, once the tradition passes into the hands of the folk, hidden transcripts proliferate.

There is just one more matter of vocabulary before we return to medieval Spain. I know of no single term that embraces all the royal entertainments, civic spectacles, church processions, calendar rituals, mock battles, and narrative dances that have blossomed on this particular theatrical family tree. I have therefore chosen to describe all these performances, whether high- or low-born, as "traditional" or "folk" theater. Folk theater is, after all, what the tradition, for all its aristocratic roots, became by the seventeenth century. For some people, "folk theater" conjures up an image of quaint incoherence. But it is the politics of domination and resistance, rather than any lack of sophistication on the part of folk artists, that requires hidden transcripts to be inscribed on a mask of innocent confusion. Switching the masks in the *danza de los santiagos* was not the consequence of rural ignorance; rather, it invested the dance with a richly layered significance.

PART TWO
SPAIN, 1150–1521

3

A Royal Wedding (Lleida, 1150)

THE Moors ruled parts of Spain for nearly eight centuries. The first and decisive invasion took place in 711, and by 732 Muslim forces had advanced as far as central France. Defeated at Poitiers by the Frankish armies of Charles Martel (grandfather of Charlemagne), the invaders retreated south of the Pyrenees. For the next 350 years, Muslim and Christian rulers faced each other across an oscillating frontier that stretched more or less northeast from central Portugal to the River Ebro at Tudela, and then turned east to run parallel with the Pyrenees, north of Zaragoza and Lleida, striking the Mediterranean coast just south of Barcelona. Infighting on both sides of the border radically affected the fortunes of war. The Christian reconquest began in earnest with the fall of Toledo in 1085 and, over the next seventy years, gradually pushed the frontier south, occasionally making inroads into Andalusia, but settling, by the middle of the twelfth century, on a line meandering east from Lisbon, south of Toledo, north of Valencia, and heading into the Mediterranean north of the Balearic Islands. The decisive campaign of the *reconquista*, in which the kings of Aragon-Catalonia and Castile-León simultaneously drove south, disputing their own adjoining boundaries as they went, took place between 1227 and 1248. Thereafter, Moorish rule in Spain was confined to the emirate of Granada, stretching along the Mediterranean coast and north of the Sierra Nevada from Gibraltar to the north of Almería.

On the whole, Moors and Christians did not let their territorial conflicts unduly impede their relationships as neighbors and trading partners. *Convivencia*, the ability of Spanish Christians, Moors, and Jews to live together in a pluralistic culture, where each enjoyed in the other's territory a measure of civic, religious, and economic freedom, was at its height during the thirteenth and fourteenth centuries. Neighborliness did not, however, diminish the Spanish desire to recapture all that had once been lost. The last bastion of Muslim occupation, the city of Granada itself, fell to Ferdinand and Isabella in January 1492, just nine months before Columbus set foot in the Americas.[1]

Violet Alford assumed that the development of dramatized mock battles between Moors and Christians could be linked to the progress of the reconquest. In the wake of the advancing frontier, she wrote, the theme of the expulsion of the Moors "fastened like a leech" onto older seasonal rituals in which "dancing brotherhoods . . . were charged with the calling in of Spring" by leaping "to shake Mother Earth" and "clashing" swords and sticks and making "other noises" to expel "Winter and its evils."[2] But the surviving evidence suggests that the early *moros y cristianos* owed far more to the tournament and the epic than to pre-Christian seasonal rites and is, in any case, too fragmentary to demonstrate an orderly advance of the drama with the frontier. I am aware of very few accounts of mock battles between Moors and Christians before 1492. The two earliest reports depend on secondhand nineteenth-century citations of manuscripts now lost, and the first evidence of a sustained tradition of local performances comes from the fifteenth-century Barcelona Corpus Christi procession, which regularly included a dance of Turkish infantry and Christian hobby horses. Even in the sixteenth century, most *moros y cristianos* were occasional, staged as part of a royal entry or other special event.

Presuppositions apart, the argument for the advance of the *moros y cristianos* with the frontier stems from a reference, in a nineteenth-century history of Spanish music, to a "dance of Moors and Christians" in Lleida in 1150. "This was," according to Alford, "the first Morisca ever invented. The Moors had been driven from Lérida [Lleida] but one year previously, and a hated enemy could hardly have been converted into a Court dancer in less time than that."[3] If dance followed reconquest so quickly in Lleida, she reasoned, it must have continued to do so elsewhere.

But Alford's argument begs several questions, not the least of which is the reliability of the reference (and here the reader will have to bear with a short report of bibliographical detective work on my part). Alford had read the report of the Lleida dance of Moors and Christians in Mariano Soriano Fuertes's *Historia de la música española* . . . (1855). Soriano himself cites as his authority a scholar by the name of Teixidor, who, he tells us, was quoting a manuscript in the possession of "Don Miguel de Manuel, then librarian of San Isidro el Real in Madrid." In the absence of further bibliographical data (or even a first name) from Soriano, I have concluded that the Teixidor in question must be José Teixidor y Barceló, who, in 1804, published in Madrid the first volume of his *Discurso sobre la historia universal de la música*. Unfortunately, the first volume deals only with ancient music, such as Hebrew, Egyptian, Chaldean, Greek, and Roman. Subsequent volumes, we are assured in the introduction, were to deal with European music through the fourteenth century, but these volumes were never published. Antonio Palau y Dulcet remarks that a manuscript copy of the second volume "is in the possession of the author's heirs." I can only assume that Soriano had access to this manuscript. Unfortunately, neither I nor anyone else who has written about the *moros y cristianos* has seen either Teixidor's manuscript or the manuscript he cites. All, including Alford, have relied on Soriano or on subsequent citations of Soriano.[4]

The evidence for the Lleida dance of Moors and Christians is therefore rather shaky. Moreover, it conforms to a common pattern of fabricated nineteenth-century narratives that locate the distant origins of contemporary festivals in "a decisive moment of political transformation . . . and a courtly setting."[5] This is not, however, quite the same as saying that the evidence has been proven false. Before we dismiss Soriano's account, we should at least give it a careful reading.

According to Soriano, the Lleida *moros y cristianos* was performed during a royal wedding. We know from other sources that the bride, Peronella of Aragon, had been betrothed in bizarre circumstances to Ramon Berenguer IV, prince of Catalonia, in 1137, shortly after her first birthday. Peronella's uncle, Alfons I of Aragon, known as the Battler, had died in 1134, leaving no children and an eccentric will. His closest relative was his younger brother, Ramir, who had been enrolled in a monastery at the age of six or seven, but Alfons had named as his heirs three separate religious orders, to none of which his brother belonged. The crisis of succession was resolved, with the approval of the bishops and nobles of Aragon, by the monk Ramir unilaterally suspending his vows long enough to inherit the throne, marry the widow of a French viscount, sire an heir, cede his kingdom and his infant daughter to Ramon Berenguer IV of Catalonia (then twenty-three years old), and return to his monastery. Thus were the kingdoms of Aragon and Catalonia united.[6]

Although Ramon Berenguer ruled the combined kingdom from the time of the betrothal onward, the wedding was postponed until the fall of 1150, some time after Peronella's fourteenth birthday. Lleida was chosen as the site of the ceremony to commemorate the surrender, one year earlier, of the besieged Muslim city to Christian forces led by Ramon Berenguer himself. The fortified place of worship in which the wedding took place had served first as a Visigothic cathedral and then, for 435 years, since the fall of Lleida in 714, as a mosque. It had been reconsecrated as a Christian cathedral within a week of the Muslim surrender of Lleida in October 1149.[7]

The wedding was celebrated, according to Gerónimo Pujades, with suitable "majesty and ostentation," and the city was filled with "many, very joyous fiestas."[8] The details, however, are hard to come by. Joan Amades claims it was the occasion of the first *entremès* (dramatic interlude or processional drama) in Catalonia: "a combat between devils and angels, the latter captained and commanded by Saint Michael the Archangel." There was also, he adds, a "*ball de bastons* [stick dance]." But he cites no source for his information.[9] Scholars have therefore ignored Amades and followed Soriano's paraphrase of Teixidor's source, in which, we are told, the festivities immediately surrounding the wedding were described: "In the cathedral, a Te Deum was sung by innumerable singers, and the prince and the queen were accompanied to the sanctuary by most of the prelates and nobles of Catalonia and Aragon, preceded by a large choir of male and female minstrels and singers, as well as by many dances, among which particular mention is made of a company of Moors and Christians who represented a fierce combat."[10]

The account is not inherently implausible. *Juglars* (minstrels) were common in the kingdom of Aragon-Catalonia and performed at both Christian and Muslim weddings. In 1180 the mosque at Tortosa complained to Alfons II that it was being forced to accommodate too many minstrels and singers at its weddings.[11] Lleida itself had a strong musical tradition. At least one well-known Muslim performer learned his trade in Lleida and left the city "very close to the Christian conquest." In the latter half of the twelfth century, there are several references to *juglars* in Christian Lleida.[12]

There is also scattered evidence from elsewhere in Europe of earlier dramatized combats between Christians and non-Christians: a dance of Gothic tribesmen in masks and deerskin cloaks, from the Byzantine court of Constantine VII, c. 953, that celebrated both Gothic and Old Testament warriors; and a complaint from Bamberg, c. 1060, that the city's bishop was spending too much time "playing the part of Attila the Hun, Amalric, and such-like heroes." Others were soon to follow: the *Play of Antichrist* from the German court of Frederick Barbarossa, c. 1160, pitted Christian forces against the pagan King of Babylon; and, in a prophet play from the Latvian port of Riga, 1204, Gideon was about to defeat the Philistines [sic], when "the pagans [in the audience], fearing they were about to be killed, started to run away and had to be called gently back."[13]

As for Spain, some have suggested that military exercises in the city of Valencia, after its capture by the Cid in 1094, involved the mock siege of a Moorish castle. But this appears to read too much into a line from the *Poema de mio Cid,* a later minstrel epic celebrating the adventures of the Spanish hero.[14] Twelfth-century performances of the poem's lengthy battle scenes, on the other hand, may well have constituted a form of solo *moros y cristianos.* John Walsh proposes that these scenes were the "peaks of epic performance," and that "every adept *juglar*" was expected to have mastered "virtuoso techniques, within a prescribed performance tradition, . . . for performing and narrating battles." In Muslim Andalusia in the middle of the twelfth century, "the staging of a good battle was a standard item in the repertoire of minstrels."[15] One of Ibn Quzman's poems, for example, simulates the voice of a minstrel directing a popular performance of some kind. The imagined minstrel, according to James Monroe, is "a very busy impresario who directs his musicians, singers, dancers, actors, and trained animals, while seeing to the comfort of his audience to whom he interprets the action being performed onstage by commenting upon it." The poem includes "a description of a mock battle and its accoutrements: swords, fighters, Arabs, a warcry, wounds, flight," all of which, the reader is led to believe, is being mimed by the minstrel's company while the minstrel himself sings his account of the action. Since, in Muslim Andalusia, the Moors would have won such a mock battle, Monroe calls it "a *moros y cristianos* in reverse!"[16] Whether the *Poema de mio Cid* was performed by a single minstrel, miming the action as he delivered the lines, or by a small company of singers and actors, Walsh concludes that "innumerable audiences" would have heard and witnessed "the spectacle of the poem," with its dramatic renderings of battles between Moors and Christians, "at festivals and weddings, in the squares and sometimes in the castles."[17]

Few of these early mock battles, with the exception of the Gothic entertainment at the Byzantine court, were dances. Others were evoked by the mimicry of a minstrel troupe or by a *juglar's* words and gestures alone. Yet others were large-scale battle plays modeled, in all probability, on the newly popular tournament *mêlées*, in which teams of knights on horseback charged one another and engaged in fierce hand-to-hand combat. Interest in this competitive military exercise was sometimes enhanced by the addition of a quasi-dramatic allegorical or historical framework.[18] Even if the chain of references back to the "fierce combat" between Moors and Christians in twelfth-century Lleida were trustworthy, therefore, we would need to be cautious in guessing at its form. Early mock battles displayed considerable formal variety.

Mention of a "company of Moors and Christians" precludes the work of a solo minstrel but not of a minstrel troupe of the kind described by Ibn Quzman. Linking the performance to the "many dances" that went ahead of the royal couple suggests a processional sword dance of the kind that still precedes the image of the town's patron saint in parts of Aragon and Catalonia. But this is almost certainly misleading, since *danza* is a term used, at least by modern writers, very loosely in this context, and there is, in any case, no verifiable record of a *danza de espadas* in Spain before 1451. Indeed, the earliest documented reference to a sword dance anywhere in medieval Europe comes from Bruges in 1389.[19]

The performance, if it happened at all, may therefore have been modeled on the tournament *mêlée*. The setting is not decisive in this respect, for Soriano does not tell us whether the *moros y cristianos* was performed outdoors, on the way to the ceremony, or in the cathedral itself. Even the latter would not preclude a large-scale combat. *The Play of Antichrist,* first performed in Germany a decade or so later, has multiple speaking (or singing) parts, and its stage directions speak of armies being marshaled, advancing to battle, rushing together to fight, and attacking Jerusalem. Because the stage directions also specify that the formal speeches be "sung" in Latin, the play is sometimes assumed to be a form of liturgical drama, taking up "the whole nave of some great church."[20] While I suspect that the tournament lists were a more likely setting for the *Play of Antichrist,* an ecclesiastical setting cannot be ruled out, and the cathedral at Lleida was large enough to accommodate a play of this magnitude. Moreover, although the phrase used to describe the performance ("*un reñido combate*") might, at a later date, have referred to a particularly vigorous sword or stick dance, it more naturally suggests even now the ferocity of a large-scale mock battle.

As for the tone of the putative Lleida *moros y cristianos,* Alford's language of "a hated enemy" being "driven from" Lleida is too strong. Later Spanish examples of the tradition stress the conversion of the Moors at least as much as their defeat and usually end with a vision, albeit a Christian one, of *convivencia* rather than humiliation. It is unlikely that a Lleida *moros y cristianos* would have been an exception. In both Lleida and Tortosa, the victorious Ramon Berenguer IV allowed Muslims who wished to do so to remain in their houses for a full year and then to move from within the city to its extramural suburbs, taking with them all their goods and furniture and retaining ownership of their cultivated fields. Lleida's Muslim community enjoyed a significant measure of religious freedom and civic autonomy for several centuries, building a new mosque in the city suburbs as late as 1382.[21]

A performance at the wedding that formalized the union of Aragon and Catalonia in a city where Christians and Muslims were hoping to live peaceably alongside one another is likely to have celebrated a vision of *convivencia* rather than a memory of bloodshed.

In the end, however, the Lleida *moros y cristianos* may be nothing more than a legend. Unless we can locate and verify Teixidor's source or some independent account of the Lleida performance, we must remain, at best, agnostic.

4

A Medley of Battles (Zaragoza, 1286–1414)

IT is another 150 years before we find the next suggestion of a Spanish mock battle between Moors and Christians. Meanwhile, there were other festive combats, including juicy "battles with oranges" between men in galleys that were dragged through the streets on "small wagons." When such a battle was staged in Zaragoza for the coronation of Alfons III in 1286, "more than fifty cart-loads" of oranges were imported from Valencia, where a similar event had taken place for a royal visit in 1269.[1] We will meet citrus fights again in sixteenth-century Mexico, and readers familiar with the annual tomato battle of Buñol (Valencia), during which some fifty-five tons of tomatoes are trucked into town to be dumped in the streets, thrown, and wallowed in by residents and visitors alike, will know that the Spanish still enjoy a festive fruit fight.[2]

Some Spanish mock battles and tournaments in the late twelfth and thirteenth centuries may have adopted a quasi-dramatic frame of Moors and Christians, but none of the accounts say so. The next specific allusion is to the reign of Jaume II, ruler of Aragon-Catalonia from 1291 to 1327, and this, too, depends on the secondary citation of a manuscript now lost. An article in a popular nineteenth-century magazine claimed that, in a sermon preached in the chapel of Our Lady of the Pillar in Zaragoza on the feast day of Santiago, 25 July 1616, Justo Armengol had referred to an ancient manuscript, written in Languedocian, that he had read a few days earlier in the library of the monastery of Poblet.[3] According to this nineteenth-century summary of Armengol's sermon, the Poblet manuscript described how, "in order better to entertain Jaume II on the day of Santiago, the Aragonese [nobles] presented to the court their servants, some dressed as Moors and others as Christians."

The entertainment began with "a pitched battle" between the two sides "in the courtyard of the king's palace." The account no doubt had in mind the large, rectangular courtyard of the fortified Moorish Aljafería, which had served as a royal residence just outside Zaragoza since the fall of the city to Alfons the Battler (uncle of Peronella) in 1118. Because of its well-documented use for spectacular theatrical festivities later in the fourteenth and fifteenth centuries, the building has been dubbed Spain's first permanent indoor theater.[4] Following the pitched battle, the Moors and Christians "went out to the open country that surrounded" the palace. There, in an artificial "castle mounted on a scaffold," they inflicted heavy wounds on one another. But, in the midst of the battle, "a captain of the guard dressed as Santiago" appeared, riding "a spirited white horse." Taking the side of the Christians, he hacked away at the Moors with his sword until they fell to their knees at his feet and surrendered.[5]

Then Santiago's squire handed him a small banner of white silk, on which was painted, by way of explanation of the Christian victory, a flesh-colored cross and the Constantinian motto "*In hoc signo vinces* [In this sign you will conquer]."[6] Seeing this, the Moors begged to be "received into the company of Christians." As a token of their conversion, they were dressed in white tunics with a red cross over the chest, drawn up in ranks to watch the burning of their standard, and given, in its place, a large cross. Afterward, they were led to King Jaume himself, who "was present at the festival." The king placed a kiss of peace on the face of the Moorish captain. This was the signal to begin "a great sport of dancing between the Christians and the converted Moors to the sound of instruments of war."[7]

I am more inclined to believe this account than I am that of the Lleida "dance of Moors and Christians." Although the chain of references back to the Poblet manuscript and thence to the Aragon court of Jaume II is tenuous, the report contains a number of plausible details, and the date of the supposed performance is later. With due caution, therefore, we can venture a conditional appraisal of the entertainment it describes. The "pitched battle" in the palace courtyard would have been smaller in scale than the subsequent assault on the "castle" in "the open country." The latter would have owed its formal origin to the outdoor tournament. If the pattern of later *moros y cristianos* can be read back into this early (and uncertain) example, the Moors would have won the first battle, setting up a Christian victory, emblematic of the advancing reconquest, in the second. Although it is not specified that any but the actor playing Santiago was mounted, the precedent of the tournament *mêlée* and the convention of subsequent festivals of Moors and Christians would suggest that, during the outdoor assault on the castle, he was not alone. Some, such as Santiago's squire, would have remained on foot, while those playing the more important characters would have fought on horseback.[8]

The closing dance is harder to imagine. What were the "instruments of war" that accompanied the dance? If they were weapons rather than musical instruments of a martial kind, did the costumed Moors and Christians engage in a closing sword dance, in which the clashing of their swords provided the rhythm of the dance? There is no known precedent for so early a sword dance, let alone its adaptation to the theme of Moors and Christians. Moreover, a sword dance would seem a strange way to celebrate the play's denouement of conversion and peace. Did the ladies of the audience join hands in a courtly dance with the newly converted Moors? This would have been dramatically more satisfying and, if the actors were not really "servants" but knights in the service of the nobility, would not have violated social order. But why would martial music have accompanied such a dance of reconciliation? A remote but intriguing possibility is that the "instruments of war" were neither swords nor musical instruments but some of the very first firearms, saluting Christian victory even as Moors and Christians danced joyously together. We can only speculate.

There are two other formal elements of this reported *moros y cristianos* that are worthy of note. First, there is the matter of the artificial castle. A castle (or pavilion) made of rich cloths and furs had been used in a dramatized battle of the sexes at Treviso, Italy, in 1214, where women and young girls defended the castle against male attackers armed with exotic fruits, flowers, perfumes, and spices. Unfortunately, a real fight developed and the show had to be suspended.[9] Armengol's account, if it can be trusted, points us to the earliest example of an artificial castle being used in a mock battle between Christians and non-Christians. This will become a common feature, in various shapes and sizes, of mock battles in general and of festivals of Moors and Christians in particular in both Spain and Mexico. It is still prominent in the large-scale festivals of Moors and Christians of Valencia, in many of their smaller counterparts in Andalusia, and, in Mexico, in the *morismas* of Bracho in Zacatecas.

Second, there is noticeable slippage, as is often the case in both ceremonial and folk theater, between the fictional world of the drama and the real world of the audience: the fictional Moorish captain is given a kiss of peace by the real Christian king. The most striking example of this characteristic "integration of the theatre and real life"[10] that we will encounter will be the genuine baptism of several adult Indians, duly instructed and prepared, who received the sacrament in Tlaxcala in 1539 while playing the role of defeated (and converted) Turks. But I also know of fictional Moors in Benamaurel (Granada) who capture an image of the Virgin Mary that is the object of real Christian devotion in the undramatized daily life of the villagers.[11] And, I have seen *matachines* dancers representing converted Aztec warriors take the offering and present the bread and wine to the officiating priest during a fiesta mass in Bernalillo, New Mexico.

This slippage is sometimes an important indicator of the significance of the play to its performers or its immediate audience. Jaume's reported kiss of peace strengthens my suspicion that, from the beginning, the Spanish *moros y cristianos* were more about a yearning for peace and *convivencia* than they were about war. Christian victory is characteristically gained, in the festivals of Moors and Christians, not by superior military prowess but by supernatural intervention, and the victory is manifest not in the slaughter of the enemy but in their conversion. The dramatized Christian goal is not, to use a phrase from modern U.S. sports and warfare, "to kick butt," but to incorporate and to live at peace with one who is an enemy no longer. The kiss of peace affirms the royal acceptance of the Moors' profession of faith and authorizes the dance that celebrates their incorporation into the company of Christians.

The kiss of peace also acknowledges Jaume's authority. It is he who must ratify the inclusion of the converted Moors in the Christian kingdom of Aragon-Catalonia. At the same time, however, the script has him do so in a manner that reminds him of his own humanity. While the Moors kneel and prostrate themselves before Santiago and worship the cross, the Moorish captain stands before King Jaume and is greeted, in a manner fitting for equals rather than for subordinates, with a kiss on the cheeks. If the account can be trusted, I suspect that the Aragonese nobles who designed the performance were making a point here.

On one level, they wished to flatter Jaume. They staged the play on the feast day of his namesake, Saint James, to whom they gave the redemptive role in the drama. Moreover, the manuscript describes their motives in mounting the show as being "to better entertain [*obsequiar*]" the king. *Obsequiar* bears connotations of ingratiation. Jaume's immediate predecessors had not enjoyed smooth relationships with the Aragonese nobility, but Jaume had "won over Aragon from its usual opposition."[12] The nobles may now have wanted to express their support for the king. We are hampered by not knowing the year in which the Zaragoza *moros y cristianos* was staged (if indeed it was staged), but a couple of possible contexts suggest themselves. The summer of 1304 saw a violent incursion of Muslim forces into southern Valencia, culminating in the fiery siege of Cocentaina. And, in 1308, Jaume led an expedition into the emirate of Granada that failed to capture the key port of Almería.[13] Depending on the date, the Aragonese nobles may have wanted to encourage Jaume in his expeditionary plans or to console him for his losses.

At the same time, they may also have wished to remind him that he ruled over Aragon only by their consent. Court documents make clear that the Aragonese nobles considered Jaume II's grandfather, Jaume I, "little more than their feudal superior, with . . . a limited right of leading them to battle," and that, in 1283, they had sworn "not to hold [Pere II, Jaume II's father] for king or to obey him," and to depose him if he did not respect the laws of Aragon.[14] That the Moorish captain in the Zaragoza performance should receive the kiss of an equal from Jaume II rather than pay him homage may well reflect an Aragonese concern to remind the king of their own equal standing with him even as they flatter him. Ambivalence toward those in power is a characteristic feature of the tradition of *moros y cristianos*.

The next century saw, across Europe, the adaptation of the dramatized battle to a variety of topics: Greek epic in the indoor *Siege of Troy* that entertained those assembled for a royal banquet in Paris in 1389; the conflict of demonic vices and Christian virtues for Mankind's soul in the English morality play, *The Castle of Perseverance* (c. 1405); or, at the coronation of Fernando I in Zaragoza in 1414, the struggle of rival claimants for a Christian throne. In this last instance, the festivities included an outdoor representation of the siege of Balaguer, at which Fernando had one year earlier defeated his rival for the throne of Aragon-Catalonia, Jaume of

Urgel. The period also saw the development of increasingly complex scenic devices: wheeled castles, ships, pavilions, and rocks, often made of painted canvas wrapped around a wooden frame and propelled by men hidden inside; elaborate fireworks displays to simulate gunfire and explosions; and, during the reenactment of the siege of Balaguer, "siege-engines which shot missiles made of leather stuffed with wadding, as big as a boy's head," at a wheeled castle "so realistically made that it seemed as if there were really houses and roofs and towers inside it."[15]

Surprisingly, given the long history of the reconquest in Spain, the Crusades in the east, and the growing power of the Ottoman Empire on the margins of eastern Europe, few of these performances concerned themselves with conflict between Muslims and Christians. The quintain, a wooden device mounted on a pole at which a charging knight practiced aiming his lance, usually represented a Saracen with a shield. The defenders at an English joust in 1331 all dressed as Tartars. The king's guests at a banquet in Paris in 1378 were entertained by a *Siege of Jerusalem*, which dramatized the triumph of the First Crusade in 1099. Also in Paris, in 1389, the *Pas Saladin* represented a supposedly historical tournament from the Third Crusade in which Richard I of England and twelve companions challenged Saladin and a team of Saracens.[16]

The Parisian performances must have been quite spectacular. For the *Siege of Jerusalem,* Christian knights arrived in "a well-made . . . sailing ship," propelled on wheels "by people secretly hidden inside" so that "it seemed it was . . . floating on water." The knights then besieged "a float made to look like the city of Jerusalem," one of the towers of which "was so high that the man on top nearly reached the beams of the hall." If the city was the same device used to represent Troy eleven years later, it measured "forty feet high, twenty feet long and twenty feet wide." Scaling ladders were used to climb its walls, which were defended from within by "Saracens." In the outdoor *Pas Saladin,* a mock castle representing Jerusalem overlooked the street, where "a fierce mock battle took place, which lasted for some time and delighted the spectators."[17]

An outdoor battle between two wheeled galleys took place in Valencia in April 1373 during the celebrations preceding the wedding of Joan el Caçador, prince of Aragon-Catalonia, and Mata d'Armanyac. One galley was loaded with Christians and the other with Saracens, although, the chronicle assures the nervous reader, "all were [really] Christians on both sides." Played by sailors from the city's seamen's guild, the Christians and Saracens were armed with "shields and wooden swords." Francesc Massip suggests that, like its thirteenth-century forbears in Valencia and Zaragoza, this was not so much a full-scale mock battle as a fruit fight in which the rival sailors fought with oranges, cucumbers, "and other fruits."[18]

An allegorical *moros y cristianos* took place in Zaragoza's Aljafería in 1414 at a banquet celebrating, as the mock siege of Balaguer had done earlier in the day, the coronation of Fernando I. "A painted, wooden castle," carrying a gilded eagle and six maidens singing, was wheeled into the courtyard between courses. The castle bore the insignia of one of the Aragonese orders of chivalry, a vase with white lilies associated with the Virgin Mary. When a gilded, fire-breathing gryphon, as large as a horse, and a company of men dressed as Moors attacked the castle, the damsels defended it from within and the eagle sallied forth to confront the gryphon and peck at the Moors. In the midst of the battle, the vase on the castle facade opened to reveal a child, sword in hand, dressed in the regal panoply of Aragon. At this manifestation of royal power, sanctified by association with the Virgin, the gryphon and Moors collapsed and lay as if dead.[19] The performance seems to have combined the theme of Moors and Christians, recalling Fernando's renowned victory over the Moors at Antequera (Málaga) in 1410,[20] with the titillating courtly entertainment of a battle of the sexes or the siege of Chastity by Lechery. It would not be the last time that the tradition associated Moors with sensuality.

5
A Martyrdom with Hobby Horses (Barcelona, 1424)

THE Barcelona *Martyrdom of Saint Sebastian* differs from its predecessors in several ways.[1] It was performed annually, the knights rode hobby horses rather than live animals, the Muslims were designated Turks rather than Moors, and it was one in a series of processional dances and pageants. Traces of its battle between Turkish infantry and Christian hobby horses survive in Catalan festivals today. It is, moreover, well documented. It is thus not only the first undisputed example of an annual festive Spanish mock battle between Muslims and Christians, but it is also the oldest root to which current festive practices can be clearly traced.

The first mention of the *Martyrdom of Saint Sebastian* comes toward the end of a list of 108 "representations" carried through the streets of Barcelona during the festival of Corpus Christi in 1424. These began with the creation of the world, the fall of Lucifer, the dragon of Saint Michael, and a sword fight between twenty-three devils and an unspecified number of angels. Stories from the Old Testament followed, including Adam and Eve, Noah and the Ark, David and the giant Goliath, "the twelve tribes of Israel marching two by two," and several prophets. Then came a nativity sequence, starting with angels singing the annunciation to the Virgin Mary and ending with the slaughter of the innocents. The remaining pageants, almost two-thirds of the total number, portrayed various saints, some of them tempted by devils and two, Saint Margaret and Saint George, locked in battle with a dragon. Toward the end of the saints' pageants came "the martyrdom of Saint Sebastian with the hobby horses and with the Turks."[2]

Three other fifteenth-century references to the Barcelona pageant of Saint Sebastian survive. In a contract between the city council and the confraternity of cotton weavers, drawn up in 1437 and supplemented in 1439, the latter agreed to pay "the bearers and all other expenses" of two *entremesos* (floats),[3] one of which bore the "great Turk," while the other carried Saint Sebastian. The pageant was again accompanied by hobby horses and Turks.[4] In 1446, the city council of Barcelona hired a painter, Tomás Alemany, to supervise work on "the floats of the martyrdom of Saint Sebastian and the hobby horses of the battle with the Turks that have to serve at the feast of Corpus Christi."[5] And, in 1467, the "pageant of the Turks" and the "pageants of the hobby horses" appeared together in a shortened version of the Corpus Christi procession staged for the visit of the Duke of Calabria.[6] Since the Corpus Christi procession had first been celebrated in Barcelona around 1320, some of these pageants had by 1424 been part of the procession for some time.[7]

The hobby horses were of the variety that Alford calls tourney horses and the French *chevaux jupons* (skirted horses).[8] The rider carried around his waist a frame of wood and compressed papier-mâché, shaped, glazed, and painted to represent the upper body, neck, and head of a horse. From the frame was hung a cotton skirt, concealing the dancer's legs, with which the animal was made to gallop, prance, and charge. The Barcelona hobby horses were sponsored and prepared by the confraternity of cotton weavers, from which the animals derived their name: in Catalan, *caballs cotoners,* and in bastardized Castilian, *cavalls guodoners.* Such hobby horses still fight Turks in the annual Corpus Christi festivities at Berga, in the foothills of the Catalan Pyrenees, and dance in several other Catalan communities. In Vilafranca del Penedès, they are known as *cotonines.*[9]

The reader may wonder why hobby horses and Turks should accompany a float depicting the martyrdom of Saint Sebastian, for Sebastian is believed to have been martyred in Rome, c. 288, long before the birth of Muhammed or the Spanish conflict with Islam. Legend has it that Sebastian was born in Narbonne or Barcelona and that, despite his customary portrayal by Renaissance painters as an effeminate youth, he was a captain in the Roman army. There, his evangelistic zeal offended the emperor Diocletian, who sentenced him to execution by a squad of archers. The archers provide the anachronistic link to Islam, for, according to some versions of the story, those assigned to carry out the order were from Mauretania, then a tribal kingdom stretching across much of northwest Africa. Since most of the archers in the Roman army were, in fact, mercenaries from either Mauretania or its eastern neighbor Numidia, this detail has a measure of historical verisimilitude. Although the people of Mauretania were not Muslims three centuries before the birth of Muhammed, it is from their name (Mauri) that the general European designation of North Africans as "Moors" derives. By the time the Moors invaded Spain, they had converted to Islam. The legend of Saint Sebastian was thus construed in Barcelona as yet another confrontation between Islam and Christianity. Since the Moors never occupied Barcelona, the executing archers were portrayed as Turkish. This designation reflected instead the heroic military adventures of the Catalan Company in Constantinople, recorded between 1325 and 1336 in Ramón Muntaner's influential *Crónica,* and an ongoing Catalan interest in the eastern Mediterranean.[10]

The contract with Alemany gives a detailed list of the characters and properties required in 1446 for the *Martyrdom of Saint Sebastian.* Alemany agreed to "paint, repair, prepare, and paint again, as necessary," the "float" or "castle" bearing the Great Turk. He would prepare the idol and the canopy for the Great Turk's throne, and provide bearers to carry the float, "as the cotton weavers used to lead or carry it in their time." Further bearers, wearing false beards, would use "frames" to carry a second float or "rock," on which, according to the earlier (1437) contract, Saint Sebastian rode.[11] An artificial tree sprouted from the "rock."

Alemany was responsible for "eight hobby horses with their bits or reins and cruppers and blankets and armoured collars and lances and swords and everything necessary for the said horses and knights, except the little bells and wood [for the frames]"; clothing and properties for the Turks, including twenty-four beards and slippers, from which we may deduce that the Turks outnumbered the Christian knights three to one; "three bucklers decorated with silver moons, one for the standard bearer and two for the scouts, and everything else necessary for all those involved in the battle against the said horses"; a crown, beard, and wig for the Turkish king; a staff of office, beard, and wig for the bailiff; the Great Turk's banner and its pole; and a mace, beard, and wig for its bearer. In fact, beards and wigs were provided for "all those who go on the float with the Great Turk." The emperor Diocletian got a beard and wig to go with his scepter, as did the man who carried "the yellow flag with silver moons." The Christians carried "the flag of Saint George." Beards and arrows were to be supplied for "all those who will shoot arrows at Saint Sebastian."

As for musical instruments, Alemany provided "two large drums with their stick" and a "small drum" with its bells. Sebastian received a cloak, underwear (to simulate nakedness once his cloak was removed), a shroud, a diadem (to signify, one assumes, a martyr's crown), and, according to the earlier contract, the inevitable beard and wig. Finally, the contract required the provision of "the Jesus," with no indication of what he was to wear, and "four pairs of wings for the angels and four pairs of hooks for the said wings."[12] The 1437 contract adds that two judges accompanied the Great Turk, and that the large drum was beaten "amongst the Turks who go on foot."[13]

The *Martyrdom of Saint Sebastian* was an elaborate affair. It involved two separate floats and a cast of about fifty-five. Whether there was any dialogue or, as N. D. Shergold assumes of Barcelona's Corpus Christi representations in general at this time, it was a pageant "of a primarily visual kind,"[14] we cannot be sure. Clearly, it entailed action, for the hobby horses battled the Turks at street level, and it required a device whereby the Turkish archers created the illusion of piercing Saint Sebastian with their arrows.

The contracts also enable us to reconstruct a tentative narrative of the *entremès*. After Diocletian set the action in motion by handing Sebastian over to the Turks, the Great Turk assumed the dominant role of imperial villain. Holding court from his canopied throne and worshiping an idol (as no true Muslim would!), he was served by two judges, a bailiff, a standard bearer, a mace bearer, two scouts, twenty-four Turkish foot soldiers, and an unspecified number of archers. Sentenced to death by the Great Turk's judges, Sebastian was stripped of his cloak, leaving him naked (or, at least, in his underwear), and tied to the tree. The Christian cavalry charged, but eventually succumbed to the overwhelming number of Turkish infantry. The archers filled Sebastian with arrows. The martyr's corpse was then taken down, wrapped in a shroud, and buried, perhaps in a cavity in the "rock." This was the low point in the drama, the apparent moment of defeat. But spiritual victory followed: awoken from death by the angels, Sebastian (or, strictly, his soul) was escorted to "the Jesus," possibly an image rather than a live actor, from whom he received his martyr's crown.

Support for this reconstructed narrative comes from a dance of Saint Sebastian that used to be performed in the hamlet of Valldellop, in the lower Penedès region southeast of Barcelona, on the saint's feast day (20 January). According to Amades, "They used to represent the martyrdom of the saint, whom some Moors tied, undressed, to a tree, after having robbed him of his robe while he was bathing. A pair of knights, represented by lads who rode papier-mâché horses, defended the saint. The protagonist, in order to simulate nakedness, wore only long knitted underwear, something that, if the year was cold, made the spectators shiver." Amades adds that the dance fell into disuse "many years ago," a demise that I assume to be within living memory, for he includes both the melody of the dance and a drawing, "collected by the author," of Sebastian tied to a tree, a Moor brandishing a scimitar, and a charging Christian hobby horse (Fig. 8).[15] The Valldellop dance preserved, on a smaller scale, the core of the Barcelona pageant. Although the action at Valldellop was initiated by the Moors' accidental discovery of Sebastian bathing[16] and seems to have ended without the martyr's coronation, the central image survived: Chris-

8. Dance of Saint Sebastian. Valldellop, early twentieth century. Drawing by Marianne Cappelletti after Amades, *Costumari,* 1: 572.

tians on hobby horses fought Muslims on foot over Sebastian's fate, while the saint, stripped to his underwear and tied to a tree, looked on.

The Barcelona *Martyrdom of Saint Sebastian* was remarkably well suited to its Corpus Christi context, for it would seem that deliberate parallels were being drawn between the death of the saint and that of Christ, whose atoning sacrifice and its perpetuation in the mass was the official occasion of the Corpus Christi celebrations. The Roman emperor Diocletian resembled the Roman governor Pontius Pilate, handing over the innocent victim to the Turks or Jews. The Great Turk recalled the Jewish high priest; both were construed in medieval Europe as the real instigators of their respective crimes. Sebastian's trial before the Turkish judges corresponded to Christ's appearance before the Jewish Sanhedrin. Sebastian, like Christ, was stripped of his robe, which, in the case of Christ, was divided up among his torturers. Both Sebastian and Christ were then bound, naked, to a tree, or cross, where their bodies were punctured by sharp weapons: arrows, or nails and a spear. Both were wrapped in a shroud and buried, as Luke's Gospel (23: 53) says of Christ, in "a tomb cut in the rock." Finally, both were woken from death by angels, welcomed in triumph to heaven, and there crowned.

The *Martyrdom of Saint Sebastian* thus nicely stimulated that mixture of weeping and joy that Urban IV, in his papal bull establishing the feast of Corpus Christi in 1264, recommended to its observers.[17] The pageant invited its onlookers to weep as they were reminded by Sebastian's martyrdom of the passion of Christ and to rejoice as Sebastian's death (and in faith their own) was, by the power of that passion and subsequent resurrection commemorated in the mass, transformed into victory. If every one of the 108 "representations" in the Barcelona Corpus Christi procession were as elaborate and as carefully linked to the overall theme of the festival as the *Martyrdom of Saint Sebastian,* then their combined dramatic effect must have been impressive indeed.

At least once, the Barcelona Turks and hobby horses went on tour without the Saint Sebastian pageant. In June 1442, Alfonso the Magnanimous, ruler of Aragon-Catalonia, conquered the Italian city of Naples. Nine months later, after a successful campaign to subdue the smaller towns of southern Italy, he returned to Naples. His triumphal entry, in February 1443, was staged "in the style of the Roman Caesars."[18] According to Antonio Beccadelli's eye-witness account, the sumptuous procession included soldiers, clergy, civic officials, music, salvos of gunfire, trumpet fanfares, several allegorical tableaux, and a mock battle between Turks on foot and Christians on hobby horses. The mock battle, whose organizers were specifically designated as Catalan, was modeled on or directly imported from the Barcelona Corpus Christi pageant, which Alfonso had seen in 1424.

Beccadelli writes of "artificial horses," each ridden by "a young man" whose foot movements made the horses charge and rear just as a real horse might. Each of the riders had in his left hand a shield displaying the royal arms of Alfonso and in his right hand a drawn sword. The Christian knights encountered "a large squadron of Turks on foot, . . . armed and dressed in the Persian style" with scimitars and fearsome helmets. The music struck up, the two sides danced, and, as the dance became more "fiery," the encounter developed into a battle. After a while, the Turks signaled defeat and fled, leaving some of their number behind as captives. A wooden castle followed, bearing an angel and four virtues, one of whom pointed to the defeated Turks and announced that, if Alfonso wanted to wage war against "those barbarians," he should not hesitate, for the Spanish were ready to serve him, accustomed as they always were to victory and sure that they would not fail. One wonders at the confidence of such a boast, given that Alfonso's obsessive campaign to capture Naples had taken a full seven years and had encompassed many preliminary failures along the way.[19]

The Neapolitan performance adds a few details of iconography (Turkish scimitars and fearsome helmets, Christian shields and drawn swords) and choreography (progression from elegant dance to fiery battle) to our understanding of the Barcelona Turks and hobby horses. More important, the reassignment of victory to the Christians shows that the meaning of such *entremesos* is not constant but changes with context. Linked to the *Martyrdom of Saint Sebastian* in the Barcelona Corpus Christi procession, the office of the hobby horses was to lose, pointing away from human military prowess to the greater victory to be won, even in death, by those who trust in Christ. In Naples, as part of a triumphal military parade, their office was to defeat the Turks and thereby to exalt the earthly monarch who had conquered Naples and might yet launch a successful crusade against the Moors. Formally, the two mock battles may have looked very much alike. Only the distinct contexts and the final moments of the drama, when one side or the other fled in defeat, would have signaled opposing readings. In folk theater, the festive context and the details of each performance, rather than a prescribed literary text or a fixed interpretive tradition, determine meaning.

The Barcelona *Martyrdom of Saint Sebastian* also began to spawn offspring closer to home. In 1402, Antoni Ferrer of Igualada traveled the forty miles or so to Barcelona "to see how that city's dragon and other . . . games from the Corpus Christi procession were made." Two years later, in November 1404, the Igualada city council paid Ferrer for the construction of a Corpus Christi dragon. References to other *entremesos* in Igualada soon follow: a "*castell* [castle or float] of Paradise" in 1406; "*jochs* [games or plays]" that required the participants to bear arms and may, therefore, have involved sword dances, in 1409; a "pageant of Saint

Michael and the dragons" in 1451; and, joining Paradise by at least 1453, a "*castell* of Hell."[20]

The first indication of a Saint Sebastian pageant in Igualada may also come from 1453, for in that year María, wife of Alfonso the Magnanimous, wrote to the city council to protest the presence of "nude men" in the Corpus Christi festivities. Saint Sebastian may have been among those she saw, for when, in 1560, the council banned partially or wholly undressed actors and actresses, it was the roles of angels, virgins, virtues, Saint Sebastian, and other martyrs that were singled out for attention. In 1489, there is mention of a "drummer of the Turks" in the procession, and, in 1587, refreshments were provided for "17 Turks." In 1596, the city accounts record payments made to "twenty-two persons who danced *la Turquía* [the dance of the Turks] and nine who danced the hobby horses" and to "Joan Torrer, carpenter, for repairing the dragon" and for working on the hobby horses. Although no complete list of the Igualada Corpus Christi pageants survives, Saint Sebastian is listed among those honored in the procession in 1604.[21] None of these references explicitly links Saint Sebastian with the hobby horses and the Turks, but the cumulative evidence suggests that something akin to the Barcelona *Martyrdom of Saint Sebastian* was taking place in Igualada during the latter part of the fifteenth century. A final mention of the Igualada "*Turquía*" comes from the 1660 Corpus Christi records. By 1679, the performance had acquired the name of "*la patera*," from the insistent rhythm of the accompanying drum (pa-té-ra, pa-té-ra). Under this name a danced battle between Moors and Christians survived in Igualada for a further three centuries. By 1896, when it was last performed, it had forty-two parts, but had abandoned Saint Sebastian and the hobby horses and moved to the city's patronal festival, held every 24 August in honor of Saint Bartholomew.[22]

Alford cites a reference to "all eight hobby horses" from Valencia in 1437 and another to "a game of hobby horses" from a royal entry in the same city in 1588.[23] Although neither of these mentions Saint Sebastian, we do know that a *Martyrdom of Saint Sebastian* was part of the Valencia procession at least by the early sixteenth century and that it survived as late as 1709, when payment was made to "the person who danced '*el turquet*,' or the part of the Turk, in the dance accompanying the float of St. Sebastian."[24] And, in "a reconstruction of antique usage, followed in Valencia in the last quarter of the nineteenth century," one of the floats was described as "harness makers with Saint Sebastian," which suggests that the harness makers may have taken over the traditional cotton weavers' role of sponsoring the hobby horses for this pageant.[25]

A Saint Sebastian pageant appeared in the Mallorcan Corpus Christi procession in 1424. Since "new heads" were made for the procession's "old hobby horses" in

1458, it is probable that Saint Sebastian and the hobby horses were linked there, too.[26] The *cavallets* (hobby horses) of Pollensa (Mallorca), which "retain much of their traditional purity," still dance on the feast day of Saint Sebastian (20 January).[27] Farther afield, we know that there was a Saint Sebastian pageant in Salamanca's Corpus Christi procession by the beginning of the sixteenth century. Between 1500 and 1531, payments were made for several items, including a mask, a diadem, painted arrows, lengths of cloth, and wig rental "for Saint Sebastian," as well as to the actors who played the saint, a "duke or judge," and two "torturers," for whom "skins of kid goats" were also provided. Hobby horses first appear in the Salamanca Corpus Christi records in 1531, and a sword dance is mentioned on several occasions, but there is no indication that either was linked to Saint Sebastian.[28]

As for Barcelona, it would appear that the hobby horses and their riders were fighting "little devils" rather than Turks by the middle of the seventeenth century. Expense lists from both 1642 and 1694 link the procession's hobby horses and devils but make no mention of Turks.[29] We know that the city's Corpus Christi procession was suspended during the War of Spanish Succession (1701–1714) and that, when the festivities resumed in 1715, the best-known figures were gradually reintroduced. The hobby horses reappeared in 1717, linked once again with devils rather than Turks. There is no mention of a pageant of Saint Sebastian.[30] The disapproval of the Bourbon monarchy during the eighteenth century exerted further pressure on the dramatic elements of the Spanish Corpus Christi in general.[31] The hobby horses appeared intermittently in the Barcelona procession "until the beginning of the nineteenth century," by which time they were in the company of a "stick dance."[32] By 1807, if the *Auca de la processó,* a series of popular illustrations and rhyming couplets that told the story of the Barcelona Corpus Christi procession, is correct, some of the hobby horses were ridden by Turkish archers.[33]

Although this is the last we hear of "the martyrdom of Saint Sebastian with the hobby horses and the Turks" in Barcelona, traces of the tradition survive in the smaller towns and villages of Catalonia and the Balearic Islands. While Valldellop's dance of Saint Sebastian seems to have been the last instance of an explicit narrative link between Saint Sebastian and the hobby horses, there are still cases of hobby horses appearing each year on the saint's feast day. The Pollensa (Mallorca) *cavallets* dance each year on 20 January, as, according to Amades, do those of Sant Feliu de Guíxols. There the horse is shaped unusually like a large tray around the dancer's waist and is preceded by a carnivalesque character with cushions inside his shirt and a sprig of gorse in his hand.[34] In neither case, however, to the best of my knowledge, do the horses engage in mock combat.

The *cavallets* of Sant Feliu de Pallerols, however, are divided into two teams of four who are said to represent Saracens and Christians and to engage in a battle that recalls a local eighth-century Christian victory.[35] Alford, who saw the dance in the 1930s, wrote that the hobby horses there "have no enemy to fight. They perform mock jousting instead."[36] Twenty years later, John Langdon-Davies remarked of the dance that "medieval [Christian] knights . . . fight a rhythmic and highly success-ful battle against Moors."[37] Neither is quite correct. Although there is little distinc-tion in dress between the two sides, the dancers told me, when I saw them perform in May 1996, that they represent "*moros y cristianos.*" When asked who won, they said, "No one; we just keep fighting."

Although the first surviving record of hobby horses in Sant Feliu de Pallerols dates only from 1801, the nucleus of the dance is thought to be much older.[38] Of the four parts into which the dance is divided, the second is generally believed to be "the central, original, and primitive nucleus of the pageant."[39] During this se-quence, the two sides repeatedly charge one another, lances (or, in the case of the two captains, swords) raised for attack. Two giants, each made of a costumed wooden frame and a papier-mâché head supported by a dancer who sees only through a tiny window in the character's waist, charge alongside one or other of the teams of *cavallets* (Fig. 9). One giant is male, dark-skinned, and turbaned; the other is female and pale-skinned. Possibly the riders are identified as Moors or Christians by the giant who joins their charge. Amades judges the Sant Feliu de Pallerols *ball de cav-allets,* which lasts about twenty minutes, to be "the most complete of those that have come down to us."[40] It is certainly the most elaborately choreographed and skillfully executed hobby horse dance that I have seen. Although the dance is per-formed at Pentecost, there is still, according to the town archivist, a link with Saint Sebastian: "At Sant Feliu, devotion to Saint Sebastian is long-standing. Data from the thirteenth century confirm the existence of a chapel dedicated to the martyr. Thus, we should bear in mind the possible connection between the performance of the hobby horses and the spiritual rootedness of the saint in the community."[41] The tiny chapel survives, and a mass is held there every 20 January.

Berga is the only town that has preserved the Corpus Christi setting of the "*en-tremès dels turcs i cristians*" and the original distinction between Christian cavalry and Turkish infantry. Berga's weeklong Corpus Christi festival is better known as the Patum, after the rhythmic striking of the big bass drum (pa-túm, pa-túm) that accompanies the festivities. The first record of a Corpus Christi procession in Berga dates from 1527. The "*turcs i cavallets*" were part of the first surviving enumeration of Patum *entremesos* in 1632.[42]

The dance begins with "a bright brassy march" as four Turkish foot soldiers, four Christian knights on hobby horses, and their handlers push against the crowd to

9. Hobby horses and giants. Sant Feliu de Pallerols, 1996.

clear a small circle near the center of the densely packed square. The dancers form two rows and bow to the authorities in the balcony of the town hall. "Then, the music turns to a 2/4 time. The Turks form an inner circle," which "skips" in a counterclockwise direction, while the horses form an outer circle, which gallops clockwise, "the last *cavallet* spinning on himself. When the music reaches its cadence, each *turc* strikes the wooden block in the hand of the nearest *cavallet* with his scimitar. The melody and the blow is repeated three times." On the last repetition, the riders draw their daggers, some tossing them in the air and catching them again, and three of the four Turks "kneel in submission." [43]

Berga's dance of Turks and hobby horses is a simpler, rowdier dance than the intricately choreographed dance of hobby horses of Sant Feliu de Pallerols. The Patum as a whole, to which we will return in Chapter 20, is one of the world's great communal festivals. As for hobby horses, we will meet them again in the New World.

6
A Game of Canes (Jaén, 1462)

EVERY report of a mock battle between Moors and Christians before the middle of the fifteenth century comes from territory controlled by the rulers of Aragon-Catalonia. There is no mention of the tradition in Castile-León until 1462,[1] when Miguel Lucas de Iranzo, governor of the southern frontier town of Jaén, presided over a *juego de cañas* (game of canes) in which half of the participants dressed as Moors and the other half as Christians. The *juego de cañas* was a form of "equestrian exercise," introduced to Spain by the Moors, which required teams of some thirty knights to charge one another at full gallop while hurling spears made of reed, rush, or bamboo canes and defending themselves with shields.

Miguel Lucas was the son of a poor farmer. Through noble patronage, he had been introduced to the royal court, where he became a favorite of the future Enrique IV. A patent of nobility, a substantial annual income from royal taxes, and marriage to a wealthy heiress were among the benefits he enjoyed. A few years after Enrique's coronation in 1454, Lucas fell out of favor, but he wisely negotiated, in return for his departure from court, the retention of his title and income and an appointment to govern the city of his choice. In 1460, he chose Jaén, a fortress city on the troublesome frontier with Granada, close to the official Moorish enemy and on the margins of growing national unrest. A bitter struggle for power between the king and various noble factions plunged Castile into civil war between 1464 and 1468. The anarchy ended only with Enrique's death and his half sister Isabella's ascent to the throne in 1474. Loyal to the king, Lucas avoided the worst of the quarrel. He was content to consolidate his own power in Jaén, to lead bloody incursions into the kingdom of Granada (while, at other times, entertaining Moorish guests), and, especially in the early years of his governorship, to sponsor one lavish fiesta after another. His death in 1473, at the hands of an unknown assassin, probably had more to do with local than with national politics: he is believed by many to have been killed over his defense of Jaén's *conversos* (Jewish converts to Christianity).[2]

A detailed eye-witness account of Lucas's years in Jaén survives.[3] From it, we can learn much of the theatrical side of Lucas's festivities. In 1462, for example, over a dozen knights, Lucas among them, rode through Jaén wearing masks and crowns "in commemoration of the three Magi." Pausing before Lucas's house, they doffed their masks and tilted at the ring for "two or three hours," an exercise at which, the chronicler assures us, the governor "shone." Dinner followed, after which "a noble lady on a little ass entered the room, with a boy child in her arms; she represented our Lady the Virgin Mary with her blessed and glorious son; and with her [was] Joseph." Lucas, who had been sitting with his wife, sister, mother, and other

noblewomen, yielded his seat to the Virgin (no mention is made of Joseph's seating arrangements) and went into an adjacent room. He returned shortly with two
fifteen-year-old pages, all three "well dressed, with masks and crowns on their
heads, in the manner of the three Magi, and each with a cup in his hands containing gifts." Following a star, which was moved by means of a cord strung across the
room, they approached the Virgin and Child and offered gifts, to the accompaniment of "a very great noise of trumpets, drums, and other instruments."[4]

A performance such as this, which seated the Virgin Mary among the women
of the governor's family and cast Lucas himself as the senior of three wise kings paying chivalric homage to virtuous womanhood, may well have been intended "for
devotion," but it also seems to have been designed to exalt Lucas and his family in
the eyes of its audience. It displays, too, an ease with anachronism and a characteristic slippage between the fictional world of the drama and the real world of the audience. While the nativity of Christ is being restaged in Lucas's dining room, the
real fifteenth-century governor yields his seat to the represented first-century Virgin, leaving her to chat with his real wife and mother. He then dons the costume
of a wise man to pay homage simultaneously and across the centuries to Virgin,
wife, and mother.

The representation of the Magi took place annually between 1461 and 1464. On
other occasions, dancing *momos* (bizarrely masked figures whose arrival signified
the beginning of a dance) and short theatrical "inventions" entertained the governor's guests.[5] There were also mock battles using unorthodox weapons. In 1461,
Lucas took part in an "egg battle." On Easter Monday, Lucas and his friends gathered in a tower and on the galleries of his house, as well as in the streets outside. An
artificial, wooden castle was wheeled into view, triggering a mock battle between
those of the house and those in the castle, in which some "nine or ten thousand
eggs" were hurled and broken. As if this weren't enough eggs, boiled eggs and fresh
cheese were then served to all present. The *combate de huevos* was repeated in 1463.
Earlier that year, during carnival week, "three or four Moorish knights of the King
of Granada" had been treated to a seventy-two-hour reception. On Tuesday, by order of the court fool, the victor at tilting at the ring was set upon by "all the pages,"
armed with "leather clubs stuffed with wool." The subsequent distribution of food
may have been so generous that guests began hitting one another with, rather than
eating, surplus chickens. Finally, there were dances by masked *momos* and a mock
battle between 150 men, each of whom wore a protective helmet and was armed
with three or four dried pumpkins. These fights may have been "burlesques of the
equestrian combats," a kind of mockery of the knights' own mock battles.[6]

For the most part, however, Jaén's mock battles in the early 1460s were opportunities for Lucas and his knights to hone and display their military skills. The

chronicle is replete, at times almost on a daily basis, with *juegos de cañas* and other varieties of tournament *mêlées*. Most of these were competitive exercises with no dramatic framework. Sometimes, however, the knights dressed as Moors and Christians, thereby enhancing the spectacle and predetermining the outcome. In 1465, the visit of the Magi was not staged, because the governor's wife was in labor. Instead, on the evening of January 7, when the *condesa* had safely given birth to a daughter, "two hundred Christian knights" and "two hundred Moorish knights with false, blackened beards" skirmished and engaged in "war games" in the square outside, to the sound of church bells, trumpets, drums, and *añafiles* (Moorish trumpets), and by the light of lanterns and torches. The new mother no doubt hated the din! On other occasions, all the combatants dressed as Moors. This may have been a way of retaining the competitive element of the war games, or, more likely, a preference for such exotic costumes as "Moorish shirts and Turkish bonnets and elegant *almayzares* [gauze veils worn by Moors] and Moorish hoods, well made and of very fine material."[7] Those who today prefer to dress as Moors rather than Christians in Valencian festivals of Moors and Christians often invoke the argument that "the Moors get the better costumes."

When Enrique IV visited Jaén in February 1464, the predominance of Moorish costumes appears to have been designed to portray the king as a hero who could ride unscathed through (or at least along the borders of) Moorish territory. As he approached the city, under escort by Lucas's knights, the king was met by "as many as five hundred horses, well harnessed, [their riders] hooded in the Moorish fashion and wearing false beards." This mimetic Moorish cavalry, carrying "very thick *cañas*" tipped with "silver-plated corks" that "truly looked like spears," skirmished for a while before the king. Perhaps Lucas's troops drove them off, for, a little further on, "some thirty men [*onbres*], cross-dressed as Moorish women [*moras*], with tambourines and rattles," appeared, wailing loudly over the loss of their men in battle. Yet further on, "four thousand boys" in "wicker hobby horses" appeared, dressed in white Moorish tunics and hoods and accompanied by drums. Finally, "another thousand boys" armed with toy crossbows made of supple osier or willow twigs fought a mock battle. We are not told whether Lucas's troops drove off the diminutive Moors or whether it was more impressive for the king to pass unharmed through the midst of a Moorish army whose threat was represented as childish. In any case, there seems to have been some reference to the king's recent visit to Gibraltar, which he had inspected for the first time since its recapture from the Moors in 1462, and his subsequent northward passage along the edge of Moorish territory. Meeting Lucas and his retinue in Alcalá la Real, to the south of Jaén, the king had joined forces with the governor in attacks on Montefrío, just across the border, demolishing two watchtowers, killing two Moors, and wounding others. The king's arrival in Jaén was thus portrayed as a triumphal entry. The Moors, on the other hand, were disparaged by being played as easily defeated men, by cross-dressed mourning "women," and by children with toy weapons and horses.[8]

A more detailed script framed the game of canes fought on the day after Christmas 1462.[9] Earlier in the year, Lucas had conducted several successful raids deep into Moorish territory, burning, pillaging, and returning to Jaén in triumph with captive Moors, livestock, and jewels. The Christmas "invention" pretended that word of these reversals had reached both Morocco and Mecca. After lunch, "the prophet Muhammed" arrived "with great ceremony" in front of Lucas's house, riding a richly decorated mule and clutching the Koran and other books of Islamic law. He rode under a canopy of lush cloth, held aloft by four "*alfaquíes* [Muslim doctors of law]." Behind him came "many trumpets and drums," "the king of Morocco," and a hundred of Lucas's best knights, wearing Moorish garb and false beards. Two of the Moors then rode to the governor's door, where they announced that they wished to deliver a letter from their king.

Being well received, they dismounted and entered a large room, where Lucas, his wife, and many of his well-dressed friends awaited them. The letter, which was no doubt read aloud, began by saluting "the valiant, strong, and noble knight, don Miguel Lucas, governor of Castile." "I have heard," the king wrote, "of the great destruction and shedding of blood that you, honored knight, have inflicted on the Moors of the king of Granada, my uncle." Struck by the contrast between the apparent forgetfulness of Muhammed and the help afforded by the Christian God in these battles, the king proposed to test their respective supernatural powers in a *juego de cañas*. "If your God," he wrote, "helps you to come out on top in this game as he has in war, then I and my Moors will forswear our prophet Muhammed and the books of our law." This is the first recorded instance of a feature that will become very common in subsequent *moros y cristianos*: the initiation of mock battles by the formal delivery of a letter or prepared speech by a royal ambassador.

Lucas accepted the challenge, ordering another hundred of his best knights to "play canes with the Moors." Since the *juego de cañas* itself had been introduced to Spain by the Moors, the stage was set for a dramatization of Christians beating the Moors at their own game. The chronicler does not offer a detailed description of the contest, other than to tell us that it took place in a square near the governor's house. But, if it followed the general pattern of such games, it began with the entry of each side's seconds, who greeted one another in the center of the plaza, retired, and then returned with a train of pack mules, lavishly harnessed and loaded with decorated canes. Then the colorfully dressed knights rode into the plaza, divided into several bands of Moors and Christians. Each knight carried in his left hand a shield with the band's device and motto. Ordinarily, there were eight bands of six or eight knights apiece, but the number of participants in this instance was greater and required either more or larger bands. The several bands joined forces into two large groups, Moors at one end of the plaza and Christians at the other. After galloping at one another in opposed pairs, they drew their swords and brandished them with great flourish and dexterity. Then, they formed up again in their bands, took canes three to four meters in length, charged the full length of the plaza hurling their canes at one other and defending themselves with shields, and returned at a gallop to the starting point.[10]

The *juego de cañas* lasted more than three hours until "the horses could no longer move." Conceding defeat, the king of Morocco, preceded by Muhammed and followed by "all his Moors," approached the governor. He acknowledged that the Christian God had proved himself to be a help in the game as he had in battle. "Your law is better than ours," the king concluded. "And, since this is so, I and my Moors renounce the Koran and our prophet Muhammed." To prove his commitment, he seized Muhammed's books of law and threw them to the ground. This dramatic conversion initiated a noisy parade across town, enlivened by trumpets, drums, and "many joyous shouts," to the Church of the Magdalena, a site surely chosen for its architectural reminder of Christian reconquest. The church, which still stands, is built over a former mosque, whose minaret now serves as a Christian bell tower. A patio at the rear preserves a pool used in Moorish times for ritual ablutions. The actor playing Muhammed was thrown into this pool and a pitcher of water was poured over the head of the king of Morocco in a token baptism. Then, as a sign of submission to Christian civil authority in general and to the governor of Jaén in particular, the king and all the Moors kissed Lucas's hand. Finally, all returned noisily to the governor's house for a festive distribution of wine and fruit.[11]

The performance embodied several layers of symbolic territorial appropriations and, once again, considerable temporal and spatial slippage between the fictional world of the drama and the real world of the audience. In a city from which, earlier in the year, fatal raids had been launched into Moorish territory, real Christians beat fictional Moors (played by real Christians) at their own game of canes. The Christian appropriation of, and (albeit fictional) victory over Moors in, an Arabic sport was a symbolic conquest of no small emotional significance. (Consider how embarrassing it is for Team USA to be beaten by Cubans in Olympic baseball.) A fictional king of Morocco then recognized the religious import both of the scripted loss on the playing field and of the unscripted losses on the battlefield and led his troops in renunciation of Muhammed and his law, a second representation of Christian conquest, this time in the spiritual arena of ideology and faith. Then, the fictional seventh-century Muhammed was unceremoniously dunked and the fictional fifteenth-century king mimetically baptized outside a church, which had colonized a mosque, in a pool once used by real Moors for ritual washing. The once sacred Moorish space, already historically conquered by Christian soldiers and priests, was thus dramatically reconquered by being put to fictive Christian purposes. Finally, the fictional Moors paid homage to the real Spanish governor, the point of contact between actors' lips and governor's hand marking the physical boundary between fiction and life, and all (real Christians and fictional Moors) feasted on wine and fruit cultivated according to methods first developed in that region centuries ago by real Moorish farmers.

Joseph Roach has written that the Mardi Gras Indian gangs in New Orleans, whose African American members roam the streets each year dressed as fancy Indians, "perform a rite of territory repossessed." He explains more fully: "I believe that one deep purpose of the gangs, their secret preparations, and their spectacular but nomadic performances is publicly to imagine a space, a continent, from which the white man and his culture have vanished or retreated to the peripheries."[12] One could say much the same of *moros y cristianos* performed by indigenous peoples in Mesoamerica over the last five hundred years. But it is not quite the same in Spain. It is true that the tradition of *moros y cristianos* was developed there to imagine and to celebrate the repossession of territory. One could argue, too, that many late-medieval Spaniards imagined a peninsula from which dark-skinned Africans and their culture had vanished or retreated to the peripheries. But, at least in Jaén, a more complicated vision of the Christian reappropriation of Moorish territory was at work.

The territory really possessed by the actors within the fiction of the drama was both ludic (the other's game) and sacred (the other's place of worship). Together, these symbolic territories pointed away from themselves to land still held by real Moors and therefore not yet possessed by their Christian neighbors. The direction of symbolic transfer, however, was not all one way. To enact the defeat and conversion of the Moors, Lucas's Christian knights spent three hours playing a Moorish game and ended up at a church whose bell tower was a minaret. The Moors in play were converted by Christians who had in life learned to imitate Moors. Who had become like whom? The Moorish heritage in southern Spain, in everything from place-names to architecture, agriculture, and facial features, is still stronger than the Greco-Roman heritage in the rest of Europe. The defeated other may, in some ways, exert greater influence on disputed territory than the conquering self.

The festivities in Jaén, then, imagined and embodied, consciously or unconsciously, not so much a territory cleansed of Moorish influence as a kind of local "land of Cockaigne,"[13] in which Christians took the best of Moorish culture and improved rather than expelled it, Moors became Christians, and all together played and feasted abundantly. This is an ethnocentric vision, to be sure, staged by and for

Christians alone; no *moros y cristianos* were performed for the Moorish visitors to Jaén in 1463. And it is arguably an eccentric vision. Lucas's passion for tournaments was exceptional for his time. Richard Barber and Juliet Barker, in their comprehensive study of the medieval tournament, note that "the reign of . . . Enrique IV saw the almost complete disappearance of court jousts" in Spain, and that those held in Jaén in the early 1460s were "the last we hear of the sport in the troubled years before the union of Spain under Ferdinand and Isabella."[14] Chivalry, too, was in decline. Moorish knights, who had once been regarded as noblemen of equal stature with their Christian counterparts, were no longer so generally esteemed. The fifteenth century, by and large, saw a "breakdown of *convivencia*"[15] and ended, after the unification of Spain under Ferdinand and Isabella in 1474, with the conquest of Granada and the expulsion of both Moors and Jews in 1492 and the subsequent confinement of Moriscos (Moorish converts to Christianity) to the isolated mountains of the Alpujarra.

But, in Jaén, ethnocentric Christian chivalry rather than ethnic cleansing appears to have been the lingering ideal. Assassinated, in all likelihood, because of his defense of Jewish *conversos,* Lucas presided in the early 1460s over a festive world that envisioned a golden age of benevolent Christian rule (his own, of course), where kings of Spain and Morocco would be equally welcome, Christian and Moorish knights would compete on the playing field rather than the battlefield, all would finally submit to the law of the Christian God, and feasting and games would be the order of each day. Oddly enough, Lucas's festive construct is not that far from the millenarian vision of the sixteenth-century Franciscans who presided over many of the first festivals of Moors and Christians in Mexico. In Mexico, however, those whose defeat was implicitly dramatized by the tradition were for the first time required to perform it. Moors, to the best of my knowledge, never watched a Christian *moros y cristianos.* Native Americans not only watched but took part, an innovation that transformed the genre.

With the exception of a single, obscure reference to an *"entremès de moros y cristianos"* in Valencia in 1472 and the mention of a "gallant skirmish" involving "a dozen nobles dressed as Moors" at a Portuguese royal wedding in 1490, the Jaén games were the last Iberian *moros y cristianos* before 1492 of which any published record survives.[16] Even the conquest of Granada, which in that year brought the *reconquista* to its long-awaited conclusion, failed to generate a flurry of reenactments. A hastily written Latin neoclassical play and a musical allegory on the theme were performed in Rome and Naples respectively in 1492.[17] At a more popular level, a week of celebrations in Gerona, early in 1493, included a spectacular reenactment of the capture of the Alhambra and, five days later, a mock siege of "the city of Granada." For the latter, the Christian "camp" outside the city included colorful pavilions and actors playing Ferdinand and Isabella, the Duke of Seville, and "other nobles," who galloped through the streets of Gerona, displaying their banners and heraldic devices, to the sound of "drums and trumpets." The city was defended by "well-dressed" Moors.[18]

In 1513, in Valladolid, the eleven-year-old grandson of Ferdinand and Isabella, also named Ferdinand, entertained his grandfather by taking part in what was intended to be a prophetic mock battle between Turks and Christians. Sallying forth from a "fortress" representing Jerusalem, the Turks attacked another representing Rhodes, a fortified island off the coast of Turkey that had been a frontier bastion of European Christendom since its capture by crusaders in 1309. A Christian army led by the young Ferdinand not only lifted the siege of Rhodes but succeeded in capturing Jerusalem.[19] Unfortunately, the ritual of sympathetic magic did not work. In 1522, Rhodes fell to the Ottoman Turks. Besides the ongoing Corpus Christi Turks and hobby horses in Catalonia, I know of no other *moros y cristianos* staged in Spain between 1492 and 1524, the date of the first recorded Mexican *moros y cristianos*, just three years after the Mexican capital of Tenochtitlan fell to Cortés.

We are now in a position, then, to draw certain conclusions about the origins and character of the *moros y cristianos* in medieval Spain before the European encounter with the Americas. Such conclusions, of course, must be tentative, given the stories of "scholars visiting church and monastic libraries where medieval manuscripts reach to the rafters"[20] and the likelihood of further evidence emerging from local archives and other unpublished records. With due caution, however, we can note, first, that there are too few known accounts of mock battles between Moors and Christians in medieval Spain for us to speak of an already long-established tradition at the time of the conquest of America. While there was a broader European tradition of scripted mock battles, there seem to have been surprisingly few in Spain that dramatized the events of the reconquest.

Second, those for which records do survive are, with the possible exception of the minstrel epic, of courtly and ecclesiastical provenance. In the nature of the case, urban court performances and church processions are more likely to be chronicled than are early rural folk dances, but the existing evidence, such as it is, affords no ground for claiming that the *moros y cristianos* had their origin in seasonal folk rituals. Instead, it points to their beginning in royal spectacles and the quasi-dramatic practices of the courtly tournament; only later were they adopted and adapted for annual popular festivities.[21] (We can, perhaps, see the first instance of this process in Barcelona, where the battle between Turks and hobby horses may well have resembled a joust in miniature.) We should not, however, swing to the other extreme and seek a single aristocratic origin, for we are dealing not with a formally prescribed genre but with a theme that can be adapted to a variety of forms.[22] By 1492, despite the comparative paucity of evidence, we have perhaps a dance or two, several *mêlées* and *juegos de cañas,* a fruit fight, an allegorical interlude, and the use of hobby horses in Corpus Christi pageants and royal entries.

Nevertheless, the fact that the medieval *moros y cristianos* were largely courtly in provenance goes a long way to explaining their lack of hidden transcripts. Tournament-based military exercises, performed by those in power primarily for their own enjoyment (and to impress those under authority), would be unlikely to conceal a hidden transcript of resistance. These will come into play only when the tradition becomes a site for the meeting of dominant and subordinate groups, such as Indian performers and Spanish sponsors in colonial Mexico, or competing powers, such as church and street in modern Spain. But the absence of hidden transcripts should not mislead us into thinking that the plays, dances, and games were only (or even primarily) about the battles between Moors and Christians that their public transcripts claim as their referent. In most cases, the theme of ethnic and religious conflict allowed those responsible for their staging to address more immediate political interests, such as (perhaps) the union of Aragon and Catalonia in Lleida, the relationship between Jaume II and the Aragonese nobles in Zaragoza, or the long-awaited triumph of Alfonso the Magnanimous in Naples. The mock battles in Jaén may have been an exception, since Christian incursions into Moorish territory were a part of the immediate political situation, but even in this case their primary purpose was the public enactment of Miguel Lucas's own vision of himself as the benevolent ruler of a land of peace and plenty. Thus, even though they entertained no hidden transcript of resistance, the medieval *moros y cristianos* were still about the dynamics of power.

Insofar as they were also about those they named, the *moros y cristianos* offered a vision of *convivencia* rather than bloodshed. Moors do not get killed in these battles. They survive to be converted and to dance and feast with their former enemies. While such a resolution may require, as one modern scholar has put it, that the Moors lose "their very identity,"[23] it still compares favorably with the harsh treatment afforded Spanish Moriscos in the sixteenth century and with the kind of ethnic cleansing we have seen in our own day. It is hard to imagine such a festive ending if Serbs were now to stage a mock battle between Christians and Muslims in the Balkans. Muslims, on the whole, are not demonized in the medieval festivals of reconquest. They may be compared to "barbarians" in Naples and, once, in Jaén, to women and children, but otherwise they are honored as worthy opponents and as welcome partners in feasting.

The Barcelona *Martyrdom of Saint Sebastian* offered a different view of power, one that grounded victory not in military might aided and abetted by God (for there the Christian knights were defeated), but in the heavenly welcome prepared by God for Christ and martyr alike. It is not the crusading Christian knight but "Christ crucified" who is "the power of God" (1 Cor. 1: 23–24) in this play. The Christian reversal of standard hierarchies of power may also have opened the door to hidden transcripts. For Christianity claims to worship a God who, in humility, became human and, for his opposition to "principalities and powers," was put to death by an alliance of Roman and Jewish officials. In sympathy with the down-trodden, according to one of the great hymns of the Christian church, God has "exalted the humble" and "put down the mighty from their seat" (Luke 1: 52).[24]

This is all very well if the "mighty" happens to be the Great Turk who ordered the execution of Saint Sebastian, but both the hymn and the incarnation it cele-brates invite applications less flattering to the hierarchical ecclesiastical context in which they are so often proclaimed. Precisely because of that context, such applica-tions will be muted, even hidden, but they will be made. The conjunction of *moros y cristianos* and Christian procession, which was to become normative in succeed-ing centuries, makes almost inevitable the use of the one tradition to negotiate the inconsistencies inherent in the other's attraction to and condemnation of power.

For the first time, too, in Barcelona's Corpus Christi procession, the *moros y cristianos* became an annual event. In doing so, the tradition began its transforma-tion from the occasional courtly entertainments of the Middle Ages to the annual folk performances of modern Spain. We will return to this process of transforma-tion in Part Five, but for now, we cross the Atlantic to Mexico.

PART THREE
MEXICO, 1321–1521

7
The Fields of the Wars of Flowers

"AFTER the conquest," writes Inga Clendinnen, "the Mexicans were to display an early, puzzling and enduring passion for the 'dances of Moors and Christians.'"[1] Such a passion should not puzzle us too much, for the tradition was inherently susceptible to indigenous readings. Spanish colonists may have thought they were celebrating the victory of light-skinned Christians over dark-skinned "heathens," linking the defeat of the Moors in 1492 to the defeat of the Aztecs in 1521. But the theme cut two ways in Mexico, for the history being dramatized was not one of conquest but of reconquest: Spanish Christians had driven out Moorish invaders. It was this image of liberation rather than that of Spanish victory that attracted indigenous Mexicans to the imported tradition. In colonial festivals of Moors and Christians, a public transcript of Catholic triumph masked a hidden transcript of native reconquest.

Nor was it just a matter of adopting and adapting a foreign tradition. The Mexicans were already familiar with mock battles of their own. In Part Three, we will consider the pre-Hispanic tradition of skirmishes, mock battles, martial dances, and ritual combat among the Mexica, or Aztecs, of central Mexico.[2] Although the Mexica Empire, if one includes within its boundaries territories not fully subjugated but nonetheless falling under its influence, stretched from the Gulf of Mexico to the Pacific Ocean and as far south as the present borders of Guatemala,[3] we will concentrate on events in and around Tenochtitlan (now Mexico City), where festivities were most elaborate before the conquest and indigenous memories most painstakingly recorded afterward.

The Mexica engaged in both scripted and unscripted warfare. The latter included the unqualified *yaoyotl* (war) as well as the qualified *xochiyaoyotl* (war of flowers). The term *xochiyaoyotl* encompassed a range of confrontations between rival cities—from unplanned brawls to ritualized and even sporting battles—that stopped short of unrestrained warfare but often shared its goal of taking captives for sacrifice. We will consider the flowery wars in this chapter. Scripted combats of an astonishing variety formed a vital part of the frame for human sacrifice in Tenochtitlan, regularly transforming the Mexica capital into "a symbolic ceremonial battlefield."[4] In Chapters 8 through 10, we will consider the three Mexica calendar festivals in which such combat was most prominent. Finally, in Chapter 11, we will paint a tentative picture of pre-Hispanic danced dramatizations of warfare.

The study of Mexica mock battles involves two temptations that we will be wise to acknowledge at the outset. First is the temptation so to assimilate the other's cultural practices to our own that we effectively deny the degree of difference.

Early Spanish chroniclers flirted with this temptation when they compared Mexica mock battles to *juegos de cañas* and other forms of European tournament. An equal and opposite temptation is so to differentiate the other as to license our own self-righteous indignation. European revulsion at the Mexica system of human sacrifice, with which the mock battles were inextricably entwined, readily succumbs to this temptation.[5]

But consider this: After the 1571 siege of Famagusta, on the island of Cyprus, the captured Christian leader, Marcantonio Bragadino, was flayed alive by his Turkish captors and his skin stuffed with straw and paraded through Famagusta under the red parasol that had marked his rank as a Venetian Senator. The effigy was then shipped to Constantinople, where "this macabre pantomime" was repeated.[6] Or consider this bizarre account of "medieval snuff drama": In Tournai in 1549, we are told, the roles of Judith and Holofernes in a biblical play staged for the visit of the future Philip II of Spain were assigned to criminals. A youth sentenced to exile was enticed by the promise of pardon to play Judith and a man condemned to torture with red-hot pincers chose to die playing Holofernes instead. At the climactic moment, Judith took a sharp scimitar, seized the hair of Holofernes, who was feigning sleep, and cut off his head with a single stroke. Blood spurted from the victim's neck, the spectators applauded frenetically, and Philip remarked, "Well struck."[7] The Mexica were not the only ones to flay their captives and parade their skins or to confuse execution and religious theater.

But such atrocities should not drive us back to the assimilative conclusion that the Mexica were just like the Turks and Christians of Europe. Whatever may be the relative moral faults of these cultures, we need to negotiate a path between the two temptations, assuming neither that Mexica mock battles were essentially the same as those of medieval Europe nor that they were so tainted by human sacrifice as to invite only our disgust. With this caution in mind, we turn to the simplest of the mock battles of pre-Hispanic Mexico, the *xochiyaoyotl,* or "flowery wars."

At least one modern scholar, like a number of the early chroniclers, has compared flowery wars to European *mêlées.*[8] Similar in the sense that they afforded an opportunity for the honing and display of military skills, they were nevertheless different in several respects, not the least of which is that captive warriors were often sacrificed and eaten. Contrary to popular perception, however, they did not always have as their goal the supply of human fodder for the gods. The first conflict to which the term *xochiyaoyotl* has been applied began as little more than a spontaneous brawl. In 1321, according to the Indian historian Francisco Chimalpahin, a religious ritual of bloodletting, involving the then-powerful Chalca and the subordinate Tlacochcalca, turned sour. When it came time for the Tlacochcalca to leave, they were attacked with stones and "many of those who fell prisoner died."

Despite the protests of the Tlacochcalca priest, the two sides "came to blows." The Chalca put chili peppers in the water jars of the Tlacochcalca women and threw burning brands at the Tlacochcalca children. Thus began the "suffering" and the "conquest" of the "flowery war."[9] Another flowery war, between the Chalca and the nascent Mexica, began in 1376. According to Chimalpahin, captured nobles from both sides were released and only commoners were killed. The *Anales de Cuauhtitlan* designate this flowery war a source of "amusement." After several years, the flowery war changed into an "angry war," in which the nobles "were no longer set free, but sacrificed."[10] Chimalpahin mentions one more flowery war, between the Chalca and the Tepaneca, that began in 1381, but he gives no details.[11]

There is no mention of a fourteenth-century flowery war producing sacrificial victims. According to Diego Durán's *History of the Indies of New Spain,* completed around 1581, it was not until the latter part of the reign of Motecuzoma I (1440–1469) that the dominant Mexica Empire put the *xochiyaoyotl* to its more sinister use. Concern over the supply of victims for the new Great Temple and the logistical difficulty of procuring such victims from distant enemies prompted Motecuzoma's brother and chief adviser, Tlacaelel, to propose a "military marketplace" in several nearby but not yet subjugated cities, including Tlaxcala, Huexotzinco, and Cholula. There the god Huitzilopochtli would "go with his army to buy victims, men for him to eat. And this will be a good thing, for it will be as if he has his maize cakes hot from the griddle—tortillas from a nearby place, hot and ready to eat whenever he wishes them." War would be declared not for political purposes of imperial expansion or control but for religious reasons of sacrificial supply. Such wars, Tlacaelel added, would "be places where the sons of noblemen, enthusiasts in the art of war, [would] be able to train, to practice their skill and show their valor."[12]

Motecuzoma liked the idea. He "summoned all his great warriors and . . . notified them that they were now to fight in a military marketplace, as if they were going to a regular market on certain days, where they would buy honor and glory with their blood and their lives." He stressed the religious motivation and the proximity of "this human marketplace." "By going to war nearby," he told his audience, "the soldiers [will] go happily as if they were enjoying some festivity, going to be entertained." Tlacaelel then stood up and announced the honors that would be awarded to heroes of these wars and the great shame that would accrue to those "who dare not go to war."[13]

Despite this innovation, Durán mentions no instance of such a war during the reign of Motecuzoma I. The first recorded implementation of the new policy came in the reign of his successor, Axayacatl (1469–1481). Needing "war captives" to sacrifice at the inauguration of a new "sun stone" and having failed to take them from the still undefeated Tarascans of Michoacan, Axayacatl "decided to go to

Tliliuhquitepec for this purpose, since it was one of the towns indicated for this kind of war." The ensuing battle was no mere chivalric *mêlée*. After the "usual formal speeches, . . . the fighting started [and] one side mixed and clashed with the other in such a disorderly manner that they wounded and killed their opponents with much cruelty, each side struggling to capture those of the other." The Mexica captured "seven hundred" prisoners but "lost four hundred and twenty" of their own soldiers. Although the narrative tells us that "the people of Tliliuhquitepec [had] been forced into this war" and were understandably saddened by their losses, their lords were able to observe the proper rhetorical protocol, telling Axayacatl afterward, "We have participated in this skirmish and we have been entertained by it."[14] Such "skirmishes" were not distinguished from outright war by any restriction on killing. What set them apart was that the conflict was confined to the battlefield and did not spill over into the pursuit of defeated warriors, attacks on civilians, destruction of enemy property, nor (the ultimate mark of victory in the Mexica world) setting fire to the other's temple.

Wars of this kind seem to have been most common during the reign of Motecuzoma II (1502–1520). (This is the ruler, more widely known by the Hispanic form of his name, Montezuma, who succumbed to Cortés.) At one point, becoming "weary of so much idleness and of the fact that there was no war in which his soldiers could practice their arts," Motecuzoma "decided to provoke the people of Huexotzinco." He therefore sent messengers, telling the rulers of Huexotzinco "that he wished to join in some entertainment with them for a few days on the battlefield and to give the men some practice in skirmishing." The men of Huexotzinco accepted the challenge "with goodwill." "One hundred thousand" Mexica warriors gathered at the designated battlefield, "all of them in splendid array. The Huexotzinca then appeared, no less finely attired and in equally good spirits, looking as if they had come to a [dancing party or] festival." Despite the festive ambience, "men began to fall on either side" and "a great slaughter took place." Among the dead were three of Motecuzoma's brothers.[15]

On another occasion, the Cholulans notified Motecuzoma "that they wished to have the pleasurable experience of skirmishing with the [Mexica] in battle." What began as a skirmish soon developed into a battle "fought with such fierce rage that, when the [Mexica] withdrew" after a full day's fighting, they "found that they had lost eight thousand two hundred soldiers." Cholulan casualties being just as high, "the fields were covered with dead bodies." The next day, "the Cholulans sent a message saying that they had had enough recreation and practice. They bade the [Mexica] go home in peace." Durán comments that for the Mexica to wage war against the Huexotzinca or the Cholulans was akin to "Spaniards warring against Spaniards," so close was their ethnic affinity. Other nations, against whom the

Mexica waged unrestrained wars of conquest, "were to them as the Moors, Turks, heathens, or Jews are to us."[16]

For a long time, scholars accepted the notion that these wars against recalcitrant neighbors and kin across the mountains to the east existed "solely to produce sacrificial victims,"[17] but their purpose is now believed to have included "practical military training"[18] and the establishment of military and political dominance without the real or potential costs of a full-scale war.[19] One suspects, too, that the conspicuous consumption of human life was, like any other public display of waste, a mark of the power of those able to command such excess. Durán remarks that he often asked the Indians why they were not content with sacrificing "quail, turtle doves, and other birds." They replied that mere birds "were offerings for commoners and paupers," whereas offerings of human "captives, prisoners, and slaves" brought honor and reputation to "great lords and noblemen."[20]

Nowhere in Durán's account, however, are these transmontane wars, as they have come to be known, called flowery wars; on the one occasion when he does use the term *xochiyaoyotl*, it is to describe an unrestrained campaign of conquest.[21] Nevertheless, Hernando Alvarado Tezozómoc's *Crónica mexicana*, written in 1598, does occasionally refer to the transmontane wars as *xochiyaoyotl*,[22] and such a designation is implicit in their confinement to the military battlefield and in the repeated description of them as festivities staged for the entertainment of the participants. In any case, it is these wars that have come to serve as the model for most scholarly descriptions of a flowery war.[23]

Although "the data on flowery wars are sparse,"[24] we know enough to draw important distinctions between the *xochiyaoyotl* and the European *mêlées*. While the latter sometimes got out of hand, they were not intended to end in the death of participants. The flowery war between the Mexica and the Chalca, beginning in 1376, may have more closely approximated the European tournament in this respect, for there captive nobles were released and only commoners were killed. But the transmontane wars, for all their rhetoric of festive entertainment, were clearly designed as something far more deadly. Participants were killed and captives sacrificed and eaten. Moreover, tournaments were never imposed on neighboring peoples, as flowery wars were during the reign of Axayacatl.

For our purposes, which have to do primarily with assessing the *mêlée* and the *xochiyaoyotl* as potential influences on the subsequent tradition of dramatized combat, the most important difference is that the *mêlée* was often fought between teams of knights from the same city or state, while the flowery war was not. The flowery war required no pretense, for the opposition of the two sides was real and did not need to be created by a dramatic frame. The *mêlée* or the *juego de cañas,* when it was fought between arbitrarily divided knights serving the same Christian ruler, lent itself to the quasi-dramatic distinction created by dressing one side as Moors or Turks. Once the distinction in costumes had been drawn, incidentally determining the outcome, the scripted contest required a narrative to frame the Christian victory. The flowery wars never developed into drama if only because they were fought between two sides already sufficiently distinguished by contesting allegiances.

There may have been at least one instance of an unscripted mock battle in pre-Hispanic Mexico fought between soldiers loyal to the same ruler. In 1487, Motecuzoma II's predecessor, Ahuitzotl, sent emissaries to neighboring lords, inviting them to attend the dedication of the Great Temple of Tenochtitlan. Those who went to Yopitzinco, in the present-day state of Guerrero, were particularly well received. After supplying them with water, chocolate, flowers, tobacco, and food, "the king of that province" ordered that they be entertained. "A squadron of armed and well-adorned men entered the courtyard and began to engage in a mock battle. They skirmished as if in a tournament, with great cries and shrieks such as these people use when they fight. When this skirmish had ended, the king said to the emissaries, 'Do not fear! All of this has been done for your pleasure.'"[25] I know of no other mock battle in precontact Mexico apparently so close in design to the tournament *mêlée:* the combatants were not, in any sense but the mimetic, at war; there were, as far as we can tell from the account, no injuries or deaths; and, although the participants may well have enjoyed the exercise, the battle had as its immediate goal the entertainment of spectators. In this last respect, it approximates theater more closely than do the other battles we have considered in this chapter. Whether the uniforms of the soldiers distinguished one side from the other and, if so, whether they did so in such a manner as to suggest some rudimentary dramatic framework, we simply do not know.

Finally in this chapter, we should note a most unusual account of scripted warfare in which no one was killed but victory and defeat were enacted. When, according to Durán's sources, Netzahualcoyotl, ruler of Tezcoco, agreed with Motecuzoma I that the Tezcoca should enter into a lasting alliance with the Mexica, Tlacaelel insisted that the Mexica reputation not be compromised by any suspicion of weakness. It was agreed that the two armies would meet on the battlefield, that they would "pretend to fight," and that the Tezcoca would flee and the Mexica pursue "without wounding or killing anyone." On the appointed day, "with a great show of arms, insignia, splendid attire, and rich adornments," the two armies met "and the mock battle began." The conflict proceeded as scripted until Netzahualcoyotl ordered that a suburban temple be set on fire. "Seeing the flames, the [Mexica] lowered their weapons, for the burning of the temple was the sign of surrender." Thus, according to the Mexica chronicles, was warfare staged for an absent audience that needed to hear yet again of Mexica military might. It is only fair to add that the Tezcoca historian Fernando de Alva Ixtlilxochitl, writing in the sixteenth century, told a different tale. According to his account, the Mexica agreed to an alliance with Tezcoco only after the latter sacked Tenochtitlan and burned its temple in a decidedly unscripted attack.[26]

8

The Festival of the Sweeping of the Roads

MEXICA military traditions, whether displayed in flowery wars or angry wars, helped to shape the visual spectacle of early colonial festivals of reconquest. Closer to the subsequent tradition of Mexican *moros y cristianos,* however, were the scripted battles embedded in Tenochtitlan's festivals of human sacrifice, for these involved impersonation, costume, script, dance, and a festive context that flowed through the streets and surrounding countryside, engaging all the senses.

Many scholars have noted the theatricality of the Mexica festivals. Davíd Carrasco describes them as "grand theatrical displays," and Johanna Broda writes of Mexica "myth" being "enacted . . . in an overwhelming theatrical setting." Inga Clendinnen, too, writes that Mexica ritual "was a highly elastic and dynamic expressive mode, more street theatre than museum piece," and observes of "the great sensory assault of full Mexica ceremonial" that its priestly organizers were "contriving, by very different means, the kind of delirium we associate not with high reverence but with carnival." Acknowledging both the art and the horror of the Mexica festivals and of the "theatrical battles between mock gods and mock soldiers" that they included, Hugh Thomas writes aptly of "astonishing, often splendid, and sometimes beautiful barbarities." [1]

The Mexica calendar was divided into eighteen months of twenty days apiece, with five days that were deemed "not worth counting" closing each year as a kind of temporal no-man's-land. Each month was named after its dominant festival. The major mock battles of the Mexica ritual calendar were concentrated in the second, eleventh, and fifteenth months. In a ceremonial calendar that "was built out of the swing of the seasons, marking the transitions out of the time of agricultural growth into the season of war," [2] these festivals measured the season of war. Thus, Ochpaniztli (the Festival of the Sweeping of the Roads) fell in the eleventh month, which began in late August or early September; it ended the agricultural half of the year, presaged the harvest, and opened the season of war. Panquetzaliztli (the Festival of the Raising of the Banners) fell in the fifteenth month, which began in November, and marked the midpoint of the bellicose season. And, Tlacaxipeualiztli (the Festival of the Flaying of Men) fell in the second month, which began in late February or early March, closing the season of war with a prolific sacrifice of captives. Then, the planting was once again prepared and rain awaited. We will consider these festivals in the order of their progress through the season of war. [3]

Our task is complicated by the fact that the two primary sixteenth-century sources of information on Mexica ritual, Bernardino de Sahagún's *General History of the Things of New Spain* and Diego Durán's *History of the Indies of New Spain,* resist combination into a single, coherent narrative. Each refers to events that the other omits, and the two narratives lack sufficient points of cross-reference for a fully satisfactory synthesis. The situation is further complicated by the fact that Sahagún's Spanish text is a paraphrase of and interpolated commentary on his Nahuatl original, known as the *Florentine Codex;* that each version contains details that the other lacks; and that Sahagún resisted the temptation to reduce the accounts provided by his various informants to a single, internally consistent narrative. Moreover, Durán's synchronic account of Mexica calendar rituals in the first volume of his *History* is sometimes complicated, if not contradicted, by specific instances that he describes in his diachronic account of Mexica history in the second volume. Finally, we are dealing with the memories of old men, filtered through the grid of Spanish inquiry, of what life was like before the trauma of the conquest.

Nevertheless, recent excavations of the Great Temple have shown the Spanish chronicles to be surprisingly reliable.[4] And the wealth of data they contain on pre-Hispanic ritual exceeds, in both quantity and quality, what little we know of *moros y cristianos* in Spain before the fifteenth century. Nor should we forget that Cortés's expedition, while still enjoying more or less friendly relations with the Mexica, was based in Tenochtitlan from November 1519 to June 1520. There the Spaniards saw (and would later remember) some of the last full stagings of the Mexica calendar festivals, including two of the three that concern us, Panquetzalitzli and Tlacaxipeualiztli.

The chroniclers' informants offered the friars only the public transcript of Mexica ritual and history. Although the friars interpolated their own Spanish Catholic criticism of Mexica practices, they were not generally alert to hidden transcripts of Mexica resistance. We should therefore treat with some suspicion scholarly conclusions that "the great public rituals of state cult" in Tenochtitlan "directly expressed the ideological pretensions of the Aztec warrior elite." Although it is safe to say that they "were clearly connected to the legitimation of political power,"[5] we would do well to remember Scott's warning that "the public transcript, where it is not positively misleading, is unlikely to tell the whole story about power relations."[6] I will argue that traces of a hidden transcript, discernible in those details of the festivals (and especially the mock battles) that appear to be at odds with the public transcript, suggest that it was not the warriors but the priests who controlled the public transcript's ideological content. I will argue, too, that the warrior elite and their families did not unequivocally endorse but partly resented the priestly cult that annually sent them to war.

My attempts to synthesize the various accounts of ritualized battle and their festive contexts in Tenochtitlan make no claims to have solved all the problems inherent in the sources. Nor do they aim at completeness. Rather, they cull from the mass of details those that seem most pertinent to the tradition of mock battles. Nonetheless, my descriptions will, I believe, be close enough to what took place annually in Tenochtitlan in the decades leading up to the conquest to allow us to assess the role of Mexica ritual in shaping the subsequent tradition of Mexican *moros y cristianos*. To the extent that I am able to read the mask of state ritual, we will also gain access to a more nuanced understanding of Mexica power relationships. Any such reconstruction involves, of course, a considerable measure of speculation. "To hear those faint long-ago Indian voices" requires, as Clendinnen observes, not only "patience and perseverance," but, "from both reader and author, a tolerance of ambiguities and of inherently contestable judgements." Not to take the risk, however, is to decline the adventure of what Mikhail Bakhtin calls the "creative understanding" of dialogue with other cultures and past epochs.[7]

Appropriately, for a festival that marked the boundary of the seasons of agriculture and war, the festival of Ochpaniztli honored both Chicomecoatl, the corn goddess, and Toci, the woman of war.[8] Betty Ann Brown, who argues most strenuously that the mock battles of Ochpaniztli recalled a formative war between the Mexica and the Culhua, explicitly compares the Mexica festival to postcontact festivals of Moors and Christians. Both, she writes, combine "more ancient, agriculturally based festivals" with ceremonies that "recall major historic battles."[9] Since the mock battles are linked almost exclusively to Toci, I have paid closer attention to the parts that honor her.

Preparations began forty days in advance with the selection of a female slave, "forty to forty-five years of age," to play the role of Toci. This unfortunate *ixiptla* ("impersonator" or "proxy") was ritually washed and caged to keep her pure for sacrifice. After twenty days, she was costumed in the same manner as the wooden image of Toci that sat in a roadside shrine at the southern entrance to the city. The upper half of her face was painted white, the lower half black; her dark hair was crowned with white cotton; and she was dressed in a fringed, white blouse and short, white skirt. Thereafter she was taken daily through the city to receive such homage "as if she had been the goddess herself."[10]

The festival itself began with a "hand-waving dance." For eight successive days, from late afternoon until sunset, four rows of dancers, bearing marigolds in each hand, walked and circled in unified and disciplined silence, accompanied only by upright drums (*huehuetl*). Not everyone treated the dance with the requisite solemnity: drunken youths sometimes imitated the sound of the drums. After eight days of dancing, "the mock battle of the women physicians" began. Toci's impersonator appeared, followed by a crowd of healers and midwives. Dividing themselves into two "squadrons," one allied with Toci and the other opposing her, the women pelted each other with balls made of matted tree moss, reeds, cactus leaves, and yellow marigolds. The goal of this comic "skirmish" was to make Toci's impersonator laugh, for if she wept now it would signal the death of many warriors in battle or of women in childbirth. Juan de Torquemada compares the skirmish to a *juego de cañas* in which, instead of spears, *alcancías* (earthenware balls filled with ashes or flowers) were used. Clendinnen, more sensitive to the plight of the woman, remarks that "the victim so mercilessly played with must have been close to hysteria."[11]

The Toci impersonator also wove maguey fiber in the marketplace while youths danced and, on her last visit to the market, sold the cloth she had made, thus modeling, as Brown puts it, "proper female behavior for her . . . audience." On her last visit, she was accompanied by men dressed (or undressed) as caricatures of the Gulf Coast Huaxteca people (Fig. 10), whom the Mexica believed to be negligible warriors but energetic lovers, and by female healers, midwives, and priests of Chicomecoatl, in whose midst she scattered cornmeal. To her duties of weaving and selling, she thus added sexuality and the propagation of corn and children. No one spoke to her of her imminent death; on the contrary, the healers fed her the fantasy that she would soon have sex with Motecuzoma. It is just possible that a recent captive, unfamiliar with Mexica ritual and "close to hysteria," might have believed this lie.[12]

After four days of skirmishes and the last of her visits to the marketplace, at midnight on the fifth day, on a platform of the temple of Toci, the impersonator was killed. In the darkness, silently, hastily, she was stretched out on the back of a priest,

10. Toci (center), priests, and Huaxteca caricatures. Detail from *Codex Borbonicus,* fol. 30. Courtesy of Akademische Druck-u. Verlagsanstalt.

beheaded, and flayed. A naked priest, noted for his strength, power, and height, "struggled into the wet skin, with its slack breasts and pouched genitalia," producing, in Clendinnen's words, "a double nakedness of layered, ambiguous sexuality." The skin wearer was not left naked but was dressed in a blouse and skirt publicly woven, before her death, by the victim. Meanwhile, a portion of skin from the victim's thigh, a location chosen, according to Brown, to represent "ritual birth," was made into a mask for the impersonator of Cinteotl, the corn god and mythical son of Toci and Huitzilopochtli.[13]

The sacrifice of the Toci impersonator recalled an early episode in Mexica history (or myth), said to have taken place in 1343, when the daughter of Achitometl, the ruler of Culhuacan, was given to the Mexica as a bride for their god Huitzilopochtli. The girl was sacrificed and flayed and a youth dressed in her skin and "womanly garments." Achitometl was then tricked, in a dimly lit chamber, into offering incense, flowers, and the blood of birds to the adjacent images of Huitzilopochtli and Toci, the former carved in stone and the latter represented by the living male cross-dressed in the girl's skin and clothes. When Achitometl threw fresh incense into a brazier, shedding light for the first time on his daughter's colonized remains, he was outraged. The offense, as the bellicose Huitzilopochtli had intended, provoked war between the Mexica and the Culhua. The Mexica suffered a humiliating defeat, fleeing before the more powerful Culhua. It is from this incident that Toci, whose name literally means "our grandmother," derives her alternative title of Yoacihuatl, or "woman of war."[14]

The next act of the Festival of the Sweeping of the Roads appears to have recalled this loss. While the skin and, with it, the role of Toci was transferred from victim to priest, "a number of noblemen and great brave warriors" gathered at the foot of the temple steps. When the new, bloody impersonator of Toci ran down the steps, guarded by costumed priests, the terrified warriors fled, much as the early Mexica had done before the Culhua. They ran, looking over their shoulders and striking their shields together, "as if to provoke a fight." Armed with straw brooms that were drenched with blood, "a symbolic expression," according to Paul Kirchhoff, of "war," the priests "set upon" the warriors and "scattered" them. This was not so much a mock battle as a rout, a "game" that terrified both warriors and onlookers with its powerful image of Mexica defeat. "There was much fear," Sahagún's informants remembered, "fear spread over the people."[15]

Here, perhaps, we see the first signs of a break in the public transcript or, to put it another way, of immediate social conflicts being enacted under the guise of historical reenactment. Broda notes that many of the mock battles during Ochpaniztli were "fought between the servants of Toci (i.e., priests) and groups of warriors" and suggests that the battles expressed "a certain tension" between the two.[16] One can understand why the warriors (and their mothers and wives) might feel hostility toward the priests, since the priests demanded sacrifice to feed the gods, while the warriors risked their lives to hunt the victims. In this instance, the priests gained the initial psychological advantage, for the script required the Mexica warriors to enact the defeat of their own class while the priests, chasing them through the streets of the city, took the part of the victors. Moreover, in a city that boasted, in the words of a Mexica poem, that "here no one fears to die in war,"[17] the warriors were made to run, terrified (or, at the very least, acting terrified), before Toci and her priests.

Next, perhaps, "captives of war . . . were crucified upon a high scaffolding," arms and legs spread apart, and filled with arrows fired by archers dressed as gods. In his second volume, Durán writes that the "arrow sacrifice" was performed before Toci's temple "in memory of those who had been wounded with arrows when the Aztecs fled from Culhuacan and had hidden among the reeds and rushes in order not to be slaughtered." In his first volume, he places the arrow sacrifice among earlier ceremonies in honor of Chicomecoatl and describes a different sacrifice at this point. Captive victims, goaded from beneath by "executioners" armed with maguey spikes, were forced to climb tall, wooden poles. When they reached the top, they were met by others who pushed them to their deaths below. A bowl of the shattered victims' blood was given to the Toci impersonator, who dipped his finger in the blood and tasted it. (S)he then began to groan, at which everyone present "shuddered . . . with fear." Whether this, too, represented Mexica (and warrior) defeat is impossible to tell. The action conveyed, at the very least, the terrible appetite for bloodshed of the woman of war.[18]

Arriving at the Great Temple of Huitzilopochtli, the skin wearer saluted the image of the god, her husband. (S)he may, as Eduard Seler suggests, have been simulating sexual intercourse, for (s)he was soon joined by the impersonator of Cinteotl, their son, a young man wearing the mask made from the skin of Toci's thigh. If divine sexual union were represented, it would have recalled the corresponding historical union that took place a generation or so after Huitzilopochtli's gruesome marriage to the flayed daughter of the Culhua ruler, for the first Mexica emperor, Acamapichtli, was also born from a Mexica-Culhua union, in this case the marriage of the Mexica noble Opochtzin and the Culhua princess Atotoztli. Mexica rulers were believed to embody Mexica gods and therefore to reproduce their stories.[19]

Together, the impersonators of Toci and Cinteotl made their way back to Toci's temple. As the sun rose, the priestly skin wearer, naked once again, stood in full view high on the edge of the pyramid. Waiting nobles hastened up the steps to adorn her. Some applied eagle down to her head and legs, while others "beautified her face with colored make up" or pulled over her tautening skin colored, knee-length petticoats and an embroidered blouse. Yet others swung incense or beheaded quail. Then her priests crowned her with a huge, square, multicolored, paper crown, from which five paper banners hung down to the ground, one from each corner and a fifth, larger one, from the center, almost enclosing her. According to the *Codex Borbonicus,* this crown doubled her height and width, creating a figure that towered over her ministering priests (see Fig. 10). Thus accoutered, (s)he slew four captives, stretching them over the offering stone, opening their chests, and pulling out their reeking hearts.

Entrusting her priests with the task of slaughtering the remaining captives, Toci rejoined her son Cinteotl and returned in procession, accompanied by male and female singers and the beat of "a small horizontal drum [*teponaztli*]," to the temple of Huitzilopochtli. Leading the procession were the Huaxteca caricatures. In the *Codex Borbonicus,* the Huaxteca wear tall, conical caps, sport black and white face paint, and, as Clendinnen puts it, bear "magnificent [artificial] erections like banners before them" (see Fig. 10). Sexuality and war are closely linked in this festival: sex breeds warriors and childbirth is the woman's battleground. "What is most remarkable," Clendinnen comments, "is the explicit rendering of the psychological and social cost of that interdependence."[20]

The procession was met by many "seasoned warriors," who surrounded Cinteotl and ran "swiftly" with him to a mountaintop in enemy territory, "one of the side peaks of Iztac tepetl."[21] Most commentators assume that Cinteotl and his warriors ran as far as the snow-capped volcanoes Iztaccihuatl and Popocatepetl, which separated Tenochtitlan from its transmontane opponents. But Clendinnen suggests that "the delivery of the war sign 'to enemy lands'" was "symbolic, not actual,"[22] and that the mountainous border was represented by an elevated site at some distance but still visible from the Great Temple. We cannot be sure. Massed warriors still launch a running attack over surrounding hills in the late-August *morismas* of Bracho. On the other hand, the Great Temple represented twin "hills or sacred mountains revered in Mexica tradition."[23] Another temple may have served as a dramatic proxy for the designated side peak of Iztaccihuatl.

It was "not without struggle" that Cinteotl and his army accomplished their goal of setting the thigh-skin mask on a designated wooden frame atop the mountain. Often the Mexica warriors were met by enemy soldiers, pursuits developed, and lives were lost on both sides.[24] If the mountaintop goal were truly in enemy territory, these battles and their consequent deaths would have been real. If the goal were closer at hand and the enemy attacks were staged by other Mexica warriors, suitably costumed, then the "deaths" would perhaps have been enacted, much as they are in festivals of Moors and Christians. Even this is not certain, for ritual battles in Tenochtitlan sometimes ended in Mexica deaths.

With this victory, whether real or symbolic, the earlier mimetic defeat, recalling the Mexica flight from the Culhua in 1343, was avenged. So had it been in history. Just four years after their initial defeat, in 1347, the Mexica had returned to conquer Culhuacan.[25] The dramatized invasion of transmontane territory, therefore, both looked forward to the imminent season of war and back to the decisive Mexica conquest of Culhuacan. It is intriguing that we should meet here the dramatic pattern that is so prevalent in both Spanish and Mexican *moros y cristianos:* an initial defeat followed, later in the festival, by a corresponding victory for those whose descendants control the festival. Just as, in Spain, the Christians first lose to the Moors before gaining a final victory, so, in the street theater of Tenochtitlan, the Mexica first lost to the Culhua before gaining a retaliatory victory. I assume that the pattern developed independently on both sides of the Atlantic, for a final victory is almost always rendered dramatically more interesting by a preliminary defeat, but the shared pattern is one more reason the imported festivals of Moors and Christians would have seemed strangely familiar to the Mexica.

The successful Mexica invasion of enemy territory was followed by a great assembly of all "the leading warriors, the generals, the commanding generals, and all the seasoned warriors, . . . the respected brave warriors," passing in review and in a kind of victory parade before Motecuzoma. "Gifts" of "costly array" were given to "the great brave warriors" as a "reward" for their service. Torquemada suggests that this, too, may have referred to the war between the Mexica and the Culhua and to "the victory that their god Huitzilopochtli gave them against their enemies."[26] Then the "hand-waving dance" was repeated in the square before Toci's temple. The warriors who had been honored took part, proudly displaying their "insignia." But "all the onlookers," especially "the beloved old women, raised a tearful cry," mourning those of their sons who would die in the imminent season of war. The dramatic narrative had moved from past to immediate future conflicts. Toci, her Huaxteca, and the "women physicians" danced separately, behind the warriors, and sang "in a high falsetto."[27] The hand-waving dance lasted from midday until sunset and was taken up again at dawn the next day, with even more dancers, a greater assembly of warriors, and more prestigious awards of "insignia . . . covered with gold . . . [and] full of quetzal feathers." Motecuzoma himself joined in the hand-waving dance that followed the presentation of awards. The decorated dancers, we are told, filled the whole square with reflected sunlight.

But the priests did not permit the festival to end with a dance in honor of the warriors, even if it were accompanied by women wailing over the imminent death of their sons and husbands in war. Late in the afternoon, when the dancing had ended, the priests of Chicomecoatl appeared, dressed in the skins of other captives who had been sacrificed and flayed and accompanied by priestesses bearing ears of dried maize on their backs. From a smaller temple of Huitzilopochtli, the priests scattered seeds of maize and squash on the people below. Brawls developed among the members of the crowd, as they fought one another to gather the seed. Then the Fire Priest of Huitzilopochtli set a wooden bowl filled with chalk and white feathers on the lower level of the war god's pyramid. Warriors raced one another up the temple steps, the first to arrive plunging his hands into the bowl and tossing chalk and feathers into the air to waft down over himself and his companions. "Chalk and feathers," Clendinnen explains, "were the sign of the warrior victim," of those who would die in battle or on the sacrificial stone. "With that headlong rush up the stairs, and their submission to the slow drift and settling of the whiteness, the warriors marked themselves for death."[28]

The skin wearer, the living image of Toci, watched. As the whitened soldiers ran from the temple, (s)he accosted and pursued them, uttering her terrifying "war cries." Even Motecuzoma ran a little way with the warriors, subjecting himself to the demands of Toci. Warriors came to blows during this last desperate rush through the city, as the priests reasserted their dominance. But signs of resistance also emerged: wherever Toci's impersonator went, "everyone spat at her; anyone whose flowers lay in his hand," a fading symbol of imminent bloodshed, "spat at her; he cast [the flowers] at her." Scattering as they ran, the warriors left Toci to run, alone but for a few priests, to her temple at the city's edge. There, the priests removed Toci's garments, crown, and streamers, and peeled off her shriveling skin, hanging the latter on a wooden frame so that "its head looked forth." With this the festival was over.[29]

The dramatic narrative of the Festival of the Sweeping of the Roads linked the early Mexica conflict with the Culhua to the season of war that the festival inaugurated. As such, Brown suggests, it "reflect[ed] and reinforc[ed] the ideology of the necessity of war," much as Veteran's Day or the rhetoric of "mak[ing] the world safe for democracy" do in the United States today.[30] But there are obvious differences, not the least of which is the horror of the Mexica festival. "Dramatically and experientially," Clendinnen writes, "[Ochpaniztli] was a brilliantly constructed horror event, in its abrupt changes of pace and its teasing of the imagination through the exploitation of darkness, the sudden rush of feet, the whisper of brooms sodden with human blood, as in the deliberation of the slow construction of Toci, built layer by layer upon the flayed human skin, each layer revealing more of her nature, until the benign custodian of curing and the domestic stood triumphant as the pitiless mistress of war, insatiable eater of men."[31] This horror calls Brown's comparison into question, for what patriotic call to arms today would carefully construct so dreadful a patroness? Modern festive and political rhetoric conceals the horrors of war, saving its gory depictions of bloodshed for the movies, where its audience can pretend that such things are not real. The Mexica festival, while extreme in its cruelty, is at least startlingly honest about the physical and psychological costs of war.

We see, too, in the Mexica festival, forms of resistance that one cannot imagine being sanctioned in modern state commemorations of military glory. Women weep and the crowds spit on Toci as she passes, an act comparable in its context to burning the U.S. flag during the Vietnam War. What is startling is that such a protest does not seem to have drawn official condemnation in Tenochtitlan but to have been an accepted part of the emotionally charged festivities. Perhaps it was reckoned to balance (and therefore to license) the humiliation experienced by the warriors as they were twice "defeated" and thus driven bloodily to war by the priests. As humiliation provoked resentment, so resentment warranted further humiliation in an annual exchange of tense emotions that could only be safely expressed under the guise of dramatic "pretense."

It is the genius of traditional theater to provide avenues for the negotiation of such tensions, to encourage, as Clendinnen puts it, "the expression of the normally concealed as well as the approved, the contested as well as the shared."[32]

Whether such festive negotiations of power are preferable to more violent political confrontations and the possible overthrow (or retaliatory strengthening) of existing power structures depends, in part, on one's view of the particular community in which they take place. And, I suspect, the degree to which such tensions are truly negotiated rather than vented in fear and anger depends on the degree to which the festival is the shared property of various segments of the community rather than the exclusive property of a dominant group.

Modern Spanish festivals of Moors and Christians are the creative work of an entire community, marking out a festive space where tensions that might otherwise divide can find sanctioned expression. The Mexica calendar festivals, by contrast, were primarily the property of a priestly elite, who used them to impose an ideology of war and sacrifice on the warriors in particular and on the people as a whole. The warriors, if I am reading the festival of Ochpaniztli correctly, had partially internalized and still partially resisted that ideology. Although the festival's public transcript had to do with fertility myths and past military triumphs and defeats, its (not entirely) hidden transcript enacted priestly dominance and warrior subordination. The festival, in other words, appears to have been a calculated public act of intimidation and recruitment on the part of the priests, reinforced and made more palatable by the public dispensation of military honors on the part of the king, and met with a deeply ambivalent and (at times) fiercely reluctant compliance on the part of the warriors and their families. War was declared to be necessary, its psychological and physical costs were acknowledged, its participants honored (and implicitly shamed should they refuse or retreat), its deaths mourned in advance, and its goddess revealed (and reviled) as the bloodthirsty patron of breeding, curing, and slaughter. So began the Mexica season of war.

9
The Festival of the Raising of the Banners

PREPARATIONS for Panquetzaliztli (the Festival of the Raising of the Banners) began immediately after the close of Ochpaniztli. Nightly, during the intervening months, naked, fasting priests, blowing shell trumpets and pottery whistles, spread fir branches on mountaintop altars around Tenochtitlan. On the branches they laid bloodied reeds and maguey thorns that had been passed through perforations in their own flesh. Meanwhile, in the courtyard of the Great Temple of Huitzilopochtli, young men burned pine bonfires against the dark, sprinkling blood from their earlobes into the fire, while a captive *ixiptla,* dressed as Huitzilopochtli, danced.[1]

Panquetzaliztli honored Huitzilopochtli, whom we have already met as the instigator of war, the bridegroom of Toci, and the god whose appetite for sacrificial victims prompted Tlacaelel's flowery wars. He was the patron god of the Mexica, lately raised to the status of sun god, whose fiery energy "had, by extraordinary convention, to be given nourishment, in the shape of human blood."[2] He was also, according to Sahagún's informants, "only a common man, a human being," a phrase generally taken to mean that the original Huitzilopochtli had been a warrior leader of the early Mexica. Some believe that the final stages of Huitzilopochtli's metamorphosis from local hero to tribal deity and bloodthirsty sun god had been engineered by Tlacaelel as part of his transformation of the Mexica from a minor tribal power into a military empire.[3]

According to Mexica myth at the time of the conquest, Coatlicue was said to have conceived Huitzilopochtli immaculately by clutching a ball of feathers to her breast. Misconstruing her pregnancy, her daughter (Coyolxauhqui) and her innumerable warrior sons (the Centzon Huitznahua) planned to kill their mother. But one of the brothers, Quauitlicac, warned the unborn Huitzilopochtli of the matricidal (and hence fratricidal) intentions of his siblings. As the Huitznahua advanced in full "war array" on Coatlicue, Quauitlicac kept Huitzilopochtli informed of their progress. At the moment of their arrival, Huitzilopochtli "burst forth, born." Grasping a "fire serpent," he used the magical weapon to decapitate his sister. Then he pursued his brothers until they, too, perished at his hands.[4]

Following Seler's early-twentieth-century lead, many scholars have interpreted this myth as the first decisive victory of the sun (Huitzilopochtli) over the moon (Coyolxauhqui) and the stars (Huitznahua), a triumph recapitulated every sunrise.[5] Others, noting that the myth makes no mention of sun, moon, or stars, have understood it to refer to an early battle for control of the Mexica shortly after they arrived in Coatepec, near Tula, in 1163. Eduardo Matos Moctezuma writes, "From reviewing the historical evidence, it seems certain that part of the Mexica group, made up of people from the barrio of Huiznahua, opposed the authority of the human leader Huitzilopochtli. The Huiznahua, led by a warrior woman, Coyolxauhqui, . . . were defeated in the confrontation. This rebellion signifies the historical attempt to usurp the power and control of the larger group led by Huitzilopochtli. It is a matter, then, of an internal power struggle that was remembered by subsequent generations as a turning point in their history."[6] In any case, it is this narrative that lies behind much of the action of Panquetzaliztli.

Tenochtitlan's merchants also readied themselves for the festival, for this was the only public occasion on which their contribution to the Mexica cycle of war and sacrifice found dramatic expression. The merchants regarded themselves as warriors of trade, routinely penetrating enemy territory for profit, serving as royal spies, collecting tribute in the form of imposed trade, and sometimes resorting to defensive arms to protect their lives and goods. During Panquetzaliztli they appropriated for themselves the ceremonial role of soldiers bringing sacrificial victims to Huitzilopochtli. Whereas true warriors captured sacrificial offerings in the "military marketplace" of warfare, merchants bartered for them in the slave market of Azcapotzalco, to the west of Tenochtitlan. A good slave, unblemished and able to dance well, cost "forty large capes" or more than four thousand cacao beans. To enhance the illusion that the slaves were prisoners of war, the men among them were armed with shields made of flowers and their hair cut "in the manner of seasoned warriors."

The merchants stocked their homes with grains, beans, chilis, salt, tomatoes, turkeys, edible dogs, chocolate, and other foods for the upcoming feast; and they tried to ingratiate themselves with the warrior class by presenting lavish gifts to "the great chieftains" and "fearless warriors." Through the annual, ostentatious redistribution of their wealth, the merchants aimed at the status that warriors accrued through risking their lives in open warfare. But these gifts could not assuage what Clendinnen calls "the settled animosity of warriors to merchant claims of warriordom." Ceremonial battles that recalled the birth of Huitzilopochtli and his victory over his siblings offered opportunity for bloody clashes between warriors and the merchants' purchased champions. Just as the festival of Ochpaniztli betrayed a certain tension between warriors and priests, so Panquetzaliztli showed warriors and merchants at odds with one another.[7]

Nine days before the sacrifice, the merchants led their surrogate captives to the foot of the Great Temple, where they drenched them in sacred water. Then, the merchants stripped the victims of their sodden clothes and dressed them in the paper vestments in which they were to die. They painted blue stripes on the slaves' legs and arms and light blue and yellow horizontal stripes on their faces—blue being the color of the daylight sky associated with Huitzilopochtli and yellow being the color of the sun. They gave the slaves nose pendants shaped liked arrows and crowned them with feathered headdresses made of reeds.[8]

Eight days later, at nightfall, bathed and painted slaves, merchants, flag bearers, and others who would play a role in the sacrificial ritual, both men and women, joined hands in the "serpent dance." The long line of dancers that snaked around the temple grounds recalled both the serpent wall that enclosed the city's ritual district and the staff that the image of Huitzilopochtli held in its right hand, for this, too, was "carved in the form of a snake, all blue and undulating." Huitzilopochtli's staff, in turn, recalled the fire serpent with which he had beheaded and dismembered his sister Coyolxauhqui. "Winding about like a snake," accompanied by rhythmic drumming and song, and watched by an admiring crowd, the merchants and their slaves danced until conch shells sounded at midnight.[9]

The same night, young women, devoted to a year of chaste and cloistered service in the temple, kneaded ground amaranth seeds, toasted maize, and black maguey syrup into a sticky dough. With it they fashioned an edible image of Huitzilopochtli, a replica, in size, shape, and decorative detail, of the wooden one that sat atop the Great Temple. Noblemen then dressed the image to recall the meaning of Huitzilopochtli's name, "southern humming-bird" or "humming-bird on the left." "On it was placed the bird's beak of shining, burnished gold; the feather headdress on his head; his apron of plumes; his shield, staff, bracelets, and anklets, his splendid sandals; and his breechcloth, a magnificent piece of needlework and feathers." He was then set on a blue litter, blue being the color of the south and of the god.[10]

The next day was one of comparative calm before the festive storm of ceremonial marathon, mock battle, fire serpent, and mass sacrifice burst over Tenochtitlan. The merchants displayed their "captives" and watched them dance; they presided over domestic feasts and gift giving; and, in the evening, perhaps accompanied in procession by the dough image, they led those who were to die up the steps of Huitzilopochtli's temple, around the sacrificial stone, and down the other side, in an eerie dress rehearsal of the captives' final trajectory the next day. So that the victims would not fear death and thereby disgrace their merchant "captors," they were made to drink a potent wine known as "obsidian medicine." It was "as if they had drunk a great deal of wine; they were, in fact quite drunk." At midnight, just as the true warriors did during the Feast of the Flaying of Men, the merchants cut locks of hair from their "captives'" heads.[11]

The climactic day of the festival, like so many great folk performances, was packed with multiple, simultaneous, complementary actions, rendering it impossible for anyone to witness the whole of it during a single annual celebration. An hour before dawn, the young women of Huitzilopochtli's temple came out, adorned with thick crowns and necklaces of toasted popcorn, their cheeks painted red, and "their arms feathered with red parrot plumes from the elbow to the wrist." They carried the image of Huitzilopochtli to the temple courtyard, where they were met by young men also serving a celibate year in the temple. The men bore the littered image to the foot of the temple steps, where large crowds paid it homage.[12]

At dawn, the pace changed abruptly with "the eruption from Huitzilopochtli's temple of a running priest," who bore a small image, variously described as being made of wood or dough. The portable image depicted "Huitzilopochtli's lieutenant Paynal, 'He Who Hasteneth,' representation of Huitzilopochtli's terrible speed." The priest rushed to the sacred ball court, where he slew four prisoners of war; the corpses were dragged around the court, as if to "paint" it with blood. For the next two to four hours, the Paynal bearer and a great press of followers ran a circuit of fifteen to twenty miles through the city's suburbs, passing under "triumphal arches embellished with flowers and featherwork, lavishly adorned with banners," greeted at each arch by what Durán calls the "abominable, dismal sound" of "drums, trumpets, and conch shells," and halting briefly along the way for further human sacrifice. Trees and cacti throughout the city were hung with "small banners." The swift and bloody procession was met repeatedly by crowds of "common folk," who "beheaded many quail" in honor of the passing god. The Mexica believed that while Huitzilopochtli "was alive he was never caught, never taken prisoner in war, was always triumphant over his enemies, and, no matter how swift his foes, none ever caught up with him. He was the one who caught them. Therefore, this feast honored his speed."[13]

Paynal was joined en route by a priest bearing the image of Quauitlicac, the elder brother who had warned the unborn Huitzilopochtli of his danger. As the raucous marathon turned for home, the dramatization of battle began elsewhere. On their way to the Great Temple, the ceremonially purified slaves were waylaid by an army of captive warriors, armed with pine staves and shields, who represented the Huitznahua. The warriors were aided by a number of Mexica "chieftains" and "brave warriors" wielding throwing spears. The slaves were armed with "shields" and "obsidian-bladed swords" or with "bird arrows" tipped with sharpened flint. While the merchants watched, their costly representatives fought the enemies of Huitzilopochtli. Scholars often suggest that this episode "recalled a mythic moment in Huitzilopochtli's early struggles against his murderous siblings the Stars."[14] But it is hard, even if one accepts the solar reading of the myth, to draw precise lines of correspondence between the staged battle and the confrontation of sun, moon, and stars, if only because, as sun god, Huitzilopochtli wins his contest single-handedly. It is much simpler to take the mock battle to represent the clan war that divided the Mexica in Coatepec and to understand the arrival of Paynal a little later, disrupting the skirmish and scattering its participants, as the decisive victory of

Huitzilopochtli and his clan. The temple of Huitzilopochtli itself was understood to represent the hill of Coatepec.[15]

The ritual battle also had immediate import, for in it the simmering tensions between warriors and merchants suddenly found clear and fatal expression. Warriors and their hard-won captives fought the property of merchants in a confrontation that was no mere "skirmish; it was just like real fighting." Some were killed in the battle; others were taken prisoner. Captured slaves were ransomed by their merchant owners or, if sufficient ransom was not forthcoming, consigned to be eaten by their captors. Open seizure and literal consumption of individual merchants' human property thus shamed these professional purveyors of conspicuous consumption, exposing their goods, when tested in battle, as inferior. Sometimes, the human goods proved worth the investment: if a Mexica warrior was taken, he was stretched across a *teponaztli* drum by the slaves and his heart cut open.

It is not hard to understand why Mexica warriors risked their lives to defend the honor of their class against mercantile surrogates. But Clendinnen wonders why the slaves, scheduled to die anyway later in the day, fought so hard. "Perhaps," she surmises, it was "for a more dignified death on the killing stone . . . ; perhaps through drunken bravado; perhaps simply to postpone the coming of the dark." Even more intriguing is the question of why the Mexica warriors publicly allied themselves with those who played the enemies of Huitzilopochtli. Can we again detect, smuggled into the public transcript of military heroism, the traces of a hidden transcript of resistance to the priestly cult of the sun god that sent the warriors so relentlessly to war?[16]

The battle ended when an official "onlooker" announced the imminent arrival of Paynal. The Huitznahua and their allied warriors fled before "the terrible speed of Huitzilopochtli." Again the priestly script called for Mexica warriors to flee, defeated, before a priest bearing the image of a god. Swept up in the commemoration of Huitzilopochtli's victory, the crowd ran behind Paynal to the Great Temple, where the dough idol of Huitzilopochtli was ensconced, high up, in "a flower-decked shelter," having been pushed and hauled up the steps earlier in the day to the noise of trumpets, flutes, shells, and drums.[17]

It is not quite clear what happened next. Sahagún tells us, in one volume, that the warriors "captured" the dough image and took it to their homes to share with their neighbors and kin. Elsewhere, he reports that a priest who had been accorded the title of Quetzalcoatl slew the image of Huitzilopochtli, in the presence of Motecuzoma and eight other religious dignitaries, by firing a dart into its heart. It was then broken up and eaten by temple personnel, the heart being reserved for Motecuzoma. Francisco Clavijero follows the second of Sahagún's narratives, adding, in strange ignorance of the grief of mothers, wives, and daughters, that women did not eat the "sacred dough" because "the business of war did not concern them." Durán reports that the young women of the temple made several hundred dough bones that were placed at the feet of the image, that the "flesh and bones of Huitzilopochtli" were sprinkled with sacrificial blood, and that all were then broken into small fragments and distributed to the entire community, "old and young, men and women, old men and children," in a kind of pagan Eucharist.[18]

Common to all these accounts is the death of Huitzilopochtli and his consumption by some or all of the Mexica people. We may be misled by superficial similarities with the Christian Eucharist into thinking that the Mexica understood their eating of the body of Huitzilopochtli to entail a beneficial communion with their god. In Mexica calendar festivals, however, it was not penitential devotees but victorious warriors who ate the flesh of sacrificial victims. Sahagún writes of Huitzilopochtli being captured by Mexica warriors or executed by a priest known, like the god Quetzalcoatl after whom he was named, for his "compassion," for his "pure heart," and for being a "peace-maker." The cult of Quetzalcoatl was a focus of enmity to sacrifice.[19] If we take seriously the language of captivity, execution, and consumption, we are led to the startling conclusion that, at the very pivot of the season of war, immediately following the dramatization of Huitzilopochtli's decisive victory, the Mexica warriors and a priest of Quetzalcoatl opposed the flow of the festival narrative with a representation of the war god's defeat at their own hands.

The next act was a magnificent, popular display of large-scale puppetry. After the surviving slaves (and imminent victims) were led in procession around the temple pyramid, a vivid image of Huitzilopochtli's magical weapon, the fire serpent, made of brightly colored paper and feathers, snaked down the temple steps. Clendinnen imagines it as "a kind of Chinese dragon." Sahagún reports that a priest was concealed within the serpent, which was "just like a blazing pine firebrand. Its tongue was made of flaming red feathers. It went [as if] burning [like] a torch. And its tail was of paper, perhaps two fathoms or three fathoms [12 to 18 feet] long. As it came down, it was like a real serpent; it showed its tongue; it was as if it bent back and forth." According to Durán, who may have confused the pre-Hispanic fire serpent with a simpler device that he had seen "in certain dances in Mexico City and in the surrounding towns," the serpent was "made of paper coiled about a pole, all made of [red parrot] feathers," and carried by a priest. In any case, the serpent drew a large crowd: "the common people massed together; indeed all came to watch. They were spread about . . . everywhere, seating themselves in the temple courtyard." Finally, at the foot of the temple, the priest turned the serpent to the four cardinal directions, stepped out of his elaborate costume, and set fire to it. Whether the crowd understood this to represent enhancement or destruction of the fire serpent (and of the power of the warrior god who wielded it) is impossible to tell.[20]

Huitzilopochtli's thirst for blood was reaffirmed when the day's activities ended with the sacrifice of the bathed slaves. Led up the temple steps by the priest bearing the image of Paynal and by their merchant "captors," the exhausted victims were stretched efficiently across the sacrificial stone, their chests gashed and hearts gouged out, and their corpses rolled, bouncing, down the steps, whence each was taken home by its merchant owner. There, "they cooked [the slave] in a stewpot. Separately, in a stewpot, they cooked the grains of maize. They served [his flesh] on it. They placed only a little on top of it. No chili did they add to it; they only sprinkled salt on it. Indeed all [the host's] kinsmen ate of it." Thus, as Clendinnen puts it, "the offering merchant chose to act the 'warrior' fantasy through to the end, . . . sharing out the flesh of his 'captive' just as the real warriors did" during the Festival of the Flaying of Men.[21]

The next day, while the merchants relaxed in domestic singing and gift-giving, other social tensions came to the fore. It was a day, Clendinnen writes, when "blooded warriors of noble lineage were privileged to drink pulque, as were the highest ranks of the commoner warriors. But the 'rulers of youths,' or as we would say the principals or directors of the warrior schools, stood one rung below that coveted privilege." If they drank, they had to do so in secret, "crouch[ing] behind bushes in order not to be seen." And, if they were discovered, they were beaten with pine staves and their heads disgracefully shaved. Their attackers "dragged them . . . ; they went kicking them; on the ground they struck them repeatedly; they cast stones at them. . . . From time to time death came from this." Sahagún does not identify the vigilantes' motives. Perhaps recent graduates of the schools, unconsciously conflicted over a military career that brought both privilege and danger in the service of Huitzilopochtli and emotionally overwrought by the sensory onslaught of the festival, sought inarticulate revenge on those whose discipline had bound them to that course. One can imagine today's graduates of boot camp, if they were sanctioned by festive custom, similarly turning on their former drill sergeants.[22]

Student warrior resentment of Huitzilopochtli and his priests seems to have shaped the culminating event of the festival, the *chonchaiocacalioa* or "mock-fight of the Chonchayotl." Three days into the following month, a wild man appeared, wearing a "terrible mask" and bloody, disheveled hair. He represented Chonchayotl, another "image," according to Sahagún, of Huitzilopochtli (Fig. 11). Allied with Chonchayotl were the "offering priests," who slew the sacrificial victims, and their students from the *calmecac* (priest house); opposing him were the young men of the warrior school or *telpochcalli* (house of youth). From midday to dusk, the two sides struck at one another with "fir staves" and "long stout reeds," the constant clash of weapons sounding like "waves . . . breaking on the shore." Many were hurt in the

11. Mock fight of Chonchayotl. From Sahagún, *Florentine,* vol. 3.
Courtesy of University of Utah Press and the School of American Research.

fighting. If a priest was caught, the student warriors rubbed maguey thorns in his flesh (Fig. 11), causing intense itching, and, if a cadet was captured, the priests drew blood from his ears, shoulders, breast, and thighs. The goal of the battle appears, at least in part, to have been the ransacking of the other's college buildings. Successful invaders stole mats, seats, drums, and shell trumpets.[23]

If it were not for the presence of Chonchayotl, we might attribute this mock battle to an excess of student energy and intercollegiate rivalry, intensified by class distinctions. In general, the sons of the aristocracy attended the *calmecac,* while the sons of commoners were restricted to the *telpochcalli.*[24] But the image of Huitzilopochtli as a wild man with terrible face and bloody, matted hair shows us once again how the Mexica calendar festivals represented the physical and psychological cost of war with startling honesty. Just as Toci was transformed, during the Festival of the Sweeping of the Roads, from "the benign custodian of the domestic" into "the pitiless mistress of war," so Huitzilopochtli was stripped, during the Festival of the Raising of the Banners, of his warm and sunny (blue and yellow) facade, his astonishing speed, and his billowing paper serpent, and exposed as a wild, disorderly force, soaked in human blood.

Once again, too, it was the priests who defended the gods of war, and the warriors, whose lives were placed in jeopardy by the strictures of a militaristic religion, who found a way to express resistance. During Panquetzaliztli, the warriors not only stood firm against the pretensions of the merchants, whose efforts to buy warrior status belittled the true dangers of warfare, but allied themselves with the Huitznahua in their battle against the legendary hero and bloodthirsty sun god. If I have identified the pulque vigilantes correctly, young warriors beat the instructors who contrived to train them. Finally, in the closing skirmish of the festival, warriors-in-training fought hard against the impersonator of the god they were bound to serve and against the priests who shaped his image. The Mexica festivals of war provide a remarkable series of windows onto the tensions of a society that might otherwise appear united in its devotion to the forces of war.

10

The Festival of the Flaying of Men

B EFORE going on to our third and final Mexica festival, it may be helpful briefly to address the question of the festivals' theatricality. On the one hand, it would be a mistake to reduce to mere metaphors descriptions of the Mexica calendar festivals as "grand ritual dramas" and as a "state theatre of power."[1] On the other hand, the festivals do not conform to the conventional model of literary theater, in which a prescribed dramatic text is performed before a single, stationary audience intended to hear every word, see every action, and participate only with attention and applause. I regard them instead as a form of spectacular ceremonial or traditional theater, akin but by no means identical to the festivals of Moors and Christians.

Traditional theater tends to privilege action and costume over the written (and spoken) word. This holds true for the Mexica festivals. Despite the Mexica predilection for ornate public rhetoric, neither Sahagún nor Durán mention dramatic speeches being delivered during the festival rites, and only occasionally was a moralistic sermon, offering no real elucidation of what had gone before, delivered at the festival's end.[2] Almost all the data on Mexica festivals have to do with complex actions and elaborate costumes. Louise Burkhart observes that "theatre, in the sense of a prepared dialogue spoken by a group of role-playing individuals in front of an audience, did not exist among the Nahuas before the Spanish invasion." She adds, however, that "existing descriptions" of the calendar rituals, which embodied "sacred narratives" of myth and ethnic history, "suggest that these stories were represented more through details of costume and gesture than through speech."[3] In such theater, meaning inheres in what is done (and worn) without being rendered explicit by speech.

The Mexica festivals were also characterized by a profligate simultaneity of action. Although, in medieval European theater, several actions could take place at the same time, the performers made an effort to ensure that most of the audience saw most of the action. The medieval theater in the round could stage several actions at once in full view of a seated audience, while the processional theater of the Barcelona Corpus Christi festival or the York Mystery Plays staged each pageant in several locations en route, so that an extended but stationary audience could see the narrative unfold in its proper sequence. The Mexica festivals, by contrast, unrolled in such a way that it was impossible for any individual to see all the action in any given year. Like many annual folk theatrical events, they depended for their overall coherence on an accumulated communal knowledge of the totality of public actions. Performers and audience alike would know, even if they could not see, what was going on elsewhere. Theatrical events of this kind may be compared to dining à la carte in a familiar restaurant rather than eating courses stipulated by a set menu.[4] In the former case, since the diners cannot eat all that is offered at a single sitting, they choose from the many dishes that are already familiar to them. In the latter case, like the audience in the literary theater, the diners eat what is set before them. The same analogy holds true for the festivals of Moors and Christians. Like a diner trying to do justice to an à la carte menu at a single sitting, I have run between shore and castle in Carboneras (Almería) to witness the simultaneous landing of the Moors and the defensive preparations of the Christians, while townspeople, confident that they would dine again next year, stayed put in one location or the other. And, just as a Mexica spectator would have had to choose between following Paynal or watching the Huitznahua ambush the purified slaves, I followed the noisy procession of Moors and Christians through the streets of Zacatecas rather than watch the first of the *matachines* dance outside the chapel at Bracho.

Part of the difference between literary theater and traditional theater in this respect involves the absence of a clear distinction between audience and performers in religious festivities. Those who are not in costume, be they congregation or crowd, constitute a participant audience, actively taking part in rather than passively observing the action. Just as an actor, even in the literary theater, does not expect to see all the action from his or her vantage point on (or off) stage, so noncostumed festival participants do not expect to see all the action from their place within the flow of events. The attitude of Mexica audiences ranged, within a single festival, from that of the "common people" who "came to watch" the descent of the fire serpent, through the "profound obeisance" of those who worshiped the dough image of Huitzilopochtli at the foot of the temple steps, to the prolonged and exhausting participation of those who ran after Paynal. Others alternated between the poles of performer and spectator. The men who played "drums, trumpets, and conch shells" at each of the arches along Paynal's route may well, in the manner of festival musicians I have seen elsewhere, have downed their instruments after the ceremonial marathon had passed and wandered into town to see the battle of the Huitznahua or the descent of the fire serpent.

There is much more that could be said about the shared theatricality of Mexica festivals and festivals of Moors and Christians, but this will suffice to keep the question of their relationship before us and to remind us that the boundaries of theatrical art stretch far beyond the confines of the literary theater. We move now to the last of the Mexica festivals that concern us, Tlacaxipeualiztli (the Festival of the Flaying of Men) (Fig. 12). Tlacaxipeualiztli honored Xipe Totec (the Flayed One,

12. Festival of the Flaying of Men. From Sahagún, *Florentine,* vol. 3.
Courtesy of University of Utah Press and the School of American Research.

13. Xipe Totec. Detail from *Codex Borbonicus*, fol. 14.
Courtesy of Akademische Druck- u. Verlagsanstalt.

Our Cut One) (Fig. 13). Spanning late February and early March, when the season of war gave way to that of agriculture, it has long been regarded as an elaborate fertility ritual. Eduard Seler defined Xipe Totec as "the earth god" and the Festival of the Flaying of Men as "the early spring festival that fell in the season before the planting, when the soil was prepared to receive the new seed."[5] Donning another's skin thus came to be regarded "as a metaphor for the living seed bursting forth from

97

within its dead covering" and a "'new skin' of vegetation [being] placed upon the earth by the coming of the rainy season."[6] The mock battles of the festival are read as the "struggle of summer with winter, sky with earth."[7] But, other than a "Song of Xipe Totec," which speaks of the sprouting of the "tender corn" and may (or may not) have been sung during the festival, and the "bunches of ears of corn" offered by "the people" during the first round of human sacrifice,[8] there is little internal evidence to support Seler's thesis. Sahagún and Durán offer no such interpretive guidance and, as Broda points out, Seler's reading of the hymn and its possible setting in terms of a fertility cult "reflects the concepts current" in the study of folklore and religion "at the end of the nineteenth century."[9]

Some scholars, most notably Broda and Carrasco, have therefore begun to look back to the season of war, rather than forward to the time of planting, for the significance of the festival. Broda has written that, "in addition to its traditional religious nucleus," the festival, with its long parade of captives to the sacrificial stone, its gladiatorial displays of prowess, and its visiting dignitaries from other towns, was "a great occasion for the warriors to enhance their prestige," and that, as the regional dominance of the Mexica increased, it became "a festival of terrorizing other peoples." Carrasco has argued that Tlacaxipeualiztli was the "representation of an ideal battlefield" on which the Mexica warriors were always victorious and their enemies always defeated. The festival was, he writes, "a story the Aztecs told to themselves about their triumphant wars, in the way they wanted it known."[10]

I agree with Broda and Carrasco that the surviving records, while not excluding an agricultural reading, point more clearly to war as the foremost concern of the festival. But I would modify Carrasco's interpretation by suggesting that it was only the public transcript that portrayed an "ideal war." Although the resistance of the warrior class does not appear to have been as strongly expressed during Tlacaxipeualiztli as it was during Ochpaniztli and Panquetzaliztli, we can still read in the festival mask an undercurrent of regret, a chastened recognition that the survivors of one season of war may be the victims of the next and that those who gain honor as captors in Tenochtitlan may, within the year, be sacrificial captives in Tlaxcala or Huexotzinco. The Mexica festivals never strayed too far from the realities of war.

Preparations for the festival began forty days beforehand with the selection, in each of the city's twenty or so barrios, of a slave *ixiptla*. Dressed like Xipe Totec, he was paraded through the streets and honored "as if he had been the god himself."[11] Dress rehearsals for the gladiatorial sacrifice also took place. Four times costumed captive warriors were taken to Yopico, the temple pyramid devoted to Xipe Totec. There they were made to go through a mock sacrifice: corn tortillas, rather than hearts, were torn from their chests by priestly sleight of hand. Their captors also dressed for the rehearsal, "anoint[ing] themselves with ochre" and covering their arms and legs with "white turkey feathers." On the afternoon before the festival, the captives "danced the captives' dance," while the warriors, armed with shields, rattle sticks, and costly insignia, basked in the admiration of the crowd. At midnight, each warrior cut hair from his captive's head, believing that he thereby inherited the latter's "valor" and "renown." [12]

At dawn, in each of the barrios, while the people offered ears of corn, the impersonators of Xipe Totec and of several other Mexica gods were slain. After the victim's heart had been removed, "the skinners . . . cast the dead body down and split it from the nape of the neck to the heel, skinning it as a lamb. The skin came off complete. . . . Other men donned the skins immediately," together with the appropriate "garments and insignia," and "took the names of the gods who had been impersonated." [13] Daybreak also saw the start of sacrifices at the main temple of Yopico, where, all day, the younger and less prestigious of the captives were killed and flayed. Although the more fearful among them fainted or threw themselves on the ground, having to be dragged up the temple steps by their hair, others went boldly, shouting the virtues of their city out loud until they, too, were stretched over the stone and their breasts cut open "with a wide-bladed flint knife." Both those who were sacrificed and those who subsequently wore the flayed skins were known as xipeme (flayed ones) and tototecti (those "burned" in honor of Totec). [14]

The flayed corpses were then removed and butchered, one thigh from each victim being offered to Motecuzoma and the rest of the body being taken to the captor's house. There "a stew of dried maize " was prepared and distributed, each portion topped with "a piece of the flesh of the captive," to gathered relatives. Far from rejoicing in his moment of triumph, the warrior who had taken the captive was "whitened with chalk" and "pasted with feathers," the conventional adornment of a sacrificial victim. He thus openly reminded himself and his family that, although he had not yet died in war, "he would yet go to die, would go to pay the debt [in war or by sacrifice]." The clause, startlingly, is unconditional: this year's captor will be another year's captive. The warrior's relatives "greeted him with tears" and "encouraged him." The drunkenness that followed was surely more morose than joyous, designed to drown terrors rather than to celebrate triumphs. [15]

Meanwhile, secretly, a prestigious audience of out-of-town guests arrived. Rulers from conquered and as yet unconquered towns came, by invitation of the Mexica emperor (an offer they could hardly refuse), to watch the climactic day of the festival. The guests "were assigned booths adorned with flowers and reeds, within which they could sit and watch," unseen, the gladiatorial sacrifice. Thus, as Broda puts it, was the Feast of the Flaying of Men "used as a means of terror and intimidation." [16]

The day's performance began at the ceremonial skull rack. There the surviving captives assembled, their bodies and faces painted white but for their eyelids and the skin around their lips, which were highlighted in black and red. Their arms and legs had been further pasted with white down, and each wore a sleeveless paper jacket. Identifying with the prisoners' fate, their Mexica captors also came pasted with white feathers. Then, while the *teponaztli* drummers sang and the captives danced, the four "sacrificers" appeared, two "dressed as jaguars and two as eagles." Each in turn approached the captives like a warrior stalking and attacking his prey, "dancing as if stretched on the ground; they went each stretched flat; they went looking from side to side, they each went leaping upwards; they each went fighting." Each warrior raised his shield and "obsidian-bladed club" to the sun before making way for the next dancer.[17]

Then "a very solemn procession" descended the temple steps. "Many priests" took part, serving as "proxies of all the gods." Having taken over the roles of captive *ixiptla* sacrificed the previous day, the priests were dressed in gods' regalia and victims' skins. Denoting the massed forces of a largely hostile cosmos, they came ready to shed blood. The chief priest, dressed as Youallauan (Drinker of the Night), another manifestation of Xipe Totec, carried the great sacrificial knife of sharpened black obsidian. Another, dressed in animal skin, is named "the Old Bear," "the Old Mountain Lion," or "the Old Wolf." Joined by the jaguar and eagle warriors, the procession passed before the captive warriors at the skull rack and circled the round gladiatorial stone. On this was carved, as "an eternal reminder of that heroic event," scenes from the Mexica "war of liberation" against the Tepaneca in 1428. The procession ended at an arbor of branches and flowers, where the "gods" were seated on "large backed seats called roseate spoonbill feather seats."[18]

To the noise of trumpets, conch shells, singing, and "whistling with fingers placed in the mouth," combat began. The first captor led his captive to the gladiatorial stone, where the Old Bear secured a rope around the victim's ankle and through a hole in the center of the stone. As weapons, he gave the prisoner four pine cudgels, four wooden throwing balls, a wooden shield, and a war club edged only with feathers. The jaguar and eagle warriors were each armed with a shield and an obsidian-edged club. Their costumes, unlike those of the victim, were lined with padded cotton armor. As the first jaguar warrior advanced, dancing, his victim "gave forth great cries and shrieks and began to leap into the air, slapping his thighs loudly with his hand and making gestures to the sky." He threw the pine balls and cudgels at the jaguar warrior, who parried them with his shield. Then the captive, tethered to the stone, defended himself as best he could with shield and feathered club. If the jaguar "striped" the prisoner, drawing blood with the razor-sharp obsidian blades, "four priests, their bodies painted black, with long braided hair, dressed in garments like chasubles, ascended the stone and laid the wounded man on his back, holding him down by the feet and hands. Youallauan rose from his seat, went to the stone, and opened the chest of the victim with his knife. He took out the heart and offered the vapor that rose from it to the sun." Then he set a hollow feathered cane in the captive's chest cavity, stained it with blood, and offered it to the sun to drink.

If the captive warrior managed to prevent the inscription on his body of the jaguar's bloody stripe, the first jaguar gave way to the first eagle; if he, too, failed, he ceded the task to the second jaguar. Some captives fought so well that they exhausted all four warriors, only finally to be striped, now tired themselves, by a left-handed warrior dressed as the god Opochtli. Others were not so brave (or were unwilling to play a role so definitively scripted to their disadvantage) and, on first handling the feathered club, threw it down in disgust and refused to defend themselves, collapsing as if they "wished that breath might end" and that they "might cast off the burden of death." The priests obliged. The status of the captor depended on his captive's display of valor.[19] After each sacrifice, the captor toured the temples, carrying a bowl of the victim's blood. With a hollow cane he placed "nourishing" blood on the lips of all the "idols." The victim's corpse was flayed, butchered, and, except for the head, delivered to the captor's home to be cooked and eaten by his relatives. The captor himself did not eat, saying, "Shall I perchance eat my very self?"

After a full day of sacrificial combat, at which "the entire city was present," the priestly *ixiptla* and the victorious jaguar and eagle warriors danced around the gladiatorial stone. Each carried the head of a victim. The rite was called "the dance with the severed heads." The Old Bear loosened the rope from the stone and dedicated it to the four directions. As he did so, he wept, "he went howling like one bereaved; he wept for those who had suffered, who had died." After this, the visiting nobles were privately told by the Mexica ruler to "remain calm, . . . quiet and tranquil," which I take to mean compliant, and so "enjoy our friendship." They left "shocked and bewildered by what they had seen, . . . so frightened that they dared not speak." Although elements of the Festival of the Flaying of Men were distributed throughout Mesoamerica, the monstrous scale of the Mexica version horrified even visitors familiar with its basic elements.[20]

What impact it had on the Mexica themselves is hard to ascertain. On the one hand, this was an "ideal battlefield," from which all danger had been eliminated and the odds rendered "five-to-one" (and the one tied to a stone, at that!) in favor of the Mexica.[21] On the other hand, the Mexica warriors repeatedly and explicitly identified themselves with their captives, smearing themselves with the same white chalky paste and feathers, staking their own reputation on the other's performance, refusing to eat the victim's flesh on the grounds that it would be a form of self-consumption, and telling themselves that the victim's fate would, another year, be their own. The Old Bear wept over the fate of "his sons," whom he had tied to the gladiatorial stone. Once more, we may discern a distinct ambivalence, on the part of the Mexica warriors, toward a divinized cosmos (and its priests) that demanded their blood.

This ambivalence also found expression in a mock battle between warriors and priests. At sunrise the next day, priests dressed as multiple representatives of Xipe Totec, in flayed and still-dripping skins, gathered on a patch of whitened earth in the temple courtyard of Yopico. They were armed with shields, war clubs, and rattle sticks. Against them came "the great chieftains" and noble warriors, armed with pine staves. "Daring, foolhardy, full of spirit, lively, proud of their valor, playing the part of men," the warriors "kept provoking" the priests, "menaced them, kept starting a fight, provoked them to battle." The irresistible insult, to which the warriors at last resorted, was to snatch at the *xipeme*'s navel. The priests, the skin of their victims' hands and feet flapping loosely from their own wrists and ankles, gave pursuit. Behind them, menacingly, came the chief priest, still dressed as Youallauan, the Drinker of the Night. Once more, warriors fled before priests.

Sahagún compares the ensuing battle to a *juego de cañas* in which the two sides fought for and against Xipe Totec. Xipe Totec won. Although the warriors threatened the priests with their staves, the priests of the flayed (and flaying) god seized warriors, beat them with their rattle sticks, trampled on their fallen bodies, and took them captive to the temple, where they had to be ransomed for a "turkey hen" or "a great cotton mantle."[22] The skirmish afforded another opportunity for warriors to express covert hostility toward the god and his priests, who insisted that the warriors risk capture and flaying themselves in order to provide an ample supply of flayable captives. And, in its scripted defeat of the warriors, it identified them again with the festival's victims and reminded them that they were powerless, for all their anger and military prowess, to change the rules by which their universe ran. Their reprieve, in exchange for a turkey or a cloak, lasted only until the next season of war.

For the next twenty days, poor men borrowed the skins of the *xipeme* and, as individual proxies of Xipe Totec, set out, one to a barrio, to beg alms in the form of food, clothing, and jewelry. If they encountered one another, they were supposed to "fight until the skin and clothing had been torn." We read both that the skin-wearing mendicants frightened children and that mothers asked the *xipeme* to hold and bless their children. The two responses are quite compatible. I have seen screaming children "blessed" against their will by men in the "skins" (now cloth) of animals: a "bull" in Jemez Pueblo (New Mexico) and a "*mulassa* [large mule]" in Sant Feliu de Pallerols (Gerona). Other mothers would pinch the *xipeme*'s navel or, with their long fingernails, cut off a piece of skin, eating it, giving it to their children, or keeping it, according to Gerónimo de Mendieta, "like a relic." Each night, the skins were stored in the temple, along with a growing cache of alms. At the end of twenty days, the alms were divided between the mendicants and the warriors whose captives had once claimed the skin as their own. The now "reeking skins," some still worn by *xipeme*, others so dried and fragile that they had to be carried in baskets, were taken to the Yopico pyramid by their original captors. There, before a large crowd, the *xipeme* peeled off the withered skins one last time and watched as they were thrown into a subterranean chamber at the foot of the temple.[23]

How relieved, Clendinnen observes, must the Mexica warrior have been thus to conclude the "bitterness" of his festival experience. If his captive had performed well, the captor had enhanced his status, but he had done so at considerable psychological cost. For forty days, he had ushered a captive skin from its still-living incorporation of a valiant warrior's captive body to its stinking disintegration and burial, so rehearsing "his own death and decay." Tlacaxipeualiztli's "representation of an ideal battlefield" turns out to be much more ambiguous than Carrasco imagined it, for, as Clendinnen observes, "an analysis sustained over the whole parabola of the action from the perspective of the warrior and his kin suggests a much darker vision." Indeed, she concludes, "beneath the immediate and superficial message of the high rituals ('the Mexica, gloriously differentiated, gloriously dominate'), the darkest aspect of the human condition" and the Mexica hierarchy's own "necessary final dissolution" before the implacable forces of the cosmos were "dramatized through this brilliant human making." Such, as she intimates, was not the public transcript, for that spoke of Mexica dominance, but it was, consciously or unconsciously, the hidden transcript of hopeless resistance.[24]

For all that the form of the Mexica mock battles may have reminded early Spanish ethnographers of *juegos de cañas* and other European skirmishes, their "messages," both public and hidden, were very different from those of the Spanish *moros y cristianos*. The latter, for all their ostensible glorification of military might, pointed beyond war to a vision of *convivencia* in which former enemies lived together in peace. The former saw war inscribed in the very fabric of a universe that nightly teetered on the brink of disaster. Although the Mexica mock battles allowed Mexica warriors and their families to express their resentment toward the way things were, they held out no hope of change. At best, the horrors of war and human sacrifice were believed to postpone the greater terrors of final, universal dissolution. The Mexica festivals, one could argue, were more honest about the nightmare of war; the Spanish festivals of Moors and Christians, shaped unconsciously by Christian eschatology, were more hopeful about the possibility of peace. How these two strands merge and influence one another in sixteenth-century Mexico will be the subject of Part Four.

First, however, in the final chapter of Part Three, we will tackle the question of whether there was a pre-Hispanic tradition of danced dramatizations of combat and, if so, what form it might have taken. For this, too, will prove important to our understanding of how festivals of reconquest were staged after the fall of Tenochtitlan.

I I

The Dance of the Emperor Motecuzoma

"As well developed as we know it was both before and after the conquest," Mexica dance has left too little "tangible evidence" to yield any certain reconstruction.[1] Other aspects of the Mexica festivals have left an elaborate architectural and archeological grid on which to map their remains, but dance is a fleeting and kinetic art whose performers need only time and an open space. While the accounts provided by Durán and Sahagún affirm the importance and variety of Mexica dance, they offer little in the way of detailed choreography. We may do well, therefore, to begin our inquiry with later descriptions of indigenous dance in Mexico City, reading backward from these toward the more incomplete evidence of danced combat in precontact Tenochtitlan.

In 1645, Andrés Pérez de Ribas published an account of a dance, "formerly dedicated to pagan custom and now dedicated to the honor of him who is king of kings, our lord Jesus Christ." It was called "the dance of the emperor Motecuzoma," and was "so agreeable that it [had] provided great pleasure, entertainment, and celebration for important persons, lords, and archbishops who have come from Spain." Fourteen dancers divided into two lines were led by another representing Motecuzoma. All were dressed "in the costume and adornment of the ancient Mexican princes," with "pyramid-shaped diadems covered with gold and precious stones" on their heads and finely embroidered cloaks hanging from their shoulders. Their cloaks were "of two fabrics, the [outer] one transparent, so that the embroidery and beautiful flowers of the inner one [could] show through." Motecuzoma's costume was similar but made of richer material and more highly ornamented. Each dancer carried in his left hand a "wand" of bright green feathers or "branches covered with aromatic flowers," and with his right hand shook a rattle made from a brightly painted gourd filled with pebbles. To one side of the flower-strewn dance floor was a *teponaztli* drummer and a group of native elders who "entoned the song that always accompanied the Mexican dances." To this native music the Spaniards had added instruments of their own, including "harp, cornet, and bassoon."

The two lines of dancers were "summoned by the music and the song," moving at first with a "slow and dignified" step. Then Motecuzoma entered "with a noteworthy display of majesty." He was preceded, "at either side and a step ahead," by two children who swept his path with feather wands and scattered flowers at his feet, and he was followed by another who shaded him with a "large fan of rich feathers." They danced toward "a kind of low stool" at one end of the dance area. Made of red wood, it represented Motecuzoma's throne. Once the emperor was seated, his nobles bowed toward him and, as the pace of the music quickened, danced for him. ("Today," Pérez de Ribas added, the dancers show reverence not to the emperor but to "the Blessed Sacrament on the altar.") After a while, Motecuzoma rose from his throne and danced with the children between the two rows of nobles, who shook their rattles in time and bowed low as he passed. "Having completed his tour, the emperor resume[d] his seat," and the dancers began a new series of steps.[2]

Adrian Treviño and Barbara Gilles have suggested that the dance seen by Pérez de Ribas was an ancestor of Oaxaca's *danza de la pluma* and New Mexico's *danza de los matachines*.[3] (The latter dance is related to but different from the Zacatecas dance of the same name.) Both these surviving dances build on two rows of a dozen or so richly costumed dancers, representing Motecuzoma's court, who carry *palmas* (fans, now made of painted wood rather than flowers or feathers) and rattles. Led by another who plays Motecuzoma, they perform a series of intricate dance routines that periodically require Motecuzoma to be seated on a wooden "throne" at one end of the line of dancers. Motecuzoma dances with one or two young girls. Although European instruments now predominate (guitar and violin in New Mexico and a brass band in Oaxaca), the Tewa Indians of Santa Clara Pueblo (New Mexico) still accompany their *matachines* with indigenous drums and chanting. Because they enact conflict between Spanish invaders and native warriors, the dances are commonly assumed to have their roots in an introduced European tradition of dances of Moors and Christians.[4] Treviño and Gilles propose instead that they stem from an indigenous tradition that flourished in central Mexico before the arrival of the Spaniards. Pérez de Ribas's comment that the "dance of the emperor Moctezuma" was "formerly dedicated to pagan custom" lends credence to their argument.

Such a dance tradition may have dramatized historical or legendary battles to songs from the Nahuatl collection known as the *Cantares mexicanos*. John Bierhorst, in a theory disputed by other Nahuatl scholars, regards the songs as evidence of a late-sixteenth-century "ghost-song ritual," in which "warrior-singers summon[ed] the ghosts of ancestors in order to swell their ranks and overwhelm their enemies." James Lockhart regards the songs, more simply, as recollections of past military glory. He notes the elaborate drumbeat notation and repeated references to dancing and agrees that they "appear to have been performed before an audience" and to have had a strong theatrical flavor. Motecuzoma is the ruler most often invoked in the combat songs as leader of the Mexica warriors. The dance of the emperor Motecuzoma seen by Pérez de Ribas may link the modern *matachines* to the combat dances of the *Cantares*.[5]

Although many of the *Cantares* refer to the conquest or express a form of acculturated Christianity, others do not and may have been composed before the conquest. Questions of authorship and original composition are notoriously tricky in an oral tradition in which performers rework their material within the conventions of an established genre rather than recite a fixed text. Song 66, which reads in one stanza, "See them dancing with their shields," and, two stanzas later, "With shields and swords they come to chase him, they the Tlaxcalans, aya! and they the Castilians," acquired its present form after the conquest. Song 15, which embeds such lines as "Let there be dancing!" and "There's combat!" in a description of a fifteenth-century Mexica defeat of Acolhuacan, may have been composed before the conquest, transcribed in its present form in the second half of the sixteenth century, and may testify to a battle dance that survived the Spanish invasion. There is no way of telling. Lockhart insists that, whatever the date of particular songs, "the genre itself must be a survival from before the conquest."[6]

I am more sympathetic than Lockhart to the idea that the postcontact songs imagine some kind of restoration of Mexica power, both because I have long been immersed in dramatizations of reconquest and because the *danza de la pluma* and Native American versions of the *danza de los matachines* build on such an expectation. There, the warriors led by Motecuzoma are both historical figures and, in keeping with the cyclical view of time prevailing in native Mesoamerica, their anticipated structural equivalents. In the latter capacity, they are not the "ghosts" of deceased warriors—such a word implies the survival of a constant soul—but the embodiments of some of their scattered powers. Something similar may have been at work in the combat dances to which the *Cantares* testify. In any case, whether those dances represented preconquest battles, postconquest revisions of those battles, or imagined future triumphs does not change the simple fact that they bear witness to an indigenous tradition of danced battles. Before going on to other evidence of precontact danced battles, therefore, it is worth looking at a few of the songs most likely to have accompanied martial dances.

Song 15 recalls the defeat, around 1415, of Acolhuacan, Tlaxcala, and Huexotzinco by the Tepaneca ruler, Tezozomoc, and his Mexica allies. In Song 24, Chalcans and Amecamecans flee before the Mexica onslaught, as "spears are broken, blades are shattered," and "shield dust spreads upon us."[7] Song 65 recalls the campaign of the Mexica king Axayacatl against the Matlatzincans of Toluca in 1474. The song begins:

> I strike up a song, I, Macuilxochitl, pleasuring Life
> Giver. Let there be dancing.
> A song! Let it be carried from where He dwells in the Place
> Unknown. It's here! And here are Your flowers. Let
> there be dancing.
> Your prize is a Matlatzincan! O Blade Companion, O
> Axayacatl! You've come to tear apart the [Matlatzinca]
> town of Tlacotepec![8]

Perhaps a version of this song was composed for the triumphant return of Axacayatl to Tenochtitlan, when the priests "made the drums sound and played flutes and shell trumpets" and "the people celebrated with song and dance."[9] Treviño and Gilles wonder if it was this song, which the manuscript calls Matlatzincayotl (Matlatzinca piece), that later lent its name to the genre as a whole and hence to the *danza de los matachines*, which in central Mexico is still spelled *matlachines*.[10] Just as the European *morisca* was not always a Moorish dance but often a Christian dance about the defeat of the Moors, so perhaps the *matachines* was not originally a Matlatzinca dance but a Mexica dance about the defeat of the Matlatzinca.

Song 66, which refers to the Spanish conquest, is divided into five cantos. In the first two, warriors from Tlaxcala and Huexotzinco assist Cortés, for whom the Nahuatl text borrows the Spanish term *capitán*, in an initial successful assault on the Mexica capital. The text refers to "the Captain's boats" and the "iron weapons," possibly shipboard heavy artillery, with which "they're wrecking the city, they're wrecking the Mexican nation," as well as to dancing warriors on both sides armed with "shields and swords." The central, third canto reverses the fortunes of war. A Mexica hero named Atl Popoca "comes to do a shield dance here in Mexico," "lays hold of withered stripers," which Bierhorst understands to mean that Atl Popoca gathers up the corpses of sacrificed Tlaxcalan captives, and "take[s] a lance from the Spaniards." The Mexica gain a great victory. In successive stanzas we read twice, "When they've captured the conquistadores' guns, then Rabbit says, 'Let there be dancing!'"

Historical reality and the need to conform to a public transcript of Spanish victory reassert themselves in the fourth canto. The "Castilians" return "in boats," and their indigenous allies advance along the causeways. Although the singer seems reluctant to concede victory and names among the Spanish forces only Fulano Guzmán, who was killed during the siege,[11] the Mexica warriors are in the end surrounded and their last emperor, Cuauhtemoc, captured. Of particular theatrical interest is the line "It thunders and thunders from out of a turquoise arquebus, and the vapor rolls," an apt description of the clouds of smoke arising from repeated arquebus fire. The mock battle described by the song may have been staged, like many colonial festivals of Moors and Christians, on a large scale, with some companies of Indian actors armed with arquebuses and others fighting from boats on the lake or from wheeled ships on land. In that case, the dances would have alternated with or accompanied the spectacular mock battles. In Zacatecas, I saw *matachines* dance even as cannon thundered from the surrounding hillsides and thousands of Moors and Christians fired their arquebuses.

In the final canto, Bierhorst suggests, the song "gives the lasting victory to Mexico, whose dead reach paradise and whose women, uniting sexually with Cortés and his men, perpetuate Mexican blood." Perhaps this ending, in which the "cuck-olded" Mexica are compared to "tom turkeys" and Cortés wins Cuauhtemoc's consort Tecuichpo (Doña Isabel), is not to be taken too seriously. It may have served as a kind of ribald coda that further deflected attention away from the Mexica victory in the central canto. Part of the joke may have been that Tecuichpo's marriage to Cuauhtemoc was a political stratagem (she was only eleven years old at the time) and probably unconsummated (Cuauhtemoc had an older wife by whom he had children). After Cuauhtemoc's death, Tecuichpo married and survived three conquistadors in succession, as well as bearing Cortés a daughter some time after her second marriage. The "coded" message of the song's final canto may not have been that the Mexica men were cuckolded (Cuauhtemoc, after all, did not lose his sexual partner) but that even their second wives were too demanding for the sexually feeble Spaniards.[12]

Much work remains to be done on the relationship between the *Cantares mexicanos* and the long tradition of mock battles in Mexico before and after the conquest, but it will have to be done by someone more skilled in classical Nahuatl than I. I am confident at least that some songs bear witness to a postconquest tradition of martial dances in which the descendants of the Mexica nobility enacted military victory over indigenous enemies. At times, perhaps obliquely, they also danced military victory over the conquistadors themselves. Since I am not prepared to argue that a preconquest genre of songs somehow quickly adopted and radically adapted a Spanish tradition of dances of Moors and Christians for which there is in any case little prior evidence, I assume that the *Cantares* made use of an existing indigenous dance tradition and that battle songs and martial dances accompanied one another in central Mexico before the conquest.

There is some independent evidence of this. Francisco López de Gómara was Cortés's chaplain, secretary, and biographer after the conquistador's final return to Spain. In 1552, he published the first history of the conquest of Mexico. Although Gómara was not an eyewitness of the events he describes, his sources, including Cortés himself, were. Cortés and his army spent nearly eight months inside Tenochtitlan before the conquest. During this period, according to Gómara, they often saw a dance performed publicly for Motecuzoma. "It was called *netotelixtli*, a dance of rejoicing and merriment," and it was performed to the rhythm of two large drums, one of them "called a *teponaztli*." The accompanying songs were either "joyful and merry" or "ballads in praise of past kings, reciting their wars, victories, deeds, and the like." "When the time comes to start," Gómara wrote, "eight or more men whistle very loudly and beat the drums softly. Then the dancers come on, dressed in rich mantles woven of many colors, white, red, green, and yellow; in their hands, bunches of roses or plumes, or fans of feathers and gold. Many carry wreaths of flowers, very fragrant; others wear feather caps or masks made to represent the heads of eagles, tigers, alligators, and other wild beasts." The feathered headdresses or masks would have been similar to those worn in battle and sacrificial ritual by Mexica warriors, extending the head but not impeding the vision and identifying the wearer as an "eagle" or "jaguar" warrior.

Thus far, the *netotelixtli* dance performed for Motecuzoma in 1520 sounds not unlike the "dance of the emperor Motecuzoma" seen by Pérez de Ribas a century later. The masks have been set aside in the latter instance, as is often the case with pre-Hispanic dances performed in Christian contexts, but otherwise the two accounts suggest that we are dealing with kindred dances. The difference appears to have been in scale and in choreography. "At times," Gómara wrote, "there are as many as a thousand dancers, or at least four hundred, all of them noble and important persons, and even lords. . . . They dance in rings, their hands joined, one ring within the other. . . . Everyone follows the time set by the leaders, save only the outer ranks, which, because they are so far away and so many, must dance twice as fast as the others and work twice as hard. Nevertheless, all of them raise and lower their arms, their bodies, or their heads alone, at the same moment." [13]

Pérez de Ribas saw just fourteen dancers in two rows, a diminished variant perhaps of another *netotelixtli* performed during the Festival of the Flaying of Men. According to Sahagún, dancers from Tenochco and Tlatelolco each "formed two rows. They went facing each other. Very slow was the dancing; very much in harmony went the dancing. Then there was emerging through the palace entrance; there was stopping. Motecuzoma brought them forth; he went dancing. Two great rulers, Neçaualpilli of Texcoco [and] Totoquiuaztli, ruler of Tepaneca land, came each following him, went facing him. Great solemnity reigned while there was dancing." [14]

Another distinctive feature of Gómara's *netotelixtli* is the presence of what are now known in New Mexico as sacred clowns: "At times, the buffoons come out, mimicking other people in dress and speech, playing the drunk, the fool, or the old woman, to the vast entertainment of the spectators." [15] Although Pérez de Ribas does not mention such clowns, their descendants may well include the comic *abuelos* (ancestors) and cross-dressed Perejundias of New Mexico's *danza de los matachines* and the black-masked, tusked *negritos* of the *danza de la pluma*.

What is missing from all three of these accounts is any mention of the mock battles to which the *Cantares* seem to bear witness. Gómara's *netotelixtli* included dancers masked as eagle and jaguar warriors and was accompanied by "ballads in praise of past kings, reciting their wars, victories, deeds, and the like," but there is no explicit indication that the dance included mock battles of any kind. We find confirmation of this aspect of the tradition in the various forms of *netotelixtli* described by Francisco Hernández, physician to Philip II and chronicler by royal commission of the medicinal properties of herbs and plants in the New World. Hernández spent six years (1571–1577) in Mexico, during which he wrote an anthropological study of pre-Hispanic Mexico, now known as the *Antiquities of New Spain,* that contains a brief chapter on the *netotelixtli.* As many as three or four thousand men took part, he writes, singing and dancing in unison and "represent[ing] in the manner of a comedy or a tragedy some image of their heroic feats." There were "many kinds of dance," to which "they sometimes sang praises of the king and sometimes of some hero or chief and perhaps of the god in whose honor the festival was being celebrated and in others they boasted of their victories." Among the varieties of dance he describes are the Cuextecayotl (Cuextlan piece), "in which they imitated the style of dancing, the ornamentation, and the appearance of the Huaxteca people [of Cuextlan], and represented the war in which they conquered them, with an appropriate variety of sounds and martial tumult." Several other "pieces" named after particular enemies are listed, among them the Huexocincayotl, Michoacayotl, Cempoaltecayotl, and Tlaxcaltecayotl. Some of these names reappear in the *Cantares mexicanos.* Tlaxcaltecayotl is the title of song 66, which describes the assault on Tenochtitlan by Cortés and his Tlaxcalan allies.

Many of the dances listed by Hernández must have been martial in nature, for he writes of the dancers in general that "their dress consisted of various animal skins, feathers, and plumes of various colors, [and] the kinds of weapons and spears [that they carried], such as bows, lances, arrows, and shields, were innumerable." The dancers also made considerable effort to catch the nuances of dress, movement, hair color, and jewelry of the various ethnic enemies they depicted, even down to such small details as ear and nose piercings. Sahagún, too, noted that Mexica singers and dancers took care to imitate the speech patterns and decorative foibles of their enemies: "If a song were to be intoned after the manner of the Huaxteca, their speech was imitated, and their headdresses were taken, with which to imitate them in coloring their hair yellow; and the masks [had] arrow marks [painted] on the face, noses pierced like jug handles, teeth filed [to a point], and conical heads." Musical and rhythmic accompaniment was provided by voices, loud noises, whistling, *teponaztli* and *huehuetl* drums, cane flutes, striated bones, and gourd rattles (Fig. 14).[16]

While we cannot definitively reconstruct any of the indigenous Mexican dances as they were before the conquest, I find the cumulative evidence that one class of pre-Hispanic dances involved drumming, singing, and mimetic combat to be compelling. Indeed, there is more evidence of danced dramatizations of warfare in

14. Two drawings of *huehuetl* and *teponaztli* drummers with singer-dancers.
From Sahagún, *Florentine,* vols. 5 and 9.
Courtesy of University of Utah Press and the School of American Research.

precontact Mexico than there is in medieval Spain. At the very least, this should caution us against the assumption that all influence on the subsequent tradition of dances of Moors and Christians traveled from Spain to Mexico.

There remain two undeniably pre-Hispanic dances for us to consider in this chapter. The first was performed in honor of Xochiquetzal, the goddess of flowers. During the dance, boys dressed as birds and butterflies, "richly decked with fine, green, blue, red, and yellow feathers," ascended "artificial trees covered with fragrant flowers." The boys "climb[ed] from limb to limb, sucking the dew of the flowers." Then, as they descended, they were met by men and women dressed as "gods," who fired blowguns at the "birds." Juan de Tovar adds that "there were witty words in favor of some and against others, with which they greatly enter-

tained the onlookers, followed by a great *mitote,* or dance, of all these personages."
Sahagún records the belief that "those who died in war" were later "changed into
birds of precious feather" and "large, varicolored butterflies, which sucked [honey
from the flowers] there where they dwelt. And here upon earth they came to suck
[honey] from all the varied flowers." Bierhorst sees the descending birds and butterflies, the combat, and the dancing as evidence of a "ghost-song" ritual. Kay Read
disputes the specificity of Bierhorst's interpretation, but acknowledges that there is
a "link" between the dance and warfare.[17]

The second dance, still popular in central Mexico, is the *danza de los voladores*
(dance of the flyers). It requires four *voladores,* accompanied by a fifth playing a flute
and small drum, to climb a stripped tree trunk, some seventy feet tall, by means of
knotted rope footholds. The four flyers then tie themselves by the waist to a large
wooden spool nestled on top and fling themselves backward from the top of the
pole. As the ropes that link the dancers to the spool slowly unwind, the flyers descend heads down in a widening gyre, and the spool revolves, forming a tiny, rotating dance floor for the remaining musician. Just before they reach the ground,
the flyers right themselves and hit the ground running. The musician slides down
one of the ropes. The dance can be repeated several times. Colonial accounts and
illustrations of the dance suggest that the dancers originally wore wings of elaborate featherwork.

The dance of the *voladores* is generally understood to be a religious ritual that
survived remarkably intact because the Spaniards took it for an acrobatic display of
skill. Explanations of its meaning vary. Juan de Torquemada explained it as a calendrical ritual in which the unwinding of the ropes produces exactly fifty-two rev-
olutions, representing the fifty-two years of the Mexica century. Today's performers have told me variously that it is "an ancient dance," that it is performed in honor
of the sun, and that the dancers represent the gods of the four cardinal points bringing messages from heaven to earth. Bierhorst sees the descent of feathered dancers
as evidence of yet another ghost-song ritual, a theory that Read rejects while allowing the possibility of a postcontact hidden transcript of resistance. Building on
Torquemada's calendrical interpretation, she suggests that the dance of the flyers may
have taunted the uncomprehending conquistadors, "Your time is now, but as time
spins back on itself, so too will our moment of power be spun back into existence.
This is how the sun spins its reality. No one lasts forever, and neither will you."[18]

Certain performances of the dance of the *voladores* in colonial Mexico City in-
cline me to suspect some such concealed challenge. In Chapter 14, we will see the
dance performed immediately after large-scale Spanish-style mock battles that represented, in one instance, the Christian defense of Malta against the Turks and, in

the other, the capture of Tenochtitlan by Cortés. If the dance allowed its performers and native audience to imagine the future restoration of Mexica power, it would have served in both cases as a spectacular vehicle for the insinuation of a hidden transcript of reversal at the close of what would otherwise have been an uncontested public transcript of Spanish Catholic triumphalism. The colonial introduction of the theme of Moors and Christians prompted many other such indigenous interventions.

PART FOUR
MEXICO, 1521—1600

12
The Conquest of Mexico (1524–1536)

HERNÁN Cortés landed on the coast of Yucatan in February 1519 with an army of some five hundred adventurers. Forming alliances with the Tlaxcalteca and other native peoples eager for the overthrow of the dominant Mexica Empire, and reinforced from time to time by fresh arrivals from the Spanish Caribbean, he managed by November to enter Tenochtitlan as the guest of Motecuzoma and there to take his host hostage. For eight months, with the reluctant blessing of the captive emperor, Cortés used the Mexica capital as his base of operations.

In May 1520, while Cortés attended to a crisis on the coast, Pedro de Alvarado was left in charge of the Spanish contingent in Tenochtitlan. During Toxcatl (the Festival of Dryness), the nervous Alvarado ordered the slaughter of several thousand unarmed Mexica dancers and spectators. Sahagún's informants remembered it well. Each of the Spanish soldiers was armed "with his leather shield, . . . with his iron-studded shield, and each with his iron sword. Thereupon they surrounded the dancers. Thereupon they went among the drums. Then they struck the drummer's arms; they severed both his hands; then they struck his neck. Far off did his neck [and head] go to fall. Then they pierced the people with iron lances and they struck them each with the iron swords. Of some they slashed open their backs; then their entrails gushed out. Of some they cut their heads to pieces; they absolutely pulverized their heads; their heads were absolutely pulverized. And some they struck on the shoulder; they split openings, they broke openings in their bodies. Of some they struck repeatedly the shanks; of some they struck repeatedly the thighs; of some they struck the belly; then their entrails gushed forth. And when in vain one would run, he would only drag his intestines like something raw as he tried to escape. Nowhere could he go." [1]

When Cortés returned, the mood was tense. In late June, in the aftermath of the massacre and the subsequent death of the compliant Motecuzoma, the Spanish expedition and its native allies were forced to fight their way out of the city. Suffering many casualties, they remembered their exodus as the "night of sorrows." By August 1521, Cortés and his allies were sufficiently recovered and reinforced to capture Tenochtitlan and defeat the Mexica (now led by Motecuzoma's cousin Cuauhtemoc), razing in the process the city they had once thought more beautiful than any in Europe. [2]

Ambition unquenched, Cortés sent several expeditions into Vera Cruz, Oaxaca, Michoacan, and, further afield, to Honduras and Guatemala. When the leader of one such expedition, Cristóbal de Olid, renounced Cortés's authority and asserted an independent jurisdiction for himself in Honduras, Cortés set out, in October 1524, to quell the insurrection. Among those he took with him were some 150 Spanish soldiers, three thousand Indian auxiliaries, two Franciscan friars, a physician, a surgeon, and, for entertainment, several musicians, an acrobat, and a puppeteer. The last Spanish settlement they reached, before launching into an arduous march of several months through thick jungle and steep mountain ranges, was Coatzacoalcos, on the Gulf of Mexico. There, the expedition was met, according to Bernal Díaz, with "triumphal arches, . . . ambushes of Christians and Moors, and other grand entertainments and quasi-dramatic games."[3]

This is the first mention of a *moros y cristianos* in the Americas. We cannot tell what form it took, although the term "*embuscadas* [ambushes]" may denote something similar to the successive groups of Moors that pretended to threaten Enrique IV when he visited Jaén in 1464. As for its intent, we can only speculate. Arturo Warman suggests that the ambushes "reflected the risk that the conquistadors were running,"[4] but the performance may also have portrayed Cortés as a conquering hero, implicitly comparing his campaigns in Mexico to the Catholic reconquest of Spain. The triumphal arches under which Cortés's army passed, with their connotations of Roman imperial triumph, would have reinforced this image. But, if the mock battles were intended to anticipate the outcome of the campaign against Olid, they bore unintended ironies, for then the victorious Christians corresponded to a largely Indian army, led by Cortés, and the defeated Moors to a Spanish force led by a rebellious Christian, Olid. A simple equation of Moors and Indians was impossible. From the outset, the Mexican festivals of Moors and Christians were fraught with the potential for complex readings. When Cortés finally arrived in Honduras, by the way, he found that Olid was already dead, that his own authority had been restored, and that the expedition had been unnecessary.

Cortés returned to Mexico City in June 1526. The people welcomed him with "all manner of spectacles," including dances, games, and, on the lake, massed canoes full of Indian warriors. These reminded Bernal Díaz of how the Mexica "used to fight against us in the time of Cuauhtemoc."[5] Perhaps a mock battle took place. Two and a half years later, when the first royal *audiencia* (a combined law court and ruling council) made its formal entry to the city, a *castillo* was among the scenic properties paid for by the city council. Assuming that it was an artificial castle rather than a simple stage or float, Linda Curcio suggests that it was used in "a mock battle of some sort."[6]

Cortés was away in Spain when the *audiencia* arrived, but he returned to Mexico in 1530. In one way or another, he appears in the narrative of four of the next five mock battles reported in colonial Mexico. The first of these narratives is a miracle story. In December 1531, on the hill of Tepeyac north of Mexico City, according to an account first published in 1648, the Virgin Mary appeared to an Indian convert named Juan Diego. A few days later, she miraculously painted her own portrait on the inside of his cloak. The bishop of Mexico, Juan de Zumárraga, ordered a chapel to be built for the image at the foot of the hill of Tepeyac, and, on 26 December 1531, the cloak was carried there in "a great procession," incorporating clergy, nobles, officials, and a great crowd of people. Zumárraga had written to Cortés inviting him to take part, and tradition has it that Cortés and his wife walked alongside the bishop at the head of the procession. Passing along a causeway between two lakes, they saw on both sides "a large number of natives in canoes, some of them engaging in skirmishes." Some were dressed in the finery of Mexica warriors and others, perhaps on shore, were dressed as Chichimeca. Of common ancestry with the Mexica, the Chichimeca were nomadic peoples who had resisted Mexica domination and were to wage a fierce guerrilla war against the northern expansion of the Spanish Empire well into the seventeenth century.[7] One of those playing a Chichimeca archer carelessly "drew his bow and, without warning, suddenly fired an arrow and wounded one of those who was skirmishing, piercing his neck." The procession halted, while the wounded Mexica actor, now taken for dead, was carried to the image of the Virgin. To everyone's joy and amazement, the dead man not only came back to life but his wound healed immediately, leaving no scar. Thus was the first miracle of healing credited to the image of the Virgin. Many believe this image now hangs in the Basilica of the Virgin of Guadalupe, where it is the most revered in all Mexico.

None of this may have happened. The authenticity of the image and its origin narratives, even the historicity of Juan Diego, have been challenged by skeptics and no less keenly defended by followers of Guadalupe. The details of the story depend, in large part, on two texts published in the mid–seventeenth century. The first, *Imagen de la Virgen María, Madre de Dios de Guadalupe*, was written by Miguel Sánchez, a highly respected priest of the archdiocese of Mexico, who claimed to have based his account on a careful compilation of Indian oral traditions. His work was published in 1648. The second was a Nahuatl text, known as the *Huey tlamahuiçoltica*, published by Luis Laso de la Vega, the vicar of the chapel of Guadalupe, in 1649. Although Laso de la Vega claimed that the work was his own, it is thought by many *guadalupanos* to have been written by Antonio Valeriano (c. 1520–1605), an Indian of noble birth, who, it is claimed, witnessed the events as a boy or later compiled his account from oral histories.[8]

Stafford Poole has concluded, however, that "there is no good reason to reject Laso de la Vega's claim to substantial or supervisory authorship."[9] Poole has also suggested, quite plausibly, that the chapel of Guadalupe dates from the mid–sixteenth century; that the oral traditions on which both Sánchez and Laso de la Vega based their work confused the putative 1531 procession, for which no written documentation survives, with a well-documented procession organized by Archbishop Alonso de Montúfar in September 1566 to honor the donation of a silver statue of the Virgin to the newly established chapel; and that the miracle stories grew up around a painted image of the Virgin, probably by an Indian artist, that was placed in the chapel from the beginning and soon surpassed the silver statue in popularity and reputed curative powers.[10]

Whatever their origins and the authenticity of their collected memories, the *Imagen* and the *Huey tlamahuiçoltica,* together with a third document that has not survived, formed the basis of Francisco de Florencia's famous account of the Virgin of Guadalupe, *La Estrella del Norte,* published in 1688. Poole calls Florencia's work "the most detailed account of the apparitions and devotion up to that time" and "one of the most influential works in the history of the tradition."[11] According to Florencia, the procession bearing the image of Guadalupe to her chapel was accompanied by "festivities, lanterns, music, and dances, especially those of the Indians, who still kept the rich and beautiful plumage that they used to wear for their *mitotes,* as they called their dances." "On the same day," he added, the Indians staged "a mock battle . . . , according to the custom of their nation, between Mexica and Chichimeca." It was this skirmish, he reminded his readers, that occasioned the first miracle associated with the image. From Florencia, the mock battle passed into an article published by Robert Ricard in 1932, and so into the canon of early Mexican *moros y cristianos.* Although, on Florencia's authority, I once described the mock battle as taking place in 1531, I am now inclined to think that, if it took place at all, it was in September 1556 as an embellishment to the procession organized by Montúfar.[12]

At least one detail of this reported mock battle rings true: the use of canoes. Tenochtitlan, like Venice, was built on an island crisscrossed by canals and joined to the lakeshore by causeways. Its people were adept in the use of canoes and, although Mexica warriors generally fought on land, war canoes were used to ferry troops and supplies to lakeshore battles.[13] Occasionally, the Mexica fought from canoes against enemies on land. On the night of sorrows, the Spaniards tried to leave secretly by the western (Tacuba) causeway. But, their retreat being discovered, "the entire causeway was [soon] under attack on both sides from innumerable canoes" filled with archers.[14] Canoes were also used by the Mexica against Spanish infantry in the final, unsuccessful defense of Tenochtitlan in 1521, but were of little effect due to the control of the lake by Spanish brigantines. It was the latter battle, "in the time of Cuauhtemoc," that Bernal Díaz recalled when massed war canoes greeted Cortés's return from Honduras in 1526.

While there is no record of canoes being used in mock battles before the arrival of the Spaniards, the record may be incomplete. Other instances of mock battles fought by Indians in canoes were reliably reported later in the century. At least one of them, in Guadalupe in 1595, may have recalled the fall of Tenochtitlan.[15] Is it possible that the mock battle between Mexica canoes and Chichimeca infantry, reputed to have taken place in honor of the dark-skinned Virgin of Guadalupe in 1531 or 1566, also referred indirectly to that disastrous fall? Were barbaric Chichimeca discreetly substituted for Spanish conquistadors and did the story of the miraculous restoration of the slain Indian implicitly reverse the outcome of the historical battle? If the Indian Virgin could resurrect a dead warrior, could she not also resurrect the Mexica nation? Such a reading of the account is highly speculative, but it may explain, as no other reading does, the enduring popularity of the legend of the mock battle and the revived warrior among indigenous devotees of the Virgin of Guadalupe.

The next reputed mock battle in colonial Mexico is equally uncertain. Aurora Lucero-White Lea writes, "In the year 1536, when the great explorer Alvar Núñez Cabeza de Vaca . . . arrived along the coast of the Pacific in Mexico on the twenty-third of July, he tells us that he was honored by Viceroy Mendoza and the Marqués del Valle, Hernán Cortés; and that there occurred the following day—the feast of Santiago—a bullfight and the play called *Moros y Cristianos*."[16] Unfortunately, this embroiders Cabeza de Vaca's own account. In his autobiographical *Naufragios,* he tells us that on his arrival in Mexico City, he was well received by Mendoza and Cortés and that, two days later, "on the day of Santiago [July 25], there was a fiesta and a *juego de cañas* and bulls."[17] While it is possible that the participants in the *juego de cañas* dressed as Moors and Christians, Cabeza de Vaca does not say so.

About this time, notices of mock battles between Moors and Christians begin to appear elsewhere in the Americas. The first of which I am aware comes from Acla, Colombia. There, in September 1532, a large crowd of Indians and Spaniards, including the governor, saw a performance that began with a solitary Christian "hunting rabbits" with nets. A band of Moors approached the peaceful hunter, carefully coordinating their attack and finally taking him captive. At once, Santiago galloped into the square, dressed in scarlet and carrying a cross and a banner. He freed the Christian and forced the Moors to the ground, threatening them with his cross. The Indians, we are told, were both "terrified" and "entertained."[18]

None of the notices of scripted mock battles in Mexico during the fifteen years following the conquest is both reliable and detailed. The first, from Coatzacoalcos in 1524, appears trustworthy but lacks detail. A mock battle, perhaps involving Mexica warriors in canoes, may have welcomed Cortés back to Mexico City in 1526. A mock siege of a castle probably accompanied the entry of the royal *audiencia* in 1528. The battle on the Guadalupe causeway, if it happened at all, perhaps took place in 1556 rather than, as reported, in 1531. The celebration in honor of Cabeza de Vaca may have involved no more than a competitive game of canes. We know too little to speak with any confidence of the way in which Spanish and indigenous traditions of military theater influenced one another in Mexico during this period. Nor can we do more than speculate on indigenous readings of these first mock battles in colonial Mexico. By 1539, however, we have substantial evidence of both mutual influence and hidden transcripts.

13

The Conquest of Rhodes (Mexico City, 1539)

THE year 1539 yields undisputed testimony of three scripted mock battles in colonial Mexico: a battle between Moors and Christians in Oaxaca, a *Conquest of Rhodes* in Mexico City, and a *Conquest of Jerusalem* in Tlaxcala. All three were prompted by a single piece of news from Europe.

Catholic Europe, in the third decade of the sixteenth century, was nervous. Its borders were contracting, threatened from within by the Protestant Reformation and from without by the armies of Süleyman the Magnificent. Luther had posted his ninety-five theses on the door of the Wittenburg castle church in 1517. The Ottoman Turks had captured the great Mediterranean naval base of Rhodes in 1521, wiped out the Hungarian cavalry on the marshy plains of Mohács in 1526, and, to all of Europe's horror, besieged Vienna for a month in 1529. Süleyman's Berber ally Khair ad-Din extended the Muslim threat westward in the Mediterranean, raiding the Spanish coast and capturing the North African ports of Algiers in 1529 and Tunis in 1534.

For some Spanish Catholics, the only hope seemed to lie in the conquest and evangelization of the New World. Even as the borders of Catholic Europe came under attack, its empire could be hugely expanded and the church restored to its pristine glory in the Americas. The twelve Franciscan missionary friars sent out to join Cortés in 1524 were compared to the twelve apostles. They believed themselves called to establish a pure church among the Indians that would, in turn, restore God's blessing to a Catholic Europe presided over by the Holy Roman Emperor and king of Spain, Charles V. The Franciscan order in Spain believed that the conquest and conversion of the New World presaged a resurgence of Spanish power and the imminent triumph of Catholicism in the Old World. Spain, it was thought, would sail the converted Indian armies of the New World across the Atlantic and into the Mediterranean to join forces with the Catholic armies of Charles V in a successful last crusade against the Muslims and Jews of the Old World. One by one, the Mediterranean ports controlled by the Turks or their allies would fall before the expanded and purified forces of the Spanish Catholic empire, culminating in the final, triumphant liberation of Jerusalem and the conversion of vast numbers of Jews, Muslims, and pagans. New hope was breathed into this millenarian vision by a resounding victory in the western Mediterranean. In 1535, Charles destroyed Khair ad-Din's fleet and recaptured Tunis. To the Franciscans, custodians by papal appointment of the holy places of Christendom, this celebrated triumph seemed to be the first stepping-stone on the return journey to the most holy city of Jerusalem.[1]

First, however, something needed to be done about the fierce rivalry between Charles V of Spain and the "Turcophile king of France," Francis I.[2] The latter had impeded Charles's progress by invading northern Spain, competing with his
armies for control of Italy, and engineering political alliances against him with the
Ottoman Turks. In 1538, the pope, "anxious to free [Charles] for an attack on the
Turks or the Lutherans," persuaded emperor and king "to meet with him—in jealously separate rooms—at Nice," and, on 17 June, "to sign a ten-year truce." A
month later, the two rulers met face-to-face at Aigues-Mortes, on the south coast
of France, where "they ceased to be royal and became human," embracing one
another's children and attending mass together.[3] Catholic Europe breathed a col-
lective sigh of relief, and Spanish millenarians turned their thoughts again to a final
crusade. The news reached Mexico in January 1539,[4] and at once plans were laid
for elaborate celebrations in which theatrical spectacle was to play a major role.
Of the *Conquest of Jerusalem* performed in Tlaxcala one of the resident Franciscan
friars wrote that it embodied "a prediction which, we pray, God may fulfil in
our day."[5]

On 23 January 1539, the viceroy, Antonio de Mendoza, dispatched a letter to
the *cabildo* (city council) of Oaxaca, bearing news of the European truce. When the
letter arrived, on Saturday, 1 February, the city fathers ordered general rejoicing,
including horseback parades, the ringing of church bells, and the placing of lights
in the doorways and on the roofs of houses. The celebrations were repeated seven
nights in a row "until the following Sunday," when, in addition to "bulls and *juegos
de cañas* . . . and many other festivities," there was a battle between "Moors and Christians" over "a wooden fortress."[6] Although no further details of the Oaxaca *moros
y cristianos* survive, we have more complete accounts of the *Conquest of Rhodes* and
the *Conquest of Jerusalem*. Anticipating imminent Christian victory in the Mediterranean, the inhabitants of Mexico City devised and staged the *Conquest of Rhodes*.
Some months later, their old rivals the Tlaxcalteca went one better and played the
Conquest of Jerusalem. We will deal with the former in the remainder of this chapter and the latter in Chapter 14.

The Mexican *Conquest of Rhodes* was performed in February 1539. It must have
taken place after the news of peace arrived in January and before 27 March, for on
the latter date the Mexico City council ordered payment made to one of the original conquistadors, Alonso de Avila, for materials used in the "festivities with which
this city celebrated the truce." Avila had supplied, among other things, "wood and
a set of nails . . . for the stages."[7] It is unlikely, given the scope of the Mexico City
celebrations, that they could have been effectively planned and carried out before
the smaller-scale festivities in Oaxaca on February 9, and equally unlikely, given
the gargantuan banquets that Bernal Díaz describes, that they would have taken

place during Lent. I assume, therefore, that the *Conquest of Rhodes* was performed during the week of carnival preceding Lent.

The "farces," the nightly "masquerades," the "jesters and wits," and the astonishing quantity and variety of food and drink consumed (if Bernal Díaz is not just fantasizing in the style of Rabelais) were characteristically carnivalesque. There is not space here to repeat even a representative sample of the banquet menus, so three items will have to whet the reader's appetite: "native hens baked whole with their beaks and feet silvered, and after that young ducks and great geese whole, with gilded beaks, and then heads of pigs, deer and calves whole, for grand effect"; "young oxen roasted whole, stuffed with chickens, hens, quails, doves, and bacon"; and, as a dish to startle the ladies, "some very large pies, with two live rabbits in some of them and small live rabbits in others, while yet others were full of quails and doves and other small live birds; they placed them on the tables all at once, and as soon as they took off the covers the rabbits went fleeing over the tables and the quails and birds flew off." In 1539, the first day of Lent (Ash Wednesday) was 19 February. The dinner guests of the marquis and the viceroy must by then have been ready for a little restraint.[8]

The *Conquest of Rhodes* was a sumptuous affair. Bartolomé de Las Casas remembered, in the main square of Mexico City, a number of "large structures like artificial theatres, as high as towers," each having several distinct stages. On each of these some kind of "representation" took place, accompanied by singers and musicians playing shawms, sackbuts, flageolets, trumpets, drums, and other musical instruments. All told, "more than a thousand Indian musicians and polyphonic singers" gathered "from throughout the province" for the occasion. Among the other scenic units were several "*castillos*" and, resplendent in the center of the plaza, "a city of wood" representing Rhodes (Fig. 15a). Perhaps, like its many European

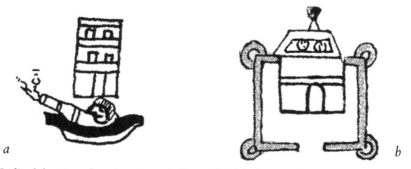

a   *b*

15. Stylized drawing of scenic units probably used in (a) *Conquest of Rhodes*, Mexico City, 1539, and (b) mock siege, Mexico City, July 1572. From *Códice Aubin* (Dibble, *Historia*, fol. 90 and 113). Courtesy of Editorial Porrúa.

predecessors, it was made of painted canvas (or some local alternative) wrapped around wooden frames and mounted on wheels for the sake of mobility. Certainly, it was impressive. Bernal Díaz admired the realism of the city's towers, merlons, and embrasures. Las Casas marveled at the silence, worthy of "a community of friars," with which "more than fifty thousand workmen" prepared the city and the other theatrical structures. Even allowing for the habitually exaggerated numbers of the times, this bespeaks the careful preparation of an elaborate stage set. There were also a number of artificial mountains, rocks, meadows, and woods (some containing live animals), serving both to embellish the government buildings that edged the square and to identify specific locations around Rhodes.[9]

The Christian army mustered in the square surrounding Rhodes. Some of the troops were on horseback, riding "*a la jineta* [with short stirrups]" and armed with lances and leather shields; others rode "*a la estradiota* [with long stirrups and stiff legs]," a position from which it was easier to break an opponent's lance; yet others were on foot and armed with arquebuses. They were led by a hundred commanders, whose badges of rank were fashioned in gold and pearls. Bernal Díaz tells us that the captain general of the Christian forces and the great master of Rhodes (so called in anticipation of his victory) "was the Marquis Cortés." Most scholars take this to mean that Cortés himself played the role.[10] We do know that the marquis was injured in the foot while taking part in a *juego de cañas* later in the festivities.[11]

The army was joined by four three-masted sailing ships that circled the plaza three times as canon on board fired (Fig. 15a) and trumpets blared. No doubt mounted on wheels and propelled by men hidden within,[12] the ships brought the audience to its feet with astonishment and seemed to Las Casas to move over the ground "as if they were on water." Among those on board were some Indians dressed as if they were Dominican friars arriving from Spain, "plucking hens and fishing." The specific meaning of this joke at the expense of the Dominicans is now lost on us, although it would appear to be one more indication of Franciscan influence on the *Conquest of Rhodes*. In the spring of 1539, Franciscans and Dominicans were embroiled in a controversy over the former's practice of abbreviating the ceremony of baptism when faced with large numbers of Indian applicants. Maybe the fishing, chicken-plucking friars in the *Conquest of Rhodes* referred to this controversy in some way; or perhaps they implied that the Dominicans fished for souls while "plucking the goods from helpless Indians."[13] Las Casas, a Dominican, makes no mention of the caricature.

The opening skirmish involved two companies of mounted Turks, adorned with "much gold" and dressed, "like real Turks," in silk, fine scarlet cloth, and pointed hoods. Emerging, one assumes, from an artificial wood (made, at least in part, with real trees), the Turks ambushed some shepherds and their sheep while the latter were peaceably grazing "near a spring" that flowed from an artificial meadow. "Artificial" should not, in this instance, conjure up visions of indoor painted stage sets. Probably the grass, water, and sheep were real, for we know that a herd of sheep appeared in the *Conquest of Jerusalem,* that a working copy of "the spring of Chapultepec and . . . some small subsidiary springs" greeted guests at a viceregal banquet, and that the Indians had "a singular talent" for combining nature and artifice to "mak[e] a thing look natural." [14]

After the Turkish raiders had carried off both men and sheep, an escaped shepherd fled to Cortés for help. The Christian armies were able to free the captives before several squadrons of Turkish reinforcements arrived. A subsequent series of battles ended with the capture of "many Turks." Finally, bulls were released to "disperse" the remaining infidels. These skirmishes, involving the protection of Christian shepherds and the flocks under their care (who had been feeding, in the words of Psalm 23, "in green pastures" and "beside quiet waters"), no doubt had symbolic import. Portraying Cortés as a benevolent guardian of Christian peace, they served as a prelude to and justification for the conquest of Rhodes. Although Bernal Díaz gives no details of the siege that followed, Las Casas mentions that the "wooden city" was "attacked by Indians from without and defended by those within."

The whole performance was watched, from windows surrounding the square, by "many ladies, wives of the conquistadors and other residents of Mexico City," richly dressed in "silk and damask and gold and silver and jewels." As they watched, they were served "marzipan, candied citron, almonds, and comfits," some of the delicacies literally "gilded and silvered." To quench their thirst, they drank fine wines, mead, fermented fruit drinks, and frothy chocolate.

At first reading, the *Conquest of Rhodes* seems to present only a public transcript of Spanish Catholic triumphalism, enacting the anticipated recovery of Rhodes and flattering Cortés by casting him in the role of millenarian hero and protector of the church against Ottoman Turks in the Old World. Like most courtly *moros y cristianos,* however, it was flavored by local politics, most notably Cortés's uncertain status in the colony. Cortés and Mendoza had cautiously negotiated their opposing claims to power since the latter's arrival in 1535, and by early 1539, former bitterness had given way to a tenuous friendship. Bernal Díaz reports that the marquis and the viceroy together "decided to hold great festivals" to celebrate the European truce and no doubt, under the circumstances, Cortés plotted and Mendoza permitted the scenario, highly flattering to the former, of the *Conquest of Rhodes.* But it was to be Cortés's last hurrah in Mexico. Shortly afterward he clashed with Mendoza over the profit and prestige to be gained from further exploration of the Pacific and, at the end of the year, sailed for Spain for the last time. There, sustaining the millenarian dream expressed in the *Conquest of Rhodes,* he fought alongside Charles V in 1541 in the emperor's storm-wracked and ultimately disastrous naval campaign to recapture Algiers.[15]

But neither Cortés's indulgent self-portrayal nor the joke about the Dominicans offers evidence of a hidden transcript of subordinate resistance. This we may find in the *Battle of the Wild Men and the Blacks* that preceded and, I believe, commented on the *Conquest of Rhodes*. Bernal Díaz describes the preparation of an artificial forest in the main square. In addition to standing trees draped with various kinds of moss and creeper, there were others that looked as if they were long fallen and already rotting. In the forest were many animals and birds, the smaller ones ("deer, rabbits, hares, foxes, jackals, other small predators, . . . and a great diversity of small birds") running and flying free, the more dangerous ones ("two puma cubs and four small jaguars") enclosed in pens. Elsewhere in the plaza were two similar glades, each concealing a squadron of "wild men," some armed with "clubs [made of] knotted and twisted [rope],"[16] others with bows and arrows. When the pens in the central forest were opened, the two squadrons advanced and a real hunt began. After killing the animals, the two groups quarreled and the ensuing battle ended with mutual retreat to their respective glades. Then, "more than fifty black men and women" on horseback entered, escorting their king and queen. All were sumptuously dressed and bejeweled. The diversity of their masks impressed Bernal Díaz, as did the way in which the black women suckled their babies and all paid homage to the queen. The black cortège also quarreled and no doubt fought with the wild men.

"The origins of this spectacle," Fernando Horcasitas admits, "are mysterious," and may lie in some pre-Hispanic hunting rite or in a historical battle between rival tribes that the play commemorates. Something similar, he suggests, was portrayed a few decades later in the famous warrior murals of the mission church of San Miguel in Ixmiquilpan (Hidalgo). According to Donna Pierce, "the Indians carrying bows in the Ixmiquilpan frescoes can be identified as pagan, 'uncivilized' Chichimecs and the Indians carrying *macanas* can be identified as the 'civilized' Christianized Otomí" who painted the murals and worshiped at the church. It may be that, in like fashion, the wild men who carried bows and arrows in the first part of the *Battle of the Wild Men and the Blacks* represented "uncivilized" Chichimeca and those who carried clubs represented "civilized" Mexica. Perhaps the spectacle was accompanied by a song akin to one of those in the *Cantares mexicanos*.[17]

The artificial woods were inherited from Mexica calendar rituals. We have already noted a dance in honor of the goddess Xochiquetzal in which boys dressed as birds and butterflies climbed "artificial trees covered with fragrant flowers" and were hunted by "gods" with blowguns. In Tenochtitlan, "dances, farces, and games" in honor of the god Tlaloc had been performed in an artificial "forest," containing "many bushes, little hills, branches, and rocks, . . . a tall tree of luxuriant foliage, and around it . . . four smaller ones," all set up in the courtyard of the Great Temple. Dancers disguised as "hunters" and "wild men" had also appeared in Mexica festivities.[18]

But the spectacle may also have had Spanish roots. A glance at the index of Shergold's *History of the Spanish Stage* shows that "*salvajes* [wild men]" were a common feature of medieval plays and festivities in Spain.[19] In 1399, at the coronation banquet of Martin I in Zaragoza, an artificial rock was wheeled in, on top of which was crouched "a great tawny lioness." The lioness was artificial, but the wildlife that emerged from the rock was not. The chronicler describes wild boars and "rabbits, hares, partridges, doves, and other birds that flew around the courtyard in which the banquet was being held." "Armed men" then attacked the lioness, but "many men dressed as *salvajes* appeared from the rock and sought to defend her. The *salvajes* beat the armed men." According to the chronicler, the performance was "in imitation" of similar "games" in ancient Rome.[20] Bernal Díaz also recalls the Roman games before describing the battle of the wild men in Mexico City, adding that the "inventor" of the Mexican festivities was a Roman gentleman, Luis de León, who was proud of his descent from the great Roman patricians.[21] Probably the first part of the *Battle of the Wild Men and the Blacks* combined elements of Italian, Spanish, and Indian pedigree.

The entry of the black cortège introduced an African presence to the proceedings. There were about ten thousand blacks in Mexico in 1539, the largest number being employed in the capital city. Many belonged to black confraternities that "fostered a spirit of camaraderie among the slaves" and provided a framework for their participation in processions and other public festivities.[22] In some parts of the New World, the confraternities were thought of as "nations," ruled by elected kings and queens. Coronation rituals were conducted at black churches and each "nation" sent its diplomatic representatives to the coronation.[23] The participation of a black "king and queen" in the performance in Mexico City may well reflect this practice.

The confraternities became "the cloak under which the members plotted rebellion in Mexico City."[24] A year and a half earlier, on 24 September 1537, Mendoza had uncovered the first slave rebellion in Mexico. "I was warned," he writes, "that the blacks had chosen a king, had conspired to kill all the Spaniards and to rise up and take the land, and that the Indians were also involved." Incredulous at first, the viceroy corroborated the rumor and then moved swiftly to arrest and execute the black king and other leaders of the rebellion.[25] Although Mendoza does not mention the election of a queen on this occasion, it may not have come to light. Certainly, in a later abortive rebellion in 1608, it is known that the "election of a king and queen was the first procedural business" at the clandestine gathering of conspirators. This was followed by an elaborate coronation of the new monarchs. Similar elections preceded failed slave rebellions in 1611 and 1612.[26] The "king and queen" who led the black cortège into the main square of Mexico City in 1539 may well have been elected in a similar fashion.

But why did a black confraternity take this particular role in the festivities? Why did the blacks fight with the wild men? Why were they on horseback, a mode of transport usually reserved for Spaniards and privileged Indian leaders?[27] And why were they wearing fine costumes and masks? Clearly, the blacks were not simply participants in a festive display but were engaged in some kind of mimetic activity. Jerry Williams offers an intriguing explanation. He wonders whether these richly caparisoned "black riders, with their masks and exaggerated full-dress uniforms, could have been satirizing or imitating the Spaniards," both the conquistadors who were to take part in the *Conquest of Rhodes* and "the caballeros and their ladies" who watched from the windows.[28] Such dramatized mockery of Spanish caballeros was not unknown in Mexico. In 1586, Tarascan Indians greeted the Franciscan commissary general with a battle play whose public transcript honored the Spanish visitor but whose hidden transcript drew gales of laughter from the Indian crowd for its depiction of "savage" Chichimeca "burlesquing . . . Spanish horsemen."[29]

Equally pertinent is the practice of Peruvian colonists who made their African slaves enact "the struggle between Moors and Christians." Officially, "the idea was twofold: to affirm the superiority of white over black and to affirm the superiority of the Christian over the pagan." But the slaves found ways of subverting the imposed text in performance, turning it into a dramatization of "African tribal struggles" and incorporating "traditional ceremonies from their country of origin."[30] Manuel Fuentes, who saw the black festivals of Moors and Christians in Lima in the first half of the nineteenth century, wrote with distaste of "the ridiculous figures of those black kings parodying the sons of Granada."[31] A similar black parody of Spanish caballeros still takes place in the fiestas of Santiago Apóstol staged annually in Loíza, Puerto Rico.[32]

Thus I am inclined to agree with Williams's suggestion that, whatever may have been the purpose of the Spanish organizers of the Mexico City festivities in inviting (or allowing) the blacks to take part, the blacks' own purpose was to parody their indulgently overdressed Spanish rulers. Their masks would not have been, as one is first inclined to suppose, traditional African masks but would have had pale faces and European features to denote the conquistadors and their women.

If Williams's hypothesis is correct, an interesting connection between the *Battle of the Wild Men and the Blacks* and the subsequent *Conquest of Rhodes* suggests itself. Might the battle between the two groups of wild men, he asks, have referred to intertribal warfare before the conquest and might that between the wild men and the blacks dressed as conquistadors have recalled the Spanish invasion of Mexico?[33] The Spanish organizers of the festivities might well have invited the Indians and black slaves to take these roles as a prelude to the millenarian *Conquest of Rhodes,* but they would not have anticipated that the blacks would insinuate a parodic hidden transcript into the public transcript of Spanish Catholic triumph. Indeed, in the manner of many dominant groups, they may never have noticed.

If Williams is right, these first two mock battles would then have formed a trilogy with the subsequent *Conquest of Rhodes.* The first battle would have dramatized past conflicts in native Mexico, perhaps pitting "civilized" Mexica against "uncivilized" Chichimeca; the second would have recalled the Spanish conquest; and the third would have anticipated the future triumph of the combined Christian armies of the Old and New Worlds over the infidel Turks. Williams's hypothesis suggests a masked reading of the *Battle of the Wild Men and the Blacks* that, for those in the know, would have reverberated throughout the subsequent performance of the *Conquest of Rhodes.* Cortés and his commanders, sumptuously attired, mounted, and armed, would, according to the public transcript of the play, have won a magnificent victory. But the Indians and blacks in and around the square would have remembered the way in which that very magnificence had been burlesqued by the black actors and would have been able to laugh at Spanish assumptions of natural superiority and pretensions to grandeur. Jonathan Kandell may be right when he suggests that Cortés "was exposing himself to ridicule as he shouted and brandished his sword . . . and bowed to the applause and drunken praises of the festive audience," but I do not suppose, as Kandell does, that it was the Spanish audience that laughed nor that Cortés "suspected" his own vulnerability to ridicule.[34]

14

The Conquest of Jerusalem (Tlaxcala, 1539)

TLAXCALA in 1539 was very different from Mexico City. Apart from two or three minor Spanish government officials and half a dozen Franciscan friars, the population of Tlaxcala, estimated at between 200,000 and 250,000, was almost entirely Indian. Local government was in the hands of the Indian *cabildo,* presided over by an elected Indian governor. Perhaps for this reason, the Franciscan mission in Tlaxcala, founded in 1524, had been remarkably successful. By the late 1530s Christian festivals were being celebrated with an enthusiasm and extravagance that astounded Spanish observers.[1]

These festivals drew on both indigenous and European traditions. In 1538, the candlelit Corpus Christi procession included "many crosses" draped with fine "gold and feather-work"; a dozen or more platforms, similarly decorated, "bearing the images of saints"; "many banners"; "many kinds of dances"; and a boy's choir that "sang and danced before the Most Holy Sacrament." The "entire road" over which the procession passed was "covered with sedge and mace reeds and flowers"; "roses and carnations" were strewn along the way. The procession passed through "ten large triumphal arches" and "one thousand and sixty-eight" medium-sized arches, each covered with seven bushels of flowers and decorated with floral shields and rosettes. Along the way the procession paused at several chapels and four artificial "mountains." The mountains were decorated with rocks, meadows, "forest trees, fruit trees, and flowering trees, . . . mushrooms, fungi, and mosses." Falcons, crows, owls, deer, rabbits, jackals, and "a large multitude of snakes," their fangs removed and their bodies pinioned to the stage, crowded the forests, where they were hunted by "carefully concealed hunters, armed with bows and arrows." The hunters were played not by Tlaxcalteca but by mountain Indians "of another tongue," probably Otomí.[2]

The festivals were the occasion for splendid outdoor theater. In 1538, on the day of Our Lady of the Assumption (15 August), Las Casas saw an *auto* performed there before an audience of "more than eighty thousand people." The play ended with Mary rising "in a cloud" from one stage to another representing heaven. The cloud, one assumes, was painted on wood or canvas and was raised, in the manner of European theater of the Middle Ages, by means of ropes and pulleys. (Even now, in the Valencian town of Elx, at the close of the annual *Mystery of the Assumption of the Virgin,* performed there since the fifteenth century, four angels bear an image of the Virgin into the roof of the basilica by means of ancient ropes and pulleys.)[3] The speeches in Tlaxcala were in Nahuatl, and the action was accompanied by flutes and a large choir. "The apostles," Las Casas wrote, "or those who represented them, were

Indians, as was the case in all the *autos* that they had previously performed (and it must be taken for granted that no Spaniard takes charge of nor meddles in the *autos* that they put on with them), and the one who represented Our Lady was an Indian man, as were all those who took charge of the play."[4] This is an important observation. "All sources agree," Ricard remarks of the Mexican missionary theater in general, "that the participants, the actors proper, the supernumeraries, singers, and dancers were Indian, and that everything spoken or sung was in the native language, most frequently Nahuatl."[5] Las Casas goes one step further, affirming that at least in Tlaxcala even those who "took charge" of the play were Indian. In this respect, therefore, the *Conquest of Rhodes* did not serve as a model for the Tlaxcala *Conquest of Jerusalem,* for in the former Europeans directed the festivities and uncharacteristically took the leading roles.

Earlier in the year, on the Wednesday following Easter, a *Fall of Our First Parents* notable for the luxuriance of the Garden of Eden had been staged. Four "rivers or springs" flowed from paradise, nurturing a profusion of trees and flowers, some natural and others "made of feathers and gold," all crowded with birds and animals. Among the birds were parrots, as many as forty to a single tree, "whose chattering and screeching was so loud that it sometimes disturbed the play." Among the animals were two tethered wild cats (*ocotochles*). "Once, during the play, Eve was careless and went near one of them and, as if well trained, the beast went away. This was before the sin," we are told by a friar who saw the play; "had it occurred after the sin, she would not have been so lucky." There were also "artificial animals, all well simulated, with boys inside them," including an artificial lion that pretended to tear to pieces and devour the body of a real deer. The Tlaxcalteca paradise included carnivores.

The fall was delayed by Adam's indignant rejection of Eve's summons to share the forbidden fruit. Finally, she accused him of not loving her, "threw him into her lap" (or, possibly, "threw herself into his lap,") and "so importuned him that he went with her to the forbidden tree." Thus the Tlaxcalteca staged a characteristically male reading of the source of human sin in female sexuality. Then, "God entered with great majesty, accompanied by many angels," to banish Adam and Eve. Six angels bore the weeping humans, all singing in polyphonic harmony,[6] to a second stage. There, in a world now "full of thistles and thorns and many snakes," an angel taught Adam and Eve postlapsarian gender roles, showing one how to "cultivate the land" and the other how to "spin and make clothes for her husband and children." A closing carol linked the first human sin to the redemptive incarnation of Christ. "This stage play," comments the friar, "was presented by the Indians in their native language, so that many of them were deeply moved and shed tears, especially when Adam was banished from paradise and placed in the world."[7]

Four more plays were performed on the Monday following Corpus Christi. Since it was the feast day of John the Baptist, they dramatized the biblical story of John's birth to the elderly Zechariah and Elizabeth and the virginal conception of Jesus by Elizabeth's younger cousin Mary. In the first play, the angel Gabriel struck Zechariah dumb for doubting God's promise of a son. In the second, "on another stage," the same angel announced Mary's role in the birth of the Messiah. Then all "marched in procession to the Church of Saint John," where, on yet another platform, "gracefully . . . adorned and embellished," Mary's visit to the pregnant Elizabeth was staged. Finally, after mass, the company played John's birth, taking full advantage of its comic potential. Luke's gospel reports that "the neighbors and kinfolk" of Elizabeth "made signs" to Zechariah, who then "asked for a writing tablet" on which to inscribe the name of his son (Luke 1: 58–63). The false assumption that a man struck dumb must be addressed in signs, combined with mute Zechariah's necessarily signed request for a writing tablet, suggests all kinds of visual comic routines. It was amusing, Toribio de Motolinía recalled, "to see the things they handed mute Zachary before giving him the slates which he had asked for, acting as if they had not understood him." The play ended with a real baptism. "In place of the circumcision [of the infant John the Baptist], the sacrament of baptism was conferred on a child nine days old, whom they named John." Then "the relations and neighbors of Zachary" brought "presents and food of all kinds." All joined in a communal meal in simultaneous celebration of the birth of John the Baptist and the baptism of his Indian namesake. Such "integration of the theatre and real life" was a characteristic feature of missionary drama in Tlaxcala.[8]

All these plays pale by comparison with the *Conquest of Jerusalem,* which was arguably the most spectacular and intellectually sophisticated theatrical event in postcontact sixteenth-century Mexico. A group of Tlaxcalteca may have traveled to Mexico City to see the *Conquest of Rhodes.*[9] Hoping to surpass their former enemies in the Mexica capital, they decided to stage the *Conquest of Jerusalem* in their own city and, "to make the play more solemn, . . . to postpone it to the feast of Corpus Christi," Thursday, 5 June 1539.[10] A detailed eyewitness account of the performance was published, in the form of a letter, in Motolinía's *History of the Indians of New Spain.* For many years, it was assumed that the letter was written by Motolinía, but his most recent Mexican editor has argued that Motolinía was elsewhere during June 1539 and that the letter was written by another friar living in Tlaxcala at the time.[11]

Some of the Indians in Tlaxcala had firsthand experience of the European politics embedded in the play. A delegation of five Tlaxcalteca had traveled to Spain with Cortés in 1527. A second group had left for Europe in 1534, gaining an audience with Charles V and winning a Spanish coat of arms and the guarantee of royal protection for the city.[12] Perhaps as a result of this embassy, it had been decided to build a new provincial capital, distinct from the numerous Indian settlements that collectively bore the name Tlaxcala, on a previously unoccupied site on the south bank of the River Zahuapan. By 1539 the church and monastery were almost completed, the plaza had been surveyed, and the first government buildings, intended to house the Indian *cabildo,* were in process of construction along the northwest side of the square.[13] The same square, though now surrounded by colonial buildings of a later date, still serves as the main plaza of Tlaxcala. Tall ash trees reduce the appearance of horizontal space, and pacing out the square's dimensions, as I did in September 1988, yields something of a surprise. Each side of the square measures approximately two hundred yards, encompassing an area about the size of four football fields. It was in this still unfinished but nonetheless "large and pleasant plaza" that the *Conquest of Jerusalem* was played.[14]

Six scenic units were prepared for the performance.[15] One made innovative use of on-site material: the unfinished *cabildo* buildings were leveled off to a height of about six feet and filled with earth. On top was built Jerusalem, a five-towered scenic city, complete with ramparts, merlons, windows, and arches, "all covered with roses and flowers." The upper story was perhaps made of painted cloth or palm mats wrapped around a wooden frame.[16] All the scenic units representing cities or camps were "surrounded by walls, on the outside of which were paintings that very realistically simulated mason-work." The others may have been mobile. The emperor Charles V lodged in one, beyond the southeast margin of the unfinished square, prior to his entry onto the battlefield. Two more, to the right and left of Jerusalem (that is, on the southwest and northeast edges of the square), represented the military camps of the armies of Spain and New Spain. A fourth, in the center of the square, was named Santa Fe, after the impromptu city built by Charles's grandparents, Ferdinand and Isabella, as the base for their successful siege of Granada in 1492.[17] Here Charles would lodge during his assault on Jerusalem. A final unit, a decorated platform on which the consecrated bread was to be displayed, was "located near Jerusalem, in order that all the festivities might be enacted before the Most Holy Sacrament."

The play began when the Corpus Christi procession reached the square. Fernando Horcasitas estimates that some fifteen hundred Indian actors took part. Considering that Tlaxcala mustered an army of ten thousand for Cortés's final assault on Tenochtitlan in 1521, and that Gómara wrote of sixteenth-century Tlaxcala, albeit with characteristic exaggeration, that "when thay have fiestas or welcome a viceroy, sixty or seventy thousand of them come out to skirmish and to fight," the number of participants in the *Conquest of Jerusalem* may well have been many more than Horcasitas supposes.[18] After the sacrament and its attendant "pope, cardinals,

[and] bishops, all impersonated," had taken their seats on the platform, ten squadrons of Indians marched five abreast into the dusty square from the northeast end, some playing trumpets, fifes, and drums. Representing the "army of Spain," they passed "in excellent order" in front of the papal platform and settled into their camp at the far end of the plaza. In a flattering piece of fiction, the Spanish army was led by an Indian actor representing Antonio Pimentel, Count of Benavente, a substantial benefactor of the Franciscans, to whom Motolinía would dedicate his *History of the Indians of New Spain*. Behind Pimentel were troops from the kingdom of Castile and León, to which the county of Benavente belonged. Then came soldiers from several other Spanish provinces and from "Germany, Rome, and the Italians," countries subject at the time to the Holy Roman Emperor. All were dressed "as Spanish soldiers."

The friar explains this uniformity in terms of Indian ignorance: "Not having seen European soldiers, the Indians do not know how each group dresses, and hence they are not wont to differentiate." But it is also possible that the Indians were establishing a contrast between the comparatively bland uniforms of the Spanish army and the more impressive and varied dress of the Indian army of New Spain. Indigenous sympathies are often signaled aesthetically in Mexican folk theater. In Oaxaca's *danza de la pluma,* the textually victorious Spanish soldiers wear plain, blue or black uniforms, while Motecuzoma and his warriors dance their exuberant way to official defeat in multicolored costumes and high, feathered headdresses. Perhaps the uniformity of Spanish costumes in Tlaxcala was due not to Indian ignorance but to Indian opinion. Whereas the Africans in the *Battle of the Wild Men and the Blacks* may have mocked the ostentation of the Spaniards, the European soldiers in the *Conquest of Jerusalem* may have aimed at a different effect, serving as a foil for the splendor of the Tlaxcalteca warriors.

The entry of the army of New Spain, from the southwest side of the square, was impressive. This army, too, was divided into ten companies, each "attired in keeping with the costumes that they wear in war. . . . All wore their richest plumage, emblems, and shields, for those who took part in the play were lords and chiefs." In another piece of dramatic flattery, an Indian actor represented Viceroy Mendoza as captain general of the army of New Spain. In the vanguard of his army were warriors from Tlaxcala and Mexico-Tenochtitlan. Behind marched eight more squadrons, portraying tribal armies from various regions of New Spain, Peru, and the Caribbean. This army, too, crossed the square in front of the sacrament and settled in its walled camp at the other end of the square. Meanwhile, an army of Moors and Jews had ensconced itself inside Jerusalem.

We must postpone the clash of these vast armies for a few pages to consider the first sign of a hidden transcript in the play: in passing and without further comment, we are told that "the Great Sultan of Babylon and Tetrarch [*tlatoani*] of Jerusalem," the leader of the infidel army and the villain of the piece, "was the Marqués del Valle, Hernando Cortés." Later, the friar's letter mentions, again without explanation, that the captain general of the Moors "was . . . Pedro de Alvarado."[19] There is no question of Cortés and Alvarado themselves acting these roles. Alvarado was in Honduras at the time, and Cortés was lame from a wound incurred during a *juego de cañas* in February. (As late as October or November, Cortés delayed his final return to Spain for two months "because he was ill from the blow from the reed[-spear] which he had received on his instep.") In June, Cortés was devoting whatever energy his injury left him to equipping three ships to explore the Pacific coast between Acapulco and Baja California. He did not sail with the ships, but hoped to profit from their voyage. Moreover, it is hard to imagine that Cortés, whose status in Mexico by June 1539 was at a low ebb, would have consented to undermining what little glory he thought he might have accrued as the dramatic victor in the *Conquest of Rhodes* by playing the infidel villain in the *Conquest of Jerusalem*. No scholar has suggested that he did.[20]

Commentators have therefore puzzled over these references. García Icazbalceta cannot understand why "the friars, authors of all these fiestas, should have offended the conquistadors by placing them in the party of the infidels." Georges Baudot insists that "there could not have been the least intention of offence." Rather, it was nothing more than "a mischievous joke that the proven friendship of Fray Toribio [de Motolinía] for the conquistadors fully authorized, as everyone surely understood." Roland Baumann wonders if the Tlaxcalteca were swaying with the political winds. Cortés's relationship with Mendoza had soured since the *Conquest of Rhodes*. Both men claimed the right to equip and profit from new voyages of discovery, and Cortés's Pacific expedition was to sail from Acapulco on 8 July in open defiance of Mendoza's claim. On 24 August the viceroy seized control of all ships leaving or entering Pacific ports, and Cortés promptly dispatched envoys to Spain to appeal what he took to be an encroachment on his own privileges. Four or five months later, Cortés himself sailed for Spain to plead his cause. Since he never returned to Mexico, Mendoza easily took control of the Pacific expedition. In the *Conquest of Jerusalem*, Mendoza is pointedly assigned the role of captain general of New Spain, a title jealously guarded by Cortés since it had been conferred on him by Charles V in 1522. Alvarado was a less dangerous rival. He had recently returned from Spain with a royal contract to "discover and conquer islands in the Pacific," but his contract recognized Mendoza's claims, granting the viceroy a third interest in Alvarado's profits. Perhaps, Baumann suggests, "the Tlaxcalans ridiculed the two conquistadors because they felt it could not displease the viceroy."[21]

Baumann's hypothesis has merit. Undoubtedly, this was one of several strands of more or less concealed references to contemporary Mexican politics in a play whose public transcript was a "prediction" of future events in Europe. Moreover, it explains why Cortés and Alvarado were placed among the Moors, while an Indian playing another conquistador, Andrés de Tapia, fought with the Christian forces. But Horcasitas wonders if the tactical flattery of Mendoza masked a further hidden transcript of indigenous resistance. "Could it be," he asks, "that the Indians found satisfaction in seeing their own conqueror routed by a native army?" Answering his own question affirmatively, he continues, "Only in this way can one explain the mysterious role in which he was made to appear in the Tlaxcalan play." Othón Arróniz is of the same opinion, finding in "the incredible audacity" of making Cortés chief of the Muslim infidels "clear indication . . . of a natural resentment in the conquered people, which could only rise to the surface at moments of festivity and under theatrical guise." [22]

I agree. The *Battle of the Wild Men and the Blacks* and the *Conquest of Rhodes*, if my reading is correct, involved both the participation and the mockery of Cortés. The Tlaxcalteca may well have seen the Mexico City performance and decided to imitate the *Conquest of Rhodes* by having one of their own actors play the role of Cortés taking part in a mock battle between Turks and Christians. By having the pseudo-Cortés play the role of the infidel villain who loses the campaign, however, they were in their own way mocking the real Cortés's heroics in the *Conquest of Rhodes*. If challenged, they could have protested that they were merely following Mendoza's lead in opposing Cortés. Under the guise of flattering the viceroy, of course, they were able surreptitiously to enact an Indian defeat of Cortés.

Moreover, the Tlaxcalteca were proud of the war they had waged against Cortés only twenty years before and were used to restaging it. Gómara reported that "when they have fiestas or welcome a viceroy, sixty or seventy thousand of them come out to skirmish and to fight, as if they were fighting against Cortés." Baumann discounts this report on the grounds that, in official accounts of their history, the Tlaxcalteca minimized their initial resistance and stressed their acceptance of Christianity and their subsequent military alliance with Cortés. [23] But public acceptance of the status quo does not preclude a hidden transcript of opposition. It should not surprise us that Gómara's report of Indians pretending to fight against Cortés should follow his account of an official Tlaxcalteca speech in praise of Cortés. Indeed, the Tlaxcalteca alliance with Cortés may have been prompted more by the "intoxicating . . . prospect of destroying" their traditional enemies, the Mexica, than by any particular liking for Cortés and his troops. When "the Tlaxcalans and other Indian allies realised . . . that their collaboration with the Castilians was not going to lead to their own succession to the Mexica as masters of the valley," they soon came to resent the dominance of the Spanish Empire. A modest attempt at rebellion in 1523 was repressed.[24] That the Tlaxcalteca should have embraced Christianity with apparently genuine fervor does not, as we saw with the Cuetzalan *danza de los santiagos,* preclude their resistance to the secular legacy of the conquistadors. Finally, we should note that the Indian governor of Tlaxcala in 1539 was Luis Xicotencatl, nephew of the Axayacatzin Xicotencatl whom Cortés hanged in Texcoco in 1521.[25] There may have been some personal or familial hostility at work in the assignment of Cortés to the losing side in the *Conquest of Jerusalem.*

One strand of the hidden transcript in the *Conquest of Jerusalem,* therefore, seems to have celebrated past resistance and enacted a form of theatrical vengeance. Another strand dreamed of future liberation, for the assignment of Cortés and Alvarado to the head of an army that would soon, from the Franciscan point of view, be expelled from its illegal occupation of Jerusalem allowed the Indians to enact their own "prediction" of reconquest. Conceding the claims of Christianity to Jerusalem, the Tlaxcalteca appear to have asked: If the Turks have no right to hold Jerusalem, by what right do the Spanish now hold Mexico? From the perspective of a Tlaxcalteca Christian, the liberation of Jerusalem from illicit Turkish occupation and the liberation of Mexico from illicit Spanish occupation may not have seemed so different. It is striking, too, that whereas the European army is consistently identified as "the Spaniards," the Indian army is designated "the Christians." The friars often compared Indian piety to the "infidelity of the countless nominal Catholics" who had come from Spain,[26] and the Tlaxcalteca performers seem to have incorporated that perception into their dramatized argument for an indigenous reconquest of Mexico. If, as the play insisted, God helps Christian armies, the identity of the true Christians was a matter of real significance.

This appropriation and reversal of Spanish rhetoric conforms to a broad pattern of "disguised reconciliations" between Indian and Spaniard at this period of Tlaxcalan history. "Situations occurred" in Tlaxcala, Charles Gibson remarks, "in which Indians accepted one aspect of Spanish colonization in order to facilitate their rejection of another. . . . Spanish colonization was such that Indians were able to range with some freedom between attitudes of affirmation and attitudes of dissent. In certain instances they came close to fulfilling the most idealistic expectations of Hispanic imperial theorists. At other times Indians seemed almost to be exploiting Spaniards, so effectively were they able to take advantage of the humanistic colonization."[27] Although Gibson does not cite it as such, the *Conquest of Jerusalem* is a splendid theatrical illustration of the kind of cultural and political maneuver that he has in mind.

As to whether the friar who wrote the eyewitness account was alert to the hidden transcript or simply puzzled when he wrote that the Sultan of Babylon "was . . . Hernando Cortés" and the Turkish captain general "was . . . Pedro de Alvarado," we may never know. Although, in the early years, the friars regarded Cortés him-self as a friend, they vehemently opposed the abuses to which the conquistadors and their successors subjected the Indians, and Motolinía had on a number of occasions sided with the Indians against the civil authorities in Mexico City. So greatly had he angered the corrupt first *audiencia,* under the presidency of Nuño de Guzmán, that in 1529 he had been charged with planning "a conspiracy with the Indians to overthrow the civil government in Mexico, slay its officials, and send the Spanish soldiers and settlers back to Spain." The government's chief witness later recanted, but Motolinía's reputation as a friend of the Indians so impressed the Franciscan chapter that in 1530 he was given his first appointment to the region of Tlaxcala as a kind of "itinerant missionary, charged with winning back dissatisfied tribes" and healing wounds inflicted during the Nuño de Guzmán regime.[28] We do not know how the friars in Tlaxcala dealt with the heightening of tension between Cortés and Mendoza in 1539. Perhaps they, too, swayed with the political winds.[29] But one need not suppose that they endorsed the theatrical demonizing of Cortés and Alvarado to grant that they were willing to hear the Indian point of view expressed theatrically.

With three armies and a theory of Cortés and Alvarado's place among the Moors now in hand, we can let battle commence. The Spanish squadrons advanced on Jerusalem, and the Sultan Cortés led his troops out to meet them "with much shouting and noise of trumpets, drums, and fifes." The Spanish gained the advan-tage in the first encounter, taking some Moors prisoner and leaving others lying on the field, "although," the friar notes with some relief, "no one was wounded." The friar's concern for the safety of the actors reflects the ferocity with which the mock battles were fought. Once the Spaniards had returned to camp, the army of New Spain also took the field and inflicted casualties. During a break in the fighting, re-inforcements bearing food and ammunition reached Jerusalem. A third skirmish, between Moors and Spaniards, ended in Spanish retreat with some of their number captured or "[left] for dead on the field." From the safety of his camp, Benavente sent a message to Charles V, claiming that the Spaniards had "fought like tigers and lions," singling out the bravery of the soldiers of León, and reporting the unfortu-nate losses. The emperor advised that guards be posted to prevent more reinforce-ments reaching Jerusalem.

His advice was not taken soon enough. As the emperor's reply was being read in one corner of the plaza, the army of New Spain was advancing on Jerusalem in another. In the ensuing skirmish, all the Indians "fought valiantly," with the ex-ception of the two Caribbean companies, who "finally began to weaken and lose ground to such an extent that between the fallen and the captured none of their men survived." Afterward Mendoza sent a message to Charles, reporting that most of the Indians had "fought like elephants and giants," but that the Moors had received "huge reinforcements of men and artillery." In the end, he wrote, all the Caribbean islanders, "since they neither were adept in the use of arms nor had defensive weapons nor knew how to invoke the help of God," fell into enemy hands. Horcasitas proposes that this be understood as "a parody of the historical reality of the Spanish conquest of the New World," to which the Indians of the Caribbean, unlike their counterparts on the mainland, offered no effective resistance. Their defeat in the *Conquest of Jerusalem* "shows a certain scorn on the part of the Indians of New Spain and of the Europeans towards the Caribs, perhaps for their more simple culture and for their easy extinction at the hands of the first conquistadors." [30] If so, the incident formed part of the hidden transcript of the play, in which only those who resist and finally overcome the conquistadors are celebrated. It also reinforced the identification of Moors and conquistadors, linking a predicted defeat of Caribbean islanders by the former to their historical defeat by the latter.

Charles's reply to Mendoza assured him "that our help will come from above, from heaven," and promised (not entirely trusting heaven) that he would "travel all night without sleeping" so as to reach Jerusalem by daybreak. Mendoza was told to forward the news to Pimentel, thereby giving the audience at the other end of the square a chance to hear Charles's message. Charles arrived shortly afterward, accompanied by "the King of France and the King of Hungary, all wearing crowns." The former represented Francis I, now formally at peace with, but in this play carefully subservient to, Charles V. The latter denoted Charles's younger brother, Ferdinand, who, as a little boy, had enacted his own version of the conquest of Jerusalem for his grandfather and was now ruler of Hungary and Bohemia and active in the war against the Ottoman Turks. The imperial army was greeted "with much rejoicing and great pomp," its progress to Santa Fe being marked by the shrill rhythm of trumpets and drums and the discharge of many fireworks imitating artillery.

The Moors "gave signs of being in great fear" at this turn of events, but when all three Christian armies besieged Jerusalem, the Moors "defended themselves very well." Some captives were freed. "The camp-master, who was Andrés de Tapia, had gone with a squadron to reconnoiter in the rear of Jerusalem, where he set fire to a place, and then through the center of the plaza led a herd of sheep which he had taken." The liberation of the sheep recalled the similar episode in the *Conquest of Rhodes* and probably signified the rescue of Christian civilians from Moorish captivity. Why Tapia should have been given this role is not clear. Clearly Cortés, who had himself led the liberation of the sheep in the *Conquest of Rhodes,* was not going to be assigned any such heroic role in the *Conquest of Jerusalem.*

Their concerted attack on Jerusalem proving ineffective, the three Christian armies returned to their separate camps. The Spaniards set out alone to renew the assault, but the Moors charged out of Jerusalem to capture some of the attackers.

Stung by this defeat, Charles dispatched a messenger to the pope, asking for prayer. The pope responded with a commitment not only to pray himself but to ask "all the children of the Church" to do so. The alternation of noisy battles and set speeches is characteristic of festivals of Moors and Christians, which, unlike the literary theater, offer little or no dialogue. There can be none during the battles, for the martial music, the explosions of gunpowder and fireworks, the shouting, and the clash of weapons would drown it out. In this tradition, there is little room for the Shakespearean practice of soldiers locking swords and declaiming blank verse. Rather, dramatic speech is confined to formal declamation, often of messages or embassies between one camp and another, during breaks between skirmishes. Often, too, if modern practice is anything to go by, the speeches cannot be heard by a majority of the vast outdoor audience.

Finding itself twice repulsed and its camp surrounded by Moors, the Spanish army fell to its knees facing the sacrament. The pope and cardinals did likewise. In response, an angel "appeared at the corner of the camp," atop the wooden frame and painted battlements, and told them that God was pleased with their willingness to die for the recovery of Jerusalem, "since he would not have so holy a place in possession of an enemy of the faith." Their hardships, he added, were only a test of their "constancy and bravery." They need not fear defeat: Santiago, patron saint of Spain, was on his way. To loud cheers, an Indian playing Santiago rode into the square on a horse "as white as snow." Encouraged, the Spaniards attacked again. The Moors fled, locking themselves in Jerusalem and not even daring to show their heads over the ramparts so long as "Santiago on his horse, always turning up in all parts," led the Spanish forces. Afterward the Spaniards returned to their camp "with their standards unfurled." They had been unable to enter Jerusalem.

Seeing this, "the Nahuales or people of New Spain" also set out against the city, but the Moors, undaunted by an army that boasted no saint, rushed to the encounter and, after fierce fighting, drove the indigenous army back to its camp. Chastened, the army of New Spain also resorted to prayer. An angel appeared above their camp, which was now called "the camp of the Christians." "Although you are newcomers to the faith," the angel declared, "God has . . . allow[ed] you to be conquered [by the Moors], in order that you might know that without his help you can do little." It was a common ploy of missionaries to argue the supremacy of the Christian god over pagan idols by pointing out that "the true and omnipotent God had allowed his faithful servants, the Spaniards, to conquer Mexico."[31] Do we hear an echo of that argument here (for the Moors are, after all, led by Cortés), and do the Indian performers reply that theirs is now the true "camp of the Christians"? The Tlaxcalteca may have reasoned that the God who had defeated their idols might now help them, as Christians, to drive out the conquistadors. The angel's next remark may be read as a reminder that it was as much the Tlaxcalteca as the Spaniards who had conquered Mexico, and that, if the missionary argument were to hold, continued possession of the land would be contingent on piety, not ethnicity. "Since you have humbled yourself," the angel announced, "God has heard your prayer. . . . St. Hippolytus, on whose feast day the Spaniards with you Tlaxcaltecas gained Mexico," would come to the aid of the new "Christians." (It had been on the feast day of St. Hippolytus, 13 August 1521, that the Mexica had finally surrendered Tenochtitlan to the conquistadors and their allies.) Soon, an Indian representing St. Hippolytus galloped in "on a brown horse" to lead "the army of the Nahuales" in its war on the Sultan Cortés.

All three armies now renewed the assault, led by the exalted triumvirate of Santiago, Hippolytus, and Charles V. The special effects were ingenious. Earthenware balls made of "mud dried in the sun" and "filled with moistened red earth" were discharged, "so that the one who was struck by them seemed badly wounded and covered with blood." The same was done with "red prickly pears." The archers "fastened to their arrowheads little pockets filled with red earth, so that [they] seemed to draw blood whenever they struck." Thick stalks of corn and balls made of reeds were propelled. Finally, a house of straw, which had been built on the shoulders of a bastion between two of Jerusalem's towers, was set on fire. Perhaps it ignited the entire upper story of wood and canvas. A similar technique (setting fire to a wooden and paper frame mounted on a single-story stone facade) simulates the burning of the captured Moorish castle at the end of the annual *morismas* of Bracho. Setting fire to stage *castillos* may derive from the Mexica practice of burning enemy temples as a sign of victory.

In the midst of this final battle, supernatural intervention settled the outcome. The sudden appearance of the archangel Michael, standing amidst the charred scenery on the main tower of Jerusalem, filled both Moors and Christians with such fear that they stopped fighting and fell silent. The archangel told the Moors, "If God considered your evil deeds and sins instead of his great mercy, you would already be buried in the depths of hell; the earth would have opened up and swallowed you alive." But, because they had "showed reverence for the Holy Places," God had mercifully allowed them time to repent and to "believe in his dearest Son Jesus Christ." Turkish respect for Christian holy places in Jerusalem pleased the Franciscans, who were guardians of those sites. Perhaps the archangel's remark was intended to rebuke the conquistadors for their failure to demonstrate a similar respect for the indigenous holy places of Mexico. In any case, the archangel concluded, it was now time for the Moors (or, in terms of the indigenous hidden transcript, the conquistadors) to "appease [God] with true tears and penance." His warning delivered, "St. Michael disappeared." [32]

Impressed, Sultan Cortés addressed his troops: "Great is the goodness and the mercy of God, because he has in this way deigned to enlighten us who are so greatly blinded in sin. . . . So far we thought we were fighting with men. But now we see that we have been fighting with God and his saints and angels." Resistance was impossible and an appeal to God's mercy would be wise. The Moorish captain general, Pedro de Alvarado, concurred and, together with all the soldiers, asked the sultan to sue for peace and for baptism. The sultan sent a letter to Charles V admitting, in terms that only a miracle would have wrenched from the historical Süleyman, "You alone are captain of God's armies," and we are "your natural vassals."

This confession is a remarkably sophisticated theatrical appropriation and subversion of the hostile rhetoric of a foreign invader. Aristotle's language of natural slavery was used by Spaniards to justify their conquest of Mexican "barbarians."[33] At the close of the *Conquest of Jerusalem,* the charge of natural slavery was applied to the Moors. We might even say that it was deflected from Indians to Moors. But in terms of the play's hidden transcript, the language of natural slavery was used by the Tlaxcalteca to suggest a radical idea. Cortés surrendered to an army played in large part by Tlaxcalteca "lords and chiefs" and declared himself and his troops to be their "natural vassals." The Tlaxcalteca nobles, proud of their own social standing and confident of their nation's inherent superiority over others, appropriated their conquerors' Aristotelian ideology and reversed its Eurocentric application.

Acknowledging his natural servitude, the penitent Sultan Cortés left Jerusalem "with a great retinue," knelt before the emperor (played by a Tlaxcalteca lord), "rendered him obedience and tried hard to kiss his hand." It must have been a stunning moment for those in the know. Then, as the play closed, apocalyptic missionary theater and the real sacramental life of the church were integrated. The emperor led Sultan Cortés to the pope, who received him "with great affection. The sultan brought also many Turks, or adult Indians, who had been designedly prepared for baptism. They publicly asked the pope that they be baptized. The pope immediately directed a priest to baptize them; whereupon they were actually baptized."

The baptisms were an act of ecclesiastical defiance. For some years conflict had simmered in Mexico over whether it was proper to abbreviate the ceremony of baptism in view of the shortage of priests and the large number of Indians requesting baptism. Motolinía estimated the number of Indians baptized between 1524 and 1536 at five million, a figure that Ricard considers "not inadmissable."[34] Faced at times with baptizing "two or three thousand Indians . . . in the course of one day," many of the Franciscans resorted to reading the ritual of baptism over a crowd of candidates, applying the full ceremony, including "the anointing with the sign of the cross, the breathing, the salt, the saliva, and the white cloth," to a few and then baptizing the rest with water alone. The other orders objected to what they considered too hasty an approach. So great was the acrimony that the dispute reached Rome, and in 1537 Pope Paul III issued a bull, recognizing the Franciscans' good intentions but instructing that the full ceremony be used in all cases but those of "urgent necessity." On 27 April 1539, a synod of Mexican bishops issued a specific definition of "urgent necessity," requiring that all other adult baptisms be confined to the seasons of Easter and Pentecost. Since Easter had just passed (Easter Sunday in 1539 fell on 6 April) and Pentecost followed shortly (25 May), the decree meant the effective suspension of adult baptism, other than that of the infirm or those otherwise in danger of death, for almost a full year after Pentecost. For "three or four months," according to Motolinía, the prohibition held. But then, in Huaquechula (Puebla), "the friars resolved to baptize all who applied for the sacrament, regardless of what the bishops had directed." Motolinía, who was visiting Huaquechula at the time, was one of the two friars involved. Over a period of five days, he and the resident friar baptized "Indians numbering by actual count 14,200 or so." They were careful to observe the full ritual, although "it proved quite a job."[35]

The *Conquest of Jerusalem,* with its concluding baptism of "many . . . adult Indians," took place during the feast of Corpus Christi, less than six weeks after the episcopal announcement and eleven days after Pentecost. If Motolinía's chronology is correct, it anticipated the mass baptisms at Huaquechula by two or three months. Arróniz therefore considers the *Conquest of Jerusalem* to have been a calculated "defiance . . . of the colonial authorities" and "a deliberate act of support for the sacrament of baptism such as it was administered by the Franciscans." It dramatized, he suggests, a "triumphant" reading of the papal bull, interpreting it as a vindication of the Franciscan eagerness to baptize.[36] It was, after all, an actor representing Pope Paul III who ordered the play's baptisms. Apparently, the Indians were not the only ones in Tlaxcala willing to use the drama for subversive purposes.

This entanglement of Spanish Franciscan and indigenous Tlaxcalteca hidden transcripts in the same play raises the question of authorship. Who was responsible for weaving indigenous Tlaxcalteca resistance, Franciscan defiance of episcopal authority, and flattery of Viceroy Mendoza into a single performance whose official referent was none of these but was, rather, a future liberation of Jerusalem from the Turks? Baudot believes Motolinía himself to be the author of the *Conquest of Jerusalem.* Arróniz, on the other hand, suggests an Indian playwright.[37]

But folk theater on this scale is rarely the work of a single author. Rather, an acceptable narrative provides the basis of the public transcript, a scenario is developed (or inherited by way of tradition), several different groups are given (or take) responsibility for various parts of the action, and rehearsals ensue, such that the performance itself issues from a kind of organic communal authorship. Hidden transcripts are consciously or unconsciously insinuated into the proceedings without being formally scripted. In the case of the *Conquest of Jerusalem,* I would guess that Tlaxcalan friars and natives saw the *Conquest of Rhodes* in Mexico City and decided, perhaps on their return journey, that Tlaxcala should outshine its old rival in the staging of theatrical spectacle. The conquest of Jerusalem was quickly chosen as the theme: it would supersede the earlier play in the greater significance of its prophetic referent, it would appeal to Franciscan millenarianism, and, as the friars waxed enthusiastic about the justice of retaking Jerusalem, the Indians recognized the opportunities in such a scenario to enact their own dreams of reconquest. After their return to Tlaxcala, friars and Indians brought other community leaders into the discussions. Plans were drawn up, a mutually acceptable scenario developed, actors recruited (with the usual rivalries over who played the leading roles), and companies of Moorish, European, and native soldiers were formed and rehearsed (perhaps with a certain competition as to which company looked, sounded, marched, and fought the best). Costumes were designed and sewn, and scenic units constructed on the model of the besieged city in the *Conquest of Rhodes.* Set speeches were composed in Nahuatl by one or more Indian authors, perhaps along lines suggested (but not dictated) by a friar. Sometime during the preparations, the Indians had the idea of dressing the sultan of Babylon and his captain general so as to signal that they also represented Cortés and Alvarado. They may well not have told the friars of their intentions. The friars decided that the traditional ending of a *moros y cristianos* (the baptism of the Moorish king) could be used for actual baptisms and quietly began to prepare candidates for that rite. Both sides agreed that it would be politic to have Mendoza lead the army of New Spain. And so it went on, with neither a single friar nor a single Indian taking charge as the "author" or "director" in the sense that these terms are used in the literary theater. This mode of organic communal composition and rewriting is the way annual festive performances develop today, and I suspect that something similar took place for the original composition of the *Conquest of Jerusalem* in Tlaxcala in 1539.

After the baptisms, the Corpus Christi procession reformed. The road was "strewn with many fragrant herbs and roses" and straddled by "ten large triumphal arches" and "more than fourteen hundred" smaller arches "entirely covered with roses and flowers." At intervals beside the road were "three artificial hills" on which "three good mystery plays" were performed.[38] The first, *The Temptation of Our Lord,* began with a "consultation" among many demons "to decide how Christ should be tempted and who should be tempter." Lucifer, being chosen, disguised himself as a hermit, finding it difficult to hide his two horns and the long, thick claws on his fingers and toes. For the third temptation he offered Christ all the natural wealth and crafted merchandise of the Old and New Worlds, including "many kinds of excellent wine." Christ resisted this potent temptation, and Lucifer "collapsed" into hell. Angels "seemed to come down from heaven," perhaps by means of ropes and pulleys. They brought food for Christ and, once they had "set the table, . . . all began to sing."

A saint play, based on incidents from the life of Saint Francis, followed. Francis preached to the birds, "who seemed to ask his blessing," and tamed "a wild beast . . . so ugly that those who saw it about to attack became frightened." During a subsequent sermon to a human audience, Francis was interrupted by an Indian feigning drunkenness and singing "what the Indians sing when they are drunk." Perhaps this made the audience laugh, but the drunkard was finally carried off by "very ugly" demons, shouting loudly, to "a fierce and fearful hell which was nearby." So were some "well-simulated witches," offering "potions concocted in this land [that] very easily cause pregnant women to miscarry." Other "vices" followed, probably engaging in banter with the spectators, encouraging them to join in ribald songs, purchase abortives, and pay no attention to Francis's sermon. Each vice in turn was carried away by the demons. Unknown to the audience, "the simulated hell had a secret door through which those who were inside could come out." So, when hell was set on fire at the close of the play and "burned frightfully," to the accompaniment of vicious and demonic shrieking, it caused "great horror," for "no one seemed to have escaped." Even those in the know were deeply affected.

It being by now late in the afternoon, the third play, *The Sacrifice of Abraham*, although "very well staged," was shortened. The friar gives no further details,[39] except to add that after it the procession finally returned to the church. It had been a full day.

15

The Tensions of Empire (Mexico City, 1565–1595)

THE scattered records of *moros y cristianos* in Mexico during the rest of the six-teenth century do not support the idea that there was a "rich pageant staged annually in the central plaza of Mexico City to reenact the conquest of the Aztec capital" or that there was anywhere "an annual battle of Moors and Christians."[1] As in medieval Spain, with the single exception of the Catalan Turks and hobby horses, mock battles between Moors and Christians in sixteenth-century Mexico were occasional rather than annual.

In October 1565, Alonso de Avila, son of the conquistador of the same name, rode into Mexico City, dressed as Motecuzoma, with twenty-four friends disguised as Indian nobles. The party was warmly greeted by a group of simulated conquis-tadors, led by Martín Cortés, the second Marqués del Valle, who played the role of his own father. After a fanciful reenactment of the first encounter of the two lead-ers, in which Motecuzoma, "to the murmur of instruments and the applause of the assembly," placed feathered wreaths on the heads of Cortés and his wife, all the par-ticipants "dined in native style." Afterward, in the street, the two sides fought a "dainty skirmish" with shields and with balls made of dried mud and filled with ashes or flowers.

The fathers of Cortés and Avila had both taken part in the *Conquest of Rhodes*. The 1565 affair staged by their sons was theatrically less ambitious, a private mas-querade rather than a public performance, but it may secretly have set its sights higher, motivated less by theatrical than by conspiratorial ends. At a dinner that fol-lowed the skirmish, the actors may have discussed a plot to overthrow the colonial government and crown Martín Cortés king of an independent New Spain. Ten months later, in August 1566, Avila and his brother were beheaded for their part in what Henry Bamford Parkes calls "the last movement for Mexican independence among the creoles for more than two hundred years." Martín Cortés was sent to stand trial in Spain.[2] Although the Mexica had already adapted their own songs and companion dances to represent the conquest, the 1565 masquerade is the first record of a Spanish-style mock battle whose public transcript recalled the history of Mexico rather than that of Europe. If the conspiracy theory is correct, it was de-signed not to indoctrinate a passive Indian audience with notions of Spanish in-vincibility but to mask a hidden transcript of creole insurgency.

In 1572, events in Europe, much as they had done in 1539, prompted a cele-bratory *moros y cristianos* in Mexico City. On 7 October 1571, a Christian navy under the command of John of Austria destroyed the Ottoman fleet in the bay of Lepanto. The Turks lost 30,000 men, 117 ships, and 650 cannon. This is the naval battle recalled by the *morismas* of Bracho. Although the impact of the victory proved short-lived, it appeared at the time to guarantee Christian control of the Mediterranean and to justify fresh hopes of reclaiming Jerusalem.[3] News of the victory arrived in Mexico early in 1572, and a mock battle was planned that year for 25 July, the feast day of Santiago.

The *Códice Aubin* provides our only record of the play: "A scenic wooden building [*quauhteocalli*] was raised so that the lords might be represented as the Moors who were scattered. They were conquered as they were in their own land. This is how they did it: first they arrived and fought in boats; then they fought on horseback; later they arrived on foot and went on the flat roof. This happened today, Friday 25 July 1572." The codex includes a drawing of a four-dimensional single-story scenic unit, with a front doorway, an open roof with a ledge around the top of the wall, and what may be a rear central tower. Two faces peer over the ledge. The building sits in the center of a square walled yard with a tower at each corner and a front gateway (see Fig. 15b). Although *quauhteocalli* literally means "wooden god house" or, as Charles Dibble translates it, "*iglesia* [church]," it seems in this instance to signify a scenic city or castle. The codex uses the same word elsewhere to describe what Horcasitas believes to be an illustration of the scenic city of Rhodes in 1539 (see Fig 15a).[4]

It would appear from this data that a massed entry of Moors and Christians ("they arrived") was followed by three battles. The first, in boats, represented the naval battle of Lepanto. The text does not specify whether the mock battle was fought in wheeled ships or, as Horcasitas prefers, in real vessels "in the ship canal." Nor does Horcasitas spell out whether he thinks the boats were Indian canoes or Spanish brigantines.[5] There is precedent for each of these options. The second and third battles conformed to traditional European modes of mock combat. One was fought on horseback. The other, after a further parade of the troops, involved the siege of a fortified scenic unit. While one party attacked the building, the other defended it from the roof. Perhaps the mock siege represented, like the 1539 Tlaxcala play, a predictive conquest of Jerusalem, anticipated once again in the afterglow of the victory at Lepanto.

The most interesting detail of this account is its admission that the play was staged "so that the lords might be represented as the Moors who were scattered [*ixcuitilloque tlatoque in quenin tepeualloc moros*]." Horcasitas misses this altogether, translating the line as "the lords . . . see a representation of how the Moors were conquered," but Dibble properly captures the identity of lords and Moors: "the lords were dressed as the conquered Moors." If the "lords" were Spanish, then the conquistadors were once again surreptitiously identified with intrusive but finally defeated Muslims. If the "lords" were indigenous, the performance may have expressed native sympathy for the Moors who, like the Mexica, had been "conquered in their own land." The codex itself provides no guidance, using *tlatoque* variously to signify both Spanish and Mexica authorities,[6] but the precedent of the *Conquest of Jerusalem* inclines me to favor the former reading.

In September 1586, the Indians of Xochimilco, a town just south of Mexico City, entertained the new viceroy and his wife with large-scale festivals of Moors and Christians. The mock battles "cost the community dearly, for in one of them two or three [Indians] died" and "the leading Indian of the city was badly wounded" when a weapon, presumably an arquebus, "was fired and exploded."[7]

In Guadalupe Tepeyac, site of the possible 1556 (or 1531) mock battle between Mexica and Chichimeca, a spectacular series of festive battles was staged in 1595, involving both Spanish and native traditions. There was the usual "artificial wood," in which Indians armed with bows hunted deer and rabbits, "as they had done before the conquest." Afterward Indians in "innumerable canoes, decorated with tree branches and bunting," fought a mock battle on the lagoon "on both sides of the causeway." The action then shifted to a castle "made of matted palms painted to look like hewn stone." The castle was large enough to hold "fifty men on horseback and fifty on foot" who fired arquebuses at regular intervals from within. At night the castle was illuminated with sticks of burning torch-pine that were secured in tubs of glazed earthenware so as not to set the castle itself on fire. The next day, two companies formed by "some of the most illustrious caballeros of New Spain" fought a "magnificent skirmish." The defenders of the castle were joined by "twelve Knights of Malta," whose clothes were red with a white cross. The Knights of Malta were the same aristocratic order of Christian knights as the Knights of St. John that had been driven out of Rhodes in 1523. Only their name had been changed to reflect their new location. The Christian defenders were attacked by thirty-six caballeros in Turkish costumes with turbans and blue *marlotas* (Moorish gowns). The mock siege may have recalled the successful defense of Malta against an overwhelming surplus of Turkish forces in 1565.[8]

The order of battles in the 1595 performance was remarkably similar to that in the trilogy that had been staged in Mexico City in 1539. Both began with a representation of preconquest hunting. Where the earlier performance had continued with the *Battle of the Wild Men and the Blacks,* the Tepeyac hunting scene was followed by a naval battle that may also have recalled Cortés's conquest of Tenochtitlan, much of which had been fought from Mexica canoes and Spanish brigantines. Finally, in both cases, Christians battled Turks for control of a fortified Mediterranean island. That the pattern was still being repeated fifty years later strengthens Williams's hypothesis that the order of the 1539 performance was by design and confirms the continued strong appeal of its intertwined public and hidden transcripts to both Spaniards and Indians.

It is not clear from the Tepeyac account whether the conquistadors were mocked during the naval battle as they had been by the blacks in 1539. Indigenous sympathies were perhaps expressed in this instance not by mockery but by reclamation of the performance space. For, after the defense of Malta, the Indians were ordered through interpreters and their native "governors" (and one suspects they had arranged to be so ordered) to perform an indigenous dance with "*volador* poles and featherwork." The featherwork almost certainly referred to the large wings still worn at that time by four *voladores* who "flew" to earth at the end of ropes unwinding from a rotating spool at the top of the pole. In any case, the dance began at two in the afternoon and, by virtue of multiple repetitions, continued "until long after nightfall."[9] If, as Read suggests, the dance contains an implicit declaration that "as time spins back on itself," Mexica power will "be spun back into existence," then its repeated performance on that long afternoon and evening in Tepeyac formed a powerful rebuttal to the enactment of Spanish imperial triumph that preceded it. Even if it represented only the worship of the autochthonous gods of the sun, earth, and four cardinal points, it still constituted a symbolic reclamation of stolen space. In either case, only the Indians knew, since the Spaniards thought of the dance as an acrobatic spectacle.

This was not the first time that the dance of the *voladores* had closed a festival whose public transcript glorified Christian victory. Some time during the viceregency of Martín Enríquez (1568–1580), Torquemada saw "festivals . . . of the conquest of Mexico," mounted by the Mexica, that "recalled the memory of Hernán Cortés and all that happened until the capture of the city." At the end of the day, as Torquemada watched the *voladores* dance one more time, an unwinged dancer (either the musician or one of the additional dancers who sometimes climbed the pole with the *voladores*) reached for a circling rope to slide down after his fellows. He missed. Perhaps, says Torquemada, his hands were full with a drum and rattles or his head was heavy from too much wine. He plunged to his death before the slowly rotating flyers reached the ground.[10] In this instance, the reclamation of desecrated space was marred by the death of an Indian actor.

Some of the late-sixteenth-century *juegos de cañas* and skirmishes may also have had dramatic elements. One, on the occasion of Martín Cortés's arrival in Mexico City in 1562, involved "more than three hundred [men] on horseback" in "a very well arranged skirmish, with many inventions, that lasted many hours."[11] Another, in Guadalupe Tepeyac in 1585, was preceded by an "invention" involving four "nymphs" and twelve "hunters," all on horseback and "richly dressed." Since some of those who fought wore "Moorish gowns and hoods," the skirmish may have been a competitive variant of the *moros y cristianos.*[12]

A dramatized *juego de cañas* on a much smaller scale took place during a procession, on 1 November 1587, in honor of a recently arrived shipment of relics. When the procession halted at a decorative arch along the route, three boys dressed as angels presented a serious play, after which twelve others from a Jesuit school appeared, carrying lances and shields, and imitated to music "a famous *juego de cañas,* ending with an ingenious dance of lances and shields, which gave much pleasure to the viceroy and to all those present, especially the caballeros, to see their military exercises reduced to music."[13]

Oddly enough, despite the later popularity of the genre, this is the first clear reference to the specific performance of a combat dance in colonial Mexico and may suggest that, as in Spain, some were the result of courtly tournaments and dramatic military festivities being scaled down and "reduced to music." Others may owe little but their overt theme to an imported Spanish tradition, having deeper, covert roots in pre-Hispanic dance. It is striking that not one of the examples I have found of mock battles between Moors and Christians in sixteenth-century Mexico offers even the slightest evidence of an imported Spanish tradition of dances as distinct from large-scale festivals of Moors and Christians. Some of the *Cantares mexicanos,* however, do suggest that the theme of the Spanish conquest of Mexico was grafted onto indigenous dances in the mid to late sixteenth century.

We now have an idea of the formal limits (and, within those limits, the variety) of *moros y cristianos* and quasi-dramatic skirmishes that took place in and around Mexico City during the latter part of the sixteenth century. But the most powerful evidence for the widespread popularity of festivals of Moors and Christians, not only among Spanish colonists in the capital but among Indians in many of the smaller towns and villages, comes from a single work that recounts the travels of Alonso Ponce. We will consider this in the next chapter.

16
The Travels of Alonso Ponce (New Spain, 1584–1589)

BETWEEN September 1584 and June 1589, Alonso Ponce traveled relentlessly through Mexico, Guatemala, El Salvador, and Nicaragua, visiting 176 Franciscan convents in fulfillment of his calling as commissary general of the Franciscan order in New Spain. His companion and secretary, Antonio de Ciudad Real, kept a daily record of their journeys. Published most recently under the title *Tratado curioso y docto de las grandezas de la Nueva España*, Ciudad Real's account offers valuable insight into the ecclesiastical politics of the day and much anthropological, archaeological, and geographical detail about the regions through which the two friars traveled.

Less often noted are the dances, plays, and mock battles staged by indigenous peoples along the way. Although my main interest here is in the mock battles, the other performances also warrant our attention. Ciudad Real provides a detailed (and, to the best of my knowledge, unique) description of a *danza de los voladores* in sixteenth-century Guatemala (1586).[1] The friars also admired the acrobatic skill of a *juego de palo* (log game) in the village of Mazatlan (Jalisco) in February 1587. One dancer lay on his back, with his feet in the air, juggling a carved and painted pole some five and a half feet in length and "a hand's breadth around" in time to the beat of a *teponaztli* drum, while others danced around him, singing and shaking gourd rattles filled with small stones or grain. The juggler repeatedly hurled the pole in the air with the soles of his feet, his thighs, or the backs of his calves, catching it again in time to the music; spun it around on one foot while controlling it with the other; and finally allowed two of the younger dancers to sit astride the pole, one at either end, while he created a seesaw effect in time to the music. Although, according to Ciudad Real, this game was widespread in New Spain, few knew how to do it well. But the friar judged the Mazatlan performer "very skillful," adding that "if he were in Spain, he would soon be rich." This is not as far-fetched as it sounds: two Indians who performed the *juego de palo* had traveled to Europe with Cortés in 1528, performing to great acclaim before both pope and emperor.[2]

The friars also saw several "dances of imitation blacks." In September 1588, in Tekax (Yucatan), a troupe of young men "in the form of blacks, representing demons," greeted Ponce with a dance. But when a choir sang several stanzas of polyphonic song that included the name of Jesus, the *negrillos* "all fell to the ground and trembled, making a thousand faces and shakings in token of their fear and dread." And in San Jerónimo (Michoacan), in November 1586, an Indian dressed and speaking "like a newly imported black" exchanged pleasantries and played cards with another dressed as Death.[3] Other dances included "a dance of masked Indians" and "an artificial bull," who performed together to the beat of a hand-held drum; and a "dance of ironsmiths" who set up their forge, with all its trappings and a large pair of bellows, on the patio of the convent in Acámbaro (Guanajuato), and hammered in time to a timbrel while "stonecutters" danced and worked in time to another. In Kantunil (Yucatan), the friars saw an "ancient" dance known as *zonó* in the local language. Six dancers carried a litter that supported "something like a pulpit, over five feet high, covered from top to bottom with sheets of painted cotton," in which a splendidly dressed Indian, carrying rattles in one hand and a feathered fly-flap in the other, shook and whistled in time to a *teponaztli* drum while the bearers and the many other dancers also sang, whistled, and shook their feet to the drum beat, all together "making much noise."[4]

Of some dances Ciudad Real tells us only that the dancers wore "many beautiful feathers," carried "many rattles," or wore masks, moved beautifully, and imitated the song of "certain nocturnal birds of the region." On one occasion, in Tlaxcala, in September 1584, he mentions tantalizingly that "twelve teams of Indians" came out to greet the commissary general, each performing a different dance "in their old way" and all dressed "as they used to for the great feast days in the time of their paganism," but offers no further details.[5] Although Ciudad Real habitually distinguishes between dances of Indian origin and those of Spanish heritage, not one of the dances he records offers any evidence of indigenous dances adopting the theme of Moors and Christians or of a Spanish tradition of dances of Moors and Christians being introduced to Mexico.

Of the few explicitly Christian plays that the friars saw on their travels, the most intriguing was an Epiphany play staged outside the church of Tlajomulco (Jalisco) on 6 January 1587. Images of the Christ Child, Mary, and Joseph had been placed inside a portico of branches, twigs, and hanging moss. An arbor housed the actors who played Herod and his court. Three kings on horseback began to descend a nearby hill, followed by an Indian, more than eighty years old, who bore a basket of offerings for the Christ Child on his back. Because of "the gravity of their role, the height of the hill, and the uneven surface of the path," they took nearly two hours to reach the church.

The crowd of "ten or twelve friars, many lay Spaniards, and more than five thousand Indians" was entertained, in the meantime, by a brief *danza de ángeles* and a much longer, comic *danza de pastores*. The angels danced, sang verses in Nahuatl, and performed "many humiliations and genuflections before the Christ Child." The shepherds, loaded with bags of provisions and gourds, the latter perhaps full of wine, carried crooks and wore poor shepherds' clothes. When an angel sang "Gloria in Excelsis Deo" from the top of a wooden tower representing heaven, they fell to the ground, but the angel comforted them, in Nahuatl, with the news of Christ's birth, whereupon the shepherds offered gifts to the child: a kid, a lamb, some loaves, and a bonnet. Then "they began to dance and sing in Nahuatl in praise of the Child, questioning one another, asking what they had seen and what they had heard; they replied with great joy, repeating many times the words of the angel and saying, 'goria, goria, goria,' jumping and leaping with their crooks with very great merriment and pleasure."

Thus far, the play adheres to the traditional narrative, but what follows is unexpected. The shepherds "wrestled one another," tumbling down and rolling along the ground, locked in each other's arms. Others blocked their passage by placing crooks in their way, but the wrestlers reversed, still grasping one another tight, and returned the way they had come. After a while, two shepherds penned the others in the center of the dance floor with their crooks. Subdued, the wrestling shepherds stood. The head shepherd called on each one by name to step forward and "to jump and leap." Finally, "seeing that the kings were approaching," all but two of the shepherds joined hands to form a circle. The other two ran around outside the circle "as if they were bulls," using their crooks to knock over those in the circle and then to roll them "this way and that." While the shepherds' antics could be interpreted as exuberance over the birth of the Savior, they could also be read as a disruption—deliberately prolonged by the slow descent of the three kings—of the imported Christian narrative. There is a strong tradition in European medieval drama of comic shepherds spinning out their own dramatic narrative before approaching the Christ Child with unassuming gifts. But recent students of the ongoing tradition of Mexican *pastorelas* regard "the prominence of the shepherds and the relative insignificance of the Holy Family" in these Christmas dramas as a form of resistance to the dominant ecclesiastical narrative.[6]

When the three kings finally arrived at Herod's arbor, the play reverted to the biblical story. As his wise men read the messianic prophecy from "a large book," Herod became infuriated, "displaying great anger and irritation, pride and presumption." He flung the book to the floor and made his trembling counselors read it aloud on their knees, only to insist that it could not possibly say what they claimed and to demand another reading. As the three kings left the court, Herod was still mistreating the text and scolding his wise men. There is implicit criticism of all tyrants in this traditional depiction of Herod, but there is no telling from Ciudad Real's account whether the crowd was reminded of any particular local official. If it had been, it would not have been the last time that a character in an American shepherd's play represented both a biblical character and an overbearing outsider. John G. Bourke, a U.S. Cavalry captain stationed in South Texas between 1891 and 1893, left one of the earliest accounts of a *pastorela* in Texas and notes that he was asked to lend his own uniform for use in the performance. "According to Bourke's own seemingly naive admission," Richard Flores reports, "the character of Lucifer in *Los Pastores* dressed as a cavalry officer." Bourke's military exploits in the region had not endeared him to the local *mexicano* population, and the dramatic identification of Lucifer as Bourke was no accident.[7] That the performers could pull this off with Bourke's unwitting aid is typical of the habitual blindness of the dominant group to all but the most blatant insinuation of a hidden transcript into the public transcript of fealty and devotion.

In Tlajomulco, after leaving Herod to his ranting, the kings knelt to offer silver to the Christ Child. Each made a short speech in Nahuatl. Then the old Indian who for two hours had carried the gifts down the hill on foot, while the kings who bore no such burden rode on horseback, spoke for the first time. Standing some way off, he turned to the Christ Child and said that "he had no other gift to offer him but this load that he bore and the fatigue that he had experienced in bearing it." The villagers told Ponce that the same man had played this part for thirty years. While his length of service is impressive, the villagers may have wanted to signal the importance of his role. For if anyone besides the shepherds represents the native viewpoint in this performance, it is the old man. Although the three gentile kings compare favorably to the tyrannical Herod, the Indian in turn compares favorably to the kings. His poignant closing words may well speak, on behalf of the "five thousand Indians" watching the play, of the exploitation of his kind by those in possession of power and wealth. And, despite his low position in the social and economic hierarchy, he is afforded the dignity of standing to address the Christ Child, while the kings he serves kneel and "prostrate themselves."[8]

Several historians and folklorists have briefly noticed Ciudad Real's theatrical testimony, but only Richard Trexler has given it any sustained consideration. Although he rebukes earlier scholars for failing to attend to "the political and cultural messages and contexts of this theater," Trexler pays little attention to the Epiphany play. He does, however, argue that the staged battles between Christians and Moors or Chichimeca, to which we now turn, constituted a "military theatre of humiliation," in which the indigenous performers "exhibited their [own] defeat." "We accept and rejoice in your culture and our defeat," Trexler imagines the Indians to be telling their Spanish rulers in these plays. The latter, he adds, "were moved by the message."[9]

But colonial *moros y cristianos* were never as simple as Trexler imagines. One cannot help noticing, for example, how often the Indians who greeted the commissary general chose to dress as Chichimeca (or, to a lesser extent, Moors) and how rarely they chose to dress as Spaniards. In Tinum (Yucatan) in July 1587, Ponce and his party were greeted by "many Indians dressed in the manner of Moors, with painted lances, adorned with colored feathers, . . . and round shields." To the sound of a drum, they ran ahead of the friars, whooping and yelling without pause. None were dressed as Christians.[10] In January 1587, the friars passed through a series of villages in Nayarit where they were met, in each case, by Indians dressed as Chichimeca. In one, "there were imitation Chichimeca on foot and on horseback" who threw lemons at each other and defended themselves with painted shields. In the next, the "Chichimeca" attacked one another with "very heavy clubs that they call *macauitles*" and parried the blows with "shields made of small rods covered with crocodile skin." As the friars approached a third, "two scantily clad Indians, painted like Chichimeca warriors and armed with shields and *macauitles,* leapt out of the bushes," so startling the Spaniards' mules that the friars barely avoided falling off. In none of these villages is there any mention of "Christians" appearing to fend off the Chichimeca attacks.[11]

The Spaniards were no doubt intended to believe that the Indian actors, in a kind of sympathetic magic, were identifying the warlike Chichimeca to the north with the Moors whom the Spaniards had already defeated. But it seems that the Indian actors were also posing as Chichimeca because they found it to be a safe guise under which to express resistance to Spanish rule. This is still the case with the festival of Moors and Christians performed annually during carnival week in Huejotzingo (Puebla). There, Chichimeca, Apaches, Turks, bandits, mountain Indians, and soldiers of North African origin all appear, but there are no Christians, no Spaniards, and, despite the public transcript's reference to the defeat of French imperial troops at Puebla on 5 May 1862, no unequivocally French troops. All the performers surreptitiously represent victorious Indian warriors who have driven the conquistadors from the field. "We are all Aztecs," one performer told me. "The Spaniards have been defeated."[12]

So it was with much of the military theater seen by Ciudad Real. Christian Indians imitated Chichimeca because they could not openly enact their own resistance, and the absence of Spaniards implied Spanish defeat. This is clear in the reception prepared for the friars as they approached Charapan (Michoacan) in November 1586. Some three miles from town, "many Indians on foot and on horseback" appeared. Those on foot were all dressed as Chichimeca and carried bows and arrows. Two riders were similarly attired. The latter "galloped their horses without holding the reins, secured by the stirrups [alone], dancing and shaking their heads and their bows and arrows. Those on foot shouted and all issued great bursts of laughter, in the way that the true Chichimeca generally do when they capture Spanish horses and in this fashion burlesque and ridicule [the Spaniards]."[13] Victorious Indians and captured Spanish horses were represented; the absent Spaniards had evidently been overcome.

On the comparatively rare occasions when Spaniards did appear, they were outnumbered, outwitted, and defeated or, if the politics of the situation prevented the portrayal of indigenous victory, held at bay. In March 1587, in the street out-side the convent of Atoyac (Jalisco), "a dozen Indians on foot came out, dressed as Chichimeca warriors, together with a single horseman, with a lance and shield, clothed in [Spanish] livery, at whom those on foot shouted and made faces and shook their bows and arrows, and although he worked hard, exerting all his power, to en-ter [the ranks of the Chichimeca] with his horse, he made no progress, because the horse was frightened to see them and to hear their shouts, and kept turning back; and so, they say, it often happens in the wars that the Spanish wage with the true Chichimeca, for [the Spanish] are unable to enter for the fear of their horses on see-ing [the Chichimeca] and hearing the shouts and whoops that they raise."[14]

Although the Spaniards introduced the horse to the New World, it was the In-dians who were portrayed in these plays as having mastered the animal. As the friars approached Zacapu (Michoacan) in November 1586, "more than thirty Indians on horseback, in many disguises, came out and, for more than a league, were galloping and breaking in the horses," thereby demonstrating their control of the animals. The riders were also "playing and rejoicing with twenty other Indians on foot, who were dressed as Chichimeca with bows and arrows and long hair." Closer to the town, an Indian dressed as a Spanish constable appeared, but his was a more plodding mount. The "Spaniard" rode a huge ox, "which was so mild that the Indians led it by a halter around its neck." To make it move at all, they had to prod it, through the cheap cloth that covered it from head to foot, with the point of a knife. The slow passage of the ox considerably delayed the entry of the friars.[15] Trexler may well be right to characterize these performances as "a military theatre of humiliation," but it is surely the Spanish and not the Indians who, none too subtly at times, are being ridiculed.

A few days later, the friars arrived at "a pretty village called Patamban." There, "more than twenty Indians on horseback, poorly adorned, all dressed as Spaniards," came out. They carried a hodgepodge of mostly ineffective weapons such as wooden pikes, which lacked their iron point, and stick swords. One bore an arquebus. An-other wore Spanish sidearms. The last delivered a speech, assuring Ponce of pro-tection against Chichimeca attack. Then the "Spaniards" began to gallop in and out of the pine trees that lined the road, shouting over and over again, in what one sus-pects was mockery of the Spanish battle cry, "Santiago, Santiago." Suddenly, ten or twelve Indians on foot, dressed as Chichimeca and brandishing bows and arrows, leapt out of the bushes, startling the horses. The two sides attacked one another and, finally, the Spanish captain managed to capture one of the Chichimeca, leading him, by a chain round his neck, to the friars. But the Spaniard's triumph was short-lived. The captive slipped his chains and ran off "like a buck." Although those on horseback gave chase, the Chichimeca warrior "remained free as before." Indeed, the roles were soon reversed, for, while the Spaniards continued their fruitless charges in and out of the pines, crying all along, "Santiago, Santiago," those on foot danced in the manner of Chichimeca and led in their midst a captured horseman. Once the party arrived in the village square, "the Chichimeca climbed onto a large rock and a very tall wooden castle that they had made, in which they danced, while those on horseback kept galloping around." A conventional mock battle would have ended with the capture of the artificial castle by the Spanish knights, but the Tarascan Indians of Patamban avoided that outcome by prolonging the siege until nightfall. Then, it being too dark to continue the play, the "Spaniards" dismounted, the "Chichimeca" descended from the castle, and all joined in a Tarascan dance to the sound of the *teponaztli* drum.[16]

Spanish victory was also postponed in a *moros y cristianos* staged in the city of Puebla, in October 1585, ostensibly to honor the new viceroy on his way to Mexico City. The viceroy was greeted by "many people on foot and on horseback, drawn up in readiness for battle. They had made a castle, which the Christians attacked and the Moors defended." But word came to Ponce, from "those in the know," that the defenders of the castle were in possession of a cask of wine and that the Moorish captain "was saying that they did not have to surrender until the cask was finished."[17] Whether drunkenness or darkness finally prevented surrender, or whether, in the presence of the viceroy, the performers had finally to conform to the official discourse of Christian victory is unclear. Ciudad Real's silence on the matter may suggest that the Indian performers here, too, managed to suspend the play before the scripted defeat of the Moors.

Indeed, it is striking that, despite Trexler's assertion that this was a genre in which the indigenous performers "exhibited their own defeat," not one of the *moros y cristianos* described by Ciudad Real unequivocally ends with a Christian victory. Spaniards were absent, nightfall interrupted the play, the Moors had to finish their wine, or, in Tlaxcala, just four days before the Puebla *moros y cristianos,* whether by accident or design, the stage castle went up in flames and the performance had to be canceled. Ciudad Real tells us that, for the arrival of the viceroy in Tlaxcala, the Indians had built "a wooden castle of two or three storeys, with many windows and alcoves." Here, a combined army of Tlaxcalteca warriors and Spanish soldiers, all played by Indian actors, was to have fought against a second army of Indians dressed as Chichimeca. But the viceroy never saw the play. In the early afternoon, the castle caught fire and, despite all efforts to save it, was soon completely destroyed. "It was," comments Ciudad Real, "the mercy of God that there was no wind at the time, so that no house in the vicinity caught fire, the flames going straight upwards and climbing to the clouds." The Indians, he reassures us, were most distressed.

Perhaps. One cannot prove arson at this distance in time, but one may suspect it. The Tlaxcalteca had a history of using *moros y cristianos* to enact their own vision of reconquest, but the 1585 script, which insisted that the Tlaxcalteca and the Spaniards were to be allies against the Chichimeca, may have left them no room for maneuver. The Tlaxcalteca could not, in this instance, identify with the Chichimeca against the Spaniards without also cheering on their own defeat. One wonders if, under those circumstances, someone felt that it was simpler just to set fire to the castle and so end the charade altogether. Whatever the cause of the fire, the portrayal of Spanish victory was once again avoided. The requirements of ceremonial subordination were later satisfied by a brief performance in which four old Indians, dressed as Tlaxcalteca "kings," delivered the keys of the city to the viceroy and recited sonnets in Spanish, asking the viceroy to preserve the privileges granted the city by Charles V.[18]

Ciudad Real's account confirms that, by the penultimate decade of the sixteenth century, various indigenous peoples in Mexico were staging festivals of Moors and Christians as a mask for their own myth of territorial recovery. Rural performances were, as one would expect, smaller in scale than those in urban centers such as Puebla, Tlaxcala, and Mexico City. In view of the prevailing scholarly opinion that dances of Moors and Christians were imported from Spain by the early conquistadors and friars, however, I have been surprised to find no evidence of such dances in sixteenth-century Mexico. Apparently, in Mexico as in Spain, lavish, large-scale mock battles, first sponsored by powerful rulers and civic authorities, initiated the tradition of *moros y cristianos*. Only later, as the tradition spread and attached itself to local, annual festivals, did conflict between Spanish Catholics and dark-skinned non-Christians become the theme of smaller, more economical dances.

17
The Conquest of New Mexico (1598)

FROM New Spain, the tradition of mock battles between Moors and Christians traveled north to New Mexico. On 30 April 1598, on the banks of the Río del Norte (now the Río Grande), Juan de Oñate formally "took possession of all the kingdoms and provinces of New Mexico, in the name of King Philip [II of Spain]."[1] Oñate may have "staged" the conquest of New Mexico as a reenactment of Cortés's conquest of old Mexico, employing such "legendary props" as Tlaxcalteca allies, a female native interpreter, twelve Franciscans, and the same banner as Cortés had carried into Tenochtitlan.[2] Oñate's expedition can also lay claim to mounting the first European "play" and the first mock battle between Moors and Christians in what is now the territory of the United States.

The reading of the act of possession on 30 April was followed by "a sermon, a great ecclesiastical and secular celebration, a great salute and rejoicing, and, in the afternoon, a comedy."[3] Although the text of the play has been lost, a brief account of its subject matter can be found in Gaspar Pérez de Villagrá's epic poem *Historia de la Nueva Mexico*. Villagrá was a captain under Oñate's command in New Mexico and published his account of the expedition in 1610. He wrote:

> And when the services were done
> They did present a great drama [*comedia*]
> The noble Captain Farfán had composed,
> Whose argument was but to show to us
> The great reception of the Church
> That all New Mexico did give,
> Congratulating it upon its arrival,
> Begging, with thorough reverence,
> And kneeling on the ground, it would wash out
> Its faults with that holy water
> Of precious Baptism which they brought,
> With which most salutary sacrament
> We saw many barbarians cleansed
> When we were traveling through their lands.
> There were solemn and pleasing festivals
> Of splendid men on horseback. . . .[4]

The description of the play ends with the phrase "which they brought." The sight of "many barbarians" being "cleansed" by the water of baptism refers to subsequent events, although such baptisms may also have been enacted predictively as part of the *comedia*. And the "splendid men on horseback" took part not in the *comedia* but in some kind of equestrian display.

We know the name of the play's author and its theme. The playwright, Captain Marcos Farfán de los Godos, was "one of the first to enroll under the royal banner to serve his majesty in this expedition," and had invested heavily in the venture, bringing with him to the initial muster "thirty equipped men and eighty horses of [his] own."[5] The theme of his play was the imminent conversion of the people of New Mexico.[6] If we can trust Villagrá's summary, the play made no reference to armed conquest, the ordinary condition of religious conversion in the New World. Instead, "all New Mexico" fell reverently to its knees and begged for baptism. Spanish possession of New Mexico was to be justified by the natives' voluntary and eager embrace of the Church.

The historical encounter was not as peaceful as Farfán imagined. In 1539, a small party, led by the friar Marcos de Niza and accompanied by a black Moroccan slave, Esteban, had been the first to enter New Mexico. Esteban had been killed by Zuni Indians. According to Joe Sando, this first encounter is still remembered in Pueblo folk performance: "The Pueblos often say, 'The first *white* man our people saw was a *black* man.' Every year, on the annual feast day at Jemez Pueblo, the two historical figures [Fray Marcos and Esteban] are portrayed. One figure wears a white skull cap, and his face is painted white. He wears a long black coat with a knotted white rope tied around his waist in the fashion of a Franciscan priest. A black sheep pelt covers the head of the other to indicate curly hair. His face is painted black, and he carries a snare drum that he plays whenever the friar walks about." A subsequent colonizing expedition, led by Francisco Vásquez de Coronado, had spent two winters (1540-1542) near present-day Bernalillo and had engaged in a number of armed clashes with the Pueblos. Coronado's venture is represented during Pueblo fiestas by men on skirted hobby horses.[7] Several missions had taken place in the intervening years, with blood being shed on both sides, but Oñate's was the first to establish a lasting Spanish settlement in New Mexico. Oñate's success, too, was by force of arms.

Subsequent spectacles during the Oñate expedition gave implicit recognition to the role of force in the Spanish conversion of other peoples. Two months later, at an abandoned pueblo about five miles north of present-day Bernardo,[8] the expedition celebrated the feast day of St. John the Baptist (24 June) with a "skirmish." Villagrá describes it thus:

> Here, taking precautions with great care,
> They celebrated the fair morn,
> The soldiers on their war horses

Divided into two opposing groups
Whose nimble flanks were captained,
In a well-contested skirmish, by
The Army Master good and the Sergeant,
Whirling their powerful lances
With gay and carefree skill.
And when the others of the men
Had broken mighty lances and had proved
The courage of their hearts in tournament
Which they had ridden with great skill, . . . [9]

This may have been an unscripted *mêlée* or, as T. M. Pearce suggests, "drama on horseback," in which the two groups of horsemen were designated Moors and Christians and speeches were delivered by leaders of each party.[10]

There were no Indians present at the skirmish on 24 June. But a noisy *moros y cristianos* staged at the Spanish headquarters of San Juan de los Caballeros in early September made a profound impression on its Indian audience.[11] Villagrá's description reads:

A solemn feast that did endure
For a whole week, in which there were
Tilts with cane-spears, bullfights, tilts at the ring,
A jolly drama, well-composed,
Playing at Moors and Christians,
With much artillery, whose roar
Did cause notable fear and marveling
To many bold barbarians who had
Come there as spies to spy on us,
To see the strength and arms possessed
By the Spaniards. . . .[12]

The week of festivities included several dramatic or quasi-dramatic events: a *comedia*, about which we know only that Villagrá found it "jolly" and "well-composed"; a *juego de cañas;* and a *moros y cristianos* whose sustained artillery fire generated considerable fear and wonder in the many Indians who had come "as spies" to watch the proceedings. The official record of the expedition confirms the use of gunfire. On the afternoon of 8 September, "the whole camp celebrated with a good sham battle between Moors and Christians, the latter on foot with arquebuses, the former on horseback with lances and shields."[13] It is not surprising that the *moros y*

cristianos, with the deafening noise and acrid smell of its repeated discharge of arquebuses, terrified its Indian audience. It may well have been a factor in the decision of
several Indian leaders "voluntarily" to "render obedience and vassalage" to the Spanish Crown at an assembly held in the main kiva of San Juan the following day.[14]

Military conquest and religious conversion, sometimes linked and sometimes, as
in Farfán's *comedia,* idealistically kept apart, were the themes of the spectacles staged
during the Oñate expedition. They are still the subject of folk theater in both Hispanic and Native American communities in New Mexico. While it is highly unlikely that any twentieth-century performance can trace its origins directly to a
continuous tradition of local performance begun by Oñate's settlers, many can claim
a generic kinship with the custom first introduced in 1598.

The most spectacular of the subsequent New Mexican *moros y cristianos* were those
that adapted the medieval European narrative to reflect armed conflict between
Spanish settlers and marauding Comanches in New Mexico in the 1770s. It is not
known how soon after the historical events the adaptation took place, but it was
certainly before the middle of the nineteenth century, for the oldest known manuscript of *Los Comanches* "was copied from another manuscript in 1864."[15] In 1931,
Gilberto Espinosa wrote that "almost every one of the older generation of New
Mexicans can repeat [the speeches] by memory, so generally is the play enacted."[16]

Lorin Brown described a performance of *Los Comanches* near San Ildefonso on
28 December 1938. During mass, actors dressed as Comanches in "fringed buckskin garb, beaded vests, and plumed bonnets" pilfered articles, which they would
later offer for ransom, from vehicles parked outside the church. After a procession,
the play took place "on the sandy bottom of an *arroyo* close by the village church."
Cuerno Verde, the leader of the Comanches, delivered "a lengthy harangue from
the back of his ever circling horse, in which he boast[ed] of his prowess and the
bravery of his warriors." The Spanish general "warn[ed] the Indians of the fate
which they [would] meet if they should be so rash as to fight against him and his
men." Between challenging speeches and the comic antics of a Spanish glutton and
braggart, Barriga Dulce [Sugar Belly], the Comanches and Spaniards engaged in
"several fierce fights. . . . In the final encounter, the Indians [were] vanquished and,
fleeing from the Spaniards, [were] overtaken one by one as they race[d] their horses
up the *arroyo* and over the hills."[17]

Brown makes no mention of gunfire, but the published versions of the text of *Los
Comanches* speak of the "powder and ball" used by the Spanish troops,[18] and Arthur
Campa refers to "the constant discharge of firearms" and "the crack of the Spanish musket." He also describes a performance "on the mesa between Taos village
and Ranchos de Taos to the south" in the summer of 1929 in which "real Indians . . . took the part of the Comanche braves. . . . Hundreds of warriors and sol-

diers took part on both sides. They presented such a realistic scene, to the accompaniment of rifle shots and arrows, that the [tourists] took cover, thinking that real warfare had broken out."[19] The scale of *Los Comanches* has shrunk in recent years. A performance of *The Comanches and the Spanish Soldiers* at Alcalde on 27 December 1971 involved just "ten men on horseback, wearing simple costumes to distinguish Indian from Soldier. [They] carried out a formal routine, declaiming in Spanish to the accompaniment of fiddle and guitar music, and acting out a pantomime."[20] I am told that such versions of *Los Comanches* are still performed "occasionally" in Alcalde and Taos.[21]

The original narrative of Moors and Christians has also survived on a small scale in New Mexico. Writing in 1953, Lucero-White Lea described the *moros y cristianos* that had been performed "until recently" in Santa Cruz: "A cavalcade of men wearing red bands on their hats represents the Moors; a cavalcade wearing white, the Christians. The spectacle is performed in the village plaza or square. Here, mounted on New Mexico ponies, the Moors clash swords with the Christians; the Christians with the Moors. A dialogue goes on between the two and, if one understands Spanish, it is possible to follow the lines. There are no props of any kind, other than a wooden cross set in the center of the square. Nothing out of the ordinary happens, and the piece ends almost as unostentatiously as it began." An earlier witness had described, in 1931, "a jumble of men on cow ponies, charging at each other with raised lances, dressed according to their ideas of Moorish and Spanish soldiers."[22]

Nowadays, the play is best known in Chimayo. On the feast day of Santiago (25 July), an audience gathers in the large field behind Holy Family Church to watch two dozen men and women on horseback enact the loss and recovery of "the standard of the Holy Cross."[23] The riders wield painted wooden swords and scimitars and bear shields marked with a crescent or a cross. The play begins as the Moors, wearing black veils to create the illusion of darker skin, gather in their "castle" on one side of the field and the Christians assemble in their "camp" on the opposite side. Both are open spaces, unmarked by scenic properties. A wooden cross, about six feet high and four feet across but light enough to be carried in one hand by a rider, "is given a place of honor in the middle of the field." In the first scene, a Moorish spy captures the cross, by professing himself ready for baptism and then offering a celebratory wineskin to the Christian guard. Once the guard is in "a drunken stupor," the theft is easy. The loss triggers the first Christian assault on the Moorish castle. Horses gallop, swords clash, and the actors "exhibit their equestrian skills." After the attack fails, a messenger goes back and forth between the camps; he offers, on behalf of the Moors, to release the cross for "a thousand doubloons" and, on behalf of the Christians, refuses all terms. In a second attack, the Christians recover the cross and capture the Moors. The sultan and his followers, convinced of the power of the Christian God, are granted full pardon. The play ends with all joining in a song of praise to the Holy Cross and riding round the field to the cheers of the crowd. Although I cannot prove direct influence, the play reminds me of the small-scale Andalusian festivals of Moors and Christians, many of which are characterized by horseback harangues and the struggle for possession of a sacred image or cross.

The *moros y cristianos* have declined in scale and popularity in New Mexico, I suspect, because they lack a hidden transcript. Whether the defeated enemy be Moors or Comanches, the heirs of the victors have felt no need to insinuate into the public transcript of Spanish triumph a hidden transcript of resistance. As the communal memory of European battles against Moors and Turks faded, the narrative was adapted to reflect the more recent threat of Comanche raiders. As the memory of those campaigns also faded, the practice diminished in importance. It has been revived in Chimayo as a means of honoring the village's Hispanic heritage. If it becomes the site for more pointed resistance to the dominant Anglo culture, it may well flourish. If it does not, it too may slowly disappear. In this respect, the history of the *moros y cristianos* in New Mexico is instructive, for the tradition has thrived in so many different geographical and chronological contexts because of two factors: its flexibility of historical referent and its capacity to mask hidden transcripts. Flexibility extended its life in Hispanic New Mexico. The lack of a hidden transcript may bring about its demise.

In New Mexico's Native American pueblos, however, aspects of the tradition have taken on a hidden transcript of resistance to outside cultures. Skirted hobby horses are used to represent the arrival of the conquistadors. In 1935, Leslie White described the *sandaro* (Sp. *soldado* [soldier]) ceremony held in Santo Domingo in late January or early February. Early in the morning, two men on hobby horses, representing Santiago and San Gerónimo, enter the pueblo. The former's horse is white, the latter's is black. Each rider carries a sword and shield and wears a buckskin shirt, a metal crown topped with an eagle feather, and a bandanna that masks his face below the eyes. The saints are followed by the *sandaro*, who "dress up like Spaniards." They paint their faces black, wear a false beard or mustache, and carry suitcases packed with food, clothes, cutlery, and "other articles which the Spaniards might have brought with them when they arrived in the pueblo country." From time to time, while the *sandaro* mimic Spanish settlers, building fires, cooking, eating, and feeding their "animals," a bull, made of painted canvas over a wooden framework and carried by a man within, charges them. Later, the *sandaro* "fight" the bull by throwing their hats at it. Finally, San Gerónimo and Santiago also fight the bull, Santiago "killing" it with a single blow of his sword. The performance concludes with the *sandaro* "telling the Indians 'goodbye,' that they are going back

16. Hobby horse, San Felipe Pueblo, c. 1940. From White, "Impersonation," p. 561. Courtesy of Michigan Academy of Science, Arts, and Letters.

to Mexico," and trading European goods (coffee, sugar, pots and pans) with the Pueblo women for Indian goods (bread, beads, buckskin, and so on).[24] Sando confirms the continued popularity of the hobby horses. "Today," he wrote in 1992, "most of the pueblos still commemorate the arrival of Coronado's party, portraying him on their feast days as a figure on a dancing horse, holding a sword in his right hand (Fig. 16). Another figure plays the snare drum, and the horseman dances to the tune of the drum. In some villages, the horseman is called 'Santiago,' who appears to have been the conquistador's patron saint. Thus do the Pueblo people . . . gain a wry revenge upon their persecutors."[25]

In August 1993, I saw hobby horses dance in Santo Domingo and Jemez Pueblos. The annual feast day in Santo Domingo (4 August) hosts the largest of the Pueblo Corn Dances. For much of the day several hundred men, women, and children performed their line dance to the beat of the drums and the rhythmic chanting of singers. Members of the Squash and Turquoise kivas alternated, beginning in the plaza just across the stream from the church and continuing in the main plaza where the two kivas are located.[26] At about 2 P.M., during a pause in the Corn Dance, two "horses" (one white and one black) and their riders (presumably, Santiago and San Gerónimo) emerged from a house on the south side of the plaza. Each dancer carried a sword in his right hand. The saints were accompanied by a drummer and four "cowboys," wearing cowboy hats, holsters and pistols at their hips, false goatees, and colorful western shirts. Rather than Spanish settlers, these seemed to represent more recent Anglo "invaders." The saints danced toward the fiesta "shrine" at the east end of the plaza where the image of Santo Domingo had been placed. As the drum beat and the "cowboys" chanted, the horses faced the shrine and danced in unison a series of intricate, quivering steps. After fifteen minutes, they returned to their house, and the Corn Dance resumed. The "cowboys" passed through the crowd, dispensing fruit and candy. No one offered me an explanation of the "horse dance." "We are not allowed," I was told.

Two days earlier, at the annual fiesta of Porcingula in Jemez Pueblo, I had seen the Pecos Bull Dance.[27] As mass ended, a canvas "bull" arrived outside the church. It was accompanied by a drummer; two *abuelos* (ancestors), each wearing a pale-faced, horned leather mask with a mustache and bushy eyebrows, and carrying a whip; about fifty men and boys in white face, some dressed as women but most wearing clothes associated with whites (jeans, T-shirts, an occasional hard hat, and a disproportionate number of Dallas Cowboys T-shirts and U.S. military fatigues); and a saint on a hobby horse. No longer imitating Spanish settlers, they recalled more recent armed intervention by whites. Some were "cowboys," wearing leather chaps or, in a nice visual pun, Dallas Cowboys shirts. Another had a note, which read "#001 Coca Cola Cowboy," pinned to his back. Others, making silent reference to the most recent outbreak of "Arabs and Christians," the U.S. liberation of Kuwait, wore T-shirts that proclaimed "Desert Storm" or "Support Our Troops." There was, I suspect, a discreet and not very flattering comparison being drawn between the U.S. military, bellicose Christians, and "cowboys."[28]

The bull group noisily preceded the solemn procession that bore the image of Porcingula from the church to her arbor in the main plaza. There the bull repeatedly charged the "whites," who scattered in fear. Finally, the bull was lassoed and led on a lengthy tour of the pueblo, stopping at houses to be given food, money, and blankets. Protesting children were made to "ride" both the bull and the hobby horse. By then, the Corn Dance had begun in the main plaza.

All this is a long way from the Catalan Turks and hobby horses, but it gives us an idea of how a folk theatrical tradition can adapt to successive environments. The hobby horse was introduced to Mexico by Spanish settlers. From there it traveled to New Mexico, where it was adopted by the Pueblo Indians. In all three countries, it is still part of a dance that dramatizes the armed conquest of one culture by another. In Catalonia, the defeat of the Turks provides the historical referent. In Mexico, Santiago sometimes rides a skirted hobby horse into battle against the heathen.[29] In New Mexico, the narrative has to do with the arrival of the Spaniards and other foreign invaders. Armed conquest is not enacted but signaled obliquely by the holsters and guns of the "cowboys" in Santo Domingo and by the references to Desert Storm in Jemez. Moreover, the victory of light-skinned "Christians" is not a matter for celebration. The Spaniards and other "whites" are portrayed as comic characters, traders, "women," and cowardly "soldiers" who flee the bull. Thus, as Sando observes, the Pueblo people "work their history into living ceremonies" and "gain a wry revenge upon their persecutors."[30]

The same may be said of the *danza de los matachines* as it is performed in Native American pueblos in New Mexico. But the story of the *matachines* in New Mexico is a more complicated one, to which we will return in our final chapter. In the meantime, we will look at the further development of the *moros y cristianos* in Spain, where one of our questions will have much to do with the vexed history of the *matachines:* in which direction did such folk dance traditions cross the Atlantic? We should not, because European ships first sailed westward, assume that subsequent cultural traffic always flowed in the same direction.

PART FIVE
SPAIN, 1521–1600

18
Touring Aztecs (1522–1529)

"IT is possible," María Soledad Carrasco Urgoiti wrote in 1963, "that a complete study of American festivals would discover currents of mutual influence linking *moros y cristianos* in the New World" to their Spanish counterparts.[1] Her suggestion of mutual influence is one that few have considered, let alone pursued with any rigor. We know that food traveled eastward: tomatoes, potatoes, corn, chocolate, turkeys, and tobacco all originated in the Americas and were unknown in Europe before the sixteenth century. In this chapter, we will weigh the earliest evidence that native artifacts and performers did likewise, that some of the artifacts wound up as costumes worn by European performers, and that some of the native routines were imitated by Europeans.

Native art was soon displayed in Europe. Among the souvenirs Columbus brought home with him in 1493 were "masks made of fish bones carved to look like pearls, and belts of the same material, admirably contrived." Three years later, after his second voyage, he presented Ferdinand and Isabella with "many masks . . . with eyes and ears of gold."[2] Portuguese ships soon brought artifacts from Brazil, where they had first landed in 1500. In an *Adoration of the Magi*, painted for the Cathedral of Viseu (Beira Alta) around 1505, one of the oriental wise men wears "a radial feather crown like those worn by several tribes of Brazilian Indians" and "carries an accurately rendered Tupinamba arrow." Europeans still thought of America as an outpost of Asia. Along the same lines, a German woodcut from 1517–1518, claiming to depict the "people of Calcutta," mixes an "elephant and its turbaned mahout" with figures wearing "the feather skirts and head-dresses of American Indians," some of whom carry "clubs of a Brazilian type" while others hold "a large Brazilian macaw" and "two ears of maize." Reversing the positive judgment of the *Adoration of the Magi,* an anonymous Portuguese *Inferno,* painted around 1550, crowns both "the devil presiding over the torments of the damned" and one of his assistants with "Brazilian featherwork."[3] William Sturtevant remarks that "the Tupinamba attire and weapons" in such works "must have been based on direct observation of . . . the artifacts."[4]

An exhibition of the first shipment of treasures sent back by Cortés to Charles V was mounted in Brussels in 1520, a full year before the fall of Tenochtitlan, and so impressed Albrecht Dürer that he wrote, "All the days of my life, I have seen nothing that reaches my heart so much as these, for among them I have seen wonderfully artistic things and have admired the subtle ingenuity of men in foreign lands." Although Dürer never reproduced any of these treasures in his own art, some have suggested that his scheme for an ideal city was influenced by Cortés's map of

Tenochtitlan and that other northern European artists, such as the Dutch painter Jan Mostaert and the anonymous sculptors who carved masked and plumed faces atop the columns in the palace of the prince-bishop of Liège, produced work directly influenced by the Mexican treasures.[5]

Cortés sent a further "vast hoard of treasure" eastward across the Atlantic in 1522. Two shiploads were distributed in Spain, mostly to the Crown but some to influential politicians and clergy. Bishop Juan Rodríguez de Fonseca, Charles V's chief adviser on colonial affairs and something of a connoisseur of the arts, received "two specially made cloaks in the style of a bishop's robe, one in blue, with a heavy gold border, the collar with elaborate plumes and a white border; the other in green, with a collar decorated by masks." A third ship, captured by French pirates, was diverted to Dieppe. Some of its treasures showed up in a private masque staged at nearby Varengeville in 1527. Dressed in American gold, jewels, and feathered cloaks, Alexander the Great and other "heroes of antiquity" strode across a platform that "had been made by Indians and brought from America."[6] On the whole, "the artistic impact of Mexico" was modest: "cultured Europeans, still busy shedding the influence of the Middle Ages, were in no mood for 'barbarism.'"[7] Nevertheless, in playful rather than high artistic mood, they were happy to dress up in exotic costumes. And, at times, they were intrigued by native performers.

Native Americans, some of them dancers, acrobats, jugglers, and costumed warriors, traveled to Europe very early in the history of cultural traffic between Spain and the Americas. Several were taken, probably from the island of Hispaniola, on Columbus's first voyage. Of these, six traveled with Columbus across Portugal and Spain to take part in his triumphal entry into Barcelona in April 1493. "Painted," as Washington Irving put it, "according to their savage fashion, and decorated with tropical feathers, and with their national ornaments of gold," they were followed by "various kinds of live parrots, together with stuffed birds and animals of unknown species, and rare plants supposed to be of precious qualities." "The streets," Las Casas remembered, "were crammed with people who came to see." Over the next twenty-five years, several hundred Native Americans were shipped back to Spain, Portugal, France, and England from homes as far apart as Newfoundland and the Caribbean. Some were exhibited; most were sold as slaves.[8]

The first to arrive from Mexico were five Totonac Indians who had been saved from sacrifice by Cortés and were sent to Spain in 1519 as presents for Charles V. On arrival in Seville, the Indians were fashionably tailored and bejeweled at Charles's expense (gloves being provided against the cold of the Castilian winter) and, after an exhausting journey, presented to the court at Valladolid. The Archbishop of Cosenza admired the treasures that they brought but found the Indians themselves disconcerting: the women were "short of stature and of disagreeable . . . appearance," and the men's bodies were "pierced and cut all over." Nor, he thought, did the labrets in their lower lips improve their appearance. "We know nothing," Hugh Thomas remarks, "of what the Indians who had come to Spain thought of their hosts." One of the Totonacs died in Seville, but the others returned to the Americas, settling in Cuba.[9]

A second group of Mexican Indians was sent to Spain on one of the treasure ships that arrived in Seville in 1522. Two of these Indians performed before a private audience that included the papal legate, the Venetian ambassador, the nephew of the Duke of Milan, and Pietro Martire d'Anghiera, the first European to gain fame by writing about the New World. Martire described how "a young native slave" advanced onto the terrace where the audience was seated. The Indian "wore a robe of woven feathers, half blue and half red, . . . cotton trousers, a handkerchief . . . suspended between his hips, . . . [and] beautiful sandals." In his right hand he carried "a simple wooden sword," a war club stripped of its obsidian blades, and in his left hand "a native shield, made of stout reeds covered with gold." The shield was "lined with tiger skin" and decorated with a fringe of feathers. The Indian "gave an exhibition of a battle; first hurling himself upon his enemies, then retreating." Then "he seized [another Indian servant] by the hair, as they do their enemies whom they capture with weapons in their hands, dragging them off to be sacrificed. After throwing the slave on the ground, he feigned to cut open his breast above the heart, with a knife. After tearing out the heart, he wrung from the hands the blood flowing from the wound, and then besprinkled the sword and shield." Finally, he pretended to light a fire, "in which he burnt the heart," and to cut the victim's body into pieces.

After a short break to change into "his gala costume," the main actor reappeared, "holding in his left hand a golden toy with a thousand different ornaments, and in his right hand a circle of bells, which he shook, gaily raising and lowering his golden toy. He accompanied himself by singing a native air, and danced about the room where we were assembled to see him." The dance included a "representation of the salutations with which they honor their sovereigns when offering gifts." Could this have been a solo version of one of the *netotelixtli* dances in which Motecuzoma took part and received homage? And could the "native air" have been one of the *Cantares mexicanos?* If so, the Indian may have acted two different parts of the same dance, for, after a further costume change, he "played the part of a drunkard, and never was the rôle more faithfully sustained."[10] The reader will remember Gómara's description of the *netotelixtli* "buffoons" who, "to the vast entertainment of the spectators," imitated "the fool," "the old woman," and "the drunk."[11]

Four years later, in March 1526, another Venetian ambassador, Andrea Navagero, saw "sons of [Indian] lords" in Seville. They may have been two young Mexica nobles who traveled to Spain that year to speak with Charles V. The young men demonstrated the traditional Mexica ball game, striking the lightweight wooden ball "not with their hands or feet, but with their sides." [12]

The largest delegation of Mexican Indians to travel to Spain in the immediate aftermath of the conquest arrived with Cortés himself in 1528. There may have been as many as seventy of them, among whom nearly thirty were entertainers: jugglers, dwarfs, ballplayers, prestidigitators, and dancers. Most were from Mexico City but others came from Tlaxcala, Texcoco, Culhuacan, and Cempoala. A German artist, Christoph Weiditz, made a series of drawings of Cortés and his party. Among those depicted are a native warrior in a feathered skirt, two playing a game with stones (Fig. 17a), two ballplayers (Fig. 17b), and a juggler who lay on his back, tossing and catching a log with his feet (Fig. 17c), like the dancer whom Ciudad Real was to see in Mazatlan in 1587.[13] Cortés's "touring Aztecs," as Howard Cline calls them, performed at least once en route to their audience with Charles V. While "paying his respects to" a group of ladies, Cortés "ordered the dexterous Indian jugglers to perform with the stick with their feet so as to give entertainment to those ladies, and [the jugglers] passed the stick from one foot to the other, a thing which pleased [the ladies]."[14] When they arrived in Valladolid in July, according to Diego Valadés, several of the group introduced an incredulous Charles V and his court to the marvels of Mexican dance, the demonstration lasting "a whole morning."[15]

The two "Indians who juggled the stick with their feet" proved to be the most popular act, even performing before Pope Clement VII in April 1529. Perhaps, Cline suggests, some of the dancers performed at Cortés's wedding to Juana de Zúñiga earlier the same month. One imagines, too, that they must have performed, if only for practice and the gratification of applause, before many less prestigious audiences along the way. Although most of the other Indians returned to Mexico, Cline admits that "we know nothing about the fate or repatriation of Cortés's entertainment troupe." Thomas grants that "some of these Indians appear to have remained behind, and were presented in various parts of Charles's domains." Is it possible that some of Cortés's traveling Aztecs made good in Europe as professional entertainers and that their success lay behind Ciudad Real's comment that the foot juggler in Mazatlan was so skilled that "if he were in Spain, in a short time he would become rich"?[16]

Some of these early Indian performers generated European imitations. A version of the Mexica ball game was part of the festival repertoire in both Toledo and Burgos. In Toledo, in February 1560, forty dancers, "clothed, masked, headdressed, and shod very naturally as Indians," greeted the arrival of Elizabeth of Valois, Philip II's third wife. They danced to a tabor, shook rattles and tambourines, and played with a ball "twice the size of their heads." The dance had been performed in

17. Aztecs in Spain, 1528: (a) gambling with stones, (b) playing with a wooden ball, and (c) foot-juggling a log. Drawings by Christoph Weiditz. From Weiditz, *Tratenbuch,* pls. XI–XVI. Courtesy of Dover Publications.

previous festivals, although on this occasion the actors and costumes were new.[17] In Burgos, one of the "carriages" that greeted Philip II's fourth wife, Anne of Austria, in 1570, carried "an Indian chief dressed in velvet and brocade, accompanied by six male and six female Indians. In front of the carriage twenty-four Indians, dressed in doublets, culottes, and taffeta cloaks of various colors, played with the inevitable ball and wore masks encrusted with precious gems."[18] (For those who may be wondering, Philip, unlike one of his fathers-in-law, Henry VIII of England, was honorably widowed four times.)

The earliest festival imitation of Indian costumes and, perhaps, dance steps in Spain may have taken place in Toledo in 1525. There an elaborate candlelit pageant wagon carried fourteen dancers ("four savages, four blacks, four Amazons, a black king, and an Amazon queen") through the city streets for three nights of August festivities honoring the Assumption of the Virgin. Thirty-two and a half yards of buckram were used on the Amazons' skirts and doublets alone; and "four dozen" small bells were provided for each wild man and black. The blacks wore painted masks, made of cloth covered with wax, loincloths, and white shoes. They carried silver-plated clubs and shields, and had their legs and arms dyed with a mixture of bitumen, eggs, and oil. "Three small bonnets of leather and short, black cords" were used as wigs, a fresh one for each night, by the white actors playing blacks. The "savages" wore masks and long-haired wigs. They carried sticks shaped on a lathe (perhaps to resemble Aztec war clubs), silver-plated bows and arrows, and wooden shields. The Amazons carried knives made of silver-plated wood and wore rented wigs. Since "three" wigs are listed, one assumes that they too wore a different one on each successive night. The list of stage properties does not yield a clear dance narrative, but the provision of "four collars and chains," the latter made of rope, suggests that one group ended up as captives. C. A. Marsden assumes that the "savages" represented "Indians of the New World," and Emilio Cotarelo y Mori remarks that this is the "oldest complete description . . . that we have found" of a Spanish danced battle.[19]

If both are correct, they would together lend startling support to the idea that traditional Spanish combat dances may have their roots not in medieval Europe but in native America. Unfortunately, we have too few details of the dance to be sure that the "savages" were intended to represent American Indians rather than medieval "wild men" or that the "Amazons" were of Brazilian rather than classical Greek pedigree. They may have been, but we cannot be sure. I know of no solid evidence, however, that refutes Cotarelo y Mori's claim.

19
Royal Entries (Toledo, 1533, and Naples, 1543)

WE will return to the influence of indigenous traditions on European festivals in due course. For now, we turn our attention to the opulent entries and other pageants of royal power in which sixteenth-century Europe negotiated the relationship between the imperial pretensions of the monarchy, the universal claims of the church, and the rights and privileges of its urban citizens. The most splendid of these spectacles were "great compilations of imperial mythology on a scale unknown since the Roman Empire." [1]

Amidst a welter of classical allusions, chivalric fantasies, and ecclesiastical grandeur, representations of American empire and Muslim conflict, too, found their place. In the next three chapters, we will look at clusters of such representations in five different countries: land and sea battles between Turks and Christians in Toledo (Spain) in 1533; jousts involving real Moors in Naples (Italy) in 1543; pyrotechnic battles between Turks, centaurs, giant wild men, and devils in Trent (now in Italy, but then part of imperial Germany) in 1549; sword dances and artillery barrages featuring "wild men" or Turks in Binche (Belgium) in 1549; and tribal warfare, starring fifty naked Brazilians, in Rouen (France) in 1550. All but the last of these took place in cities ruled by the Spanish monarch. It is in these mock battles before royal audiences that the modern Spanish festivals of Moors and Christians have their roots.

In May 1533, the citizens of Toledo celebrated Charles V's return to Spain after an absence of four years in Germany and Italy. Brooking no delay, they began the festivities while Charles was still on the way from Barcelona. An unsigned letter, written in Toledo after eight days of religious processions, dances, *juegos de cañas*, bull runnings, masquerades, and "many inventions," describes the festivities as "the best ever," but claims that they will do "much more once his majesty comes to this city." [2] An anticipatory royal entry was part of the celebrations. Competing for a prize offered to the guilds for the best "invention," the fruiterers prepared a "triumphal car covered with brocade and cloths of gold and silver," on which sat actors playing "the emperor" and "the empress." Accompanied by "richly-dressed grandees and advisers" and surrounded by "a dance of the most magnificent gentlemen ever seen," the surrogate emperor "seemed to have subdued the whole world." Preceding the imperial carriage were "all the crosses of the parish churches," their "many relics," the archbishop, and all the canons, chaplains, priests, and friars of the city. These were followed by the nobles, the confraternities, and the guilds, all interspersed with large numbers of musicians. Even in the absence of the monarch, the triumphal entry drew more participants than the city's Corpus Christi procession.

This is a telling comparison, for Toledo's Corpus Christi procession officially celebrated the victory of Christ, through the perpetual reenactment of his death in the sacrament of the mass, over the forces of darkness; and it offered a vision of the nations of the world voluntarily submitting to the risen Christ's gracious rule. The Renaissance royal entry, modeled on the imperial triumphs of pagan Rome, substituted human emperor for divine lord, claiming always that the emperor was not only Roman but now also holy and that he ruled, in some tension with the pope, as Christ's representative on earth. For all the lingering crosses, relics, and clergy, the focus of the renaissance entry was on human rather than divine triumph.

Among the competing "inventions" that filled the week of festivities in Toledo were two mock battles between Moors (or Turks) and Christians, mounted by carpenters and masons on the one hand and gardeners on the other. Perhaps the battles were intended to recall imperial victories over the Ottoman Turks in Austria the previous summer and to prophesy future naval victory in the Mediterranean. If so, history imitated art, for two years later Charles led a naval force of some 25,000 men in the sack of Tunis. (The sack of Tunis was celebrated in Nuremberg, at the other end of the empire, in 1535, with a pyrotechnic mock siege, in which a giant figure of a Turk stood atop the castle battlements, much as the giant Muhammed still does in Valencian festivals of Moors and Christians, while smaller Turk-dolls were thrown into the air by rockets [Fig. 18].)

18. Mock siege of a castle defended by Turks. Nuremberg, 1535.
Drawing by Marianne Cappelletti after an engraving by Erhard Schön.

For the first of the two mock battles in Toledo, a "very tall" castle was built in the Plaza de Zocódover, then as now the main square of the city, by "more than seven hundred . . . carpenters and masons." Many of the same artisans would begin work a few years later on renovating the Alcázar, the fortified imperial residence in whose imposing shadow they now built their stage castle.[3] The involvement of masons suggests that the artificial castle was more substantial than the medieval structure of painted canvas wrapped around a wooden frame. Having built the scenery, the carpenters and masons fought for it in military uniforms of "silk and gold." For most of the late afternoon and evening, "the Great Turk" led the "Moors" in a spirited defense of the castle. "More than forty thousand" spectators watched from windows decorated with canopies and hung with tapestries or from vantage points within the square, as they still do during Toledo's annual Corpus Christi procession. At last, the Great Turk and his Moorish soldiers yielded and, together with their flags, which had been unceremoniously "dragged down" from the castle walls, were led captive through the city. In what was, to the best of my knowledge, the first instance of such deliberate destruction in a Spanish *moros y cristianos,* the castle was set on fire. Incendiary consumption of costly scenery seems to have been an innovation dictated by the Renaissance impulse to "prodigal expenditure."[4]

Three days later, Toledo's gardeners staged a battle on the river Tagus. No doubt the guild chose this setting to display its skill at decorating the boats with latticework "shelters" made of masses of supple branches. The boats, one half designated Christian and the other half Moorish, were further crowded with "artillery and musicians." After a naval battle "that was something to see," the Moors dismasted their boats and fled up the bank to ensconce themselves in the "rock" of the Moorish king. The Christians pursued them. Although, for fear of "prolixity," the letter writer abandons his account at this point, we can assume that the Christians ousted the Moors from their stronghold and defeated them.

Despite the involvement of the popular guilds and the potential for parody in a royal entry staged without a monarch, I can detect no trace of a hidden transcript in the Toledo festivities. The lack of evidence in a single eyewitness account is, of course, no proof that the public transcript of imperial splendor reigned unchallenged. When Charles had first arrived from the Netherlands, speaking no word of Spanish, surrounded by foreign courtiers, and harboring imperial ambitions that were decidedly unpopular in Spain, it was Toledo that had led the revolt (1519–1521) of the Castilian *comuneros* against the teenage monarch.[5] It is hard to believe that such resistance had faded from civic memory in only a dozen years. I would love to know more about the fruiterers' representations of the absent emperor and empress and of the grandees, advisers, and gentlemen who danced attendance on them. Perhaps the portraits were not entirely flattering. But the bait of prizes is often more effective than the threat of punishment in regulating folk performers on a public stage, and this may have been the case in Toledo.

Even prize money soon proved to be too risky an investment. By the middle of the century, authorities in the larger cities were reluctant to entrust the management of civic pomp to guilds whose popular tastes included too much "extraneous matter."[6] City councils preferred instead to hire professional humanists, poets, and artists who could be trusted to adhere to a neoclassical aesthetic and to construct a unified political program. The active involvement of the guilds in Toledo may have marked the first intervention of "the popular element" in the organization of a Spanish mock siege,[7] but the convergence of guilds, mock sieges, and royal entries was not to last long. For, in the context of such an entry, even a mock battle celebrating royal victory entailed "a delicate negotiation of power and prestige." Explicitly celebrating "the royal spectator's own military prowess and accomplishments" elsewhere, it implicitly referred to the defensive battle that the city was choosing not to mount then and there. It served, in other words, to remind the visiting monarch that his entry was granted rather than forced and that it bore with it certain reciprocal obligations to the city. Steven Mullaney observes: "Rather than lay siege to gain entry, the monarch granted an entry was entertained by the comfortably displaced spectacle of a siege, a dramatic entertainment that at once represented the potential for conflict manifested by a royal visit, and sublimated that potential, recasting it as a cultural performance to be enjoyed by city and crown alike."[8] Replacing the heterogeneous medieval guild procession with a professionally constructed, unified royal entry gave greater control of both form and content to the civic authorities, ensuring that the city's message to the visiting monarch was delivered with proper clarity, tact, and taste.

Professional political scripting of royal pageants will be evident in the elaborate entertainments (including those at Trent and Binche) offered to Philip II during his tour of Europe in 1549 and to Henry II at Rouen in 1550. But the "potential for conflict" is perhaps most dramatically apparent in Geronimo de Spenis's account of the visit of al-Hasan, ruler of Tunisia, to Naples in 1543.[9] On the morning of Sunday, 3 June, four ships entered the bay of Naples bearing the king of Tunis, his wife, a substantial escort of Moorish soldiers, "many Moorish women," horses, exotic merchandise, and two captive lions. The women stayed on board, but that evening the king and a group of Moorish warriors were greeted outside the city gates by the Spanish viceroy, a company of nobles, and "innumerable common people on foot and on horseback." Carefully escorted and preceded by trumpet fanfares, the king made his formal entry into the city. He was followed by a cavalcade of fifty Moorish soldiers armed with "spears [zagaglie]" and "very long muskets." It must have been an impressive and somewhat unnerving sight, to which the Spanish hosts responded in kind. As the Moors approached the palace where they were to lodge, they were met by a furious barrage of artillery that lasted a full fifteen minutes and "made the earth shake." Although the royal Moorish entry and its Neapolitan reception were not quite as daring as they first sound, since al-Hasan was an ally of Charles V, installed as puppet ruler of Tunis after the Spanish conquest of the city in 1535, they constitute a striking example of historical conflict between Moors and Christians being "comfortably displaced," to use Mullaney's phrase, by public pageantry.

The visit was not without tension. Two days later, the viceroy's herald toured the city's streets threatening death to anyone who mistreated a Moor. On 6 June, with both sides reassured by the other's good behavior, the king's wife landed and was escorted to the palace by a further five hundred armed Moorish warriors. On 12 June, a Spanish soldier who had robbed and wounded a Moor was publicly hanged. On 31 June, the king of Tunis ordered one of his own men hanged for offending a Christian. The most intriguing feature of the visit, from the point of view of our study of mock battles between Moors and Christians, took place on Sunday, 1 July. What de Spenis calls a "Moorish joust" was held in one of the main streets of the city. His brief account does not permit a detailed reconstruction of the event, but we do know that the son of the viceroy and an Italian nobleman dressed as Moors. Other similarly costumed Christians may have taken part, but the Tunisian warriors were the star attraction. Armed "as if for war," some with spears and others with muskets, they galloped to and fro on their light cavalry horses.[10] "When the game of spears was finished, they took up canes" for a further round of jousting. For once, as Benedetto Croce puts it, "authentic Moors" competed in a game of canes on European soil.[11]

There is no evidence that either game was scripted, although the costuming of at least two Christians as Moors gave the event a degree of theatricality. In the diplomatic nature of the case, the joust could not have been staged as a conventional European *moros y cristianos* in which the Moors were finally defeated. Nor could the Moors have reversed the outcome and defeated the Christians. By dressing the Christian nobility as Moors the event was ostensibly stripped of its usual connotations of ethnic conflict and presented as a competition among Moors alone rather than as a dramatic mock battle or sporting contest between Moors and Christians. Nevertheless, to have seen Moorish warriors charging through the streets of Naples, brandishing spears, firing muskets, and displaying consummate skill at their own martial game of canes, must have been somewhat disconcerting to a European audience for whom the fear of Muslim invasion was still very real. Invasion, to use Mullanay's term, was temporarily recast as "cultural performance."

20

Great Balls of Fire (Trent, 1549)

THE most spectacular series of sixteenth-century Spanish royal entries greeted the future Philip II on his long tour of Italy, Germany, and the Netherlands between October 1548 and May 1550. The tour was intended as a triumphal buildup to his proclamation as heir to the Holy Roman Empire. Having defeated the Lutheran League of Schmalkalden at the battle of Mühlberg in April 1547 and so consolidated his power in Germany, Charles V had decided that the time was ripe to secure the imperial succession for his son. As it turned out, Charles abandoned these ambitions in the face of strenuous objections from the eastern Hapsburgs, but at least for the duration of his tour, Philip believed himself to be the future emperor. So did many of those who entertained him. Philip was twenty-one when he set out from Valladolid in October 1548. Keeping records of his journey were Cristóbal Calvete de Estrella, the prince's former tutor and official chronicler of the tour; the royal steward Vicente Alvarez, who wrote a journal when he was not supervising the food; and, until he left the tour in Trent, a trumpeter in the cardinal's service called Cerbonio Besozzi.[1]

When Philip sailed from the Catalan port of Rosas, the salvos of artillery from the boats at sea and the castle on shore were so frequent and so furious that "it seemed as if the sky and earth were drowning in thunder and fire; and that the galleys and other ships [were] . . . burning with living flames."[2] Similar gunfire greeted the royal fleet as it sailed past Monaco and again when it arrived in Genoa. There, "the smoke was so thick that one could hardly see the city and the mountains." Jenaro Alenda y Mira interprets an unpublished Italian verse account of the Genoese reception to mean that Philip was entertained with mock battles offshore.[3]

From Genoa, Philip headed north, arriving in Trent on Thursday, 24 January 1549. Philip's host was the thirty-six-year-old bishop of the city, Cardinal Cristoforo Madruzzo, who had traveled with the royal party from Spain. Although Trent was then just within the German boundaries of Charles's empire, the majority of its population of between seven and eight thousand was Italian.[4] The Council of Trent had convened there in 1545, but had been fragmented two years later when delegates loyal to the pope moved to Bologna and those dependent on the emperor remained in Trent. It was to begin a second, more or less united session in 1551.

Philip was greeted by a fireworks display in the cathedral square. A wooden castle, decorated on all sides with "many heads like those they paint to represent the winds" and with two large wheels mounted on poles on its walls, stood in the center of the square. When the wheels were lit, they began to spin at great speed, throwing off "rays of fire" and other fireworks with "great and dreadful bangs." At the same time, all the heads spouted "flames of fire from their mouths, eyes, and noses, all up and down the castle, with many fearful explosions"; a drum, fife, and bugle corps made "a great din"; and artillery fired "with great rapidity" from a nearby tower. All this went on for "more than half an hour," until the castle was ignited from within and quickly consumed by "huge flames."[5]

A little further on, at the gate of the bishop's palace, a painted globe, surrounded by "a dozen heads representing the principal winds," hung from a cord stretched across the square. Above the globe were a "wheel" representing the sun and a crowned imperial eagle. As Philip reached the center of the square, artillery opened fire, "trumpets, fifes, drums, and other instruments" struck up, and a fireworks dragon (Fig. 19) raced along the suspended cord to ignite the globe, which was full of fireworks "skillfully arranged to go off in order." In an instant, the sun wheel was revolving and the winds were blowing furiously, flashing and sending off fireworks, some high into the air and others into the crowded square. People didn't know where to turn for safety. The display lasted "a long time."

Afterward, the prince entered the bishop's palace, a magnificent Renaissance castle built for Madruzzo's predecessor. There the royal party dined and drank heavily "in the German style" and Philip danced with "the most beautiful of the Italian women."[6] Later that night, outdoor entertainment included "a disorderly dragon, which threw fire in all directions and progressed with its head held so high that it reached the windows" from which beautiful Italian and German women were watching. While the "dragon" attacked second-story windows, a live ass was released into the piazza, with several "explosive tubes" attached to its ears and tail so as to scatter fire without endangering the animal. But the poor beast was terrified rather than terrifying and ran braying among the crowd until, to much laughter, it had to be led away. Then, at the entrance to a "horrible hell mouth," a giant Hercules appeared, struggling with another "disorderly monster" that spat fire continually. Suddenly Cerberus, the three-headed canine guardian of classical hell, emerged, spraying fire from its several mouths and ears. Although, later in the week, Hercules and Cerberus were to be represented by immobile figures, this confrontation seems to have required live actors to manipulate the giant and his monstrous opponents. Hercules conquered both animals.[7]

Friday night brought a series of individual jousts and another pyrotechnic display. For an hour and a half, fireworks were launched from two hillside castles outside the city walls, illuminating the night sky with "a thousand different shapes," spinning wildly from two enormous pyrotechnic wheels, and pouring massive fire balls down a steep precipice toward the city. So abundant and uninterrupted were the explosions that "it seemed as if the peaks and the precipices were burning." But all this, Calvete remarks, was nothing compared to the "battle for the castle" the next day.[8]

19. Pyrotechnic dragon on a string. Drawing by Marianne Cappelletti after a 1627 engraving by Joseph Furttenbach, Ulm.

It began mildly enough. On Saturday evening, to the noise of artillery fire, four "centaurs" and "some soldiers dressed as Turks" marched around a "wooden castle" in the center of the square, guarding and defending it. Then the fireworks began. To one side of the square was a sculpted relief of Hercules leading the defeated Cerberus on a chain out of hell. Four "giants in the form of fierce and terrible wild men" appeared near the cavernous hell mouth and eight "armed men" bearing sidearms and helmets entered from another side of the piazza. On each of their helmets was a crest representing Hercules overcoming a lion, which, by means of some pyrotechnic device, blew a stream of fire from its mouth. The men all carried "hollow pikes," packed with gunpowder, over their shoulders. From both ends, with loud bangs, the pikes scattered sparks and fireworks that fell among the crowded audience in the square, sending people scurrying from one place to another to keep from being burned. The armed men marched around the castle, "jumping [*saltando*]" to keep the pikes alight. As they reached the cave, they were attacked by the wild giants, each of whom wielded a club, packed with powder, that poured out smoke and flames.[9] When the centaurs, bearing hollow lances that also spewed fire and smoke, joined the battle on the side of the giants, the armed men divided their forces, four taking on the giants and four trading blows (and fire) with the centaurs. The ensuing skirmish, marked by an uninterrupted "rain of sparks" and thunder of explosions, lasted "more than half an hour."

This was only the first round. As the fighting temporarily died down, a wheel on one corner of the castle began to spin furiously, scattering fireworks in all directions. The giants retired to their cave, the centaurs to the castle, and the armed men to the side of the square. But, when the large fire wheel stilled, the combatants returned to battle, the armed men bearing flaming torches that scattered huge sparks; the giants carrying fresh fire-clubs that expelled multiple "balls of fire"; and the centaurs shooting fiery arrows from bows that made a noise like gunfire. So furious was the battle and so fierce the flames "that it seemed more infernal than human." The second round lasted forty minutes. When it ended, a second fire wheel was ignited to the same splendid effect as the first.

While the fire wheel spun, the actors replenished their weapons. For the third round, the armed men carried iron maces and shields. Each shield had five mouths that together shot flames and sparks with loud reports, as did the maces. The men attacked the castle, which was ably defended by the giants, armed with fresh fire-clubs, and the centaurs, sporting small shields and iron maces, all packed with powder and fireworks. The centaurs "jumped" and "turned swiftly" like horses, always firing flames into the night air. Finally, the armed men set fire to the third wheel, which made everyone (including the actors) take shelter, as the fifes, drums, and trumpets struck up and the last splendid shower of fireworks descended on the piazza. The performance lasted "more than two hours." [10]

More was to follow the next evening, but it is worth pausing at this point to ask what was intended by this pyrotechnic drama. While we may not be able to unravel all the threads of meaning, we can at least discern the broad patterns. A similar "fireworks pantomime" at Düsseldorf in 1585, including giants Hercules and Atlas, monstrous animals Cerberus and the Hydra, a burning castle with devils hanging over the walls representing hell, and a boatload of soldiers storming hell with swords, shields, and blazing arquebuses, is said to have entailed a contemporary application of the third act of Seneca's *Hercules Furens* (Fig. 20).[11] But it is hard to see how, and there is in any case no such specificity in the Tridentine accounts. Nor can we ascribe to the display a definite historical referent, as had been the case in 1547 when Madruzzo celebrated news of Charles V's victory at Mühlberg with an attack on an artificial city that must have represented the defeated Protestant stronghold.[12]

Clearly, the armed men in the 1550 mock battle, linked by their crested helmets to the heroic Hercules, were "good," and the wild giants, centaurs, and Turks were "bad." One strand of the narrative may have entwined a mythical battle in which Hercules used firebrands to repel an attack by centaurs with another in which he came to the aid of the gods in their struggle against the giants. Both battles were understood to signify the struggle of civilization against barbarism.[13] So, in western

20. Pyrotechnic dramatization of Act 3 of Seneca's *Hercules Furens,* Dusseldorf, 1585.
Drawing by Marianne Cappelletti after a contemporary print.

Europe, was the more recent battle of the Holy Roman Empire against the Turks,
which forms another strand of the pyrotechnic narrative. In this context, Renaissance kings, including Charles V, were often compared to Hercules and analogies
drawn between their victories and those of the classical hero.[14]

The pyrotechnic battle may also have contained an allusion to the prince's losing
battle against intemperate sexuality, for the fight between civilization and barbarism
was also thought to be waged within the individual. When Philip had disembarked
in Genoa two months earlier, he had passed beneath a triumphal arch depicting the
Roman proconsul Publius Scipius, "a young man who with great continence,"
while commander of the imperial forces in Spain between 217 and 211 B.C., "declined the most beautiful young women his soldiers offered him." The arch had also
portrayed the mythical battle between the centaurs and the Lapiths. According to
Greek legend, Perithous, king of the Lapiths, invited the centaurs to his marriage
to Hippodamia, but the barbarous centaurs spoiled the feast by drinking too much
and trying to rape the Lapith women. The arch showed the centaur Eurytion forcibly
carrying off the bride and meeting his death at the hands of Hercules.[15] Centaurs
were classical symbols of drunkenness and lust and no doubt also bore these connotations in Trent.

One has to feel a little sorry for the young prince. He was already three years a
widower, his first wife, María of Portugal, having died in childbirth when both were
just eighteen. Before he had married, he had received bizarre sexual advice from

his father. The emperor had written to his son that he should "keep away from [María] as much as possible" and, when with her, "let it be briefly." Philip's second wife, Mary Tudor, whom his father chose for him for political reasons in 1553, was eleven years older than Philip and, by her own account, not "disposed to be amorous."[16] In a world of such dysfunctional attitudes to royal sexuality, Philip paid little heed to the Genoese warning and, before the tour was out, engaged in several affairs.

Turks, centaurs, and giants represented all that Christian Europe believed itself and its rulers called to resist. To see its princes and their armies in Herculean terms upheld the official position that they were strong enough to win both territorial and moral battles. But to take such delight in "infernal" fireworks, banquets, heavy drinking, and dancing with beautiful women, all at ruinous expense to Cardinal Madruzzo, suggests a certain ambivalence about the message even on the part of those who paid for its staging. In any case, victory for the forces of civilization in the pyrotechnic battle was postponed. The first day's siege of the castle ended indecisively.

On Sunday evening, the royal audience returned to the piazza to see the conclusion of the mock battle. The four "centaurs" entered the square, accompanied by "many men of war dressed as Turks." All bore small shields and iron maces; one had a lance. Once the Turks and centaurs had taken up defensive positions inside the castle, "a terrifyingly ugly, wild giant," wielding a dreadful "fire-club," came out of the hell mouth. In an apparent collapse of barbarism into internecine warfare, the Turks and centaurs left the castle to attack the giant. For "over half an hour," nothing could be heard but explosions and nothing seen but the flames and sparks of maces, lance, and clubs. When, at last, the giant was left for dead on the field, the Turks and centaurs returned rejoicing to the castle.

A group of "devils" then scurried out of the cave, leading an "ass" or "she-mule," presumably the same poor creature that had been so terrified on Thursday night. The ass wore a "mask" and a "mantle," both laden with fireworks, and "threw great sparks of fire, with deafening bangs, from its nostrils, ears, and tail." The devils carried fiery cylinders in their hands and scattered "flames and sparks" from their horns. But they were also comic characters, playing "a thousand jokes" with the mule. Then, while the devils were trying to load the burning body of the giant on the ass, a "huge and dreadful winged serpent" came out of the castle to dispute possession of the corpse. The dragon had five "fires" on each wing, a fiery disk on its head, and sparks pouring with loud bangs from its mouth and its tail. It was "full of powder and rockets" and "hurled fire everywhere incessantly." After a prolonged battle that "seemed more truly hellish than artificial," the devils beat off the serpent and carried the giant's corpse to hell.

As if the battle between the winged serpent and the devils weren't noisy enough, fifty arquebusiers then led an enlarged force of "many" armed men, bearing hollow pikes spitting fire and accompanied by flag bearers, fife players, and drummers, in a furious attack on the castle. A continuous display of fireworks from the surrounding mountains extended the setting of the mock siege. Hurling explosive grenades, the Turks and centaurs successfully repelled the first wave of what, one assumes, again represented the Herculean forces of European civilization and moral restraint. Some of the fireworks fired from the hillside formed bright crosses against the night sky, perhaps identifying the attacking army more specifically as Christian. As the armed men and arquebusiers retreated, a huge fire wheel burst into action on one corner of the castle, giving the actors a chance to grab fresh firearms. A second attack was equally fierce, fiery, and failed. During a third attack, some of the soldiers managed to scale the castle walls; others maintained a barrage of arquebus fire. When a final fire wheel was lit, the assailants did not retreat, despite the storm of sparks that the spinning disk poured down on them. Instead they persevered, finally capturing the castle and planting their flag on its walls.

Seeing his side defeated, the castle warden fled, with a burning mace in his hand, to hell. Inside the cave were "thirty fires, twenty fire-cylinders, and ten fire-balls packed with fireworks." The conjunction of burning mace and such a stock of explosives had the desired effect: "in an instant all of hell caught fire and burned with such a horrible noise and terror that it seemed not just artificial but truly infernal." In keeping with the denouement of apocalyptic victory for the "good," the statues of Hercules and Cerberus were unharmed, adding to the general conflagration by shooting jets of fire toward hell mouth from Hercules's handheld mace and Cerberus's three heads. This destructive "fury," consuming the symbols of evil, barbarism, and unrestrained lust in an absorbing display of pyrotechnics, lasted a good half hour.

The performance culminated with the explosion of a sphere that had been packed with powder and placed atop the castle and now hurled a multitude of fireworks in all directions. The castle also went up in flames "to the great joy of all," especially of the infantry who had laid siege to it. The victorious soldiers surrounded the burning ruin, "demonstrating their joy . . . , throwing fire and sparks with their pikes," and "charging and discharging their arquebuses" around the charred structure. At last, the crowds dispersed, full of wonder at having witnessed "so many and so varied inventions and such ingenious and never before seen artifices of fire." But for Philip and his party, the night was not yet over. Colonel Madruzzo hosted a final banquet and dance; when all at last retired to sleep, "little of the night remained."[17] The royal party left Trent on Tuesday.

Despite Tridentine claims of originality, this was not the first pyrotechnic mock siege that Philip had seen. As part of the celebrations in Salamanca in 1543, when the young prince had married María of Portugal, a fire-breathing dragon, two giants, three knights, a dozen gentlemen, a squadron of thirty soldiers, and several other combatants had taken part in the siege of a wooden, wheeled castle so loaded with fireworks that "the uproar of the explosions and the number of rockets that shot up into the sky" made "the whole square seem prey to flames."[18] Such sieges had a long history in Spain. As early as 1414, fireworks had been used to simulate gunfire during the mock siege of Balaguer staged in Zaragoza for the coronation of Fernando I, and a fire-breathing gryphon had taken part in an allegorical mock siege later the same day. Given J. R. Partington's argument that the recipe for gunpowder was introduced to Europe from Arabic sources first translated in Spain, it is possible that the first pyrotechnic mock siege was staged in Spain rather than, as Arthur Lotz claims, in Germany. Some of the details in Trent, however, may have been Italian. Vannoccio Biringucci's *Pirotechnia* (1540) mentions "stage shows, based on a story or fable," mounted on saints' days in Siena and Florence, "in which figures of wood and plaster, emitting fire from their mouths and eyes, played their part, as well as 'trunks' or cylinders for the projection of fire-balls, all arranged on a lofty pedestal."[19]

But the dominant influence on the festivities in Trent may have been Catalan. Despite the intervening distances in space, time, and class, much of the Tridentine spectacle bears a startling likeness to the annual Corpus Christi festival of Berga (Barcelona), whose dance of Turks and hobby horses I mentioned in an earlier chapter. A brief account at this point of Berga's festival, known locally as the Patum, will breathe further life into the historical record from Trent and allow us to assess the intriguing possibility that elements of the Patum's more famous ancestor, the Barcelona Corpus Christi procession, traveled to imperial Germany in the sixteenth century. I saw the Patum in June 1996.[20]

The first several days of the Patum included raucous street parades; two performances of the full sequence of *entremesos,* at noon and at night on Thursday; and, on Friday, a spectacular display of fireworks from the town's hillside castle. The festival reached its climax on Sunday. By noon, the main square, its compact dimensions made to seem even smaller by the five-story buildings that surround it, was packed with people. Those in the square wore floppy cotton hats to protect their heads and necks from falling sparks and long-sleeved shirts, scored with prestigious burn marks from previous years. Others watched from balconies, the church steps, or behind the *barana,* a waist-high stone wall shielding the rising street in front of the church from the drop to the square.

The first *entremès* was the familiar dance of Turks and hobby horses. The second pitted Saint Michael and a companion angel, both played by small boys in blond

21. Devils or *maces* from Berga's Patum.
Drawing by Marianne Cappelletti after Amades, *Costumari*, 3: 117.

wigs, against eight masked devils. Each devil carried a *maça* (club, or, in this instance, pole) that ended in a metal drum, containing pebbles and decorated with a painted devil's face. Fixed to the top of the drum was a *fuet,* a slow-burning firework about eighteen inches long. As the devils, also known as *maces,* leaped in disorderly strides from one end of the narrow space cleared by their handlers to the other, the pebbles rattled inside the drums and the *fuets* trailed sparks over the heads of the crowd (Fig. 21). The two angels skipped delicately to and fro across the devils' path, carefully avoiding any contact with their adversaries. As each devil's *fuet* reached its concluding charge and exploded, he lay down, feigning death, and was finished off with a token thrust of angelic lance and sword. When all the devils were vanquished, the *salt* (jump, rather than dance) was over.

Next came the *guites,* two long-necked giant mules made of green cloth stretched over a wooden frame and a long pole sheathed in green cloth that sported a fierce mask at the upper end. The jaws of each beast contained a metal holder for three *fuets.* Supported by two men within and several more outside, the larger *guita* reached high into balconies or attacked spectators watching from the *barana.* One of the animal's handlers jumped onto the wall and, holding the mule's giraffe-like neck, ran up and down the length of the *barana,* forcing the spectators to retreat to avoid the sparks and then surge back to regain their vantage point. The smaller *guita* suddenly dropped its neck and spun on the spot, showering onlookers with sparks.

The pace slowed temporarily with the dance of the *àliga* (eagle), a rotund and regal papier-mâché effigy worn from the waist up by a single carrier who looked out through a grille in the bird's chest. Although the eagle may once have represented John the Evangelist in Barcelona's Corpus Christi procession, it has long served as a symbol of civic power and, more recently, as an emblem of Catalan independence. Of the next three *entremesos,* only one, the *ball dels gegants* (the dance of the giants), has any roots in medieval Barcelona. The other two, the dances of the *nans vells* (old dwarfs) and the *nans nous* (new dwarfs), belong to a tradition of papier-mâché "big-heads" that seem to have appeared in Catalonia only in the late eighteenth century.[21] Even the giants have changed substantially since the late Middle Ages. Now they are elegant kings and queens, danced by men who carry towering wooden frames draped with oversized robes and topped by papier-mâché heads. When Goliath accompanied David in the Barcelona procession, he was a giant wild man played, if Amades is correct, by a man on stilts hidden by a floor-length robe.[22]

The noon performance ended with the *tirabol,* a massed counterclockwise *salt* around the square. While the band played, small groups of spectators, arm in arm, combined to form a human whirlpool in the square. The *guites* joined the fray, the fireworks clamped between their jaws scattering trails of orange sparks, and, in one corner, two of the giants spun in place. This was the most dangerous of the *entremesos,* for if anybody had fallen, the momentum of the *tirabol* would have brought others tumbling down on top of them.

At night, the *plens* (full [devils]) were added to the program of *entremesos.* Silently, a hundred or more masked dancers, dressed, like the *maces,* in red and green felt suits, but with a wreath of packed green vines around the neck and a tuft of vines tied to their tails, filed into the square. Every devil wore three *fuets* on each of the mask's two horns and two more *fuets* on his tail. The *plens* positioned themselves throughout the densely packed crowd. At a signal, all the lights went out, plunging the square into blackness; the *plens'* companions lit the *fuets* of their respective devils, creating pockets of sparkling light; the band struck up; the drum provided its own insistent rhythm; and the *plens* and the entire crowd began to jump counterclockwise around the square in a burning whirlpool of fire. Clouds of smoke roiled up the chimney of the square, dropping black ashes on those in the balconies. The *fuets* began to burst, a few at first and then many together, drowning the music in a barrage of explosions. As the last firecracker burst, we were again in total darkness before the floodlights lit up the square and the music stopped. When the last of the *plens* had left, a lengthy *tirabol,* repeated twenty times or more, gradually brought the night's activities to a conclusion. Reluctantly, despite the hour, small groups spun off and wandered slowly home, arm in arm, through the town's narrow cobbled streets.

Do the shared elements of the Tridentine and Berguedan spectacles derive from a common Catalan source? In one case at least we can be reasonably sure that they do. Turks and hobby horses were first mentioned in the records of the Barcelona Corpus Christi procession in 1424 and soon traveled to Italy, appearing in Naples in 1443 during the triumphal entry of Alfonso the Magnanimous. Although Catalan hobby horses may not have been the first to engage in mock skirmishes, the conjunction of hobby horses and Turks is almost certainly a Catalan innovation, and the mythologically unorthodox juxtaposition of Turks and centaurs in Trent is difficult to explain if it is not rooted in the Catalan tradition. The centaurs' alliance with the Turkish foot soldiers may have been suggested by the notion that both Turks and centaurs were creatures of lust.

It is hard to imagine how centaurs might have been represented in sixteenth-century Trent if not by some version of the skirted hobby horse. (The front partner in a Victorian-style pantomime horse costume can doff his equine head to represent a kind of comic centaur, but the pantomime horse was a much later innovation than the skirted hobby horse.) Several "realistic" centaurs, with naked human torsos and equine bodies, fought a single Hercules in a Viennese fireworks display in 1666, but they appear to have been represented by statues rather than live actors.[23] Skirted hobby horses with fire shooting from their mouths and tails appeared in a "mummery" with drummers and arquebusiers in Düsseldorf in 1585 and, again, with actors bearing fire tubes and a giant statue, perhaps of Hercules, near Berlin in 1592.[24] In neither case, as far as we know, were they identified as centaurs or accompanied by Turks, but they may have been modeled on the Tridentine precedent. A skirted hobby horse, of course, is not quite a centaur, for the human torso emerges too far back and the body of the horse has a head of its own, but I suspect it was close enough for representational purposes.

The absence of fireworks from the Barcelona hobby horses and their modern Catalan descendants may have been a concession to their early processional context alongside Saint Sebastian. A thirteenth-century Catalan hobby horse went up in flames when it trespassed inside a church in the diocese of Elne, now in southwestern France. While the priest claimed that the conflagration was a case of divine judgment, the more immediate cause is likely to have been wayward pyrotechnics.[25] And the description of the Neapolitan Turks and hobby horses as "fiery" may mean that fireworks were reintroduced once the *Martyrdom of Saint Sebastian* was left behind.

The other incendiary beasts, from the long-necked "dragon" and the fireworks-laden mule, through Cerberus and the "disorderly monster," to the "huge and dreadful winged serpent," are kin to a family of pyrotechnic animals that have enlivened Catalan festivals for well over five hundred years. At least three appeared in the 1424 Corpus Christi procession in Barcelona: two "dragons" that fought Saint Michael and Saint Margaret and a "serpent" that accompanied Saint George. The records in Valencia mention dragons even earlier. A "winged dragon" welcomed Juan I to the city in 1392. "A large snake, made very life-like, . . . that blew huge flames from its mouth," was defeated by "many men armed with all kinds of weapons" during a banquet at the coronation of Martín I in 1399. And dragons belonging to the pageants of Saints Margaret and George were "remade" for the Valencia Corpus Christi procession in 1400.[26] Nothing in my experience more closely resembles the "disorderly dragon, which threw fire in all directions and progressed with its head held high so that it reached the windows" in Trent than does the larger of Berga's two *guites*. The terrified she-mule that accompanied the long-necked "dragon" in Trent and later appeared masked and mantled with fireworks may also have had a Catalan ancestor. One of the origin narratives for the *guita* tells of an attack by Saracens on nearby Guardiola. The Christians there, so the story goes, took "a very bad-tempered mule, a '*mula guita*,' . . . loaded it with 'rockets and exploding fires,' set it ablaze, and sent it out to the Saracen camp in the middle of the night. The Saracens, startled . . . by the furious black thing, fled in terror, and the castle was saved." While the story may tell us little about any historical encounter between Saracens and Christians, it may suggest that the festive ancestor of the *guita* was just such a live pyrotechnic mule.[27]

As for the "disorderly monster" that spat fire continually as it battled Hercules and the "huge and dreadful winged serpent" that fought the devils, I have seen many such monsters in Catalan festivals. The difference between a "*drac* [dragon]" and a "*víbria* [serpent]" is usually one of gender: while both are winged, the latter is female and displays large papier-mâché breasts.[28] One of the most spectacular of the *dracs* is that of Vilafranca del Penedès, near Barcelona, where a single man carries the eight-foot-long body of a winged black dragon on his head, spinning on his feet while the dragon sprays bright fire from its wing tips, back, mouth, and tail (Fig. 22). Of the more recent innovations, the most creative may be the whirling, fire-spitting *bou de foc* (fire ox) of Manresa, made out of two bulky pieces of an old ribbon-making loom (itself known as an "ox"). The legs of the man who carries the ox over his upper body can just be seen amidst the ambient flashes of light and thick clouds of smoke.[29] Given the widespread tradition of processional dragons in medieval Europe,[30] a Catalan origin for the Tridentine monsters cannot be proven. But the appropriation of the Turks and hobby horses demonstrates a willingness on

22. Processional dragon. Vilafranca del Penedès, 1995.

Madruzzo's part to borrow from the Catalan repertoire. And the fact that Spanish travelers to the Netherlands routinely went by way of Barcelona, Genoa, and Trent, rather than directly through France, which was then enemy territory, makes the possibility of cultural traffic between Catalonia and southern Germany more likely.

It is precisely along this diversionary route between northern Europe and Spain that processional giants with sculpted papier-mâché heads and hands are still most common.[31] The early processional giants, spreading from Catalonia to the Netherlands in the late fourteenth century, were played by men on stilts. The first record of a sculpted giant ("*mannequin porté*") comes from Bergen-op-Zoom (Netherlands) in 1447. Amades finds evidence of sculpted giants in Castile in the third quarter of the sixteenth century and in Catalonia, alongside the older stiltwalkers, in 1593. Dorothy Noyes therefore cautions against the common assumption that sculpted giants first arrived in Flanders as a result of Spanish colonization and "wonders whether, as with painting, the influence may not have gone in the other direction."[32] In Trent, the "terrifyingly ugly, wild giant," which was eventually overcome by the Turks and centaurs, and the Hercules who fought the infernal monsters were probably sculpted giants rather than costumed men on stilts. The comic devils made much of trying to load the defeated body of the ugly giant onto the pyrotechnic mule. It is easier to imagine this scene with a cumbersome, robed wicker frame, oversize sculpted head, and unwieldy sculpted hands than it is with only a pair of stilts and a deflated robe.[33] Moreover, one suspects that Madruzzo, with his love of lavish expense and the latest fashion, would have preferred the more elaborate sculpted giant to the simpler and somewhat outmoded stiltwalker.

Devils or wild men are an even more widespread feature of European folk theater. But they were also a prominent part of the medieval Catalan repertoire, and it is intriguing that the same verb (*saltar*) is used to describe the action taken by the devilish Berguedan *maces* and the Tridentine armed men to keep their firework "pikes" alight. The devils in Trent also carried fiery cylinders in their hands. The immediate juxtaposition of pyrotechnic devils, Turks and centaurs, giants, fiery monsters, long-necked dragons, and incendiary mules in Trent cannot help but remind anyone who has seen it of the Patum. The family resemblance almost certainly derives from their common ancestry in the Barcelona Corpus Christi procession.

21

Noble Fantasies (Binche, 1549, and Rouen, 1550)

PHILIP's journey through Lutheran Germany was comparatively sedate. There were no triumphal arches until he reached Brussels in April;[1] and, apart from an occasional salvo of artillery and a joust on the Danube in Ulm, very little in the way of noise. Catholic Belgium was rowdier. In Namur, in late March, the prince saw a battle between two teams of fifty men apiece on stilts. The stilts were six feet high, and the men "seemed like giants." The battle seems to have been competitive rather than dramatic, for one side dressed in the colors of Burgundy, which was then part of the empire, and the other wore an imperial eagle. The stiltwalkers fought individually, then three against three, and finally in a general mêlée in which all took part, skillfully tripping one another so that "there were many falls and wounds." Philip gave the winning side fifty gold coins. Such stilt battles are a traditional part of the Namur folk calendar, first recorded in 1411, staged for Charles V in 1515 and Napoleon in 1813, falling into disuse in the latter part of the nineteenth century, and successfully revived in 1951.[2]

Philip was in Brussels on the Sunday after Ascension Day for the annual procession that included, in 1549, squadrons of soldiers, triumphal floats representing the lives of Christ and the Virgin Mary, and a series of "games and inventions." Among these were "a devil in the form of a wild bull, spraying fireworks from his horns, between which rode another devil"; a young man in a bear suit making music by pulling the tails of live cats with such precision that the animals howled in tune; "a graceful dance of [youths dressed as] monkeys, bears, wolves, deers, and other wild animals"; a giant and giantess dancing to a hurdy-gurdy; several boys, "naked as Indians," riding giant skirted hobby horses and camels; and "a terrible serpent hurling fire and fireworks from its mouth in all directions."[3] In Tournai, in early August, if we are to believe a handwritten note that never made it into the official accounts, Philip watched a real execution staged as a dramatization of the story of Judith and Holofernes.[4]

The most memorable political pageantry was the carefully scripted series of performances that entertained Philip during his visit to his aunt, Mary of Hungary, at Binche.[5] The royal party, which by then included Charles V, arrived at Mary's brand-new, sumptuous Renaissance palace late on 22 August. Over the next several days, visitors and townsfolk were entertained by a preliminary series of jousts and an elaborate outdoor fantasy role-playing game for knights, the *Liberation of the Castle of Gloom*.[6] Then, on the evening of 28 August, a second fantasy, involving mock battles between Europeans and dark-skinned "savages," began.

After dinner, four swordsmen entered the great hall of the palace. The several eyewitness accounts and a surviving colored drawing of the event (Fig. 23) are not easy to reconcile in every detail, but it would seem that the men wore long brocaded gowns, in the old Venetian style, lightweight helmets covered with large multicolored plumes, and masks with long white beards. Each escorted a lady of the court, who wore an ankle-length brocaded cloak of a kind "no longer used." They were followed by two more women, at least one of whom, if the drawing is to be believed, was played by a cross-dressed bearded man, and two more men whom an eyewitness describes as also wearing "old men's masks." All twelve danced "a German dance" so well that "it was beautiful to see."[7]

As the four couples danced "chastely," four more swordsmen arrived, also wearing tall feathered headpieces, but dressed "in the pastoral style" in shorter capes, and sporting trimmer, darker beards. They were preceded by two drummers. When the women began to dance with these new, younger arrivals, their original partners resorted to swordplay, jealously attacking the younger men "with many fierce sword blows." Social decorum was fast disintegrating. As urban age fought rural youth for the hands of courtly women, "wild men" from beyond the pale of civilization intervened. Eight "savages" entered the hall, dressed in skintight bodysuits, marked with pale green and blue scales and yellow kneebands, and short, tattered green capes "in the rustic style." They wore feathers that were "trifling" compared to those of their civilized counterparts and were accompanied by four attendants, similarly dressed. In a common confusion of Islam and savagery, the wild men were described by a German eyewitness as being dressed like Moors. Taking advantage of the sword fight in progress, the wild men (or Moors) seized the watching women. This had the immediate effect of uniting urban age and rural youth against the common threat. A "terrible battle" ensued, represented by a sword dance in which, at the moment captured by the drawing, the eight civilized Europeans are lined up shoulder to shoulder facing the eight wild men, all with swords drawn. This was no "disorderly *mêlée*," but a carefully choreographed dance.[8]

The Europeans soon found that their unschooled opponents were neither cowards nor easily conquered. As swords clashed and feet followed the rhythm of the drums, the wild men's attendants escorted the captive women from the hall. The women do not appear, from the drawing, to have offered any resistance. Once outside, they climbed into a chariot, covered in green silk and drawn by four white horses, in which they were carried off to an artificial castle a league distant at Mariemont. Finally, as the Europeans grew tired, their wild rivals withdrew to safety, leaving the former to notice for the first time that their women had vanished. The European dancers, young and old, petitioned the emperor to allow them to muster all possible force the next day for a concerted attack on the castle where the women were now spending the night. Charles granted their request.

23. Sword dance. Binche, 1549. Drawing by Marianne Cappelletti
after a contemporary colored drawing.

It would be a spectacular battle, but before going on to describe it, we may ask what was intended by the evening's dances and the concluding capture of courtly women by wild men. Daniel Heartz wonders if the sword dance was a kind of *moresca,* representing in stylized and allegorical form the current hostilities between Turkey and a Europe itself divided by dynastic and religious quarrels. In this case, the women might represent Christian territory seized by the Turks. Mary of Hungary had lost everything—her husband, her throne, and her possessions—to the Turks at the battle of Mohács in 1526.[9]

This may be so, but it does not explain the distinction in age between the two sets of European men, the antiquated costumes of the first dancers (both men and women), and the seduction of the old men's women, first by rural youth and then by wild men. An alternative explanation may be that the entertainment expresses, consciously or otherwise, the fear of old men that their women will be sexually attracted by young men, of city dwellers that their women will be aroused by potent country dwellers, and of white men that their women will be seized by dark-skinned savages. If so, the furious barrage of artillery that the Europeans were to launch against the castle of the wild men the next day lends itself to interesting commentary on the gun as phallic symbol. This explanation is compatible with an allusion to Moors or Turks in the dance itself or, if the German witness is correct, in the costumes of the wild men. It may be, too, that the ladies of the court were staging a quiet protest of their own. The four women, dressed in antiquated style, begin by dancing "chastely" with four old men. They end by riding off into the night, in a magnificent horse-drawn chariot, with four wild men. Perhaps Mary of Hungary and her circle would have liked in their lives fewer old-fashioned restrictions and a little more freedom and romance. It was Mary, after all, who paid for and perhaps suggested the entertainment. As for the bearded "woman," I can offer no coherent explanation except to say that such a figure is not unusual in folk performance. What her role was in this instance, I don't know.

The next morning Charles and his court repaired to Mary's hunting lodge at Mariemont, overlooking the wild men's castle. They were not the only spectators; crowds from Binche and the surrounding villages packed the lanes and fields. The facade of the moated castle was made of bricks and mortar, and its other three sides of panels were painted to look like brick. Defending it from within were several knights, eighty well-armed soldiers, thirty arquebusiers, and several pieces of artillery. Outside, other defenders were ensconced between a small stream of running water and a twelve-foot-high rampart. Clearly, the wild men did not scorn modern military technology, suggesting that we should read them as "uncivilized" Turks rather than as primitive "savages." Ranged against them were two squadrons of cavalry, five squadrons of infantry, pikemen, and arquebusiers, and several cannon. The attacking army was commanded by the prince of Piemonte, who had led the elderly dancers the previous night.[10]

The first attack was launched around midday. Artillery opened fire, and infantry advanced to the disciplined rhythm of fife and drum, but knights rode out of the castle to defend the crossing of the stream in a "robust skirmish." The Europeans were forced to retreat, "recognizing that it was not going to be as easy to destroy the castle as they had thought." They resorted to a barrage of heavy artillery from sixteen guns that "fired with such speed and fury that it seemed as if the sky were falling." (The guns had been hauled from the arsenal at Mons some ten miles away. It would take 153 horses two full days to return them.)[11] While all this was going on, lunch was served. Seated on a balcony overlooking the battlefield, the royal party was served a magnificent banquet by young women dressed as pastoral goddesses, nymphs, and fauns. Wine was poured by young men representing Bacchus, Silenus, and Pan, and musicians played gently throughout. The contrast between the refined elegance of the luncheon and the brutal bombardment going on nearby does not seem to have struck anyone as odd.

During lunch, one of the castle's two fortified towers was damaged by artillery fire, forcing the defenders of the stream to retreat and block access to the castle itself. Then the attacking forces advanced on the castle walls, climbing scaling ladders but being repelled by pike thrusts and by stones and fireworks thrown from above. An ensign and several soldiers breached the walls, but the ensign and his flag were captured and the soldiers retreated, many singed by fireworks and some wounded. Several cartloads of provisions and munitions resupplied the castle, but were attacked with swords, lances, and arquebuses as they left. Reinforcements from within came to their aid. Others were busy repairing the castle walls "with baskets full of earth and wood." Captives were required to buy their freedom with "a large sum of money that was distributed to the peasants in reparation for the damage done by the troops." Eventually, as the sun set, the defenders again ran short of munitions and the attackers focused their artillery barrage on the weak points in the walls, destroying the second tower and opening broad access to the castle. Those within defended themselves with stones, earth, wood, and fireworks. When it became apparent that their cause was lost, as many as were able fled through a secret door in the back of the castle.

Thus the Europeans reclaimed their women. One witness wrote that the women had been kept in "some low vaults, where they could not be harmed by the artillery." Another, more likely account, reports that the victors only "pretended to deliver the women, whom, in reality, they found outside." Climbing aboard their chariot, the women were carried to the hunting lodge. There they stepped back from fantasy into the world where reputation counts and established that their honor had never really been at stake: the wild men, they announced to the royal guests, had been none other than their husbands, brothers, and relatives, good Flemish and Burgundian gentlemen all. With this, the party returned to the palace at Binche, where actors and audience dined and danced together.

Real warfare arrived in Binche a few years later. In 1554, Henry II of France sacked the area, completely destroying the ephemeral splendor of Mary's palace in Binche and her hunting lodge at Mariemont. Traces of the famous fêtes of Binche may survive in the town's annual carnival. Local legend says that the "Gilles," who dance in their hundreds each year in the town's main square, their heads sprouting a splendid plume of tall, multicolored ostrich feathers, are descendants of the "Incas" who danced in the great hall of Mary's palace in 1549. There is, of course, no evidence that the "wild men" represented Incas, a fanciful reading advanced by a local nineteenth-century journalist. Local twentieth-century antiquarian authority therefore scoffs at the idea of a link between carnival and courtly entertainment, preferring the more fashionable notion of pagan roots. But the "civilized" dancers who fought the wild men did wear splendid headdresses of many-colored feathers, larger and of greater value than those of the wild men, and it is possible that they, rather than the wild men, are the ancestors of the modern-day Gilles.[12]

In October 1550, just over a year after and some 150 miles southwest of the festivities at Binche, the people of Rouen welcomed their new king, Henry II, with a royal entry intended to rival those that had greeted Philip II in the Netherlands. Of particular interest is an episode featuring native American performers. As the king approached the river Seine on the outskirts of the city, he saw a meadow, some two hundred feet long and thirty-five feet wide, made to look like a Brazilian forest.[13] In the manner of sixteenth-century Mexican theatrical forests, live birds and animals, including monkeys and brightly colored parrots, could be seen amidst the foliage of both natural and artificial trees. At either end of the meadow were two native villages, whose authenticity was vouched for by three hundred actors, fifty of whom were "natural savages recently brought from the country," while the other 250 were French sailors, merchants, and adventurers who knew well the language and customs of the region. The native Brazilians wore nothing but polished and enameled stones in their pierced lips and stretched earlobes. Otherwise, male and female, they were naked, "without the least cover for the parts that Nature commands [to be covered]." So, according to the written account, were the French actors, thus "disguising" themselves as "savages." In a contemporary engraving of the event (Fig. 24), some of the men are wearing the briefest of feathered skirts, headdresses,

24. Mock battle in a Brazilian village. Rouen, 1550. From Denis, *Fête*, p. 4.

and armbands, leading one scholar to suppose that "the Rouennaise imperson-
aters . . . sacrificed some degree of authenticity for the sake of Norman modesty." [14]

For a while the royal party watched the natives fire their bows at birds, chase after monkeys, laze in hammocks, dance, and chop and prepare wood for French trade.
Such trade, largely conducted by merchant seamen from Rouen, was represented
by a ship, offshore in the Seine, that flew the colors of both Henry and Rouen. But
then war broke out between two tribes of natives. The Tabayaras, roused by a pas-
sionate harangue "in the Brazilian language" by their "king," or *murubicha*, violently
attacked the Tupinambas, trading partners of the French. [15] The latter group defended itself valiantly with shields, stone clubs, spears, and bows, finally routing the
aggressors and setting fire to their village. The entire performance was repeated the
next day, when the queen entered the city. Many in the audience who had been to
Brazil remarked that the representation of native life, including the battle, seemed
"genuine rather than simulated."

Fiery realism also marked an extension of the Brazilian pageant, seen by the king
after he had crossed to the other side of the Seine. Two ships, one representing
France and the other Portugal, approached each other on the river. The former
seems to have been the same merchant vessel that had earlier sailed offshore, while
the latter probably represented Portuguese "pirates" interfering with "legitimate"
French trade. A mock naval battle, characterized by fierce cannon fire, ended with
the Portuguese ship going up in flames and its sailors having to swim for their lives,
much to the concern of the crowd.

Although the Portuguese claimed sovereignty over Brazil, French merchant ships
from Rouen disputed Portuguese control and conducted a profitable timber trade
with the Tupinamba. For all its value as exotic entertainment, the Brazilian pageant
was "a device to display the importance of Rouen's trade to the king and, as
such, . . . an appeal by the city for continued interest and support by the monarch." [16] Moreover, it seems to have advanced the claim that French dealings with
America, unlike those of the Spanish and Portuguese, were characterized by benevolent free trade and noninterference in Indian affairs. The pageant script required that the French merchants defend themselves against Portuguese aggression
but remain neutral during tribal warfare. [17] (The reaction of the Portuguese ambassador, who was present, is not recorded.) Such a claim is, of course, undercut for
early twenty-first-century readers by our knowledge of colonial economies and by
our distaste for the notion of shipping Brazilian natives to France and there requiring them to build and burn replicas of their own homes to pander to the demand
of royal pageantry for ostentatious display and conspicuous consumption.

Nevertheless, I know of no other royal entry that tried to stage the New World
on European soil on such a grand scale and with such concern for authenticity. Nor

do I know of any occasion within the time frame of this book when so many native Americans performed together for so prominent a European audience. In the next chapter, we will look at a Spanish mock battle that represented the encounter of Cortés and Motecuzoma, but its actors, as far as we know, were all Spanish. In the first part of the chapter, we will look at a festival in which "foreigners" closer to hand took part. In Granada, in 1561, just seven years before the bloody Morisco Revolt broke out, four hundred of the city's Arabic-speaking Moriscos joined their old Christian neighbors in a "fierce and splendid skirmish."

22

Fêted Dreams of Peace (Andalusia, 1561–1571)

IN 1561, Philip II appointed eighteen-year-old Luis Hurtado de Mendoza mayor of the Alhambra, the fortified Moorish palace that dominates the city of Granada. Luis was the fourth successive member of the Mendoza family to hold the office. Both his grandfather and father, who had preceded him in office, were still alive, the former serving as president of the royal council of Castile and the latter as captain general of the kingdom of Granada and as Philip's ambassador to the Vatican. In his father's absence, Luis had served for two years as deputy captain general. He was also the fifth count of Tendilla and, on his father's death in 1580, would become the fourth marquis of Mondéjar. The single most powerful family in the former Moorish kingdom of Granada, the Mendozas governed the Alhambra, exercised military authority in the kingdom, and enjoyed the support of the aristocracy. They were opposed by a twenty-six-member chancery, first established by Ferdinand II in 1505, that governed the rest of the city of Granada, regulated civil life in the kingdom, and enjoyed the support of the immigrant Christian population. The two sides clashed over the problem of the Moriscos.

At their surrender in 1492, Granada's Moors had been promised freedom of religion. Ten years later, they had been given the choice of exile or Christian baptism. Those who stayed paid only nominal allegiance to Christianity. Known as Moriscos, they managed, for the most part, to retain their distinctive language and culture in public and observe their Muslim faith in private. In the city of Granada, some 20,000 out of a total of 50,000 to 60,000 inhabitants were Morisco.[1] In many of the mountain villages of the Alpujarra, only the priest was not. The chancery wanted to see an end to any distinctively Morisco culture. The Mendozas defended the Moriscos against undue persecution, but there was a measure of self-interest in this aristocratic protection of hard-working merchants and laborers. Fernand Braudel has remarked that the "feudal landlords" of Granada protected the Moriscos "much as in the United States southern plantation owners protected their slaves." But there is a difference: the Mendozas' opponents did not want to free the Moriscos, they wanted to eradicate them.[2]

To celebrate his appointment as mayor, Luis ordered that the feast day of John the Baptist (24 June) be observed with a mock battle that would amply demonstrate the military force, both old Christian and Morisco, at his disposal.[3] The setting was an artificial island in the river Genil, created by redirecting the normal flow of water. It was joined to the riverbanks by a bridge at each end. On the eve of the fiesta, "four hundred horsemen, a thousand arquebusiers, and four hundred Moriscos" assembled in the grounds of the Alhambra. Divided into two companies, one led by

Luis and the other by two of his friends, they left the palace by different gates, an hour before dawn, to descend through the city streets to the river. Luis and his men were dressed "in Moorish style." A band of fifty men playing flageolets and other instruments preceded the soldiers. Then came the Moriscos, wearing loose trousers, white shirts, and colored bonnets. Some were armed with slings; others carried small lances or spears. They were followed by a dozen trumpeters and other musicians wearing silken Moorish gowns. The arquebusiers came next, accompanied by many fifes and drums. There were a dozen knights, riding "with short stirrups"; twenty more knights armed with halberds, shields, or bows; five halberdiers "with many feathers in their hats"; and twelve grooms.

Behind this escort rode Luis himself. The young count wore Moorish dress: loose damask trousers, a silken gown, and a camlet cloak, all decorated with gold and silver. He carried a shield and a long lance from which hung a pennant emblazoned with Islamic crescent moons. Behind him came twenty foot soldiers and a mounted equerry, the latter carrying a lance and standard also decorated with crescent moons. Then came three standard bearers, six trumpeters, and, marching two by two in the wake of their captain general, "all the people, dressed in Moorish style with many elegant Moorish gowns." Thus, as the sun rose, Luis reached the island in the river. A great crowd awaited him.

No description survives of the opposing army. Perhaps they represented Christians, although this would have meant either that Luis, at the head of what was clearly intended to represent a Moorish army, would have lost the ensuing battle (and his Morisco supporters would have been induced to enact their own defeat) or, equally unthinkable, that the Moors would have been allowed just this once to defeat the Christians. Perhaps both sides, whether old Christians or Moriscos in daily life, dressed as Moors for the mock battle, just as they had when the king of Tunis visited Naples in 1543. Only thus could Luis identify with the persecuted Moriscos, lead the winning side, and still avoid representing the defeat of Christians. It was enough, under the circumstances, for him to fly the crescent moon. He would not have wanted to enact the undoing of the *reconquista*.

As day dawned, Moriscos streamed across both bridges onto the island stage, the arquebusiers formed up in battle lines, and together "they began to fight a valiant and fierce skirmish as if it were real," many feigning death on either side. Artillery boomed from the walls of the Alhambra and, after a while, the cavalry joined in, four hundred strong, with the "gallant" Luis leading the charge. It was "something never seen before in that city" and so well ordered that, even though it lasted a long time, "it ended without any mishap." Once the battle was over, Luis led the troops in a triumphal parade back to the Alhambra, leaving the Moriscos in their own quarters along the way. All the knights who had taken part sat down to lunch at tables in the courtyard of Luis's grandfather's house. The colors of their costumes and the multitude of feathers that adorned their heads so impressed the courtiers that they declared they had never seen anything like it. Food was also provided for the foot soldiers and Moriscos, although apparently not at the marquis's tables. *Convivencia* has its limits.

I am aware of no other mock battle in Christian Spain in which Moriscos took part. Although it is possible that they were performing under duress, I am inclined to think that they offered a voluntary show of support for the new mayor of the Alhambra. Luis seems to have returned the favor, dressing as a Moor not simply for the splendor of the costume but to identify with his Morisco subjects and thereby to challenge the prejudices of the civil chancery. Moorish dress was a heated political issue. The chancery would soon persuade Philip to revive dormant laws forbidding Moriscos to wear traditional Moorish clothes. For Luis and his followers to have paraded in triumph through the city streets, dressed "*a la morisca*," was a politically loaded gesture. In the process, he was able to portray himself as a powerful leader, both in the fictional world of the drama and, by his ability to summon a large and well-ordered military force, in the real world of Granadine politics.

Sadly, the Mendoza policy of tolerance toward the Moriscos did not prevail much longer. The Turkish siege of Malta in 1565 heightened Christian fears of an assault on the mainland. The increased frequency and scope of corsair attacks, culminating in a spectacular raid later that year on Orgiva, twenty miles inland from the Granadine coast, added to the tension, as did the discovery that some Moriscos were spying for the Turks and others were planning to seize control of Granada. Encouraged by the chancery and without consulting the Mendozas, Philip revived a decree first issued by his father in 1526 but never seriously enforced. It required the Moriscos of Granada to learn Spanish and outlawed all use of Arabic after three years. It forbade the use of Moorish costumes, surnames, music, dances, wedding ceremonies, and public baths. It aimed, in short, at complete cultural assimilation. To enforce the decree, Philip appointed Pedro de Deza president of the chancery of Granada. In January 1567 Deza began his campaign of suppression by demolishing the beautiful Alhambra baths. Iñigo López de Mendoza, marquis of Mondéjar, Luis's father and once again Philip's active captain general in Granada, was outraged.

For a while, the Moriscos hoped that negotiations and generous donations to the royal treasury would resolve the matter, as they had in the time of Charles V, but Philip was adamant. Tension mounted and, after dark on Christmas Eve 1568, 180 armed Moriscos from the Alpujarra trooped into the city dressed as Turks. Had there not been an unexpected snowfall, their numbers might have been greater. When their brethren in the city, sensing a fiasco, failed to join the uprising, the raiders cursed them for cowards and traitors. The "Turks" killed a few guards and sacked a store before being driven off by Mondéjar's soldiers. In the morning, Mondéjar personally assured the city's old Christians that there was no cause to worry. He was wrong. When the rumor that a Turkish army had invaded Granada reached the mountain villages of the Alpujarra, the Moriscos there took up arms and massacred their old Christian priests and neighbors. The legend of the "martyrs of the Alpujarra" was born. Mondéjar was forced to raise an army and respond.[4]

This, at least, is the official version of events. Roland Baumann has suggested that Christian fear, rather than Morisco aggression, was the primary cause of the "revolt." So terrified, he argues, were the Christians of a Turkish-backed "return of the Moors" that they exaggerated accounts of the Morisco uprising, "announcing a rebellion . . . in order to justify a genocide." "The dead Christians," he adds, "were not martyrs, but colonists killed by their infuriated victims."[5]

As is often the case with ethnic conflict, the war produced accounts of terrible cruelty on both sides. The Moriscos are said to have desecrated churches, using Madonnas for target practice and holy vessels for chamber pots; tortured priests, roasting one inside a pig and filling another's mouth with gunpowder before blowing off the top of his head; and enslaved prisoners, shipping men to the galleys and women to the harems of north Africa. On the Christian side, after John of Austria replaced Mondéjar as leader of the Spanish troops, the war was fought with calculated brutality. Entire villages were razed, each house, fence, fruit tree, and vine being cut down or burned to the ground. Male captives were hanged or shot, women and children enslaved.

In the midst of all this, there was, strangely, a partial reprise of the festivities of June 1561. When John of Austria entered Granada in April 1569, he was greeted with a mock battle in which Luis led a hundred horsemen dressed in Moorish costumes against another hundred clothed in scarlet silk. All wore cuirasses and carried lances and shields.[6] Once again, while one side was designated by its costumes as Moorish, the other's identity is not specified. And, although Moriscos were surely absent from this mock battle, Luis did not flinch from leading the army that represented their cause. Perhaps he dressed in the same splendid costume that he had worn eight years before. Given that John of Austria was relieving the Mendozas of their command and that the family still hoped for a negotiated peace with the Moriscos, one wonders at the hidden transcript of this royal entry.

A few months earlier, the *moros y cristianos* tradition had been put to ingenious wartime use. In February 1569, just two months after Moriscos had dressed as Turks to spur an uprising, Christians dressed as Moors to capture Moriscos. The Christians of Almería first sounded the alarm, announcing that a Moorish fleet had been sighted off the coast near Inox. After dark, the Moriscos of nearby Dalías joyously gathered on the beach in Inox to await the liberating navy, but were attacked instead by a troop of Spanish soldiers armed with cannon and arquebuses. As the Moriscos fled, a fleet of Moorish galleys appeared offshore, guns blazing, and promptly dispatched boats to help their beleaguered brethren. The desperate Moriscos clambered aboard, only to discover that the Moorish sailors were really disguised Christians. The battle had been simulated, the artillery and arquebuses, onshore and in the boats, loaded with nothing but gunpowder. No one was killed, but the captured Moriscos were sold into slavery in Almería, Cartagena, Mallorca, and Naples.[7]

For a while, it seemed that the rebellion in Granada would ignite a broader conflagration, but, though sympathizers in North Africa sent arms and volunteers, the Moriscos in Valencia and Aragon failed to rise in support. The Turks calculated the risks and decided against intervention. A massive importation of arms and gunpowder from Italy helped the Spanish Christians. By November 1570, John of Austria was able to leave Granada, knowing that only a few thousand Morisco rebels were left, operating like bandits in the most remote parts of the Alpujarra. The Morisco Revolt was arguably "the most brutal war . . . fought on European soil during that century."[8] When it was over, tens of thousands were dead, the Alpujarra was devastated, and the Arabic civilization of Andalusia was a thing of the past. Most of the 80,000 Morisco men, women, and children who had survived the fighting were forcibly marched north in winter rain, wind, and snow, a deportation that, as the Mendoza family chronicler commented bitterly, "left the kingdom [of Granada] totally destroyed and Castile, where they were taken, unimproved."[9]

It is this war that is recalled during the festivals of Moors and Christians still staged in the villages of the Alpujarra and, to a lesser extent, throughout Andalusia. In the manner of folk theater generally, the Granadine *moros y cristianos* make anachronistic reference to such diverse figures as El Cid, Ferdinand and Isabella, and the Catalan General Prim, who fought at the Mexican battle of Puebla in 1862. But mention is also made of Farax ibn Farax, who led the ill-fated "Turkish" invasion of Granada on Christmas Eve 1568, and Mahomet ibn Umaiya, who was shortly afterward crowned king of Granada by the leaders of the rebellion.[10] Of the twenty festivals of Moors and Christians still staged in Granada, "fifteen allude to a landing of the Turks on the southern coast."[11] The fear (or hope) of such an invasion played a major part in the uprising, but was no longer a serious threat after the battle of Lepanto in 1571.

How one interprets these references is a question of perspective. One scholar regards the Granadine festivals of Moors and Christians as a monument to the martyrs of the Alpujarra. Another, more sympathetic to the Moriscos, quotes with approval the title given to the Júviles performance by the mailman who plays the part of the Christian general there. He calls it simply, "the tragedy of the Moors."[12] Pedro Gómez García believes that the *moros y cristianos* of the Alpujarra reflect "the guilty conscience" of those whose ancestors moved in when the Moriscos were driven out. Now, he argues, their descendants deal with "the trauma of the war of conquest and their remorse over the foundational violence" that cleared the way for their own possession of the land by annually reenacting Morisco hostility and the threat of Turkish invasion. Only thus, he says, can they justify in their own minds the historical slaughter and deportation of the Moriscos.[13]

I am not so sure. In neither of the Andalusian *moros y cristianos* that I attended in June 1996—in Carboneras (Almería) on the coast and in Trevelez (Granada) in the high mountains—did I sense any troubled conscience. The festive atmosphere and the structure of the narratives seemed to me to celebrate a fictive *convivencia* rather than to justify a historical slaughter. In Carboneras, although Moors and Christians fought over the old castle in the center of town, they spent much more time carrying the image of the town's patron, Saint Anthony, to and from the church, and were united in a genuine devotion to the saint. After the final battle was won by the Christians, the opposing generals hugged and called each other "brothers." The next morning, Christian and Moorish flags flew alongside one another on the castle ramparts. In Trevelez, too, Moors and Christians joined in a common devotion to the patronal Virgin of the Snows and to Saint Anthony, whose feast day had just passed. After the final battle, represented by a shuffling sword dance, both images were carried through the steep, cobbled streets of the village's three barrios, in a long and winding procession that was punctuated by deafening fireworks and periodically saluted by Moors and Christians together on horseback. In nearby Válor, where the best known of the Alpujarran *moros y cristianos* is performed each September, the text ends with the Moorish king telling his Christian counterpart, "Yesterday you were my enemy, / Today you will be my affectionate brother."[14]

Gómez García denounces such closing conversions as "false," arguing that they are guilty of rewriting history "in order to cover up intolerance and the annihilation of a foreign culture."[15] Again, I disagree. It seems to me that the nature of the Spanish folk festivals of Moors and Christians is not to reenact history but to embody a vision of what might have been and what might yet be. The performers do not believe that historical battles between Moors and Christians ended with conversion and fraternity, but they may well wish that it had been so. And they may wish, too, that human relationships now could be less conflicted and more able to encompass difference without hostility. I am persuaded that Spain's festivals of Moors and Christians, by rewriting the country's most prolonged ethnic conflict so that it ends not in exile but in reconciliation, express that yearning. Christian faith proclaims, as the priest at the fiesta mass in Trevelez told his congregation in 1996, that "in Christ we can all be brothers." Non-Christians may resent the condition of this claim. But, unless I am mistaken, it is the vision to which the Andalusian festivals of Moors and Christians aspire. Whether in Jaén in 1462, Granada in 1561, or the province's small towns and villages today, the fiestas deliberately revise history, not to deny its pain or to conceal its guilt, but to envision a better outcome.

The same is only partially true of a series of mock battles that took place in Alcalá de los Gazules and Tarifa in the late summer of 1571. There, the longing for a better outcome seems to have gone hand in hand with a specific denial of ancestral guilt. One hundred and fifty miles southwest of Granada, Tarifa faces Morocco across the Strait of Gibraltar, while Alcalá is thirty-five miles inland. Like the festivities in Granada ten years earlier, those in Alcalá and Tarifa honored powerful nobility. Per Afán Enríquez de Ribera was duke of Alcalá and marquis of Tarifa. His brother and heir, Fernando, who shared the title of duke but not that of marquis, was married to Juana Cortés, the youngest daughter of Hernán Cortés. Juana had been born in Cuernavaca in 1536 and returned to Spain some time before her marriage in 1564. In 1571, less than a year after the Morisco Revolt had reached its bitter conclusion, and as John of Austria was leading a Christian navy toward its decisive encounter with the Turks at Lepanto, the two dukes were honored in a festive progress from Alcalá to Tarifa.

Among the entertainments were a dramatization of the conquest of Mexico, a scripted *juego de cañas,* several Moorish ambushes, and a skirmish on the beach in Tarifa. Surprisingly, none of the mock battles made reference to the Morisco Revolt or to the massing of rival navies in the eastern Mediterranean. Perhaps in this instance all politics really was local. Alcalá and Tarifa had been free of Moorish rule since 1264 and 1292 respectively, and although Tarifa had fought off subsequent attacks as late as 1340, the region was not implicated in the Morisco Revolt. Nor did members of its ruling family fight at Lepanto. Of more immediate concern were the threat posed by Moroccan corsairs and the diminished reputation of Juana's father. An unsigned letter, written in Tarifa on Sunday, 7 October 1571, describes the festivities. Intriguingly, if the letter was written on the final day of the celebrations, the skirmish on the shore at Tarifa and the battle of Lepanto were taking place at the same time.[16]

The members of the ducal family were awoken from their afternoon siesta in Alcalá by noise in the square outside the palace. From the windows, they saw "twenty well-dressed horsemen," who, "to the music of flutes and Italian trumpets," were galloping back and forth across the square trying to decapitate geese that had been strung up on a cord stretched across the square. This was, the letter assures us, an "equestrian game" that required "much dexterity and strength" and provided "considerable amusement for those who watched." Probably, the birds' necks were greased and the horsemen used their bare hands. The sport continued until after dark.

Then, a minstrel appeared, singing about the capture of Motecuzoma and introducing a masquerade on the same subject. "There were more than two hundred men in the corner of the palace square, dressed in costumes and head-dresses to look like Indians." In the same place, there was a "well-painted tent that represented the house of Motecuzoma." Inside were the Mexica emperor and "his crowned chieftains." After an ambassador had come from Cortés, delivering many demands and returning with many replies, all of which failed to produce a pacific surrender, Cortés arrived with "eight horses and some soldiers." If the represented Spanish army was in fact as small as it sounds, it may have been because Cortés's Tlaxcalan allies were conveniently erased from the dramatic narrative in order to maximize Cortés's heroism against the odds and to portray him as aggrieved ambassador rather than militant aggressor.

Shortly afterward, "a great multitude of Indians came out, with Motecuzoma and his chieftains," to attack the Spaniards. In the ensuing battle, "sometimes the Indians retreated and at other times the Christians, with loud cries and shouts from the Indians, until some of the Christians fired their artillery," which "put such fear into the Indians that they were confounded and Motecuzoma was captured and hauled up on the haunches of the marquis's horse." The marquis in question was the represented marqués del Valle, Hernán Cortés, rather than the watching marquis of Tarifa. Finally, twenty horsemen, perhaps including Cortés and his captive emperor, galloped up and down in front of the palace, wearing fine masks and carrying torches.

Although one might expect festivals of Moors and Christians in Spain to have been routinely adapted to dramatize the conquest of Mexico, I know of no other instance. It seems probable, therefore, that the idea for the Alcalá performance came from sixteenth-century Mexican precedents. Juana Cortés had been in Mexico when her father led the Christian troops, some of them played by Spanish caballeros but the majority by Indians on foot, in the *Conquest of Rhodes*. Although she would have been too young to remember it and may, in any case, have been at the family home in Cuernavaca, she would probably have heard of it from her father. She may also have heard of the Tlaxcalteca armies that took part in the *Conquest of Jerusalem*. Surely she learned from her brother Martín, after his enforced return to Spain in 1566, of his role in the masquerade of Cortés and Motecuzoma in Mexico City the previous year. Juana would have been familiar with the kinds of costumes and head-dresses that Mexica warriors had worn into battle and still wore in postconquest plays and dances. Possibly, she (or someone in her retinue equally familiar with Mexico) advised those responsible for the masquerade in matters of costume, head-dress, and makeup. Maybe she even loaned souvenirs of her birthplace to those playing Motecuzoma and his court. In all likelihood, both the theme of this mock battle and details of its staging were imported from Mexico.

The next day, after a Te Deum at the church and a running of bulls in the square, there was a scripted *juego de cañas,* similar to the one staged for Miguel Lucas in Jaén in 1462. Twelve Christian horsemen, divided into three groups according to the color of their gowns, gathered at the entrance to the square. Another horseman, dressed in Moorish costume and accompanied by two Moorish grooms, rode across the square to the Christian knights with a letter from the governor of Tetouan. The letter was read aloud: "Mawlay Muhammed, governor of Tetouan and Chechaouen, subject of the Sharif, king of Fez and of Morocco, to the lord high governor of Alcalá de los Gazules. In the name of God, greetings. From some of my raider scouts I have learned that the most excellent dukes of this town are in residence and that your honor and other Christian knights are mounting many festivities. Because of the kindness that your Excellency showed me when I was your prisoner, I wanted to serve you in these fiestas. . . . " Tetouan is a port on the Moroccan peninsula that had recently launched several attacks on Spanish shipping and coastal towns. Muhammed Bureddan, designated here by the honorific *mawlay* (my master) and his personal name, became its governor after a local revolt in 1567 and remained in office until his death in 1591.[17] I have been unable to trace any corroborative evidence of his capture and kind treatment by the duke of Alcalá. It may have happened as the letter claims or, like his desire to express gratitude by taking part in the dukes' festive celebrations, it may have been a dramatic fiction.

It is possible that a narrative link was intended between the previously enacted capture of Motecuzoma and the now claimed captivity of Mawlay Muhammed. The marqués del Valle had captured the former; the marquis of Tarifa had captured the latter. One hero was related to the other by marriage. A certain dramatic kinship between the two marquises and, therefore, between Motecuzoma and the *mawlay* could hardly be avoided. Perhaps it was being suggested that Cortés, like Per Afan, had treated his hostage well and that, had it not been for Alvarado's brutality and the death of Motecuzoma in the confusion that preceded the night of sorrows, Cortés might have won the peaceful resolution of the Mexican invasion that he wanted. It would have been consistent with the impulse of the Spanish *moros y cristianos* toward *convivencia* rather than elimination to have expressed here a wish that the conquest of Mexico had ended not in the destruction of Tenochtitlan but in chivalric coexistence under Spanish Christian rule. Such an interpretation would also be consistent with the *Capture of Motecuzoma*'s probable portrayal of Cortés as aggrieved rather than aggressor. And it would have pleased Juana Cortés to see her father's reputation, which had suffered since his early years in Mexico, implicitly reclaimed. Whatever the purpose of the reference to Mawlay Muhammed's captivity, his offer to honor the dukes of Alcalá by taking part in their festivities was well received. The Moorish ambassador left the square, yielding to twelve horsemen dressed in

Moorish costumes and armed with lances and shields. Moors and Christians joined in a *juego de cañas* that lasted "just under an hour."

The next day, the ducal families left Alcalá for Tarifa, escorted by armed men who defended them against troops of "imitation Moors" who came out of villages along the way. Arriving safely in Tarifa, the dukes were met by large crowds, profusely decorated streets, triumphal arches, and loud salvos. The following Sunday, they watched from their castle as a "varied festival of canes and skirmishes" unfolded on the shore. The mock battles ended with "the taking of a daughter of the governor of Tetouan" and her presentation "in captivity to the duchess." I assume the recipient to have been Juana Cortés, wife of the younger duke, and that another link was being forged between the conquest of Mexico and the conquest of the Moors, for it was surely not accidental that the daughter of the *mawlay* was presented to the daughter of Cortés. Perhaps the gift and its reception was intended to reinforce the idea that the Cortés family treated their prisoners well.[18]

If these links were indeed part of the overall festive design, then the mock battles against the Tetouan Moors constitute a rare instance of Spanish festivals of Moors and Christians being used to render implicit comment on the conquest of Mexico. Although this was comparatively common in Mexico, it was not so in Spain, perhaps because the indigenous vision of reconquest in Mexico had a much wider appeal than the family claim in Alcalá that Cortés had sought peace and been kind to his captive emperor. If such links were not intended, the Alcalá *Capture of Motecuzoma* is still the only large-scale Spanish mock battle that borrowed its theme and its most striking visual details from the New World. In this respect, it was, as Warman observes, "extraordinary."[19]

Although individual squadrons in Spanish festivals of Moors and Christians may still dress as Indians, I know of no other instance of a large-scale Spanish *moros y cristianos* being given over entirely to a Mexican theme. It is not, therefore, in the festivals of Moors and Christians that we can trace any sustained Mexican influence on Spanish folk theater. The dances may be another story. But before we look at these, we will travel one last time with Philip II, enjoying the royal entries and entertainments that greeted him during his tour of Aragon, Catalonia, and Valencia between January 1585 and March 1586. We will thereby gain an idea of where matters stood with the Spanish tradition of *moros y cristianos* at the end of the sixteenth century. And by visiting a modern Valencian descendant of the tradition, we will gain a sense of how the tradition has developed since the sixteenth century.

23

Changing Tastes (Daroca to Valencia, 1585–1586)

ON 19 January 1585, Philip II set out on a royal tour of eastern Spain that lasted fourteen months.[1] Along the way, he attended his daughter's wedding, presided over a meeting of the Cortes (legislative assembly) of Aragon, and was entertained by lavish festivities that, in his late middle age, he was beginning to find tiresome. A record of Philip's journey was kept by a notary and archer of his Flemish guard, Enrique Cock. Trekking at first through "rain, hail, snow, and fierce winds," the party made slow progress and encountered little entertainment.

On Sunday, 19 February, the citizens of Daroca (Zaragoza) ran some bulls through the streets and "represented a Saint George killing a huge dragon, which threw flames and fire from its mouth and nostrils." They also performed twice "the mystery of the most holy corporals," corporals being the linen cloths on which the elements of the mass are laid. The play told the story of a battle between Moors and Christians near Xàtiva (Valencia) on 24 February 1239. The besieged Christians chose five captains to take communion together "on behalf of all the army," but the priest was unable to administer the sacrament before the Moors attacked. He wrapped the consecrated wafers in the corporals and hid them beneath a flagstone. After a rousing Christian victory, he was startled to discover that the bread had changed into real flesh and blood, staining the corporals. Faced with a dispute as to where the sanctified linen should be kept, the priest placed it in a wooden box, which he loaded on a mule. Unprompted, the mule walked to Daroca. The corporals, their holy stains still visible, have stayed in the city ever since, the story of their miraculous origin being remembered annually during the feast of Corpus Christi. The late-sixteenth-century play may have been performed not only at Corpus Christi but also on the feast of St. Matthew (24 February) and, in this instance, a few days earlier for the royal visit.[2]

Unfortunately, Cock tells us nothing of the form of the "*misterio* [miracle play]." Its generic designation and the lack of any mention of gunfire, which Cock is usually quick to record, suggest something quieter than the rowdy festivals of Moors and Christians. But it is unlikely that the battle would have been confined to verse, in the decorous manner of later neoclassical tragedy, rather than actually fought. Perhaps it was represented by a sword dance. If the *Misterio de los Santos Corporales* did include a mock battle of some sort, it would be one of the first recorded instances of an annual, rather than an occasional, mock battle between Moors and Christians.

The royal party arrived in Zaragoza five days later. Crowds lined the streets and hung from windows while musicians played on special platforms. That night, forty-eight horsemen, divided into four squadrons, rode up and down in front of the royal palace, "imitating the manners and ceremonies of the Moors." Afterward, two bulls with fireworks tied to their horns were released, driving the crowds from the streets. An auto-da-fé on the 27th paraded representatives of the city's confraternities, friars carrying boxes of relics, and several people condemned by the Inquisition for retaining Moorish or Jewish practices. Carnival, at the beginning of March, was fairly restrained: masked figures roamed the streets, and young men threw eggs full of colored water at young women on balconies. Philip's younger daughter, Catalina, was married on 11 March to the duke of Savoy. The celebrations included a *juego de cañas* and, despite the almost constant rain that caused its postponement for several days, a tournament. The party visited monasteries and churches in the area, including the chapel of Our Lady of the Pillar. Little of theatrical interest took place during the five weeks the king spent in Zaragoza, a remarkable contrast with the spectacular royal entries and weddings of the mid–sixteenth century.[3]

On 2 April, the royal entourage set out for Barcelona, visiting Lleida, Tarragona, and the monastery of Poblet en route. In Hospitalet, on the outskirts of Barcelona, the villagers celebrated the first of May by "raising a very tall pine decorated with flowers and oranges and dedicating it to his Majesty."[4] Philip refused the honor of a royal entry to Barcelona, pleading the ill health of many of his party and the private nature of his visit to bid good-bye to the newlyweds as they sailed for Italy. Once safely lodged, Philip reluctantly permitted subsequent festivities. On the evening of 8 May, "the sky was covered with the smoke of artillery fire while almost everyone covered their ears," the streets were lit with bonfires, and musicians played.

On Saturday, 11 May, a procession wound through the city streets, watched from the palace by the king and his family. At the head of the procession were men "dressed as devils" fighting "two dragons." Saint Michael appears to have disappeared from or gone unnoticed in this traditional Corpus Christi pageant, leaving the impression that the devils and dragons were at war with one another. Another familiar Corpus Christi *entremès* followed: "twenty-two knights on artificial horses" that "jumped and galloped" and, when signaled by a trumpet, charged into battle. The riders' feet were hidden by cloths that reached the ground, while artificial legs and feet, wearing spurs, hung down on either side. Cock makes no mention of Turks on foot, which may mean that the Turkish infantry of the Saint Sebastian pageant had become cavalry, as the *Auca de la processó* of 1805 portrays them, and were indistinguishable, to Cock's casual eye, from the Christian hobby horses they fought. Over sixty confraternities followed, some carrying images of saints and others with "inventions": "a dragon scattering fire and smoke"; "a very lifelike pelican"; and "a camel," kin perhaps to the giant skirted camel that Philip had seen in Brussels in 1549. Clergy, crosses, relics, and "twenty-four angels, their wings extended, playing various instruments," completed the procession.

On 16 May, Italian galleys arrived in port with such an exchange of friendly artillery fire between ship and shore that "one could see nothing but smoke." On 2 June, an engineer in the duke of Savoy's employ staged a fireworks display, but one of the fireworks landed on the neck of the new duchess, almost setting her ruffs on fire. The duke was outraged. A week later, the pardoned engineer arranged a more elaborate display. Two wagons shot at one another from iron tubes full of little holes that spurted fire. Another two supported spinning wheels, full of fireworks, mounted on high poles. Four "castles" were ignited. On the top of one was a fire-breathing pelican. On another was a woman surrounded by snakes (Cock counted fifty-three mouths spouting fire). The third supported a pyramid on which was painted a globe. And the fourth, in deference to the newlyweds, displayed a Cupid with bow in hand. The show, which crackled like a veritable barrage of arquebus fire, lasted until midnight. On 13 June, the duke of Savoy and his bride sailed for Italy.[5]

From Barcelona, the royal party set out for the meeting of the Cortes in Monzón. On the way, the king passed through Igualada, where on 20 June he watched the Corpus Christi procession. In a letter to Catalina, he remarks only that it was "very short."[6] In the fall, a severe epidemic broke out, claiming hundreds of lives. Cock himself fell ill, and the king was so sick that the realms of Aragon, Catalonia, and Valencia swore an oath of loyalty to his heir, the future Philip III. But the king (and Cock) recovered, and in December the royal party moved on to Tortosa. The salvos of artillery that greeted them were so loud "that all the fish in the Ebro went away to sea and didn't dare return until the king left Tortosa." Or at least, Cock adds rather sourly, one couldn't buy fish anywhere, but this may have been because the fishermen were on holiday or the city council would just as soon the king leave quickly. Confraternities danced outside the royal residence on 20 December to the music of flute, tabor, and "other paltry instruments." (The fever seems to have left Cock a little grumpy!) Members of the ploughmen's guild carried a "green house, interwoven with branches, on their shoulders," and brought with them a silver-plated plough drawn by two hardy asses, a spectacle that gave Cock "much to laugh about." They also performed "a very good dance." Another confraternity brought several "well-made blacks [*negrillos*]," who stood on other men's shoulders and made the crowd laugh by sticking out their tongues and throwing figs. Yet another group came with "dancing giants." In fact, so many were the dances that a nearby wall, loosened by the perpetual stamping of feet, collapsed, plunging spectators into the river.

The next day, the guilds staged a mock battle between Moors and Christians. A wooden tower, painted on all sides, was erected on the riverbank facing the palace. Moors, played very capably by the fishermen's guild, defended the tower while Christians attacked it with much gunfire by water and by land. At times the two sides joined in hand-to-hand fighting. By evening, the tower was destroyed and the Moors defeated. The Christians led their conquered foes in triumph through the palace gates. On the day after Christmas, another procession passed before the palace windows, led again by "devils and a fire-breathing dragon." A "dance of Moriscos" followed. The *negrillos* and the dancing giants of the earlier procession also reappeared, as did the images of saints, the clergy, the relics, the crosses, and the crowds. Finally, on 30 December, the fishermen organized a mock joust on the river, in which combatants in boats exchanged blows until the loser fell in the water.[7]

The festivities in Tortosa were a world apart from those that had greeted Philip on his journey through Italy and the Netherlands in 1549. Neither professional artists nor tight civic control were at work in Tortosa. Philip was losing interest in pomp and ceremony, and the guilds were, it seems, allowed a free reign in designing the festivities. Gone are the classical references and the alternately flattering and moralistic verses. In their place are dances and mock battles that appeal more to the folk performers than to their royal audience. It may be, if Cock's sense of Tortosa's ambivalence toward Philip's visit is correct, that the festivities in Tortosa concealed some discreet dissent, but Cock's account gives us too little to go on. I cannot help wondering, though, what was intended by the storming of the palace gates by the victorious Christians.

From Tortosa, Philip headed south along the coast to Valencia. The villagers of San Mateo took time off work to mark the arrival of the king with "dances and other public spectacles." The citizens of Castellón de la Plana erected a folk version of a triumphal arch, woven together with "ivy, oranges, foliage, and various flowers," and flowing with "three fountains of wine for all who passed by to quench their thirst."[8] Philip entered Valencia on 19 January. After passing through a triumphal arch that compared the military triumphs of his own reign to those of such heroes as El Cid and Jaume I, he saw a series of restrained reenactments of his victories. Six miniature galleys flew through the air on ropes to attack a replica of the rocky fortress of Vélez de la Gomera, on the north African coast, captured by the Spanish fleet in 1564. Six painted Moors marveled at their defeat. Plans had called for "twenty-five or thirty men dressed as Turks" to defend the fort with artillery fire, but Philip, fearing accidents in such a large crowd, had asked that gunpowder not be used. A little further on, "a large platform" supported a dozen or more galleys, each about three and a half feet long, that represented the battle of Lepanto. The ban on explosives was not enough to prevent mishap: part of the stage collapsed, plunging ships and tackle into the abyss. The king, we are told, graciously applauded the realism of the shipwreck. A third scaffold represented Philip's defeat of the French at St. Quentin in 1557. Finally, "six ships and two galleys" enacted the relief of Malta in 1565. The play's large scenic hill had originally been intended to represent the island of Terceira, in the Azores, whose resistance to Philip's claim on the Portuguese throne had been suppressed in 1583. To avoid offense to the king's new Portuguese subjects, the historical referent had been changed. Moreover, because of Philip's insistence that gunpowder not be used, the battle was "mimed, without any martial noise." This prohibition, indicative of the growing gap between royal and popular taste, was happily lifted a few nights later, when "all the mock battles were staged realistically." There is no indication that the king was present.[9]

Little else in the way of theatrical entertainment was offered the king during his stay in Valencia. For the most part, he preferred to stay indoors, venturing out only to visit the city's monasteries and to attend mass. On 3 February, Philip and his son appeared on the royal balcony to watch a series of tableaux rolled past by Valencia's confraternities. The fishermen's guild pulled a wheeled ship on which they portrayed the piscatory disciples, Peter, Andrew, and John, casting their nets into the sea. Another guild, venturing into more political waters, "represented on a triumphal car what happened in Monzón when the oath of loyalty was taken to the prince." The portrait seems to have been satirical rather than sympathetic, for Cock comments with distaste, "This comic spectacle seemed ridiculous and unworthy to be represented before the royal majesty."[10] Once again, Cock's account suggests traces of a hidden transcript. Philip left for Madrid on the 27th.

Festivals of Moors and Christians, as Warman puts it, "began their slow decline" after the death of Philip II in 1598. This decline was not so much a loss of popularity as a loss of social status, a "sinking through the varying strata of society," to use Rodney Gallop's description of the transformation of aristocratic culture into folk culture. In the first half of the seventeenth century, there is no record of a *moros y cristianos* being staged for Spanish royalty or of court nobility taking part in one. Tastes were changing. A more fastidious court began to prefer exclusive entertainment, within the palace walls and away from popular crowds.[11] But festivals of Moors and Christians were beginning to put down popular roots along the Valencian coast and inland mountains. A significant impetus may have been the formation, in the second half of the sixteenth century, of local militias, armed with arquebuses and given the task of guarding the coast against Turkish sailors and Berber pirates. In the absence of enemy troops, the militias staged mock battles between Moors and Christians, much as the fishermen of Tortosa had done for Philip II in 1568, and began to accompany the annual procession of the town's patron saint. It was the conjunction of costumed militia, the once courtly tradition of mock battles between Moors and Christians, and the popular *fiesta del patrón* that gave rise to the annual festivals of Moors and Christians in Valencia.

Intermittent references to the use of gunpowder during the procession of the patron saint and to skirmishes between Moors and Christians later in the day can be found in Alcoy (Alicante), the site of the oldest annual festival of Moors and Christians, from 1638 onward. By 1741, there is clear evidence of an annual mix of religious processions and mock battles.[12] From Alcoy the practice spread throughout the province, expanding considerably in both scale and geographical distribution during the period of industrialization and economic prosperity in the second third of the nineteenth century. Far from being threatened by modernization, the Valencian festivals of Moors and Christians are more popular today than at any time in their history. This is due, at least in part, to their capacity to host hidden transcripts.

In September 1992, I saw the fiestas in Villena (Alicante), second only to those of Alcoy in size and reputation.[13] At noon on 5 September, the mayor pronounced the fiestas open, a barrage of fireworks exploded over the main square, arquebuses sent clouds of smoke into the air, and the banners of the several *comparsas* (companies) of Moors and Christians swirled furiously. Late in the afternoon, the "grand entry of the companies of Moors and Christians" began. This was a parade of all the costumed *comparsistas,* most on foot, some on horseback, and three that year on live camels. There were seven companies of Moors and seven companies of Christians. The former, with one exception (Pirates), were all named Moors (Old Moors, New Moors, Moroccan Moors, and so on). But only one company of Christians was called *cristianos.* The rest seemed to distance themselves from their official religious affiliation, adopting such names as Corsairs and Andalusians. Despite the even division of companies, the Moors greatly outnumbered the Christians. "To be a Moor," remarks one observer, is "considered more desirable than to be a Christian."[14]

The *festeros* (those who take part in the fiestas) ordinarily explain this preference in terms of aesthetics: the Moors have the more spectacular costumes and the more stirring music. But one *festero* offered me a different explanation. There are two battles between Moors and Christians, the Moors winning the first and the Christians the second. While this reflects the historical order of Moorish conquest and Christian reconquest, it also means that the Moors rule over the "real world" of the fiestas.[15]

Their festive reign represents the temporary resurgence of all that is suppressed but cannot finally be expelled by church and state. "The Moors are not just a symbol," said one of my friends in Villena. "They are something in us. Look at our faces. Many are Moorish." Moreover, in the popular imagination, the Moors represent

25. Moorish women. Villena, 1992.

those "sensual" aspects of human nature that the Church condemns but cannot finally expel. "The Moors," I was told by the *festeros,* "are not bad." For "Moors," I read "we."

Each *comparsa* included several squadrons dressed in more expensive costumes, led by "corporals" who strutted in front, brandishing swords or scimitars and appealing to the crowd for applause. The Moorish women, in their luxuriant costumes, suggested the world of the harem (Fig. 25). Some of the female "corporals" brandished long whips. Many of the men smoked cigars. Brass and percussion bands played *pasadobles* for the Christians and *marchas moros* for the Moors. As the parade took five and a half exhilarating hours to pass, it occurred to me that, whatever their costumes, all the *festeros* were, in one sense, "Moors." "We are all Moors," one of my friends admitted later. The real Christians were bringing the Virgin to town.

For most of the year, the statue of Our Lady of the Virtues, Villena's *patrona,* resides in a chapel three miles west of town. Because of her dark complexion, she is known affectionately as *la morenica* (the little dark one). That morning, while crowds had gathered in the main square of Villena, a smaller assembly of the faithful had honored *la morenica* at a mass in her chapel. In the early evening, while the parade of Moors and Christians was in full swing, she had been hoisted onto the shoulders of her bearers and, accompanied by pilgrims carrying candles and singing hymns, had begun her procession to town. When the last of the *comparsas* had reached the intersection of Villena's main street and the chapel road, the procession of the Virgin arrived. As the two worlds met, the image of the Virgin was greeted by a sustained burst of gunfire and a swirling of flags. She was then escorted back down the parade route by the *comparsas*, each led by a group of arquebusiers who fired their guns repeatedly. Officially, the Virgin was being honored by this reception, but it could also be read as a display of resistance to and retreat before the intrusion of the religious world into that of the secular fiesta. Around midnight, the Virgin reached the parish church of Santiago in the main square across from the town hall. The church was packed with worshipers, who applauded when the Virgin entered. The costumed *festeros,* for the most part, remained outside. The Virgin was carried twice around the church and each time she passed the south door there was a barrage of gunfire from the square outside. Finally she was enthroned above the altar on a graduated series of pedestals that, propelled by hidden levers and pulleys, rose slowly into the air as candles on each level slid in front. A priest called out, "¡Viva la Virgen! ¡Viva la morenica!" The congregation shouted, "¡Viva!"

The first assault on the castle began late the next afternoon. The Christians led the parade from the main square to the old Moorish castle that overlooks the town. The Moors followed. Along the way, musicians gave way to arquebusiers, bands to gunfire. Once the Christian captains and gunners were ensconced inside the castle, the Moorish ambassador approached the gate on horseback, demanding a Christian surrender and offering a large measure of autonomy and *convivencia* in return for the payment of taxes. When the Christian ambassador refused, gunfire exploded on the castle walls and in the square outside. For ten minutes, the air was filled with noise and with smoke that in the end almost hid the castle from view. Finally the guns quieted, the defeated Christians marched out, and the image of Muhammed was placed on top of the battlements.

There was clearly a correspondence between the image of Muhammed and that of the Virgin. The Virgin had been carried to the parish church and enthroned above the altar, where she presided over the religious fiesta. Muhammed had been carried to the castle and enthroned on the battlements, where he ruled over the secular fiesta. *Mahoma* (Muhammed) is usually a masculine noun, but here it was given a feminine article: *la mahoma.* "It's easier to say that way," I was told, but it seemed to me to be another link between *la mahoma* and *la morenica. La mahoma* claimed pre-eminence: The image of Muhammed was larger than that of the Virgin, and the hilltop castle is considerably higher than the spire of the parish church. When, after midnight, the *comparsas* again paraded along the main street, the Virgin remained in church. The *festeros* ruled the streets.

The next night the secular fiesta tested the limits of its license. The *retreta* (retreat to barracks) was a carnivalesque parade in which local and national governments, the Barcelona Olympics, the Columbus Quincentennial, and the *comparsas*

26. The *retreta*. Villena, 1992.

themselves were mocked. Men dressed as women (Fig. 26), members of Christian companies dressed as Moors and burlesqued the Moorish swagger and bravado, humans dressed as animals, men stuffed *mahoma* dolls between their legs, and, despite the official prohibition on "disguise," many faces were hidden behind masks. This carnival revelry seemed to signal imminent disintegration, the danger of moral collapse should the world ruled by Muhammed not be restrained by the world of the Virgin.

At noon on the final day, therefore, the second assault on the castle took place (Fig. 27). This time, after further posturing by ambassadors and noisy firing of arquebuses, the Christians won. Muhammed was taken down from the battlements and carried to the headquarters of the Old Moors. One of my friends remarked wistfully before the battle, "If one year *la mahoma* should win, we'd have to eat and

27. Christian assault on the castle. Villena, 1992.

drink and have fiesta for 365 days!" That evening, in the Church of Santiago, one of the Moorish corporals professed faith in the Virgin and was baptized. All the Moors were implicitly converted in this act, signaling the incorporation of Moorish heritage into Spanish society and, more immediately, the reincorporation of the *festeros* into the world that is not fiesta. "It is," as one of my friends in Villena put it, "an act of forgiveness for everything done during the fiestas." *Convivencia* thus embraced both the ancestral ethnic other and the suppressed "sensual" other within oneself. An integrated squadron of Moors and Christians led a procession of all the *comparsistas* past the image of the Virgin in the church. There were some striking juxtapositions: converted Moorish warriors, still dressed for battle, marched through a Christian church (Fig. 28); women dressed as Moorish odalisques filed past the image and the banner of the Virgin. There was an almost palpable sense of relief among the worshipers in the church that the excesses of the fiesta were over and that the streets were now safe for the Virgin. For four hours the Virgin presided over this homage of the *comparsistas* before she, too, was taken from her throne and, surrounded by hundreds of soberly dressed pilgrims bearing candles, followed the *comparsistas* through the streets. Passing through every church along her way, she returned to the Church of Santiago long after midnight.

The next morning the Virgin was escorted to the edge of town and, with one last burst of gunfire and swirling of flags, seen out of town. From a religious perspective, she had rescued the town from the forces that threatened its destruction

28. Converted Moorish warriors leave the church. Villena, 1992.

and could now safely return to her chapel. But the *festeros* might argue that it was her visit that had sanctioned the sensual excesses of the fiestas, and they could take comfort in the knowledge that she would do so again next year. Three hours later, the Virgin and her pilgrims arrived at the packed chapel, where the conversion of the Moor was repeated. That evening, in Villena, there was a final parade of all the *comparsas* during which only *pasadobles* were played. There were no Moorish marches, for all, despite their still distinct costumes, were now Christians. The "real world" of the fiesta was over. The Moors and all for which they stand in the popular imagination had been allowed an honored space in the life of the community. It was a space that both challenged and was bound by the world of the church. But within that space, for several days, there had been staged the simultaneous tensions and mutual accommodations of *convivencia*.

24
Gilded Indians (1521–1600)

AMONG the triumphal floats that greeted Anne of Austria as she entered Burgos in October 1570 was one on which twelve *matachines* performed "acrobatics and feats of strength."[1] In the same year, a dance of *matachines* appeared in a civic procession in Seville.[2] As we return to the matter of mutual influence between Spanish and Mexican mock battles, concentrating now on dances rather than festivals, we face a deceptively simple question that illustrates very well the difficulty of definitive answers. What, if any, is the relationship between European and American *matachines*? The European *matachines*, who flourished from the mid-sixteenth to the early eighteenth centuries, are variously described as masked "buffoons" or sword dancers. They are generally believed to have originated in Italy.[3] The American *matachines* are widely distributed in northern Mexico and the southwestern United States. I have seen the dance performed in northern New Mexico, where it tells the story of Motecuzoma, and in Zacatecas, where it was described to me as mimetic preparation for human sacrifice.[4]

Most scholars assume that the dance traveled from Spain to Mexico and thence to the southwestern United States. J. D. Robb argued this case on several grounds. In New Mexico, the dance is popular in both Hispanic and Native American pueblos; the musical accompaniment is usually played on Spanish fiddle and guitar; Indian men dance traditional dances with bare torsos and legs, but perform the *matachines* dance fully clothed; and the Indians generally permit photography of the *matachines* but not of such unquestionably indigenous dances as the Corn Dance. Although none of these observations apply in Zacatecas, they have been assumed by subsequent scholars to "prove" that the American *matachines* dance "comes from Europe."[5] A few scholars have granted that the dance "acquired some Indian characteristics" along the way or that "native elements, perhaps entire native dances" may be "hidden under the European veneer."[6]

Many Native American performers claim that the dance has indigenous roots. Older New Mexicans believed that it was "an Aztec dance offered by Motecuzoma to the Spanish at Cortés's conquest in 1519."[7] Taking these claims seriously, Treviño and Gilles suggest that it may derive from a type of *netotelixtli* dance, known as a *matlatzincayotl*, in which the Mexica celebrated their victory over the people of Matlatzinco. The Matlatzinca, they add, "were noted for their physical strength and for their agility as displayed in acrobatic dances." These traits of the defeated enemy may then have been incorporated, in characteristic Mexica fashion, into the battle dance that remembered their defeat. Treviño and Gilles suggest, too, that a version of the Mexican *matachines* may have traveled to Europe, shortly after the conquest, and there given rise to its European namesake.[8]

I have written elsewhere in this book of the American *danza de los matachines*. In this chapter, I will restrict myself to the European side of the story, setting the first descriptions of *matachines* in Europe against the general background of a discernible influence of indigenous American dance traditions in Europe. The first recorded Native American performance in Europe, noted by Pietro Martire, was the polished demonstration offered by a Mexica slave to a private Italian audience in Seville in 1522.[9] Since this performance included many of the component parts of a *netotelixtli* dance (mimetic combat, mock sacrifice, elegant dance, homage to the Mexica ruler, indigenous song, and the comic relief of drunken buffoonery), it may well have been a scaled-down version of just the kind of pre-Hispanic dance that Treviño and Gilles find at the beginning of their history of the *matachines*. Moreover, the audience of Italian travelers might explain why, if one were to accept the theory of a Mexican origin of the European *matachines,* the term first appears in Italy rather than, as one might expect, in Spain.

Other Native American performers followed. Some may have described themselves as *matlatzinca,* either because of ethnic origin or because of the name of their dance. Two of the Indians who arrived with Cortés in 1528 (Francisco de Alvarado Matlacchuatzin and Benito Matatlaqueny) had names that could easily be Italianized as *mattaccini*. Intriguingly, the latter is the only Indian whom we can identify as being in Rome near the time of the papal performance in April 1529. Benito Matatlaqueny traveled to Rome some time before late May of that year and returned to Seville on 27 July.[10] Could it be that Matatlaqueny was one of the foot jugglers and acrobatic dancers who performed before the pope and that it was he who lent his Italianized name to the European *mattaccini?*

Nor was it long before Europeans imitated Indians. Lynn Brooks observes, "There was constant population exchange and travel between the New World, Africa, and Spain, including the transporting of 'savages' and 'Indians' back home for show, where their costumes and dances were the cause of wonder and interest. The love of novelty, which Spanish theater of this period demonstrated, made these imports prime sources from which to appropriate innovations in themes, movements, rhythms, and costumes. . . . In this way, the dance compositions, presented at court, in the theater, and in public festivals" easily incorporated new material from overseas.[11]

It is in this context that we first begin to read about the European *matachines*. Despite the casual assumption of some who favor the European origin of the dance that the *matachines* were already active "in the Middle Ages,"[12] the first verifiable use of the word is in an Italian carnival song, probably written in Florence between

1530 and 1550. Piero da Volterra's *Canzona de' Mattaccini* portrays the *mattaccini* as lively fools, whose dance involves exaggerated (and sometimes obscene) postures, pratfalls and body blows, and dubious claims of agility and youthful sexual prowess. "We are *mattaccini*," the song begins, "whose aim is to please by showing you all the games that we can do." The second verse speaks of posturing, exchanging kicks and blows to the ear, and finding themselves the wrong way round or face downward. "Every wise and very prudent / *barbaceppo* [fool] or *mattaccino*," the third verse continues, "turns his face and makes a bow." Thus bent over, he "displays his buttocks to you, / which makes him tremble [or, shit] with fear, / because he breaks a prohibition." The fourth verse boasts, "We are all as agile as cats, . . . just need something to hold on to." The next three verses engage in a series of double entendres in which the word *montare* has the same range of connotations as its English equivalent, "to mount." Young men are able to "do what is necessary," because their "flesh" is "alert," whereas an old man "mounts slowly / with anguish and much difficulty." Whether the "earth" is "dry" or "moist," the *mattaccini* "mount tirelessly," because there are always "friendly people" ready to "let them all the way inside." The "weather" can be treacherous, however, and those who, like fools, fearlessly go outside in bad weather, may fall into a latrine and find themselves mocked by others. "We move to the beat of the lute," the final verse announces, "with a dagger, pratfall, or slap, / now with a pinch, now with a scratch, / and stretch ourselves out on the ground; / stretched out, we continue to fight," while trying "to recover by rubbing our limbs."[13]

Da Volterra's song offers no clue to the origin of the *mattaccini*. Tumbling routines, comic battles, and carnivalesque innuendos are popular the world over. Perhaps the simplest solution would be to suppose that *mattaccino* was at first a diminutive of *matto*, meaning "fool," and that the carnival performers had their roots in the same Italian soil that gave rise, at about the same time, to the *commedia dell'arte*.[14] But one can also imagine, without much difficulty, that the carnival *mattaccini* were an Italian parody of scantily clad Mexica performers, who in Weiditz's drawings do indeed display their buttocks (Figs. 17a, b), and "touring Aztec" dancers, who reproduced in miniature the ritual battles of the Mexica calendar festivals. Carnival, after all, ridicules the strange and the exotic as well as the familiar. Moreover, in light of the last line of the song, it is intriguing to recall that one of the key moments in the New Mexico *matachines* comes when an *abuelo* revives Motecuzoma by massaging his legs (Fig. 30).

A few years later, an *intermezzo* (interlude) in the *Rappresentazione di Santa Uliva* involved "four men dressed as *mattaccini*, with bells on their feet and drawn swords in their hands." The stage direction has them enter "with a lot of noise" and adds, "It would be good if they could do two or three movements of a *moresca*." Although

the *sacre rappresentazione* (miracle plays) generally were at the height of their popularity in the second half of the fifteenth century, Vittorio Rossi dates the more elaborate *Santa Uliva* in the "sixteenth century." Nerida Newbigin confirms this: "My
impression from reading the play and looking at its use of *intermezzi* is that it is *very*
late, quite possibly mid-sixteenth century." She notes that the earliest known edition
of the play was printed in 1578.[15]

Other mid-sixteenth-century Italian references to *mattaccini* include an exchange
between two characters in Giovanni Cecchi's *L'Assiuolo* (1550) in which one remarks, "If we have masks, we'll look like two *mattaccini*," and the other replies,
"Little fools or big fools [*o mattaccini, o matti grandi*], it doesn't matter; / It's enough
for me not to be recognized." In 1558, Annibal Caro wrote of "*mattaccini* who, to
make people laugh more, go about with that floppy shirt and their shoes untied,
acting the fool," and listed, as after-dinner entertainment at a ducal feast, "*moresche*,
feats of strength by Hercules, galliards, *mattaccini*, and sword games."[16]

The word appears to have passed from Italian to French, where its first recorded
use is in Rabelais's *Sciomachie*, an account, written late in 1549, of elaborate mock
battles fought in Rome the previous year. Rabelais uses the word *matachins* twice.
First, he describes "some *matachins* unfamiliar with the sea, who thought they could
show off and fool around on water just as they do very well on land." Then, toward the end of the festivities, he mentions "a company of new *matachins*," who,
"to the sound of cornets, oboes, [and] sackbuts," replaced a scheduled comedy and
"greatly delighted the entire audience."[17]

The most complete sixteenth-century description of *matachins*, complete with
music, dance steps, and gestures, is given in French in Thoinot Arbeau's *Orchesography* (1589). Arbeau's *matachins* are not fools, but elegant sword dancers, ordinarily
"dressed in small corslets, with fringe epaulets and fringe hanging from beneath their
belts over a silken ground. Their helmets are made of gilded cardboard, their arms
are bare, and they wear bells upon their legs and carry a sword in the right hand
and a shield in the left." They may also be dressed as "Amazons," which seems to
imply, unusually for a sword dance, that women (or perhaps men dressed as women)
might take part.[18] It is on the basis of Arbeau's description, rather than any specific
textual designation, that Heartz reads the sword dance between Europeans and wild
men in the hall of Mary of Hungary's palace at Binche in 1550 as a version of the
matachins.[19]

It is evident that, from very early on, the term *mattaccini* or *matachins* covered a
wide range of performers from acrobats to masked fools and courtly sword dancers.
So it was in Spain, where, in the first recorded Spanish use of the term, in 1559,
Francisco de Alcocer called on all "good judges and governors" to "banish" the
"*matachines*," along with "similar inventions, childish dances, and *comediettas* that

foreigners bring with them to make money of the common people."[20] This suggests a kind of professional and not very reputable street performer, akin to the *mattaccini* of da Volterra's carnival song. At the other end of the social scale, as we have seen, in 1570 a processional *danza de los matachines* was sponsored by the city council of Seville, and a triumphal carload of *matachines* greeted Anne of Austria in Burgos. There is also the intriguing remark by Bernal Díaz, writing in Spain in the 1560s, that some of the dancers in Motecuzoma's court "seem like *matachines*."[21] Had he penned these words in Tenochtitlan in 1519, they would have established the availability for comparison, at the time of the conquest, of European *matachines*. As it is, they say nothing about the nationality of the *matachines* he has in mind, only that he saw similar dancers in Motecuzoma's court.

By 1583, the term had reached England. On New Year's Day of that year, "sundrey feates of Tumbling and activitie were shewed before her Ma[jes]tie," including a performance by a number of "matachins." In the *Arcadia,* published in 1590, Philip Sydney wrote of "a matachin dance" as one that "imitate[s] fighting." And, in John Webster's *White Devil,* first performed in 1608, two characters dressed as monks interrupt a third in the act of murder. "We have brought you a mask," says one. "A matachin it seems by your drawn swords," replies the villain, "churchmen turned revellers."[22]

Whatever the origin of the European *matachines,* there were other contemporary performances that clearly did owe much to American influence. In Toledo in 1560, Elizabeth of Valois saw forty dancers "clothed, masked, headdressed, and shod very naturally as Indians." And in Seville in 1598, the members of a black confraternity celebrated the feast day of their patron saint "with a banquet, plays, and a tourney, in which twelve blacks, dressed Indian-style, sang and played instruments."[23] Sometimes it is hard to tell whether the performers were Europeans (or Africans) dressed as Indians or genuine Native Americans on show. How are we to interpret, for example, the "triumphal chariot" of "Indians" that rolled into view in Burgos in 1570, just ahead of the acrobatic *matachines?* Riding the chariot were an "Indian chief dressed in velvet and brocade, accompanied by six male and six female Indians." Ahead went a further "twenty-four Indians," clothed in "doublets, culottes, and taffeta cloaks of various colors," wearing "masks encrusted with precious gems," and playing a version of the Mexica ball game.[24] Were the masks hiding European faces or were the fine European costumes "civilizing" native limbs? I don't know.

Equally opaque is the account of the *danza de indios* organized in Toledo for the Feast of the Assumption of the Virgin in 1585. The dancers were "eight Indians dressed in cloth of gold and silver, with gilded faces, colored taffeta cloaks, and baggy pants of colored taffeta or light Moorish wool." Each wore mirrors on his "chest, head, and forehead," carried "trinkets" in his hands, and was equipped with "small bells and rattles" and "many tall feathers." The dance was accompanied by three musicians, also dressed in Indian style, who played a large drum, a small drum, and a flute and tabor. At one point, the entire troupe entered the choir of the cathedral with a full-sized, artificial elephant ridden by a monkey that looked "natural," but may—the writer couldn't tell—have been artificial.[25] The mirrors, rattles, and feathers are characteristic of indigenous dance. So are the musical instruments used. The elephant is not. I am inclined to guess conservatively that the dancers were Spanish rather than Indian, but in either case, the Toledo *danza de indios* is a strong reminder of the influence of Native American dance traditions on Spanish festive processions.

"Indian" dances were popular in Seville. In her list of processional dances sponsored by the city between 1540 and 1699, Brooks includes ten titles that mention the name of a specific American tribe, "Indians" in general, or Motecuzoma. Others, such as the "*Sarao* of the Nations" of 1621, included Indians as well as French, Turks, Portuguese, and Gypsies among the nations and peoples represented. Although the dancers, one assumes, were ordinarily Spanish (or African), this may not always have been the case. A masque performed in 1621 included "an Indian of but few years, with a mask, gloves to his elbows, and fitted boots, which imitated on his arms and legs the toasty color of his face." Over his "short locks" he wore "a headdress of fifty red and white plumes, which encircled his face to form a half moon, or rather a heavenly arch, with pins and jewels of consummate value." Was his face naturally "toasty" (and Indian in its features) or was makeup used to darken a European face and match his mask, gloves, and boots? Whatever this dancer's natural ethnicity, he was accompanied by a torch bearer, attired in similarly colored feathers, who was, we are told, "a native Indian."[26]

At times the organizers imitated not only Indian dress but Indian dance steps. A contemporary wrote of the "dance of Motecuzoma" entered in the Corpus Christi procession in 1693 that it "was something to see for the newness and variety of the movements in the Indian style." In this instance, we know that the dancers were not Indian, for Motecuzoma wore a long wig. But Brooks speculates that the director of the dance, one "Juan Antonio de Castro, black of color," may have been "born in New World territories and later [come] to Spain to take up residence as a freed man in Seville," in which case "his contact with exotic dance style may well have been firsthand."[27] Whether or not Castro himself had been to the Americas, many others who passed through Seville would have brought personal knowledge to bear on processional dances claiming Indian heritage.

The European *matachines* did not claim such a heritage. Although sometimes said to dress as "wild men," the *matachines* were never identified as Indians. Subsequent Spanish descriptions of *matachines* yield references to dances with wooden swords in which the vanquished fall to the ground and are "despoiled"; equestrian ballets; tricks with fireworks; tightrope walkers; and dancers dressed as devils, wearing half-masks with long papier-mâché noses or waving animal bladders on sticks. The most consistent elements continue to be slapstick humor, mime (sometimes acrobatic), and sword dances.[28] While it is possible that some elements were modeled on indigenous traditions, none were designated as such in contemporary accounts. In this regard, they differ markedly from the costumes of the Toledo *danza de indios* or the movements of the Seville "dance of Motecuzoma."

Several elements were often combined in a single performance. An account from 1690 shows how sword dance and comic pantomime, cleansed in this instance of its carnivalesque obscenities, could be linked. After remarking conventionally on the Italian and French heritage of the *matachines*, Francisco de Bances y Candamo writes, "These *matachines* of today do not perform indecent movements . . . , but rather the most ridiculous ones that they can. Now two of them act as if they had bumped into each other at night. One pretends to be afraid of the other and they both draw back. Then, as they begin to realize their error, they caress each other, scrutinize each other, and dance together. They become angry again and fight, with wooden swords, striking blows in time to the music. In an amusing fashion they take fright at an inflated bladder which perchance appears between the two of them. They approach it and retreat. Finally, by jumping on top of it they burst it, and at the loud noise of its explosion they pretend to be dead. In this way other performances are devised—for two, four, or more *matachines,* as one desires—which describe in dance and in gestures some ridiculous, but not obscene, action."[29] This is close enough to the earliest Italian account, in the *Canzona de' mattaccini,* to imply some degree of consistency over the years.

Judging by European accounts alone, the European *matachines* appear to have been comic mimes, sometimes obscene, who used their mimic, acrobatic, and dancing skills to construct brief theatrical entertainments for audiences at court and in the streets. Sometimes, depending on the venue, one element might predominate. Arbeau's description suggests that the comic routines could yield to an elegant sword dance. Other elements, such as tightrope walking or pyrotechnics, might be added, depending on the skills of individual performers. At times, the *matachines* tradition might be adapted to different forms altogether, such as the precision horsemanship of an equestrian ballet. The American *matachines,* on the other hand, became a religious dance, performed at festivals to honor a patron saint or virgin, to recall the days of human sacrifice, or to anticipate the triumphant return of Motecuzoma. Although in many cases it retains a strong comic element, it is never treated lightly by its performers or its audience.

Lacking sufficient evidence to settle the question of the *matachines'* origins, I remain agnostic. With regard to the European *matachines,* the simplest explanation would be that the performers came from the same Italian soil as the *commedia dell'arte;* that the name was originally a diminutive of *matto* (fool); that the tradition passed from Italy to France, Spain, and England; and that it (or at least its distinctive name) died out in the late eighteenth century. But the absence of any reference to European *matachines* before the first Mexican dancers appeared in Europe gives me pause. As for the American *matachines,* I suspect that, like many other Mexican dances, it has its formal roots in both Hispanic and indigenous cultures, but that its meaning is to be derived from its various American contexts rather than from any European heritage it may share. In this respect, as I will explain further in my final chapter, I am entirely persuaded by Treviño and Gilles's argument that the *danza de los matachines* of native New Mexico is best understood as one of resistance rather than submission to foreign cultures.

PART SIX
EPILOGUE

25
Dancing with Malinche (New Mexico and Oaxaca, 1993–1994)

THE long popularity of dances and festivals of Moors and Christians in widely divergent cultures is due to the tradition's remarkable flexibility of historical referent and contemporary application. The Christians can be Carolingian knights, medieval crusaders, invaders of the Alpujarra, sailors at Lepanto, New World conquistadors, or New Mexican settlers. The Moors can become Moriscos, Turks, Saracens, Jews, Aztecs, Chichimeca, or Comanches. Into the public transcript of historical conflict, various hidden transcripts can be insinuated, exposing the scars left by past traumas, negotiating current power relationships, and yearning, in Spain, for *convivencia,* and, in Mexico, for freedom from external rule. It is not the public transcript's theme of ethnic and religious triumph that has retained the interest of generations of folk performers, but the tradition's inherent susceptibility to hidden transcripts. The theme of reconquest invites folk performers to imagine resistance to the larger cultures of which they are so often a subordinate part.

I have dealt more with the large-scale festivals than with the smaller dances because the early history of the tradition includes more accounts of one than of the other. In this final chapter, I will return to modern Mesoamerica, where I will concentrate on two dances: northern New Mexico's *danza de los matachines* and Oaxaca's *danza de la pluma.*[1] Whatever the dances' uncertain relationships may be to European *matachines,* Spanish dances of Moors and Christians, or precontact indigenous dances, both in their present form belong to the broad Mesoamerican tradition of dances of reconquest. When their mask is read carefully, they offer intriguing hidden transcripts.

Any serious attempt to reckon with their hidden transcripts must begin with the link between the dances' two shared main characters, Motecuzoma and Malinche. Most observers assume that Motecuzoma represents only the Mexica emperor who opposed Cortés and that the Malinche of the dances corresponds to the Malinche of the European conquest narratives.[2] Otherwise known by her baptismal name of Doña Marina, the latter was Cortés's indigenous mistress and translator. The public transcript then yields a Motecuzoma who in the *danza de los matachines* is converted to Christianity and in the *danza de la pluma* is defeated by Cortés. Malinche becomes the first native convert to Christianity, instrumental in the subsequent defeat and conversion of Motecuzoma. But just as the masks in the *danza de los santiagos* signal the presence of a hidden transcript, so does Malinche in these dances, for she is openly identified not as the companion of Cortés but as the "wife" or "daughter" of Motecuzoma.[3] The hidden transcript knows that, in indigenous Mesoamerican folklore, Motecuzoma is the name both of a past ruler and of a "messiahlike figure" who will "defeat the Spanish and initiate a new Indian hegemony." It knows, too, that, as the mythical daughter of the former Motecuzoma, Malinche (or her structural equivalent) must marry the next emperor and so legitimate his rule. As the necessary link between past and future glory, she is "the final hope for the resurgence of indigenous culture in the face of inevitable destruction."[4] Motecuzoma and Malinche, in their several manifestations, also embody the divine rulers of the spirit realm, Huitzilopochtli and Toci.[5]

Evidence for this popular understanding of Motecuzoma and Malinche is plentiful. During an armed rebellion in highland Chiapas in 1712, the summons to resist the colonial regime included the assurance that "the Emperor Motecuzoma was being resuscitated and would help the Indians defeat the Spaniards." In 1761, the leader of an indigenous rebellion in Yucatan, Jacinto Uc, added to his own name those of Motecuzoma and of Canek, the last Maya king. The official report of the rebellion states that he was crowned "Re Jacinto Uk Canek, Chichán Motezuma, which in translation means King Jacinto Uc Canek, Little Motecuzoma."[6] In 1900, Frederick Starr came across Otomí in the Sierra de Puebla who "believe that Motecuzoma is to come again. Meantime, from him come health, crops, and all good things." Each year, a feast is "given in his honor, of which he is believed to partake." And, in 1835, Ignacio Zúñiga identified a dance in Sonora as a dramatization of "the passage of the Aztecs, and the coming of Motecuzoma, whom they await as the Jews await the Messiah."[7]

Malinche's link to Motecuzoma is a long-standing one. In Guatemala City in 1608, a spectacular nighttime masquerade included clergy dressed as "Indians, Turks, Spaniards, and Moors." Among those singled out for the richness of their costumes were "those who represented the Grand Turk and the Sultana, Motecuzoma and La Malinche."[8] Not only does this indicate an early date for the popular connection between Motecuzoma and Malinche, but it implies that the relationship between them, like that between the Grand Turk and the Sultana, was one of husband and wife or father and daughter.

Similar legends abound among the Pueblo Indians of New Mexico. Several writers have recorded the conviction of the natives of Pecos and Jemez Pueblos that Motecuzoma will "return to deliver his people from the yoke of the Spaniards."[9] According to one story, the Pueblo hero Poseyemu "assumed the name of Motecuzoma" when he became the cacique of Pecos Pueblo. Shortly afterward, "the Great Spirit revealed to [Motecuzoma] that he should marry the youngest daughter of the cacique of the pueblo of Zuñi, . . . whose name was Malinche." Motecuzoma and Malinche traveled southward, founding a new capital "where Mexico City now stands" and ruling over "the great country of the Aztecs."[10] Early in this century, Noël Dumarest reported the belief of the people of Cochiti Pueblo that

Motecuzoma and his "wife," Malinche, had the "power of working miracles," and that "one day" Motecuzoma would "reappear in the world . . . to deliver his people from the yoke of their conquerors." More recently, Teresa VanEtten retold the story, which she first heard in San Juan Pueblo, of Motecuzoma asking the people to dance the *matachines* in his memory. In this version, too, Motecuzoma has a beautiful wife, Malinche, with whom he rules "the Indian people." [11]

The *danza de los matachines* is the only ritual dance performed in both Hispanic and Indian communities in New Mexico. In the Hispanic communities, the dance is thought to dramatize, in general, "the triumph of good over evil, Christianity over paganism" and, in particular, the conversion of Motecuzoma. [12] In the Native American pueblos, a hidden transcript of indigenous resistance emerges, for there the dance may be read as a dramatized victory of indigenous warriors, led by the messianic Motecuzoma, over intrusive "foreign cultures." [13] In both cases, particular performances also make reference to local politics and ethnic relationships. [14]

I saw the *danza de los matachines* in the Hispanic town of Bernalillo in August 1993 and in the Native American pueblos of Picuris (Fig. 29), San Juan, and Santa Clara over Christmas 1994. According to Richard Kloeppel, a former leader of the Bernalillo team, the dance there tells the story of the conversion of Motecuzoma to Christianity, through the agency of his daughter Malinche, and the incorporation of the Aztec people into the Catholic Church. [15] After Motecuzoma

29. *Matachines*. Picuris Pueblo, 1994.

leads his twelve *danzantes* (dancers) or soldiers in a joyful opening dance, he sits on a chair to one side. Led by an *abuelo* (ancestor), Malinche approaches him. The conversion of Motecuzoma begins when Malinche faces the Mexica king and each circles his or her extended right hand in alternating directions over and under the other's hand. There follows what Flavia Champe calls "the pantomime of the struggle forward," during which Motecuzoma moves slowly from one end of the line of dancers to the other, lunging forward with one foot and dragging the other to join it, while an *abuelo* massages his calves (Fig. 30). Champe speculates that this is intended "to symbolize Motecuzoma's struggle to accept Christianity."[16] The *toro* (bull), played by a man dressed in the demonic colors of red and black, is enraged and attacks the converts until he is shot and killed by the *abuelo*. Following the dance, a triumphal procession wends its way to the parish church, where the "con-

30. An *abuelo* massages Motecuzoma's legs. Bernalillo, 1993.

verted" *matachines* take an honored part in the fiesta mass. But even the Bernalillo dancers are not entirely satisfied with this reading. One of the men playing the part of Motecuzoma confessed to me that the meaning of the dance was difficult to ascertain and that "we need to do more research."

Treviño and Gilles's research has led them to trace the history of the *matachines* to Mexica dances that celebrated military victories over rival tribes. Although their specific reading of the *danza de los matachines* depends too heavily on Bierhorst's theory of an "Aztec ghost-song ritual," they are, I think, fundamentally correct when they see in the native version of the dance a dramatized victory of indigenous warriors, led by Motecuzoma and Malinche, over intrusive "foreign cultures." Not only does their reading make better sense of the several elements of the dance, but it explains the *matachines'* continued popularity amongst the Pueblo Indians. And it accords with the "Indian tradition," reported by Dumarest, that "this dance was instituted by Motecuzoma that the descendants of his race might have the pleasure of mocking their conquerors." [17]

A brief reading of the San Juan Pueblo *matachines* will illustrate my point. After several minutes of dancing, Motecuzoma moved backward between the two rows of dancers and each pair of dancers knelt as he passed. While the dancers remained in a kneeling position, an *abuelo* escorted Motecuzoma to a chair at the far end of the rows. "When the time comes for Motecuzoma to leave the physical world," Treviño and Gilles write, he is led "out of the dance area and to a place of honor in the spirit realm" by the *abuelo,* who represents not, as the word is usually translated, "a grandfather" but "a guardian ancestor spirit." [18] The chair denoted Motecuzoma's place of honor, and the kneeling position of the *danzantes* signaled the death of his warriors. I take this phase of the dance to portray, in a highly compressed form, the life of the Indians before the arrival of the Europeans and the subsequent death in battle of Motecuzoma and his soldiers. What follows concerns the restoration of power through the coming of his messianic namesake.

Malinche wove her way through one line of dancers after the other. "As the queen of the spirit realm," according to Treviño and Gilles, Malinche was thus purifying and uniting the warrior spirits who had died honorably in battle. When she approached the seated Motecuzoma, the entire drama focused briefly on the small space around his chair, where "the circling motion of La Malinche's extended arm [brought] Motecuzoma back to life." Rising from his chair, Motecuzoma moved with difficulty between the rows of kneeling warriors. One of the *abuelos* massaged his legs. Several times, the *abuelo* coiled his whip on the ground like a snake and then held it under Motecuzoma's foot, thereby hastening the ruler's recovery. Nothing suggested the religious conversion that Champe sees in this episode. Treviño and

Gilles offer a more persuasive explanation: "Motecuzoma arises and begins the journey back to the world of substance. He slowly stretches his legs and makes cautious steps, trying to regain control of his physical self. He has been in the spirit realm for a long time. *El abuelo* rubs Motecuzoma's legs to reduce the stiffness." Finally, Motecuzoma called on his warriors to join him in battle. Two by two, the *danzantes* rose from their kneeling position to dance their way back from "the spirit world" to "the world of substance." The revived warriors and their messianic king are best read not as "ghosts," in the sense of sharing a single soul with the deceased, but more loosely as partial embodiments of ancestral powers.[19]

After they performed several intricate and joyful dance patterns, Motecuzoma and his soldiers were attacked. The bull, which until now had only occasionally skirmished to one side with the *abuelos,* entered the playing area. As well as his bull's head and hide, he wore a sweatshirt with the word "Saints" emblazoned across the front. I have noted already the Dallas Cowboys T-shirts that were worn in performance in Jemez Pueblo to connote U.S. military aggression, and I suspect that the New Orleans Saints sweatshirt was intended to link the bull with the religious pretensions of the conquistadors and their descendants. The bull confronted Motecuzoma, Malinche, and each of the warriors in a series of brief, stylized battles. When the last dancer had fought the bull, the *abuelos* gave chase. Capturing the bull, they laid him on his back and covered him, from his neck to his knees, with a sheet. One of the *abuelos* produced a plastic laser beam that emitted electronic beeps. While the other *abuelo* lifted the bull's legs, the one with the laser crawled head first between the bull's legs under the sheet. There the *abuelo* pretended to perform surgery, from which he finally emerged with two large nuts which he displayed triumphantly to the crowd. The bull had been castrated. It was a humorous, but nonetheless very powerful, image of the defeat of the invader. During the second performance of the day, the *abuelo* hung a "Bull For Sale" sign around the *toro's* neck after the castration and led him around the crowd, collecting money in a hat borrowed from a woman tourist. Marketing the captured enemy to the new invaders (tourists) was a nice emblematic reversal of the economic exploitation Native Americans have suffered in the past at the hands of their conquerors. More aggressively, in Taos Pueblo in 1992, the *abuelo* "mock-sodomized a male tourist who was crouched on all fours to videotape the dance."[20]

The final episode in San Juan was a joyous victory dance. Although the fiesta had begun the night before with vespers in the Catholic church, the dance itself had offered no hint of indigenous conversion to Christianity. Rather, its defining moment had been the emasculation of the conquering "saints." The *matachines* dance in San Juan is best read not as a celebration of conversion to Christianity but as a cleansing of the pueblo, through the intervention of Malinche and Motecuzoma, for the unimpeded performance the next day of the pueblo's "most important public [pre-Christian] ritual," the Turtle Dance.[21]

The *danza de la pluma* is performed in several villages in Oaxaca. The most impressive version in recent years has been that of the village of Teotitlan del Valle, where I saw the entire eight-hour dance drama twice during the first week of July 1994. Earlier accounts of the dance had prepared me for some elements of the hidden transcript. Frederick Starr, in 1896, remarked on the difference between the fine costumes of the Indians and the plain ones of the Spaniards: "In dress and armament, the white men . . . present a truly ridiculous appearance." In 1925, Toor was certain that this contrast disparaged the Spaniards: "Motecuzoma and his captains looked and danced like gods," but Cortés "was accompanied by a lot of small boys, stiffly dressed in blue uniforms." Although "Cortés and Christianity conquered, the Conquest was a lie." Aesthetic victory belonged to the Indians.[22] When I saw the dance, the conquistadors wore black military uniforms, trimmed with gold braid, and each carried a sword and a toy rifle. Cortés, Alvarado, and the smallest soldier of all, known as the Cortesito (little Cortés), wore white plumes in their hats. Motecuzoma and his soldiers wore brightly colored indigenous costumes, each topped by an enormous circular headdress, three feet in diameter, made of thousands of soft downy feathers in radiating colored tiers. Amidst the feathers were small circular mirrors that reflected the sun and, when the dancers were in motion, scattered light in swirling patterns across the playing area. Each dancer carried a rattle made of a small gourd attached to a deer's hoof and a small, colorfully painted wooden "fan."

Two young girls accompanied Motecuzoma (Fig. 31). La Malinche wore a multicolored indigenous dress and a small feathered headdress, Doña Marina a bright Spanish-style dress and hat. Although some observers assume that in the *danza de la pluma* both girls represent "Malinches,"[23] they are clearly distinguished. Malinche represents Motecuzoma's wife and remains with him throughout. Doña Marina begins with Motecuzoma but transfers to the Spanish side halfway through the dance. She is also known by the Indian name of Sehuapila, derived "from the Nahuatl *cihua*, 'woman,' and *pilli*, 'noble.'"[24]

Not only did the Indians have the better costumes, they had the better dance steps. While Motecuzoma and his courtiers engaged in elaborate whirling dances, leaping high in the air, kneeling, and circling, Cortés and the Spaniards never broke into anything more complicated than a march. The Aztecs also held the playing area for a greater proportion of the time, while the Spaniards spent much of the dance seated quietly on a wooden bench. The disparity of ages, too, was significant. Cortés was represented by a middle-aged man and Alvarado by a young adolescent,

31. Malinche, Motecuzoma, and Doña Marina. Teotitlan del Valle, 1994.

but the rest of the Spanish soldiers were played by small boys (Fig. 32). Although Motecuzoma, too, was played by a middle-aged man, his warriors were represented by young men in their late teens or twenties. With their elaborate headdresses further extending their height, the adult Indian warriors dwarfed their tiny Spanish enemies. The sixteenth-century Spanish justification for the conquest of the New World depended, in part, on the notion that its indigenous inhabitants were like children and needed the civilizing government of mature Europeans. For the Indian performers to assign all the Spanish roles but that of Cortés himself to children was quietly to reverse this argument.

But the most striking evidence of the dance's hidden transcript lay in its conclusion. Some observers had suggested that Motecuzoma might occasionally gain the military victory. Frances Gillmor cites a text from Cuilapan that "ends with the defeat of the Spaniards," but she reasons that the text "must have been missing the last page or two." Elsie Parsons reports that in the dance she saw at Santa Ana del Valle, "the usual order" of victory was reversed. "Having Motecuzoma get the better of Cortés was an innovation of a nationalistic 'revolutionary' character." And Jeffrey Cohen, who saw the dance in Teotitlan in 1986, states that "Cortés's triumph is short lived. In the last act of the dance Motecuzoma is resurrected. Dancing a final time the Spaniards and the Aztecs battle again. In the end it is Cortés who is vanquished. [Doña Marina] rejoins Motecuzoma and the *danzantes* dance as a group in the open plaza. With pre-contact order restored the dance comes to an end."[25] I saw neither resurrection nor overt indigenous victory. In fact, nothing I had read had prepared me for the brief but, once spotted, unmistakable way in which Motecuzoma's victory was finally signaled. This oblique signaling of the victor's identity, however, must follow a reading of the dance as a whole.

The "dance floor" was a square, each of whose sides measured a hundred feet or

32. Spanish soldier. Teotitlan del Valle, 1994.

so. It was delineated to the east by part of the church facade and an adjacent arcade. The other three sides were marked off by long wooden benches. As the dance began, Cortés sat in a chair at the northeast corner of the playing area, just outside the church door. His diminutive soldiers occupied the bench nearest him. Motecuzoma sat on a wooden throne to the south of the dance floor, flanked by Malinche and Doña Marina, each on her own throne. The sixteen Indian *danzantes* faced one another in two parallel lines stretching across the dance floor from the seated Motecuzoma. The members of the orchestra were on benches in the shade of a large tree at the southeast corner of the dance floor. Between them, the twenty-eight musicians played two bass tubas, two baritone tubas, a French horn, three trombones, five trumpets, five saxophones, seven clarinets, a bass drum, a pair of cymbals, and a kettle drum. Such an orchestra had replaced the older *teponaztli* drum and flute at the end of the nineteenth century. According to a typed list pegged to the rim of the bass drum, the *danza de la pluma* consisted of forty-one distinct *bailes* (dances).[26]

During the first two *bailes*, Cortés marched to and fro in front of his soldiers, encouraging them for the task ahead. They were understood to be still in Spain. The next four *bailes* recalled "the life of the Indians before the conquest" and the entertainments offered "Motecuzoma in his court."[27] The best was a schottische, lasting fifteen minutes, during which Motecuzoma, Malinche, and Marina advanced, rotating around one another, between the lines of courtiers, while the courtiers, jumping, kneeling, and whirling, formed squares and circles that then developed into lines that wove complex patterns lengthways and sideways across the dance floor. During the next *baile* Motecuzoma addressed his army while two *negritos*, so named because of their black, tusked wooden masks, flirted with foreign tourists and improvised comic routines with the still-unoccupied wooden benches. When fireworks exploded, they pretended to have been shot, writhing on the ground in mock death throes. The *negritos* doubled as stage managers and "clowns." One was linked to the Spaniards, the other to the Indians; both carried whips.

Then the Indians danced and the Spaniards marched in single file around the perimeter of the dance floor, four times veering off to cross the center of the square in opposite directions, clashing Spanish swords and Indian fans as they passed. The *negritos* followed, one at the end of each file, each striking the other's whip. Next came the first "meeting" of Motecuzoma and Cortés. Flanked by Malinche and Marina, Motecuzoma walked around a series of rectangles formed by the *danzantes*. Cortés pursued them, speaking of the Spanish law and the Catholic religion to which he was going to subject the Mexica, but never quite catching his opponent. This encounter, in which Cortés threatened and chased but never actually met Motecuzoma, clearly had a comic dimension. Imperial European rhetoric was being juxtaposed to indigenous dignity and quietly mocked.

Such dissonance between speech and action is typical of the interplay between public and hidden transcripts. While the public transcript is inscribed in the text that dictates speech, the hidden transcript is encoded in the visual elements of the performance. The disparity of ages and costumes, the aesthetic dominance of the dance floor by the Aztecs, and the failure of the hectoring Cortés to catch the silent Motecuzoma were all signs that stood apart from the prescribed speeches. As in so many Mexican dances, the dialogue was delivered sotto voce and was only audible at close quarters. It made no difference. The local audience knew the story, and the hidden transcript, with which their sympathies lay, was being played out not in verbal but in visual signs.

More indigenous *bailes* followed, including a lively *jota,* danced with castanets and twirling skirts and petticoats by Malinche and Marina between the lines of *danzantes,* and a schottische that began with a lilting clarinet solo and was danced by four "kings" of Motecuzoma's court. Then Malinche removed Motecuzoma's feathered "crown," and the thrones were moved to the center of the dance floor. There, in his "palace," Motecuzoma "fell asleep" and in his dreams saw fearful omens. The dancers begged him to wake and to be strong. "If you lose, *señor,*" they told him, "we will lose, too." Finally, they formed a defensive circle around him. By this time, the dance had been in progress for nearly two hours.

Next, Cortés and his soldiers marched on Motecuzoma's "palace" from one side of the dance floor after another, stopping each time at the circle of *danzantes* and firing their toy rifles. After the last advance, Cortés performed his most elegant *baile,* a slow march from one corner of the dance floor to the next, alternately approaching and withdrawing from the circle of Indians in the middle of the dance floor. At each corner, he stood on a chair, placed there by the Spanish *negrito,* raised his sword, and imperiously demanded Motecuzoma's surrender. Afterward, the Spanish troops closed in on the palace, surrounding the Aztecs. The concentric circles of Indians and conquistadors began to move, like so many Mesoamerican ritual dancers, in "a counterclockwise, that is, sunwise, direction," increasing speed as they went.[28] Soon the outer circle of short-legged Spaniards were unable to keep up with the inner circle of adult Aztecs, and the aspiring conquistadors peeled off to return to their bench by the church door. Once again, as with the comic encounter between Cortés and Motecuzoma, the movement of the dancers had belied the text. In this instance, the sacred motion of the Aztecs in the direction of the sun's trajectory had sufficed to repel the Spaniards; the image of little boys effortlessly outpaced by grown men had added a comic dimension to the scene.

As the afternoon wore on, the crowd, sparse at first, began to thicken. Village elders sat on benches in front of the arcade, and baskets of fruit began to arrive, placed first at the elders' feet and then distributed, along with beer and *mezcal,* to the audience. The *negritos* brought water to the dancers and went through a slap-stick routine with the water bucket and the ladle. The thrones were returned to the south end of the dance floor. I climbed the tightly spiraled stone staircase inside the bell tower to watch the dancers from the church roof and to see more clearly the complex patterns formed by the *danzantes*. From time to time, they paused to let the wind, which blew against their tall headdresses, die down before they attempted one of the more difficult routines. Motecuzoma, his strength regained, danced two solo *bailes* between the rows of *danzantes*. A *zandunga* followed, in which the whirling and interweaving of the whole court alternated with a lively duet by Malinche and Marina. Then the Spaniards once again marched in pursuit of the Indians, always crossing the center of the dance floor just too late to catch the Indians, who danced away before the soldiers arrived.

Left, for once, in possession of the dance floor, the boy soldiers resorted to a "trick." Alvarado and the Cortesito approached two of Motecuzoma's captains, who were dancing a schottische. The captains graciously escorted the Spanish embassy to Motecuzoma and, after some negotiation, Doña Marina left with the Spaniards. Holding a cross and a Spanish flag, she was taken to Cortés, where she was introduced by her indigenous name, "the beautiful Sehuapila," and seated next to the Spanish leader. In exchange for Marina's "conversion" and her agreement to help the Spaniards, the Indians believed they had received a promise of peace. But Cortés had not given his word; he had tricked Motecuzoma by sending the Cortesito instead. So he announced, "Tomorrow we march on Tenochtitlan."

Thinking themselves safe from attack, the Indians danced their most beautiful sequence of *bailes:* a quadrille, an *himno grande,* a schottische, and a waltz, which together lasted over an hour. The audience had grown by now to about fifteen hundred, and the lanes leading to the churchyard were packed with vendors selling drinks, fruit, baked tamales, candies, and piles of cream cakes swarming with wasps. From time to time, one of the *negritos* wiped the face of a woman in the crowd and then tried to wipe a man's face with the same bandanna. Everybody laughed. Although Parsons complained that "nobody would tell me . . . the meaning of [this] joke," it was explained to me as a disclosure of concealed sexual desire or liaison.[29]

As the sun set over the village, lights were strung over the churchyard, and the "first war" was staged. Lines of tiny soldiers advanced on towering Indians. Cortés and Motecuzoma fought a stylized duet. Cortés and his soldiers "entered the city," where they watched an Indian waltz. After another battle, in which Cortés suffered his first defeat, conquistadors and Indians formed an alternating circle. Every Spaniard faced an Indian, to whom he surrendered his sword and rifle. This represented the night of sorrows. Outside the circle, the *negritos* enacted their own version of Spanish defeat: using his whip as a rope, the Indian *negrito* captured his Spanish counterpart, unmasked him, and displayed him in defeat to the crowd. In celebration of their victory, the Indians danced a polka and some traditional *danzas oaxaqueñas*. But their triumph was short-lived. War began again, and in the last *baile* of the official list, the circle of defeat was repeated. This time, the Indians were disarmed, kneeling and surrendering their headdresses to the Spaniards, and the Spanish *negrito* captured and displayed his Indian counterpart.

The first time I saw the dance, I had left at this point, persuaded that the narrative of the dance ended in military victory for the Spaniards. But I was puzzled, for inquiries about the victory yielded ambivalent answers. One group of older men watching the dance assured me that Motecuzoma won, but a younger man, who claimed to have danced the role of Motecuzoma for three years, insisted that victory lay with Cortés. When I asked the dancers playing Cortés and Motecuzoma, each asserted confidently (in the other's absence) that his character was the victor. But at the second performance, after the final funeral march for the capture of Motecuzoma, I was advised not to leave, for there would be two more *bailes* that were not included in the official list pegged to the orchestra's bass drum.

Motecuzoma and his soldiers replaced their headdresses. Motecuzoma returned to his throne, and Malinche sat beside him. Spanish soldiers and indigenous warriors formed two parallel lines stretching away from Motecuzoma across the dance floor. The first of the unofficial *bailes* was an exuberant dance by Malinche and Marina, at the end of which Marina returned to Motecuzoma and sat beside the restored monarch. She had returned from Cortés to her indigenous origins. I was told that the *baile* represented "reconciliation" or "joy." The final and thematically conclusive *baile* involved the *negritos*. Parsons had mentioned such a closing dance in Santa Ana del Valle, but had assigned it no meaning.[30] What I saw was quite clear. Between the two lines of Indians and Spaniards, the *negritos* engaged in a brief mime involving chairs and bandannas. It ended with the Indian *negrito* suffocating his Spanish counterpart by pressing him hard against the ground with a chair. The Spanish *negrito* imitated death throes and lay still. The final image of the entire eight-hour *danza de la pluma* was one of Spanish defeat.

The ready intelligibility of the dance of the *negritos* built on much that had gone before. We had learned to read the sign of death throes early in the afternoon when the *negritos* had comically responded to the explosion of firecrackers with the same enacted sign. We had learned, too, during the course of the performance, to associate one *negrito* with the Spanish army and the other with the Aztecs. And, finally, we had seen the *negritos* visually summarize the outcome of the two previous "wars" between Spaniards and Aztecs in their own enacted relationships as captor and captive. Whereas we had twice read the visual summary of the *negritos* in light of the more prominent action of the armies of Cortés and Motecuzoma, we were now meant to infer, from the action of the *negritos* alone, an unseen third and decisive war. We were asked, in other words, to imagine an episode (the final defeat of Cortés) whose direct enactment the public transcript could not tolerate but to whose absence the *negritos* could allude.

Although the performers, then, did not directly enact the resurrection of Motecuzoma, as they had when Cohen saw the dance, they no less clearly signaled, in the two unlisted *bailes,* the Aztec ruler's restoration to his throne and his ensuing triumph over invading forces. This was not a rewriting of sixteenth-century history, for the Zapotecs of Teotitlan do not believe that Motecuzoma rose from the dead and defeated the historical Cortés. Rather, the Motecuzoma, Malinche, and Cortés of the finale are the partial embodiments of powers that belonged to their historical namesakes in the earlier part of the dance. According to this reading, Motecuzoma represents the messianic king who will restore Indian rule, Malinche his legitimating queen, and Cortés connotes whatever foreign power the future Motecuzoma will defeat.

But there is one more layer of the mask to read before we leave Teotitlan. I suggested, in Chapter 1, that those who stage the *morismas* of Bracho have no wish to reinstate pre-Christian religion. Rather, they draw on the repertoire of Aztec ritual to imagine a world of local authority free from external control. In the same way, the Zapotecs of Teotitlan draw on the repertoire of myth to enact resistance to their immediate political situation. Cohen understands Motecuzoma's restoration in Teotitlan to speak to the tension between the nation-state of Mexico, "symbolized by Cortés and his men," and the local Zapotec community, represented by the Indian *danzantes.* "The finale of the dance and the banishment of Cortés," he writes, "are a metaphor through which the people of Teotitlan del Valle construct an alternative world. This is not a world where the Indian is subordinate to mestizo, nor is it a place where Indians are thought of as relics of an indigenous, ancient past. Generated from the success of the *danzantes,* this new world is Zapotec, with Teotitlan del Valle as its center. The Mexican state (signified by Cortés and his men) is—at least for a moment—banished. The world is purified and returned to its indigenous glory."[31] That such a vision should be enacted in *bailes* pointedly omitted from the official list of dances is consistent with James Scott's understanding of the relationship between public and hidden transcripts.

NOTES

References are designated by author, brief title, and page number(s). Further publication details are provided in the Bibliography.

CHAPTER I. BEHEADING THE MOOR (ZACATECAS, 1996)

1. *El Sol de Zacatecas,* 2 Sept. 1996, E-8. My description of the *morismas* is based on personal observation; printed materials available at the site, including a booklet (*Las morismas*) published by the Cofradía de San Juan Bautista en Bracho; and conversations with actors and spectators.

2. The purpose and story of the crusade are explained in a brochure handed out by the company of the Twelve Peers of France during the performance in 1996. With due allowance for changes along the way, this strand of the Zacatecas narrative can be traced to a medieval Charlemagne legend that originated in eleventh-century Portugal. Various literary versions exist, including a late-twelfth-century French *chanson de geste* known as the *Song of Fierabras.* Medieval adaptations of this song, "the best-seller of all medieval French epics," can be found in French, Latin, Spanish, Portuguese, Italian, German, Dutch, Irish, and English. Jehan Bagnyon's enormously popular French prose adaptation, *Fierabras,* was published in Geneva in 1478 and, in William Caxton's English translation, in London in 1484, respectively the second and fourth books ever printed in those two cities. Nicolás de Piamonte's Spanish translation of Bagnyon's work, published in Toledo in 1498, "knew inordinate success in Spain, in the French Pyrenees, in Portugal, and Latin America" (Mandach, "Evolution," p. 137). It is Piamonte's version that is the source of so many Latin American ballads and folk dramas of Charlemagne and the Twelve Peers of France, including the *morismas* of Bracho. (See Mandach, "Evolution"; Mandach, *Naissance;* and Canto-Lugo, "Danza," pp. 9–11.)

3. Flores Solís, *Morismas,* pp. 24, 32, 47.

4. Ibid., p. 23.

5. Sten, *Ponte,* p. 116.

6. Ibid., pp. 122–123.

7. Julien, *Histoire,* 1: 66–67.

8. Toro, "Morismas," p. 9.

9. Pérez de Ribas, *Life,* p. 8.

10. Seler, *Comentarios,* 1: 119. The reference is to the impersonator of the goddess Toci, who was beheaded before being flayed (see below, Ch. 8).

11. *El Sol de Zacatecas,* 2 Sept. 1996, E-8.

12. Sten, *Ponte,* p. 122.

13. I was helped, in writing these two paragraphs, by Olga Nájera-Ramírez's fine study of the *fiesta de los tastaones* in Jocotan, Jalisco.

CHAPTER 2. READING THE MASK (CUETZALAN, 1988)

1. Puthussery, "Chavittunātakam," p. 97.

2. Trexler, "We Think," pp. 197, 207.

3. For a more complete account of my visit to Cuetzalan, see my *Dialogical,* pp. 99–107.

4. Toor, *Treasury*, p. 349.

5. For a photograph of one of Huerta's masks, now displayed in the Rijksmuseum voor Volkenkunde, Leiden, see Esser, *Behind*, pl. 129.

6. Toor, *Treasury*, pl. 68.

7. Scott, *Domination*, p. xii.

8. Ibid., pp. 2–4.

9. Ibid., p. 12.

10. Ibid., pp. xii–xiii, 115–116, 122–123, 153, 157, 175–176.

11. Ibid., pp. 140, 164.

12. Ibid., pp. 206–208.

13. Ibid., p. 136.

14. Díaz Roig, "Danza," p. 194.

15. Wachtel, *Vision*, p. 33.

CHAPTER 3. A ROYAL WEDDING (LLEIDA, 1150)

1. Livermore, *History*, pp. 64–131. For maps, see ibid., pp. 102, 127; Hillgarth, *Spanish*, 1: ii; and Reilly, *Contest*, pp. 38, 128, 228. For *convivencia*, see Hillgarth, *Spanish*, 1: 155–214, 2: 126–169; and Nirenberg, *Communities*.

2. Alford, *Pyrenean*, p. 222; Alford, *Sword*, p. 17. Her theory is repeated by Foster, *Culture*, p. 222, and Louis, *Folklore*, p. 270.

3. Alford, *Sword*, p. 151.

4. Teixidor y Barceló, *Discurso;* Soriano, *Historia*, 1: 125; Palau y Dulcet, *Manual*, 22: 16. In Spain, Milá y Fontanals, *Trovadores*, p. 233; Milá y Fontanals, *Obras*, 6: 264; Capmany, "Baile," p. 390; and Brisset, *Fiestas*, p. 10, cite Soriano. In Mexico, Warman, *Danza*, p. 17, cites Capmany. In Guatemala, Montoya, *Estudio*, p. 10, cites Capmany, but misplaces the wedding in Barcelona. In England, Gallop and Alford, *Traditional*, p. 111, cite Soriano, but mistakenly confuse the betrothal of Ramon Berenguer and Peronella of Aragon in 1137 and their wedding in 1150, giving the date of the performance as 1137. Alford, *Pyrenean*, pp. 222–223, corrects the date. In France, Louis, *Folklore*, p. 270, cites Alford. In the United States, Foster, *Culture*, p. 222, cites Alford; Very, *Spanish*, p. 93, cites Gallop and Alford. In Germany, Hoenerbach, *Studien*, p. 10, cites both Alford and Foster. I am grateful to Gerald J. MacDonald, librarian of the Hispanic Society of America, for information on vol. 1 of Teixidor y Barceló and for confirming my suspicions that it was the manuscript of the unpublished second volume that Soriano must have consulted.

5. Dorothy Noyes, personal communication, 25 August 1997.

6. Schramm, "Ramon"; Reilly, *Contest*, pp. 181–187.

7. Pujades, *Crónica*, 8: 428; Schramm, "Ramon," p. 31; Cabestany, "Alfons," p. 59; Lladonosa y Pujol, *Història*, 2: 48, 55, 121–123, 239, 288; Reilly, *Contest*, pp. 215–225.

8. Pujades, *Crónica*, 8: 428; see also Balaguer, *Historia*, 1: 739.

9. Amades, *Costumari*, 3: 16; cf. Amades, *Danzas*, p. 91, where, a decade later, he mentions "una lucha de moros y cristianos," but mistakenly dates the royal wedding at 1137.

10. Soriano, *Historia*, 1: 125.

11. Milá y Fontanals, *Trovadores*, p. 234. For further evidence of *juglars* in Aragon-Catalonia, see Cabestany, "Alfons el Cast," pp. 84–90.

12. Lladonosa y Pujol, *Història*, 1: 286–287.

13. For the dance of Gothic tribesmen and the complaint about the Bishop of Bamberg, see Axton, *European*, pp. 33–34, 44. The bishop played heterodox roles: Attila fought against

Christians in central Europe, c. 450; Amal[a]ric, king of the Arian Visigoths, was defeated in battle by the kings of the Catholic Franks in 531 (*Enciclopedia Universal*, 5: 12–13). For the *Ludus de Antichristo*, performed at the court of Frederick Barbarossa, see below, note 20. For the Riga *Ludus Prophetarum*, see Young, *Drama*, 2: 542, and for an English translation of the Latin original, see Axton, *European*, p. 44. In the biblical account (Judges 6–8), Gideon defeats the Midianites rather than the Philistines. For early mock combats in general, see Axton, *European*, pp. 33–46, and Tydeman, *Theatre*, pp. 6–9.

14. Hoenerbach, *Studien*, pp. 10–11, misreading Muñoz Renedo, *Representación*, p. 11, cites line 1602 of the *Poema de mio Cid* as evidence of a *moros y cristianos* in Valencia in 1094, but the line speaks only of a military training exercise involving "*tablados*." Smith, *Poema*, p. 128, explains that "the *tablado* was a construction of boards and scaffolding (possibly an imitation castle), against which the knights threw *bohordos* (darts) in an attempt to knock it down" (see also Ledesma Rubio and Falcón Pérez, *Zaragoza*, p. 144). While it is possible that one or more of the *tablados* may have been understood to represent a besieged castle held by Muslims, or that such a castle may have been erected on top of a *tablado* (meaning in this case a stage or scaffold), as was the case in the *moros y cristianos* held at the court of Jaume II in Zaragoza (see below, Ch. 4), the text of the *Poema de mio Cid* does not so specify. Castellanos, "Costumbres," pp. 165–166, also suggests that the *danzas de moros y cristianos* had their origin in the conquest of Valencia by El Cid in 1094, but cites no authority.

15. Walsh, "Performance," pp. 16–18.

16. Monroe, "Prolegomena," prints, translates, and judiciously explains Ibn Quzman's *Zagal No. 12*; I have quoted from pp. 94, 97, 121–122 of his article.

17. Walsh, "Performance," p. 21.

18. For the early history of the tournament, see Barber and Barker, *Tournaments*, pp. 13–27.

19. Amades, *Danzas*, and Warman, *Danza*, use *danza* to designate the entire tradition of *moros y cristianos*, danced or not. Amades, *Costumari*, 3: 294–295, calls the Alcoy *fiestas de moros y cristianos*, a three-day street theater extravaganza involving thousands of actors, a *ball* (dance). For the first references to sword dances, see Corrsin, *Sword*, pp. 17, 71. Alford, *Sword*, p. 28, cites a reference to a sword dance in Nuremberg in 1350, but Corrsin told me (personal communication, 28 October 1997) that "the 1350 date apparently comes from eighteenth-century sources. . . . The earliest verifiable date [for a sword dance in Nuremberg] is 1490."

20. Chambers, *Mediaeval*, 2: 63. Young, *Drama*, 2: 394, however, concludes: "There is nothing to show that [*The Play of Antichrist*] was acted in association with the liturgy, or even within a church." For the Latin text of the play, see Young, *Drama*, 2: 371–387, and for an English translation, see Wright, *Play of Antichrist*. For a discussion of the date of the play, see Wright, p. 24.

21. Lladonosa y Pujol, *Història*, pp. 93, 253–257.

CHAPTER 4. A MEDLEY OF BATTLES (ZARAGOZA, 1286–1414)

1. Milá y Fontanals, *Obras*, 6: 233; Shergold, *History*, p. 113; Stern, *Medieval*, p. 96.

2. García Rodero and Caballero Bonald, *Festivals*, pp. 207–209, 284.

3. For the excerpt from Armengol's sermon, see Castellanos, "Costumbres," p. 165. Castellanos does not cite his source, although he implies ("we read") that he has before him a printed text. I have been unable to locate any volume of Armengol's sermons. The relevant portions of Castellanos, including his full citation from Armengol, are readily available in Caro Baroja, *Estio*, pp. 119–120.

The church of Our Lady of the Pillar, otherwise known as Santa María la Mayor, is one of Zaragoza's two cathedrals. The marble pillar is one on which Santiago is reputed to have seen a vision of the Virgin Mary. Languedocian, or Provençal, was the language of the medieval troubadours and is still spoken in southern France. The Cistercian monastery of Poblet was founded by Ramon Berenguer IV around 1150, and became, in the Middle Ages and beyond, the most prosperous monastery in Aragon-Catalonia, serving as the "dynastic mausoleum" (Bisson, *Medieval*, p. 120) for several generations of royalty.

4. Aubrun, "Débuts," p. 297. For theatrical use of the Aljafería, see also Shergold, *History*, pp. 114–121, and Stern, *Medieval*, pp. 96–99. For its history and design, see Arco, *Zaragoza*, p. 59, and Reilly, *Contest*, pp. 83 (photo), 160.

5. Castellanos, "Costumbres," p. 165.

6. "*In hoc signo vinces*" was reputedly inscribed on a pillar of light in the form of a cross that appeared to the Emperor Constantine before his victory at the Battle of Milvian Bridge, A.D. 312 (Smith, *Constantine*, pp. 101–103).

7. Castellanos, "Costumbres," p. 165.

8. Such is the practice today in the only extant French *maures et chrétiens*, at Martres-Tolosanes (Haute-Garonne), which I attended in June 1996. In a field outside the village, a lengthy pitched battle is fought between ranks of Franks and Saracens on foot and on horseback (see Boudignon-Hamon and Demoinet, *Fêtes*, pp. 132–137).

9. Bigongiari, "Theaters," p. 214.

10. Horcasitas, *Teatro*, p. 84.

11. Rodríguez Becerra, *Guía*, p. 341; Sánchez, *Guía*, p. 56.

12. Hillgarth, *Spanish*, 1: 263.

13. Martínez Ferrando, "Jaume," pp. 106–110.

14. Hillgarth, *Spanish*, 1: 250, 255.

15. For *The Siege of Troy*, see Loomis, "Secular," pp. 108–110. For the text of *The Castle of Perseverance*, see Eccles, *Macro*, pp. 1–111, and for discussions of its staging, see Southern, *Medieval*; Tydeman, *Theatre*, pp. 156–159; and King, "Morality," pp. 243–247. For the historical siege of Balaguer, see Hillgarth, *Spanish*, 2: 237, or Bisson, *Medieval*, p. 235, and for its reenactment, see Shergold, *History*, pp. 116–117. For wheeled castles and other devices, see Tydeman, *Theatre*, pp. 70–79, 86–95.

16. For the jousters dressed as Tartars and the quintain, see Barber and Barker, *Tournaments*, pp. 32, 163. For the Paris *Siege of Jerusalem* and *Pas Saladin*, see Loomis, "Secular," pp. 103–107, 110.

17. Froissart, *Chronicles*, p. 353; see also Tydeman, *Theatre*, p. 93, and Loomis, "Secular," p. 110.

18. Madurell, "Noces," p. 56; Massip, "Rei," p. 65.

19. Shergold, *History*, pp. 115–120; see also Aubrun, "Débuts," pp. 301–302, and Massip, "Rei," p. 74.

20. Hillgarth, *Spanish*, 1: 407, 2: 233.

CHAPTER 5. A MARTYRDOM WITH HOBBY HORSES (BARCELONA, 1424)

1. For an earlier and more detailed version of this chapter, see my "Catalan."

2. For the list of representations in 1424, see Milà y Fontanals, *Obras*, 6: 376–379; for a summary in English, see Very, *Spanish*, pp. 37–39, or Shergold, *History*, pp. 56–57.

3. *Entremès* (literally, "between courses" and hence "interlude" or "short play") can, in this context, signify both the scene and the float or pageant wagon on which it is represented.
4. The text of the contract is printed in Milà y Fontanals, *Obras*, 6: 255−256, and Duran i Sanpere and Sanabre, *Llibre*, 1: 87−89. See also Balaguer, "De las antiguas," p. 368.
5. Alemany's name suggests that he may have been German, perhaps of Jewish heritage. A contemporary, Jaume Alamany, is described in Beccadelli, *Fets*, pp. 122−123, as "a Christian man, but born of Jewish parents." Tomás Alemany's contract with the city council is reprinted in Milà y Fontanals, *Obras*, 6: 254−255, and Duran i Sanpere and Sanabre, *Llibre*, 1: 167−169. Tomás Alemany's son, Gabriel, succeeded him in the business of preparing Corpus Christi floats (Durán y Sanpere, *Fiesta*, p. 24).
6. Milà y Fontanals, *Obras*, 6: 248.
7. Curet, *Visions*, p. 204; Very, *Spanish*, p. 4. A list of expenses for the 1380 procession, published by Llompart in "Fiesta," pp. 31−32, alludes to many of the *entremesos* that reappear in the 1424 list but makes no mention of the hobby horses. Even at this early date, the Barcelona hobby horses would not have been the first to engage in mock skirmishes. De Roos, "Battles," p. 170, cites a 1359 Dutch reference that she found in Jonckbloet, *Geschiedenis*, 3: 600, to "'the companions . . . who jousted on wooden horses,' i.e. on hobby horses."
8. Alford, *Hobby*, pp. 3, 79.
9. For Berga, see Armengou, *Patum*, pp. 95−98, or Noyes, "Mule," pp. 45−46, 303−306; for Vilafranca, see Bové, *Penedès*, pp. 65−66.
10. For Saint Sebastian and the narrative detail of the Mauretanian archers, see *Enciclopedia Universal*, 54: 1262−1265; for his birth in Narbonne, see Mills, *Mystère*, p. xii; and for the claim that he was from Barcelona, see Amades, *Costumari*, 1: 548. For the etymology of "Moor" and "Mauri," and for a map showing the third-century boundaries of Mauretania, see Raven, *Rome*, pp. xxvi−xxviii. For Rome's dependence on Mauri and Numidian archers, see Boudot-Lamotte, *Contribution*, p. ix. For the persecution of Christians under Diocletian, which, in fact, began "in the late 290s" and was at its height between 303 and 306, see Williams, *Diocletian*, pp. 170−185. For the Catalan Company, see Muntaner, *Crónica*, 2: 79−181 (chs. 193−244), and Hillgarth, *Spanish*, 1: 233−238, 268−270. I know of one other Corpus Christi pageant, from sixteenth-century Freiburg, that features Turks and Saint Sebastian (see Martin, *Freiburger*, pp. 82−84, lines 2018−2069). I am grateful to Ralph Blasting for this reference.
11. Both *castel* and *rocha* can simply mean "float," but as Shergold, *History*, p. 140, points out, these terms, "often used as synonyms for *entremés*, may have originated from floats that actually represented a rock . . . or a castle, as many of them frequently did." In the case of the Barcelona *Martyrdom of Saint Sebastian*, the distinction between the Great Turk's "castle" and Saint Sebastian's "rock" seems to be pertinent. A further complication arises from the difference at this point between the transcriptions of the contract published by Milà y Fontanals (*Obras*, 6: 255) and Duran i Sanpere and Sanabre (*Llibre*, 1: 167). Where the former's version reads, "*la rocha e l'arbra e los bastatxos per portar aquella ab lurs bastimens he barbes* [the rock and the tree and the bearers to carry that with their frames and beards]," the latter substitutes "*águila* [eagle]" for "*aquella* [that]" and "*vestiments* [clothes]" for "*bastimens* [frames]." Grau, "Cavallets," p. 4, takes the "eagle" to be the gilded eagle that still dances in many Catalan festivals, but it is hard to see what role it would have played in the *Martyrdom of Saint Sebastian*. I am grateful to Jan Grau and Marta Ibáñez for drawing my attention to Duran i Sanpere and Sanabre's transcription.
12. Milà y Fontanals, *Obras*, 6: 254−255; Duran i Sanpere and Sanabre, *Llibre*, 1: 167−168.

13. Duran i Sanpere and Sanabre, *Llibre*, 1: 82. Milà y Fontanals, *Obras*, 6: 255, reads "*patges* [pages]" for "*jutges* [judges]." In this instance, I am inclined to favor Duran i Sanpere and Sanabre's version.

14. Shergold, *History*, p. 58.

15. Amades, *Costumari*, 1: 567–568, 572.

16. In another Catalan version of the Saint Sebastian legend, Sebastian was a Barcelona fisherman whose success was envied by the other fishermen. Catching him bathing one day, they stole his cloak, tied him to a tree, and killed him by piercing him with his own fishing canes (Amades, *Costumari*, 1: 548).

17. Kolve, *Play*, p. 45.

18. Ryder, *Alfonso*, p. 248.

19. Beccadelli (also known as Panormita) wrote in Latin. He is quoted copiously, in Spanish translation, in Ametller y Viñas, *Alfonso*, 2: 448–454. Not having access to Beccadelli's original, I have translated Ametller's version. Amades, *Danzas*, pp. 100–101, cites Ametller and mentions Alfonso's presence at the 1424 Barcelona Corpus Christi festivities, as does Durán y Sanpere, *Fiesta*, p. 18. For an account of Alfonso's campaign against Naples and a summary in English of the triumphal entry, see Ryder, *Alfonso*, pp. 210–251.

20. Segura i Vila, *Historia*, 2: 158–166.

21. Ibid., 2: 160–166. See also Castellá y Raich, "Igualada," p. 193, and "Estudi," p. 270. Amades, *Danzas*, pp. 101–102, cites many of the same references but mistakenly assigns them a single date, 1450.

22. Castellá y Raich, "Estudi."

23. Alford, *Hobby*, p. 104.

24. Very, *Spanish*, p. 49. For the sixteenth-century reference, see Stern, *Medieval*, p. 116.

25. Very, *Spanish*, p. 34.

26. Llompart, "Fiesta," p. 5.

27. Sánchez, *Guía*, p. 13; see also Alford, *Hobby*, p. 107 and pl. VIII.

28. Espinosa Maeso, "Ensayo," pp. 573–582.

29. Llompart, "Fiesta," pp. 9–10.

30. Llompart, "Fiesta," p. 13; Capmany, *Enramades*, p. 34; Very, *Spanish*, p. 40.

31. Very, *Spanish*, pp. 106–109.

32. Curet, *Visions*, p. 234.

33. Capmany, *Enramades*, p. 49.

34. Amades, *Costumari*, 1: 565–567, 2: 99–100.

35. Casademont i Donay, "Cavallets," p. 1.

36. Alford, *Hobby*, p. 106.

37. Langdon-Davies, *Gatherings*, p. 27, and illustration following p. 128.

38. Murlà i Giralt, *Gegants*, pp. 150–152.

39. Casademont i Donay, "Cavallets," p. 3.

40. Amades, *Costumari*, 1: 981; cf. 1: 1012, 3: 30.

41. Casademont i Donay, "Cavallets," p. 3.

42. Armengou, *Patum*, p. 22; Noyes, "Mule," pp. 256, 303.

43. Noyes, "Mule," p. 46.

CHAPTER 6. A GAME OF CANES (JAÉN, 1462)

1. Records of theatrical activity in medieval Castile-León are generally sparse. For a discussion of "the apparent lacuna in the Castilian theatre between the twelfth-century *Auto*

de los Reyes Magos and Gómez Manrique (c. 1412–1490)," see Surtz, "Spain," pp. 195–202, and for an attempt to fill the "three-hundred-year gap," see Stern, *Medieval*.

2. Toral Peñarada, *Estudios*, pp. 13–24, 110–117; Ruiz, "Elite," pp. 299–302; Hillgarth, *Spanish*, 2: 333–337; Carriazo, *Hechos*, pp. xxxvii–xlvi.

3. Carriazo, *Hechos*. For a discussion of the uncertain authorship of the chronicle, see Gayangos, *Relación*, pp. 517–518; Carriazo, *Hechos*, pp. xxi–xxxi; and Aubrun, "Chronique," pp. 41–42.

4. Carriazo, *Hechos*, pp. 70–76. The representation of the Magi varied from year to year, for in 1463 King Herod appears, there is no mention of Mary, and the Magi are played by three adult knights who arrive at Lucas's house on horseback, guided by a star strung up on a cord in the street (p. 102).

5. For a discussion of *momos*, see Surtz, *Birth*, pp. 69–72.

6. Aubrun, "Chronique," p. 47. For the Easter egg fights in 1461 and 1463, see Carriazo, *Hechos*, pp. 63–64, 123. Brisset, *Fiestas*, p. 12, and Stern, *Medieval*, p. 106, assume that "*huevos cocidos* [hard-boiled eggs]" were used in the fight, but the text uses this phrase only for the eggs served afterward and there seems to me to be little festive point in throwing eggs that don't erupt on contact! For carnival 1463, see Carriazo, *Hechos*, pp. 109–112. Ruiz, "Elite," p. 314, interprets the clause "*la gente se daban unos a otros con ello*," in the account of the carnival meal, to mean that "the people in the square began hitting each other with the chickens."

7. Carriazo, *Hechos*, pp. 117, 257–259.

8. Carriazo, *Hechos*, pp. 187–195. Gayangos, *Relación*, p. 201, transcribes "*moros*" rather than "*moras*" and so misses (or conceals) the cross-dressing. For a note on the meaning of "*arbórbolas* [wailing]," see Gayangos, *Relación*, p. 201 n. 2, where he relates it to an Arabic word meaning the ululation of women. Aubrun, "Chronique," p. 51, mistakenly translates "*cauallejos de caña*" as "*chevaux de bois*"; Ruiz, "Elite," p. 305, offers the better "wicker horses." They were, I assume, tourney horses made not of wood but of supple canes or osier twigs.

9. The date is usually given as 1463 (Shergold, *History*, p. 123; Ruiz, "Elite," pp. 296–297), a confusion wrought by the fact that the chronicler begins each new year with the festivities of the Christmas season. Thus, although this *moros y cristianos* is recorded under the rubric 1463, it actually took place on Sunday, December 26, 1462 (Carriazo, *Hechos*, pp. 98–100).

10. *Enciclopedia Universal*, 11: 299–300; see also Romero de Terreros, *Torneos*, pp. 3–4.

11. Carriazo, *Hechos*, pp. 99–100.

12. Roach, *Cities*, pp. 205–207.

13. Ruiz, "Elite," p. 314.

14. Barber and Barker, *Tournaments*, p. 102.

15. Hillgarth, *Spanish*, 2: 126–169.

16. Amades, *Danzas*, pp. 99–100, mentions the Valencia *entremès* but gives no source, noting only that "the chronicler does not indicate whether or not a battle was represented." Amades is inclined to think not. Brisset, *Fiestas*, p. 113, mistakenly transfers to Valencia a 1437 reference to the Turks and hobby horses in the Barcelona Corpus Christi procession. Resende, *Vida*, p. 354 (ch. cxxxi), records the Portuguese "skirmish."

17. Brisset, *Fiestas*, pp. 13, 93–94.

18. Plá Cargol, *Gerona*, pp. 131–132; Warman, *Danza*, p. 30.

19. Ricard, "Fiche."

20. Stern, *Medieval*, p. 3.

21. All the evidence, according to Ricard, "Fiche," p. 288, "shows that, although they

have today become a popular entertainment, the festivals of Moors and Christians were originally an entertainment of the court."

22. As possible influences on the *moros y cristianos* tradition, Brisset, *Fiestas*, pp. 10–12, lists *juegos de cañas*, courtly festivities, Epiphany plays ("there are similarities between the speeches of the three wise kings on horseback and those of the Christian kings and ambassadors" in the *moros y cristianos*), the "poetic duels" of medieval minstrels, carnival masquerades, Basque *pastorales*, military parades and shows, Corpus Christi pageants, and popular festivals. "I do not believe," he concludes, "that a single origin [for the *moros y cristianos*] can be found."

23. Gómez García, "Mala," p. 138.

24. I am using the familiar language of the Magnificat in the *Book of Common Prayer*.

CHAPTER 7. THE FIELDS OF THE WARS OF FLOWERS

1. Clendinnen, "Ways," pp. 118–119. I am deeply indebted to Kay Read for her careful reading and many corrections of an early draft of Chapters 7–11.

2. "Mexica" is now believed to be a more precise designation of the inhabitants of Tenochtitlan-Tlatelolco. The broader terms "Aztec" or, by reference to their common language, "Nahua" cover many Yuto-Aztecan groups in Mesoamerica, including such enemies of the Mexica as the Tlaxcalteca and Huexotzinca.

3. Thomas, *Conquest*, pp. 5, 26.

4. Carrasco, "Give," p. 11.

5. For a sympathetic attempt to understand the ethics of human sacrifice from the Mexica perspective, see Read, *Time*.

6. Beeching, *Galleys*, p. 179.

7. Faber, *Histoire*, 1: 14–15. According to Delangre, *Théâtre*, pp. 6–7, the record of the decapitation is contained not in the official account of the royal entry but in a handwritten note later published in the *Feuille de Tournai*, 23 July 1848. For a recent discussion of this account, its status as history or "urban legend," and its place in the larger history of violent entertainment, see Enders, "Medieval Snuff Drama."

8. Moriarty, "Ritual Combat."

9. Chimalpahin, *Relaciones*, pp. 152–153, 177.

10. Chimalpahin, *Relaciones*, pp. 82–83, 89, 157, 182, 189. For the *Anales de Cuauhtitlan*, see Bierhorst, *History*, pp. 73–74, and Bierhorst, *Codex*, p. 38; see also Hicks, "Flowery," pp. 87–88. The flowery war lasted, depending on the account, as little as eight years or as many as thirty-nine.

11. Chimalpahin, *Relaciones*, p. 183.

12. Durán, *History*, pp. 231–233 (chs. 28–29).

13. Ibid., pp. 233–235 (ch. 29).

14. Ibid., pp. 286–287 (ch. 38).

15. Ibid., pp. 425–427 (ch. 57).

16. Ibid., pp. 438–440 (ch. 59).

17. Brundage, *Fifth*, p. 205.

18. Hicks, "Flowery," p. 91.

19. Hassig, *Aztec*, pp. 129–130, 254–256; Hassig, *War*, pp. 145–146.

20. Durán, *Historia*, 1: 140–141 (ch. 14); English translation adapted from Durán, *Book*, p. 227.

21. Durán, *History*, p. 410 (ch. 55). On p. 402, Durán appears to use the term "flowery

war" to describe wars that have as their purpose "recreation for the army" and "pleasure and food for the gods," but this is the translator's explanatory interpolation. Durán, *Historia*, 2: 411 (ch. 54) uses only the unqualified phrase "*las guerras* [the wars]."

22. Alvarado Tezozómoc, *Crónica*, pp. 413–414, 453.

23. Brundage, *Fifth*, pp. 205–208; Hassig, *Aztec*, p. 10. For the weapons used in both *yaoyotl* and *xochiyaoyotl*, see Hassig, *Aztec*, pp. 81–85, 130.

24. Hicks, "Flowery," p. 91.

25. Durán, *History*, pp. 334–335 (ch. 43).

26. Durán, *History*, pp. 126–127 (ch. 15); Alva Ixtlilxochitl, *Obras*, 1: 445–446.

CHAPTER 8. THE FESTIVAL OF THE SWEEPING OF THE ROADS

1. Carrasco, "Give," p. 20; Broda, "Templo," p. 70; Clendinnen, *Aztecs*, pp. 5, 258; Thomas, *Conquest*, p. 24.

2. Clendinnen, *Aztecs*, p. 111.

3. For a detailed chart of the Mexica calendar festivals, see Turrent, *Conquista*, between pp. 112 and 113. Turrent, p. 70, notes that "the lack of precision as to when the months began derives from the sources."

4. Matos Moctezuma, "Templo," p. 30; Broda, "Templo," p. 81.

5. Broda, "Templo," pp. 62, 106.

6. Scott, *Domination*, p. 2.

7. Clendinnen, *Ambivalent*, p. xi; Bakhtin, *Speech*, pp. 6–7.

8. Toci's name means "our grandmother," but in this instance, she seems to have appeared in her role of Yoacihuatl or "woman of war" (Sahagún, "Relación," p. 307; Brown, "Ochpaniztli," p. 202).

9. Brown, "Ochpaniztli," pp. 206–207. It is easier to make a case for some Mexican *moros y cristianos* being grafted onto pre-Christian agricultural rites than it is for their Spanish counterparts.

10. Durán, *Book*, pp. 231–232 (ch. 15) and pl. 24. Although the wooden image represented "an old woman," the "historical" Toci was said to have been a young girl. One early account (1553) of the festival reflects the historical tradition, saying that the Toci impersonator was "the most beautiful Indian virgin that could be found" (Gómez de Orozco, "Costumbres," p. 48).

11. Sahagún, *Florentine*, 3: 118–119 (bk. 2, ch. 30); Sahagún, *Historia*, pp. 131–132; Torquemada, *Monarquía*, 3: 396 (bk. 10, ch. 23); Clendinnen, *Aztecs*, p. 201. For a proposed reconstruction of the "hand-waving dance," see Martí and Kurath, *Dances*, p. 135, and for an explanation of their system of notation, p. vii. Anderson and Dibble's translation, in *Florentine*, of the flora carried by the dancers as "flowering *tagetes* branches" is unclear. *Cempoalxochitl* denotes the Aztec marigold (*tagetes erecta*). Sahagún's description, in *Historia*, of the dancers carrying "in both hands flowers called *cempoalxochitl*, not arranged but cut with the same stem" would seem to describe a cluster of uncut marigolds.

12. Durán, *Book*, pp. 232–234 (ch. 15); Sahagún, *Florentine*, 3: 119–120 (bk. 2, ch. 30); Sahagún, *Historia*, p. 132; Brown, "Ochpaniztli," p. 203; Horcasitas and Heyden remark, in Durán, *Book*, p. 233 n. 4, that "the phrase 'disguised as Huaxtecs' may mean that the . . . men were naked."

13. Sahagún, *Florentine*, 3: 120 (bk. 2, ch. 30); Sahagún, *Historia*, pp. 132–133; Durán, *Book*, pp. 233–234 (ch. 15); Clendinnen, *Aztecs*, p. 201; Brown, "Ochpaniztli," p. 203.

14. Durán, *History*, pp. 35–39 (ch. 4); Davies, *Aztecs*, pp. xv, 30–34.

15. Sahagún, *Florentine*, 3: 120−121 (bk. 2, ch. 30); Sahagún, *Historia*, p. 133; Kirchhoff, cited in Broda, "Tlacaxipeualiztli," p. 251.

16. Broda, "Tlacaxipeualiztli," pp. 199, 251.

17. León-Portilla, *Pre-Columbian*, p. 87.

18. Durán, *Book*, pp. 227 (ch. 14), 235 (ch. 15); Durán, *History*, pp. 456−457 (ch. 62). For an illustration of the arrow sacrifice among the Chichimeca, see Broda, "Tlacaxipeualiztli," p. 234.

19. Sahagún, *Florentine*, 3: 121 (bk. 2, ch. 30); Sahagún, *Historia*, p. 133; Seler, *Comentarios*, 1: 120; Brown, "Ochpaniztli," p. 203; Durán, *History*, pp. 48, 52 (chs. 5 and 6); Gillespie, *Aztec*, pp. 26−28, 55.

20. Sahagún, *Florentine*, 3: 121−122 (bk. 2, ch. 30); Sahagún, *Historia*, pp. 133−134; *Codex Borbonicus*, p. 30; Clendinnen, *Aztecs*, pp. 202, 205, and following p. 240.

21. Sahagún, *Florentine*, 3: 122 (bk. 2, ch. 30); Sahagún, *Historia*, p. 134; for the identification of Iztactepetl and Iztaccihuatl, see López Austin, *Juegos*, p. 41.

22. Clendinnen, *Aztecs*, p. 342.

23. Matos Moctezuma, "Templo," p. 57; see also Broda, "Templo," p. 98.

24. Sahagún, *Florentine*, 3: 122 (bk. 2, ch. 30); Sahagún, *Historia*, p. 134.

25. *Códice Chimalpopoca*, pp. 29, 161, dates the collapse of Culhuacan to 1347, suggesting that the causes had more to do with internal discord than with Mexica conquest. Brown, "Ochpaniztli," p. 197, argues from other sources that "the Aztecs considered the conquest of Culhuacan of major historical importance."

26. Torquemada, *Monarquía*, 3: 398 (bk. 10, ch. 23); Sahagún, *Florentine*, 3: 122−123 (bk. 2, ch. 30); Sahagún, *Historia*, pp. 134−135.

27. For the "Song of Teteo Innan [Toci]" that may have been sung at this point, see Sahagún, *Florentine*, 3: 226 (bk. 2, app. 6); Sahagún, *Historia*, pp. 175−176.

28. Clendinnen, *Aztecs*, pp. 203−204; Sahagún, *Florentine*, 3: 124−125 (bk. 2, ch. 30); Sahagún, *Historia*, p. 135.

29. Sahagún, *Florentine*, 3: 125−126 (bk. 2, ch. 30); Sahagún, *Historia*, pp. 135−136; Durán, *Book*, pp. 235−237 (ch. 15).

30. Brown, "Ochpaniztli," pp. 195, 206.

31. Clendinnen, *Aztecs*, p. 204.

32. Ibid., p. 259.

CHAPTER 9. THE FESTIVAL OF THE RAISING OF THE BANNERS

1. Sahagún, *Florentine*, 3: 141, 197−199, 204 (bk. 2, ch. 34, app. 3), 4: 6−7 (bk. 3, ch. 1); Sahagún, *Historia*, pp. 142, 165−168, 193−194.

2. Thomas, *Conquest*, p. 12.

3. Sahagún, *Florentine* 2: 1 (bk. 1, ch. 1); Sahagún, *Historia*, p. 31; Brotherston, "Huitzilopochtli"; León-Portilla, *Aztec*, pp. 158−165; Davies, *Aztecs*, pp. 17−18.

4. Sahagún, *Florentine* 4: 1−5 (bk. 3, ch. 1); Sahagún, *Historia*, pp. 191−192.

5. Seler, *Collected*, 3: 233, 5: 93−99; Caso, *Aztecs*, pp. 12−14; Graulich, *Myths*, pp. 224−233.

6. González Torres, *Culto*, pp. 80−81, argues for an exclusively historical interpretation. Matos Moctezuma, "Templo," pp. 48−59, and *Life*, pp. 49−56, suggests that historical and cosmological explanations are not mutually exclusive. See also Davies, *Aztecs*, pp. 12−18.

7. Sahagún, *Florentine*, 10: 45−49 (bk. 9, ch. 10); Sahagún, *Historia*, pp. 506−508; Clendinnen, *Aztecs*, pp. 136−138.

8. Sahagún, *Florentine*, 3: 141–142 (bk. 2, ch. 34); Sahagún, *Historia*, pp. 142–143.

9. Sahagún, *Florentine*, 3: 142–143 (bk. 2, ch. 34), 4: 4 (bk. 3, ch. 1); Sahagún, *Historia*, pp. 143, 192; Torquemada, *Monarquía* 3: 404 (bk. 10, ch. 27); Durán, *Book*, p. 73 (ch. 2); Sten, *Ponte*, pp. 89–99.

10. Durán, *Book*, pp. 84–86 (ch. 2).

11. Sahagún, *Florentine*, 3: 143–144, 175 (bk. 2, ch. 34, app. 1), 10: 63 (bk. 9, ch. 14); Sahagún, *Historia*, pp. 143–144, 156, 512. For paintings of the image of Huitzilopochtli, see Durán, *Historia*, or Durán, *Book*, plates 3 and 4.

12. Durán, *Book*, pp. 86–87 (ch. 2).

13. Sahagún, *Florentine*, 3: 145, 175–176 (bk. 2, ch. 34, app. 1); Sahagún, *Historia*, pp. 144–145, 156; Durán, *Book*, pp. 87 (ch. 2), 457–458 (ch. 18); Clendinnen, *Aztecs*, p. 254. For a painting of Paynal, see *Codex Borbonicus*, p. 9, reproduced in Sten, *Ponte*, following p. 64. For a mapping of Paynal's route in relation to the streets of modern Mexico City, see Durán, *Book*, p. 458 n. 1.

14. Clendinnen, *Aztecs*, p. 142; López Austin, *Juegos*, p. 47.

15. Broda, "Templo," p. 77; Matos Moctezuma, *Life*, pp. 67–68.

16. Sahagún, *Florentine*, 3: 145–146 (bk. 2, ch. 34), 10: 64 (bk. 9, ch. 14); Sahagún, *Historia*, pp. 145, 513; Clendinnen, *Aztecs*, p. 142–143; López Austin, *Juegos*, pp. 47–51.

17. Sahagún, *Florentine*, 3: 146 (bk. 2, ch. 34); Sahagún, *Historia*, p. 145; Durán, *Book*, p. 87–88 (ch. 2).

18. Sahagún, *Florentine*, 3: 147 (bk. 2, ch. 34), 4: 5–6 (bk. 3, ch. 1); Sahagún, *Historia*, pp. 145, 193; Clavijero, *Historia*, 3: 169–170; Durán, *Book*, p. 88–89, 84–85 (chs. 2–3).

19. Sahagún, *Florentine*, 4: 67 (bk. 3, app., ch. 9); Sahagún, *Historia*, p. 214; Thomas, *Conquest*, p. 27.

20. Sahagún, *Florentine*, 3: 147 (bk. 2, ch. 34), 10: 65 (bk. 9, ch. 14); Sahagún, *Historia*, pp. 146, 513; Durán, *History*, pp. 191–192 (ch. 23); Clendinnen, *Aztecs*, p. 254.

21. Sahagún, *Florentine*, 3: 148 (bk. 2, ch. 34), 10: 66–67 (bk. 9, ch. 14); Sahagún, *Historia*, pp. 146, 514; Clendinnen, *Aztecs*, p. 138.

22. Sahagún, *Florentine*, 3: 148–149 (bk. 2, ch. 34); Sahagún, *Historia*, p. 146; Clendinnen, *Aztecs*, p. 118.

23. Sahagún, *Florentine*, 3: 149–150 (bk. 2, ch. 34), pl. 31; Sahagún, *Historia*, pp. 146–147; Sahagún, "Relación," pp. 312–313; Clendinnen, *Aztecs*, pp. 113–114, 129.

24. Thomas, *Conquest*, pp. 10–11; Clendinnen, *Aztecs*, p. 113.

CHAPTER 10. THE FESTIVAL OF THE FLAYING OF MEN

1. Broda, "Templo," p. 100; Clendinnen, *Aztecs*, p. 92.

2. Durán, *Book*, p. 184.

3. Burkhart, *Holy*, p. 43.

4. Massip, "Continuïtat," pp. 93–94.

5. Seler, *Collected*, 3: 284.

6. Markman and Markman, *Flayed*, p. 177.

7. Martí and Kurath, *Dances*, pp. 68, 76.

8. Sahagún, *Florentine*, 3: 240 (bk. 2, app. 6); Durán, *Book*, p. 176 (ch. 9).

9. Broda, "Tlacaxipeualiztli," pp. 197, 258.

10. Broda, "Tlacaxipeualiztli," p. 265; Carrasco, "Give," pp. 2–3, 25.

11. Durán, *Book*, p. 174 (ch. 9).

12. Sahagún, *Florentine*, 3: 46–49 (bk. 2, chs. 20–21), 9: 83–84 (bk. 8, app. A).

13. Durán, *Book*, p. 176 (ch. 9).

14. Sahagún, *Florentine*, 3: 47–48 (bk. 2, ch. 21); Sahagún, *Historia*, pp. 100–101; Motolinía, *Memoriales*, p. 51 (pt. 1, ch. 16).

15. Sahagún, *Florentine*, 3: 48–49 (bk. 2, ch. 21); Sahagún, *Historia*, p. 101; Broda, "Tlacaxipeualiztli," pp. 203–205.

16. Durán, *History*, pp. 170, 273–274, 429–430, 474 (chs. 20, 36, 57, 65); Broda, "Tlacaxipeualiztli," p. 235.

17. Durán, *History*, pp. 170, 274–275 (chs. 20, 36); Sahagún, *Florentine*, 3: 49–51 (bk. 2, ch. 21); Sahagún, *Historia*, p. 101; Pomar, "Relación," p. 18; Broda, "Tlacaxipeualiztli," p. 210.

18. Sahagún, *Florentine*, 3: 51–52 (bk. 2, ch. 21), 9: 84 (bk. 8, app. B); Sahagún, *Historia*, pp. 101–102; Durán, *History*, pp. 169–171 (ch. 20); Durán, *Book*, pp. 176–178 (ch. 9); Pomar, "Relación," p. 20; Alvarado Tezozómoc, *Crónica*, p. 220 (ch. 50); Broda, "Tlacaxipeualiztli," pp. 211–213, 220–221. For a summary of the Mexica war against the Tepanec, see Davies, *Aztecs*, pp. 70–78.

19. Sahagún, *Florentine*, 3: 52–53 (bk. 2, ch. 21), 9: 84 (bk. 8, app. B); Sahagún, *Historia*, pp. 102–103; Durán, *History*, pp. 171–172, 275 (chs. 20, 36).

20. Sahagún, *Florentine*, 3: 53–55 (bk. 2, ch. 21), 9: 85 (bk. 8, app. B); Sahagún, *Historia*, pp. 102–103; Durán, *History*, pp. 173, 276 (chs. 20, 36); Durán, *Book*, p. 180 (ch. 9); Alvarado Tezozómoc, *Crónica*, p. 222 (ch. 50); Carrasco, "Myth," p. 155. For the wide distribution of the custom of flaying and other elements of Tlacaxipeualiztli, see Acosta Saignes, *Tlacaxipeualiztli*, and Broda, "Tlacaxipeualiztli," pp. 252–257.

21. Carrasco, "Give," pp. 15, 21.

22. Sahagún, *Florentine*, 1: 65 (bk. 1, ch. 18), 3: 50 (bk. 2, ch. 21), 9: 85 (bk. 8, app. B); Sahagún, *Historia*, pp. 45, 101.

23. Sahagún, *Florentine*, 1: 65 (bk. 1, ch. 18); Sahagún, *Historia*, p. 45; Durán, *History*, p. 173 (ch. 20); Durán, *Book*, pp. 182–184 (ch. 9), 415 ("Calendar," ch. 5); Mendieta, *Historia*, 1: 110 (bk. 2, ch. 15); Broda, "Tlacaxipeualiztli," pp. 221, 226–228.

24. Clendinnen, *Aztecs*, pp. 209, 260–261; Carrasco, "Give," p. 3.

CHAPTER 11. THE DANCE OF THE EMPEROR MOTECUZOMA

1. Lockhart, *Nahuas*, p. 374. Martí and Kurath, *Dances*, represents the most sustained effort to reconstruct "the choreography and music of precortesian dance."

2. Pérez de Ribas, *Historia*, 3: 325–327 (bk. 12, ch. 11); English translation adapted from Pérez de Ribas, *Life*, pp. 244–246, and Bierhorst, *Cantares*, pp. 88–90.

3. Treviño and Gilles, "History," pp. 109–111, 121.

4. Kurath, "Mexican"; Robb, "Matachines," pp. 88–91; Champe, *Matachines*, pp. 1–6; Rodríguez, *Matachines*, pp. 6–8.

5. Bierhorst, *Cantares*, pp. 3–4; Lockhart, "Care," p. 129; Lockhart, *Nahuas*, pp. 393–394. Bierhorst believes that, as part of a larger "revitalization movement," dancers representing the spirits of ancestral warriors reenacted historical battles, celebrating past victories and reversing past defeats. The significance of the songs "was hidden from missionaries and even from younger, acculturated Aztecs . . . by virtue of its having been coded in a diction accessible only to Indian conservatives." Thus, when the songs spoke of gathering "flowers" or weeping for "songs" from another world, or of "fine-colored birds" "scattering," "raining," "flying," or "whirling" to earth, they were using traditional metaphors to signal that the dancers represented the spirits of ancestral kings and warriors returning to earth. It is to

such translation and commentary that Lockhart, "Care," pp. 125–126, strenuously objects. While he grants that "in the *Cantares*, . . . flowers, songs, and birds often have additional references to people," he denies that those people must be "revenants." "A whole series of Nahuatl verbs frequent in the texts—*malina, ilacatzoa, ihcuiya*—are uniformly translated [by Bierhorst as] 'whirl' even though their primary meaning is 'to twist elongated matter.' In the *Cantares*, flowers are the most usual object of these verbs, followed by songs, and the senses that leap to the eye are 'to entwine garlands of flowers,' secondarily 'to string together verses of a song,' and thirdly 'to entwine and bring together the present happy company.'" Moreover, "'down' is often seen in the translation with no basis in the text whatever," as in the last line of song 70, where "bringing down" is offered by Bierhorst as the translation for "*quihualaxitia*, a verb form which says nothing about up or down." Lockhart's revised translation would not have revenants whirling down from heaven, but it would allow for dancers gathering to represent ancestral battles.

6. Lockhart, *Nahuas*, p. 394.

7. Bierhorst, *Cantares*, pp. 154–159, 188–191, 434–436, 440. For Spanish translations of and alternative commentaries on Songs 15 and 24, see Garibay, *Poesía*, 2: 11–12, 90–93, lxxv–lxxviii, cxv–cxvii. For the historical defeat of Acolhuacan, see Alva Ixtlilxochitl, *Obras*, 1: 332–342, 433–439.

8. Bierhorst, *Cantares*, pp. 317–319, 471–472. Cf. Garibay, *Poesía*, 3: 53–54, xlii. For an account of Axayacatl's Matlatzincan or Tolucan campaign, see Durán, *History*, pp. 263–277 (chs. 35–36); Alvarado Tezozómoc, *Crónica*, pp. 206–217 (chs. 48–49); and, for its date, Davies, *Aztecs*, p. xvi.

9. Durán, *History*, p. 270 (ch. 35).

10. Treviño and Gilles, "History," pp. 117–119.

11. For the death of Fulano Guzmán, see Durán, *Historia*, 2: 568 (ch. 77).

12. Bierhorst, *Cantares*, pp. 318–323, 472–476. For Tecuichpo's marriages, see Thomas, *Conquest*, pp. 453, 594.

13. López de Gómara, *Cortés*, pp. 147–148.

14. Sahagún, *Florentine*, 3: 55 (bk. 2, ch. 21).

15. López de Gómara, *Cortés*, p. 148.

16. Hernández, *Antigüedades*, pp. 116–118 (bk. 2, ch. 7); Sahagún, *Florentine*, 9: 45 (bk. 8, ch. 14).

17. Durán, *Book*, p. 296 (ch. 21); Tovar, *Relación*, p. 190 (bk. 2, ch. 4); Sahagún, *Florentine*, 4: 47–48 (bk. 3, app., ch. 3); Bierhorst, *Cantares*, pp. 71–72; Read, personal communication, 30 November 1997.

18. Torquemada, *Monarquía*, 3: 434–437 (bk. 10, ch. 38); Larsen, "Notes"; Leal, "Voladores"; Bierhorst, *Cantares*, pp. 66–69; Read, personal communication, 30 November 1997.

CHAPTER 12. THE CONQUEST OF MEXICO (1524–1536)

1. Sahagún, *Florentine*, 13: 55–56 (bk. 12, ch. 20).

2. For the best recent account of these events, see Thomas, *Conquest*.

3. Díaz, *Historia*, p. 460 (ch. 174). Maudslay, in Díaz, *True*, 5: 6, incorrectly translates "*embuscadas de cristianos y moros*" as "dances of Christians and Moors." For an account of the "dreadful march to Honduras," see Prescott, *Conquest*, pp. 643–654 (bk. 8, ch. 3).

4. Warman, *Danza*, p. 74.

5. Díaz, *Historia*, p. 504 (ch. 190).

6. Curcio, "Saints," p. 68; *Actas*, 1: 186.

7. Powell, *Soldiers*; Gradie, "Discovering." For the tradition that Cortés accepted Zumárraga's invitation to take part in the procession, see Keyes, *Grace*, pp. 61–70.

8. Sánchez, "Imagen," pp. 236–238, 245–246. A facsimile of the 1649 Nahuatl text of the *Huey tlamahuiçoltica*, together with the 1926 Spanish translation and notes of Feliciano Velázquez, is printed in Junco, *Radical*, pp. 57–158. The account of the procession is found on pp. 102–105.

9. Poole, *Lady*, p. 221.

10. Poole summarizes his conclusions, for which the bulk of his meticulously researched book provides the arguments and evidence, in *Lady*, pp. 214–225. For other summaries of the debate over the authenticity of the *Huey* and its narrative, see Lafaye, *Quetzalcoatl*, pp. 231–253, and Nebel, *Santa*, pp. 207–217.

11. Poole, *Lady*, p. 156.

12. Florencia, *Estrella*, pp. 29–30, 115; Ricard, "Contribution," p. 65; Harris, *Dialogical*, pp. 73–74. For an assessment of Florencia and his sources, see Poole, *Lady*, pp. 156–165.

13. Hassig, *Aztec*, pp. 108, 133, 241; Thomas, *Conquest*, p. 486.

14. Thomas, *Conquest*, p. 410.

15. See Chapter 15 of this book.

16. Lucero-White Lea, *Literary*, p. 21.

17. Cabeza de Vaca, *Naufragios*, p. 214 (ch. 36).

18. *Documentos*, 2: 324. See also López Cantos, *Fiestas*, pp. 169–170.

CHAPTER 13. THE CONQUEST OF RHODES (MEXICO CITY, 1539)

1. Phelan, *Millennial*, pp. 5–77; West, "Medieval"; Horcasitas, *Teatro*, p. 500. In a play performed in Valladolid in 1519 to mark Charles V's election as Holy Roman Emperor, the Turkish ambassador is made to say that even Turkish astrologers have discovered signs of Charles's imminent recovery of Jerusalem from the Turks (Surtz, "Spanish," p. 227).

2. Livermore, *History*, p. 216.

3. Durant and Durant, *Story*, 6: 515.

4. Paso y Troncoso, *Epistolario*, 3: 243–244, cites a letter from Viceroy Mendoza, dated 23 January 1539, reporting that the news arrived earlier in the same month. Motolinía, *History*, p. 160 (treatise 1, ch. 15) prints a letter written, perhaps, by himself to his superior Antonio de Ciudad Rodrigo, which begins, "As you know, dear Father, the news reached this land a few days before Lent." Díaz, *Historia*, p. 544 (ch. 201), says that the news arrived in 1538. Martínez, *Cortés*, p. 710, relying on Díaz, writes that "the news of this peace must have reached Mexico in the month of September [1538]."

5. Motolinía, *History*, p. 160 (tr. 1, ch. 15).

6. Paso y Troncoso, *Epistolario*, 3: 244.

7. *Actas*, 4: 165, cited in Martínez, *Cortés*, p. 713.

8. For the banquets, see Díaz, *Historia*, pp. 546–548 (ch. 201). For the date of Easter Sunday 1539 (6 April) and hence the ability to calculate Ash Wednesday and other dates in the 1539 calendar, see Parise, *Book*, p. 327. Ash Wednesday is the seventh Wednesday before Easter.

9. Las Casas, *Apologética*, 1: 334 (bk. 3, ch. 64); Díaz, *Historia*, p. 545 (ch. 201). In the following account, I have quoted from both Díaz and Las Casas. For an English translation

of the Las Casas passage, see Versényi, *Theatre,* pp. 31–32, and for an English translation of Díaz's account, see Díaz, *True,* 5: 188–197. For a description of musical instruments used in colonial Mexico, see Horcasitas, *Teatro,* pp. 146–151. Fig. 15a reproduces what Horcasitas, p. 501, believes to be a stylized rendering of the artificial city of Rhodes and one of the sailing ships mentioned in the next paragraph. This may be so, although the date assigned to the record in the Nahuatl text is 1538.

10. Pereyra, *Cortés,* p. 406; Madariaga, *Cortés,* p. 471; Dotor, *Cortés,* p. 407; Martínez, *Cortés,* p. 711.

11. Díaz, *Historia,* p. 548 (ch. 201).

12. Williams, *Teatro,* p. 66, suggests that "the square was converted into an artificial lake." Not only would this have severely impeded the rest of the play's action, but it is explicitly ruled out by Las Casas's observation that the ships looked "as if they were on water, [while] going on land."

13. Lopes Don, "Carnivals," p. 20.

14. Motolinía, *History,* p. 158 (tr. 1, ch. 15); for the artificial spring, see Díaz, *Historia,* p. 546; and for other examples of Indian set design, see Horcasitas, *Teatro,* pp. 110–112.

15. For the relationship between Cortés and Mendoza, see Aiton, *Mendoza,* pp. 116–124, and Martínez, *Cortés,* pp. 708–718. For Charles V's Algerian campaign, see Martínez, pp. 735–737, and Livermore, *History,* pp. 223–224.

16. Díaz, *Historia,* p. 545 (ch. 201). Maudslay, in Díaz, *True,* 5: 190, translates "*garrotes añudados y retuertos*" as "knotted and twisted cudgels." Clubs or cudgels made of knotted and twisted rope are still used by the combatants in the annual "jaguar fights" in the state of Guerrero (see McDowell, "Aztecs," p. 743).

17. Horcasitas, *Teatro,* p. 503; Pierce, "Identification," p. 5. I am grateful to Susan Verdi Webster for helping me to understand Horcasitas's reference to the Ixmiquilpan frescoes.

18. Durán, *Book,* pp. 160–164, 296–297 (chs. 8, 21), pl. 14; Horcasitas, *Teatro,* p. 105; Lopes Don, "Carnivals," pp. 24–25.

19. Shergold, *History,* p. 617. See also Livermore, "Caballero."

20. Shergold, *History,* pp. 115–116.

21. Luis de León Romano was present for Charles V's triumphal entry to Rome in April 1536. This recent spectacle probably had more influence than the ancient Roman games on León's design for the Mexican festivities. Commissioned by the emperor, León soon left Rome for Mexico, where he served as the senior magistrate in the cities of Puebla and Oaxaca and died in 1558 (Ricard, *Etudes,* pp. 161–168, and Lopes Don, "Carnivals," p. 22).

22. Palmer, *Slaves,* pp. 27, 133; Davidson, "Negro," p. 237.

23. Karasch, "Commentary One," p. 139.

24. Palmer, *Slaves,* pp. 54–55.

25. *Colección,* 2: 198–199; Aiton, *Mendoza,* pp. 87–89; Davidson, "Negro," p. 243.

26. Palmer, *Slaves,* pp. 136–139.

27. Thomas, *Conquest,* p. 559.

28. Williams, *Teatro,* p. 65; see also Williams, "Teatro," p. 139.

29. Ciudad Real, *Tratado,* 2: 81–82 (ch. 73); Powell, *Mexico's,* p. 110, offers a translation of this passage.

30. Cuche, *Poder,* pp. 174, 178; see also Cuche, *Pérou,* pp. 131–132.

31. Fuentes, *Estadística,* p. 595; see also Fuentes, *Lima,* pp. 119–120, and Pradier-Fodéré, *Lima,* p. 221.

32. Zaragoza, *St. James,* pp. 106–108. I saw the Loíza fiestas in July 1997.

33. Williams, *Teatro*, p. 65.

34. Kandell, *Capital*, p. 144.

CHAPTER 14. THE CONQUEST OF JERUSALEM (TLAXCALA, 1539)

1. Gibson, *Tlaxcala*, pp. 28–41, 51, 55, 67–68, 72, 75–88, 104–106, 141, 156.

2. Motolinía, *History*, pp. 152–154 (tr. 1, ch. 15). For the relationship between the Tlaxcalteca and the Otomí, see Thomas, *Conquest*, pp. 238, 241–243.

3. Epton, *Spanish*, pp. 164–171; King, "*Festa.*" See Ciudad Real, *Tratado*, 2: 148, for another sixteenth-century Mexican play on "the assumption of our Lady."

4. Las Casas, *Apologética*, 1: 333 (ch. 64).

5. Ricard, *Spiritual*, p. 200. Although Ricard is generally correct, it was not unusual for Latin hymns to be incorporated in Nahuatl drama (see Horcasitas, *Teatro*, pp. 145–146).

6. Here, as elsewhere, Steck mistakenly translates "*en canto de órgano*" as "to the accompaniment of the organ" (cf. Motolinía, *Historia*, p. 67, and Motolinía, *History*, p. 159). Later in the same paragraph, Steck translates the same phrase correctly as "in harmony." Horcasitas, *Teatro*, p. 142, points out that "*canto de órgano* does not refer in any way to the instrument of that name" but to polyphonic song, as distinct from the older plainsong, or *canto llano*.

7. Motolinía, *History*, pp. 156–159 (tr. 1, ch. 15).

8. Horcasitas, *Teatro*, p. 84. For the account of the plays, see Motolinía, *History*, pp. 154–155 (tr. 1, ch. 15).

9. Arróniz, *Teatro*, p. 63.

10. Motolinía, *History*, p. 160, and, for the following account of the play, pp. 160–167 (tr. 1, ch. 15), and Motolinía, *Historia*, pp. 67–72. For the date of Easter 1539 (6 April) and hence the ability to calculate Corpus Christi and other moveable feasts in the 1539 calendar, see Parise, *Book*, p. 327. O'Gorman, in Motolinía, *Historia*, p. 67 n. 24, dates Corpus Christi one week later on 12 June, but other authors (Sten, *Vida*, p. 211, and María y Campos, *Guía*, p. 41) confirm the earlier date. Corpus Christi falls on the Thursday after Trinity Sunday, which is itself eight weeks after Easter Sunday.

11. O'Gorman, in Motolinía, *Historia*, pp. xxix, 63–64 n. 11, 65 n. 19. O'Gorman's argument is not conclusive, but it is consistent with the letter's otherwise odd ascription, in Motolinía, *History*, p. 155 (tr. 1, ch. 15), to "a resident friar of Tlaxcala" rather than to Motolinía himself.

12. Gibson, *Tlaxcala*, pp. 164–165.

13. Ibid., pp. 44–45, 124–127.

14. Motolinía, *History*, p. 160.

15. The play was not, as Gibson, *Tlaxcala*, p. 38, implies, performed on a single "stage," but, in the manner of the *Conquest of Rhodes*, used the entire plaza as an elaborate playing area. For a diagram of the location of the scenic units in relation to one another and to the square as a whole, see my *Dialogical*, p. 83. This diagram may be compared with the plan of central Tlaxcala provided by Gibson, p. 127, so long as it is remembered that the "*cabildo* dwellings" on Gibson's plan are those built around 1550 (p. 128). The earlier buildings, to which the description of the play refers, were, as Gibson, pp. 125–126, makes clear, on the northwest side of the square. I have followed Gibson's more precise account of the relation-

ship of the square to the points of the compass. Thus, what the friar's letter calls the western side of the square was, in fact, the northwestern side.

16. For similar effects, see Gage, *Travels*, p. 146, and Rangel, *Historia*, p. 34.

17. Hillgarth, *Spanish*, 2: 386.

18. Horcasitas, *Teatro*, p. 507; Thomas, *Conquest*, p. 455; López de Gómara, *Conquista*, p. 248.

19. Motolinía, *History*, pp. 161, 165; Motolinía, *Historia*, pp. 68, 72.

20. For the activities of Alvarado and Cortés in June 1539, see Recinos, *Alvarado*, pp. 176–183; Kelly, *Alvarado*, pp. 206–207; Madariaga, *Cortés*, p. 472; Díaz, *True*, 5: 199 (ch. 201); and Martínez, *Cortés*, p. 713. Martínez gives both 8 June (pp. 726 and 903) and 8 July (p. 713) as the date of the fleet's departure from Acapulco. Since he cites as his source (p. 716 n. 81) Captain Francisco de Ulloa's account of the voyage, which includes a departure date of "*ocho de julio*" in its title, the later date would appear to be correct.

21. García Icazbalceta, *Colección*, p. 89 n. 21; Motolinía, *Historia*, ed. Baudot, p. 43; Baumann, "Tlaxcalan," p. 143; Martínez, *Cortés*, pp. 713–718, 895; Madariaga, *Cortés*, pp. 472–473; Aiton, *Mendoza*, pp. 34–36, 121–123.

22. Horcasitas, *Teatro*, p. 508; Arróniz, *Teatro*, p. 83.

23. López de Gómara, *Conquista*, p. 248; Baumann, "Tlaxcalan," pp. 145–146.

24. Thomas, *Conquest*, pp. 455, 587.

25. Gibson, *Tlaxcala*, pp. 98–100; Thomas, *Conquest*, p. 491.

26. Phelan, *Millennial*, p. 33.

27. Gibson, *Tlaxcala*, p. 191.

28. Motolinía, *History*, pp. 14–15, 18.

29. Versényi, *Theatre*, pp. 33–34.

30. Williams, "Teatro," p. 143; Horcasitas, *Teatro*, p. 508.

31. Ricard, *Spiritual*, p. 87.

32. In *Dialogical*, p. 91, I assumed that Michael disappeared upward, in the manner of the Virgin Mary in the 1538 assumption play, "with a quick manipulation of the ropes, pulleys, and painted cloudwork." I now think it more likely, since there is no mention of "heaven" or of "high mountains" in this play, that the actor, having stepped into full view from a hiding place within or behind the tower, simply returned to his place of concealment.

33. Pagden, *Fall*, pp. 41–47; Harris, *Dialogical*, pp. 125–127.

34. Motolinía, *History*, p. 182 (tr. 2, ch. 3); Ricard, *Spiritual*, p. 91.

35. Motolinía, *History*, pp. 184–191 (tr. 2, ch. 4). See also, for a summary of the controversy, Ricard, *Spiritual*, pp. 91–94; for the text of the episcopal decree, García Icazbalceta, *Zumárraga*, 3: 149–184; and, for a discussion of the political ramifications of the controversy, Rivera, *Violent*, pp. 229–234. For the location of the baptisms in Huaquechula rather than, as Motolinía, *History*, pp. 189–190, has it, Quecholac, see Motolinía, *Historia*, p. 89 n. 13. Huaquechula is about twelve miles south of Atlizco.

36. Arróniz, *Teatro*, p. 82.

37. Motolinía, *Historia*, ed. Baudot, pp. 24, 42–43; Arróniz, *Teatro*, p. 83.

38. Motolinía, *History*, pp. 166–167 (tr. 1, ch. 15); Motolinía, *Historia*, pp. 73–74.

39. Horcasitas, *Teatro*, p. 191, suggests that a Nahuatl *Sacrifice of Isaac*, extant in eighteenth-century manuscript form, may be the text of the play performed in Tlaxcala in 1539. He prints, on pp. 208–229, both the Nahuatl text and a Spanish translation. Raviz, *Early*, pp. 83–98, has translated this play into English. Potter, "Abraham," p. 310, believes that this text "is almost certainly derived from the 1539 Tlaxcala performance." Burkhart, *Holy*, p. 238, notes both plays but offers no theory as to their relationship. Stylistic evidence for an early

date of the *Sacrifice of Isaac* is substantial. Beyond that, only the coincidence of subject matter links this text and the Tlaxcala *Sacrifice of Abraham*.

CHAPTER 15. THE TENSIONS OF EMPIRE (MEXICO CITY, 1565–1595)

1. Kandell, *Capital*, p. 144; Thomas, *Conquest*, p. 590. Beginning in 1529, Mexico City celebrated the feast day of St. Hippolytus each year with bullfights and a procession of the city's standard from the government building to the church of St. Hippolytus (see Rangel, *Historia*, p. 7; Warman, *Danza*, p. 73). Since Tenochtitlan surrendered on that day in 1521, an occasional skirmish or game of canes may have been adapted to recall the conquest.

2. For the masquerade, see Romero, *Torneos*, pp. 22–24; Sten, *Vida*, pp. 78–79; and Warman, *Danza*, pp. 97–98. For the conspiracy, see Suárez de Peralta, *Conjuración;* Parkes, *History*, pp. 95–96; and Kandell, *Capital*, pp. 190–194. Romero, citing a report by Manuel Orozco y Berra, says that the masquerade took place in October 1566, but other authorities, including Martínez, *Cortés*, pp. 525, 780, agree that the Avila brothers were arrested 16 July 1566 and beheaded in the main square on 3 August. The most likely conclusion is that the performance took place in October 1565. Further confusion can be avoided if it is remembered that Hernán Cortés named two of his sons after his father, Martín: the first (b. 1522) by his indigenous translator Marina, and the second (b. 1532) by his second wife Juana de Zúñiga. It is the latter who was implicated in the supposed plot, while the former was tortured to extract evidence against his half brother.

3. Beeching, *Galleys;* Livermore, *History*, p. 244.

4. Dibble, *Historia*, p. 82, fol. 113, reproduces in color the manuscript text and illustration, transcribes the Nahuatl text, and translates it into Spanish. Horcasitas, *Teatro*, pp. 122–124, 512–513, reproduces a detail of the illustration in black and white, transcribes the Nahuatl text, offers his own Spanish translation, and comments on both text and illustration. Horcasitas's transcription and translation differ from Dibble's. Kay Read and Jane Rosenthal very kindly provided me with a literal English translation of the Nahuatl, which Kay and I then worked on further over the phone to produce the version I have used. Dibble's text gives the date as Friday, 30 July 1572, although he notes that the British Museum MS (like Horcasitas's versions) has 25 July. I have checked the date for Easter Sunday 1572 (6 April) in Parise, *Book*, p. 372, and thus confirmed that 25 July 1572 was a Friday. As for the illustration, the reader who lives in a rainy climate and is familiar with sloping roofs may think at first that the roof of the scenic building was sloped and contained a broad window, but this is the effect of poor perspective rather than the representation of an architecture unknown in Mexico City at the time. Elsewhere in the codex (Dibble, *Historia*, p. 45), *tlapanco* denotes a flat roof: unusually heavy rain, rather than running off the roof, causes corn to grow on it. For the *quauhteocalli* that may have been used in the *Conquest of Rhodes*, see Dibble, *Historia*, p. 64, fol. 90, and Horcasitas, *Teatro*, p. 501.

5. Horcasitas, *Teatro*, p. 512. Dibble, *Historia*, p. 82, translates *acalco* simply as "*en barcos* [in boats]." Formed from *atl* (water) and *calli* (house), *acalli* literally means "water house." When the locative suffix *co* (in) is added, it contracts to *acalco*.

6. Compare Dibble, *Historia*, p. 71, fol. 98, where the entry for 6 June 1557 uses *tlatoque* to designate Mexica "lords" assembled to hear a Spanish proclamation, and p. 88 (15 June 1581), where *tlatoque* refers to the king of Spain and viceroy of Mexico.

7. Romero, *Bocetos*, p. 19 (ch. 2).

8. *Actas,* 12: 213–214, 220–223; Rangel, *Historia,* pp. 30–34; see also Warman, *Danza,* pp. 96–97. For the siege of Malta, see Beeching, *Galleys,* pp. 67–98.

9. Rangel, *Historia,* p. 34.

10. Torquemada, *Monarquía,* 3: 436 (bk. 10, ch. 38).

11. Suárez de Peralta, *Conjuración,* p. 6. See also Romero, *Torneos,* 4: 5; Warman, *Danza,* p. 95.

12. Rangel, *Historia,* p. 24.

13. Juan Sánchez Vaquero, as cited in María y Campos, *Guía,* pp. 56–57, has the performance take place indoors in a Jesuit school; Johnson, *Triunfo,* p. 13, places it during the procession.

CHAPTER 16. THE TRAVELS OF ALONSO PONCE (NEW SPAIN, 1584–1589)

1. Ciudad Real, *Tratado,* 2: 5. For a translation of this passage and for a more detailed account of dances and plays seen by the friars, see my "Dramatic," pp. 238–245.

2. Ciudad Real, *Tratado,* 2: 141–142. For other early descriptions of this dance, see Sahagún, *Florentine,* 9: 30 (bk. 8, ch. 10), pl. 64; Clavijero, *History,* 1: 404–405 (bk. 7, sect. 46) and pl. 16; and, in seventeenth-century Guatemala, Fuentes y Guzmán, 1: 364–366 (bk. 16, ch. 5). Illustrations from Sahagún and Clavijero are reproduced in Martí and Kurath, *Dances,* pp. 64, 86. For the Indian performers who traveled with Cortés, see Chapter 18 of this book.

3. Ciudad Real, *Tratado,* 2: 78, 114, 141, 363.

4. Ibid., 2: 69, 71, 331.

5. Ibid., 1: 14, 2: 19, 150, 369.

6. Potter, "Illegal," p. 143; see also Broyles González, "Native," and Herrera-Sobek, "Mexican."

7. Flores, "History," p. 170.

8. Ciudad Real, *Tratado,* 2: 100–103; see also Horcasitas, *Teatro,* pp. 329–330.

9. Trexler, "We Think," pp. 197, 201, 207. For brief references to Ciudad Real, see Robe, *Coloquios,* pp. 9–10; Ricard, *Spiritual,* pp. 199–200; Gibson, *Tlaxcala,* p. 147; and Powell, *Mexico's,* p. 110.

10. Ciudad Real, *Tratado,* 2: 326.

11. Ibid., 2: 114–121.

12. Harris, *Dialogical,* pp. 116–119.

13. Ciudad Real, *Tratado,* 2: 81–82.

14. Ibid., 2: 150–151.

15. Ibid., 2: 79.

16. Ibid., 2: 82–83.

17. Ibid., 1: 105.

18. Ciudad Real, *Tratado,* 1: 102–104.

CHAPTER 17. THE CONQUEST OF NEW MEXICO (1598)

1. Hammond and Rey, *Oñate,* p. 314, translating from *Colección,* 16: 242.

2. Gutiérrez, "Politics," p. 51.

3. Hammond and Rey, *Oñate,* p. 315, translating from *Colección,* 16: 242. The site of

the celebrations was some fifteen miles south of the present-day El Paso/Ciudad Juárez, in what is now Texas.

4. Villagrá, *Historia*, p. 131 (canto 14, lines 316–331). The Encinias, Rodríguez, and Sánchez edition, from which I quote, contains, side by side, the Spanish original and an English translation. New Mexico and the Church each seem to have been represented not by a single allegorical figure but by a group of actors, for the Spanish verbs and pronouns are in the plural ("les *labase aquella culpa* [would wash out *their* fault]" and "*traían* [*they* brought]").

5. Hammond and Rey, *Oñate*, pp. 248–249; see also Villagrá, *Historia*, p. xvii.

6. Gutiérrez, "Politics," pp. 51–52, unaccountably ignores the "nueva" in "nueva México" (Villagrá, *Historia*, p. 131 [canto 14, line 321]) and so writes that Farfán's play "recounted the most important historical event in the spiritual conquest of Mexico—the arrival of the twelve Franciscan 'apostles' in Mexico City in 1524 and the spectacular greeting they received from Hernán Cortés." Farfán's play was not historical but, like the *Conquest of Jerusalem*, predictive.

7. Sando, *Pueblo*, pp. 51–52, 170.

8. Hammond and Rey, *Oñate*, pp. 318–319, identify the pueblo as San Juan Bautista, a name no doubt given it by the Spanish in honor of the day of their arrival, and place it "four leagues" north of Sevilleta, the present-day village of La Joya.

9. Villagrá, *Historia*, p. 143 (canto 15, lines 180–192).

10. Pearce, "Moros," p. 58.

11. The pueblo of Yungueingge, on the west bank of the Río Grande, was commandeered by Oñate as his military headquarters in the summer of 1598 and renamed San Juan de los Caballeros. The evicted Tewa inhabitants moved across the river to Ohke Oweege (present-day San Juan Pueblo), taking the name of San Juan with them. The Spanish renamed their capital San Gabriel de Yunque Yunque. It was almost certainly in San Gabriel that the *moros y cristianos* took place in September 1598.

12. Villagrá, *Historia*, p. 150 (canto 16, lines 100–111).

13. Hammond and Rey, *Oñate*, p. 323, translating from *Colección*, 16: 264.

14. Hammond and Rey, *Oñate*, pp. 325, 342–347.

15. Campa, *Hispanic*, p. 232. The historical referent of the play is not precise. Leadership of the Spanish forces is ascribed to Carlos Fernández, who defeated a war party led by Cuerno Verde in 1774. Most versions of the play end with Cuerno Verde's death, which occurred during the decisive victory of the Spanish over the Comanches in 1779. Different versions of the play have been published by Espinosa, *Comanches*, and Campa, *Comanches*. An English version can be found in Espinosa, "Comanches," pp. 133–144. For the historical background, see Campa, *Comanches*, pp. 7–11, 21, and Kenner, *History*, pp. 29, 47–51.

16. Espinosa, "Comanches," p. 134.

17. Brown, *Hispano*, pp. 40–43.

18. Espinosa, *Comanches*, p. 31; Campa, *Comanches*; p. 32, Espinosa, "Comanches," p. 140.

19. Campa, *Comanches*, p. 21; Campa, *Hispanic*, pp. 231–233. See also Roeder, "Comanches." A brief account of a performance of *Los Comanches* can be found in Jaramillo, *Shadows*, p. 46.

20. Champe, *Matachines*, p. 3.

21. Josie Espinosa de Luján, personal communication, 26 September 1993.

22. Lucero-White Lea, *Literary*, p. 22; Barker, *Caballeros*, pp. 236–237. Lucero-White Lea includes, on pp. 107–112, an edition of the Santa Cruz text. An earlier edition, in Spanish with an English translation, may be found in Pearce, "Moros," pp. 60–65. For a similar description of a *moros y cristianos* in Alcalde in 1928, see Austin, "Drama."

23. Espinosa de Luján, "Moros." For an edition of the Chimayo text, in Spanish with an English translation, see Espinosa de Luján, *Moros*. I am grateful to Josie Espinosa de Luján for showing me photographs of the performance during a visit to her home in 1993 and for providing further details in subsequent phone conversations.

24. White, *Santo Domingo*, pp. 149–154. See also White, "Impersonation." White, *Santa Ana*, pp. 272–276, describes a similar performance in Santa Ana Pueblo. There, the *konyisats* ceremony is "a dramatization of the coming, long ago, of the Spaniards from the south to Santa Ana pueblo." It involves a bull and several *konyisats* ("the people who came up from the south"), who "wear old clothes to represent Mexicans, wearing hats and shoes. They put on wigs and mustaches and beards." The *konyisats* also burlesque other outsiders, such as "Roman Catholic priests, officials of the US Indian Service, American tourists, their Mexican neighbors," and even "their own priests and medicine-men."

25. Sando, *Pueblo*, p. 52.

26. For descriptions of the Santo Domingo Corn Dance, see Fergusson, *Dancing*, pp. 56–60, and Sinclair, *New Mexico*, pp. 54–61.

27. For a description of the Pecos Bull Dance and the accompanying Corn Dance, see Parsons, *Jemez*, pp. 96–100. The patron saint of the old Pecos mission was Santa María de los Angeles de Porciúncula, named after the vision of Mary surrounded by angels that St. Francis is reputed to have seen at Porciuncula, near Assisi. Porcingula is a corruption of Porciuncula (Fergusson, *Dancing*, p. 62).

28. Such mockery is compatible with honorable service in the U.S. military. I heard at least one performer speak of his own tour of duty in Kuwait. Parsons, *Jemez*, p. 96, describes a similar mimicry of whites during the Pecos Bull Dance in 1922: "They are caricaturing Whites, their face and hands painted white; one wears a false mustache, another a beard of blond hair. 'U.S.A.' is chalked on the back of their coat or a cross within a circle."

29. Starr, *Notes*, p. 70; Heth, "American," p. 5.

30. Sando, *Pueblo*, p. 52.

CHAPTER 18. TOURING AZTECS (1522–1529)

1. Carrasco Urgoiti, "Aspectos," p. 481, or Carrasco Urgoiti, *Moro*, p. 39.

2. Las Casas, *Historia*, 1: 332, 435 (bk. 1, chs. 78, 112).

3. Honour, *European*, pp. 27–30.

4. Sturtevant, "First," p. 421.

5. For Dürer's reaction to the exhibit, see Dürer, *Records*, pp. 47–48. For the influence of Cortés's map on Dürer's ideal city, see Palm, "Tenochtitlan." For various efforts to date and interpret Jan Mostaert's *Picture with a Colonial Theme*, which is now in the Frans Hals Museum in Haarlem, see Michel, "Tableau"; Snyder, "Mostaert"; and Honour, *European*, pp. 30–32. For the sculpted faces in the palace of the prince-bishop of Liège, see Collon-Gevaert, "Art." For a summary of these and other materials, see Thomas, *Conquest*, pp. 536–537, 755–756.

6. Thomas, *Conquest*, pp. 564–569; Michel, "Tableau," pp. 138–139.

7. Thomas, *Conquest*, p. 537.

8. Irving, *History*, 1: 178, 190 (bk. 5, chs. 6, 8); Las Casas, *Historia*, 1: 333, 421 (bk. 1, chs. 78, 107); Las Casas, *History*, pp. 38, 56; Foreman, *Indians*, pp. 3–10.

9. Thomas, *Conquest*, pp. 220, 344–351; Cline, "Hernando," p. 81. For the archbishop's comments, see Carey, "Translation."

10. Martire d'Anghiera, *Orbe*, 2: 195, 202–204 (decade 5, bk. 10).

11. López de Gómara, *Cortés*, p. 148.
12. Gibson, *Tlaxcala*, p. 164; Navagero, "Viaje," pp. 851–852, and "Cartas," p. 886.
13. Weiditz, *Trachtenbuch*, pls. XI–XXIII; Cline, "Hernando"; Thomas, *Conquest*, p. 597.
14. Díaz, *True*, 5: 144 (ch. 195); Cline, "Hernando," p. 88.
15. Palomera, *Valadés*, p. 218; Thomas, *Conquest*, p. 598. Martínez, *Cortés*, pp. 503, 514, doubts Valadés's account, believing instead that the gout-ridden emperor "would only have devoted a few minutes to the Indian exhibitions prepared for him by Cortés."
16. Cline, "Hernando," p. 88; Díaz, *True*, 5: 152 (ch. 195); Ciudad Real, *Tratado*, 2: 141; López de Gómara, *Cortés*, p. 145 (ch. 68). Martínez, *Cortés*, pp. 514–518, 532, cites a letter, written 2 April 1529, that reports Cortés's departure from Toledo, 29 March, for his wedding in Béjar, and he dates the departure of the Indians for Rome at 16 April. Probably the foot jugglers left for Rome after the wedding.
17. Uhagón, *Relaciones*, p. 79; see also Marsden, "Entrées," p. 392.
18. Marsden, "Entrées," pp. 400–401.
19. Marsden, "Entrées," p. 392; Cotarelo y Mori, *Colección*, 1: clxxi–clxxii, prints the contract that lists the stage properties and other supplies needed for the dance; Massa, "Monde," p. 111, misreading Marsden, assumes that the "savages" were genuine Indians.

CHAPTER 19. ROYAL ENTRIES (TOLEDO, 1533, AND NAPLES, 1543)

1. Strong, *Art*, p. 76.
2. The letter is printed in Alenda y Mira, *Relaciones*, pp. 31–32. For Charles's campaign in Austria, passage through Italy, and return to Barcelona, see Martínez de Campo y Serrano, *España*, 1: 172.
3. According to Martín Arrúe, *Historia*, pp. 73, 77, Charles V ordered the restoration of Toledo's Alcázar in 1535 and work began by 1538. The *New Encyclopaedia Brittanica*, 2: 830, however, claims that work on the Alcázar "began about 1531."
4. Strong, *Art*, p. 22.
5. Lynch, *Spain*, 1: 35–41; Livermore, *History*, pp. 207–213.
6. Strong, *Art*, p. 48.
7. González Casarrubios, *Fiestas*, p. 149.
8. Mullaney, "Strange," p. 70.
9. De Spenis, "Breve," pp. 519–525. For al-Hasan, see Abun-Nasr, *History*, pp. 165, 177.
10. De Spenis, "Breve," p. 521, uses the term "*jomenta*" to describe the Moorish mounts. In modern Italian, *giumenta* means a mare, mule, or beast of burden, but in the late Middle Ages and early modern period, it also meant a small riding horse and hence, in this instance, the kind of lightweight Moorish cavalry horse for which De Spenis perhaps knew no more specialized term. I am grateful to John Dillon for help in translating this passage.
11. Croce, *Spagna*, p. 193.

CHAPTER 20. GREAT BALLS OF FIRE (TRENT, 1549)

1. Calvete, *Felicísimo*; Alvarez, *Relation*; Besozzi, *Crónica*, pp. 54–71. Kamen, *Philip*, p. 324 n. 12, observes that, although "Spanish writers call him Calvete, . . . Calvet always

wrote his name thus." He was probably Catalan. I am grateful to Marco Gozzi and Jeff Mueller for their bibliographical help with the first part of this chapter.

2. Calvete, *Felicísimo*, 1: 7–13.

3. Calvete, *Felicísimo*, 1: 29; Alenda y Mira, *Relaciones*, pp. 45–46.

4. Jedin, *History*, 1: 545, 556. For Madruzzo, see Jedin, *History*, 1: 566–574, and for the Madruzzo family, Dal Prà, *Madruzzo*.

5. Calvete, *Felicísimo*, 1: 124; Besozzi, *Crónica*, p. 69. For a recent study of pyrotechnic and other special effects in the medieval theater, see Butterworth, *Theatre*.

6. Calvete, *Felicísimo*, 1: 131–133; Besozzi, *Crónica*, pp. 69–70; Alvarez, *Relation*, p. 56. For the bishop's palace, see Jedin, *History*, 1: 563–564.

7. Besozzi, *Crónica*, p. 70. Neither Calvet nor Alvarez mentions the outdoor entertainment on Thursday night. Perhaps, having traveled all day, they retired earlier than Besozzi, who had arrived in Trent some days beforehand with Madruzzo.

8. Calvete, *Felicísimo*, 1: 134; Besozzi, *Crónica*, pp. 70–71. Besozzi seems to have left Trent at this point, for he makes no further mention of the festivities.

9. For an illustration of wild men and their "fire-clubs" from early-seventeenth-century Denmark, see Brock, *History*, pl. ii, and the explanatory text, pp. 32–33.

10. Calvete, *Felicísimo*, 1: 134–137; Alvarez, *Relation*, pp. 56–57.

11. Lotz, *Feuerwerk*, p. 33; Erdmann, "Theatrical," pp. 22–23; Schaub, "Pleasure," pp. 193–194.

12. Bertoldi, "Spettacoli," p. 194.

13. *Oxford*, pp. 220, 466.

14. Strong, *Art*, pp. 24–25, 54, 84, 171.

15. Calvete, *Felicísimo*, 1: 26–35; *Oxford*, pp. 220, 961.

16. Kamen, *Philip*, pp. 11, 54.

17. Calvete, *Felicísimo*, 1: 138–142; Alvarez, *Relation*, pp. 57–58.

18. Varey, "Spectacles," pp. 619–620.

19. Partington, *History*, pp. vi, 42–90; Lotz, *Feuerwerk*, pp. 22–23; Brock, *History*, pp. 29–30, summarizing Biringucci.

20. For the Patum, see Noyes, "Mule"; Armengou, *Patum*; Noguera i Canal, *Visió*; and Farràs, *Patum*. For a more detailed presentation of the argument that follows, see my "Fireworks."

21. Noyes, "Mule," p. 361.

22. Amades, *Gegants*, pp. 54–58; Amades, *Costumari*, 3: 73–75; Noyes, "Mule," pp. 326–333.

23. Schaub, "Pleasure," pl. 47.

24. Erdmann, "Theatrical," pp. 21–22; Schaub, "Pleasure," pp. 162–166, pl. 35.

25. Noyes, "Mule," pp. 265–268; Schmitt, "Jeunes," pp. 130–132, 154.

26. Milá y Fontanals, *Obras*, 6: 376–379; Very, *Spanish*, p. 67; Shergold, *History*, p. 54.

27. Noyes, "Mule," pp. 316–317; Amades, *Folklore*, 1: 1307–1308; Bartrina, *Castell*, pp. 96–97.

28. Amades, *Gegants*, pp. 179–189.

29. Bové, *Penedès*, pp. 73–85; Torras, *Manresa*, pp. 60–62.

30. Dumont, *Tarasque*; Very, *Spanish*, pp. 55–62; Noyes, "Mule," pp. 311–316; Amades, *Gegants*, pp. 163–165.

31. Noyes, "Mule," p. 326; Meurant, *Géants*, pp. 320–330.

32. Noyes, "Mule," pp. 326–328; Meurant, *Géants*, pp. 227–248, 325; Amades, *Gegants*, pp. 45–58. For the Bergen-op-Zoom Goliath, see also Autenboer, "Ommegangen," p. 112,

who cites a payment to "Willem the basketmaker" for braiding the frame of "Golias" out of "*teene* [twigs]."

33. According to Meurant, *Géants*, p. 74, the frames of the first sculpted giants were made of wicker ("*osier*") rather than wood.

CHAPTER 21. NOBLE FANTASIES
(BINCHE, 1549, AND ROUEN, 1550)

1. Calvete, *Felicísimo*, 1: 143.
2. Calvete, *Felicísimo*, 1: 163–164; Alvarez, *Relation*, p. 74; d'Haenens, *Folklore*, pp. 159–160.
3. Calvete, *Felicísimo*, 1: 204–211.
4. Enders, "Medieval."
5. For eyewitness accounts of the events in Binche, written by members of Philip's party, see Calvete, *Felicísimo*, 2: 1–69, and Alvarez, *Relation*, pp. 89–110.
6. For the *Liberation of the Castle of Gloom*, see Calvete, *Felicísimo*, 2: 19–50; Devoto, "Folklore"; and Barber and Barker, *Tournaments*, pp. 134–135.
7. Calvete, *Felicísimo*, 2: 50–52; Alvarez, *Relation*, pp. 105–106. Heartz, "Divertissement," reprints and comments on Italian and German eyewitness accounts as well as on Calvet's report. For comment on the drawing and its possible artist, see Van de Put, "Two," and Popham, "Authorship."
8. Heartz, "Divertissement," p. 332.
9. Ibid., pp. 333–339.
10. For descriptions of the mock siege, see Calvete, *Felicísimo*, 2: 53–61, and Alvarez, *Relation*, pp. 106–108. Wellens, "Compte," publishes extracts from the royal accounts detailing payments made in connection with the festivities. Calvete, 2: 54, identifies the prince of Piemonte as the captain general of the besieging army. Both the Italian and German witnesses quoted by Heartz, "Divertissement," pp. 341–342, name him as the leader of the dancers. Wellens, p. 281, identifies him as Emmanuel-Philibert de Savoie, who was to become duke of Savoie in 1553.
11. Wellens, "Compte," p. 295.
12. Glotz, *Carnaval*. I attended the Binche carnival in February 1999.
13. For discussions of the Brazilian pageant, including reproductions of a French eyewitness account and two contemporary illustrations, see Denis, *Fête*; Fruth, "American"; McGowan, "Form," pp. 218–220; Massa, "Monde"; and Mullaney, "Strange," pp. 70–73.
14. Fruth, "American," p. 27.
15. Denis, *Fête*, pp. 12–13, 60–63, identifies the "Tabegerres" as Tabayaras, the "Toupinabaulx" as Tupinambas, and "Morbicha," or *murubicha*, as a title rather than a name.
16. Fruth, "American," p. 28.
17. Massa, "Monde," p. 114.

CHAPTER 22. FÊTED DREAMS OF PEACE
(ANDALUSIA, 1561–1571)

1. Cortés Peña and Vincent, *Historia*, pp. 47–56.
2. Rodríguez de Ardila y Esquivias, "Historia"; Caro Baroja, *Moriscos*, pp. 141–150;

Lea, *Moriscos;* Braudel, *Mediterranean,* pp. 785–790; Cortés Peña and Vincent, *Historia,* pp. 169–175, 185.

3. For an account of the mock battle, see Rodríguez de Ardila y Esquivias, "Historia," pp. 112–114. Brisset, *Fiestas,* p. 125, cites the late-seventeenth-century paraphrase of Ardila by Gaspar Ibáñez de Segovia, eighth marquis of Mondéjar.

4. For accounts of the war and the events leading up to it, see Rodríguez de Ardila y Esquivias, "Historia," pp. 94–110, 116–125; Lea, *Moriscos;* Caro Baroja, *Moriscos,* pp. 173–204; Braudel, *Mediterranean,* 2: 1055–1073; Lynch, *Spain,* 1: 211–218; Beeching, *Galleys,* pp. 99–123; and Kamen, *Philip,* pp. 128–132.

5. Baumann, "Matanzas," pp. 86–91.

6. Bermúdez de Pedraza, *Historia,* p. 243 (pt. 4, ch. 89); Brisset, *Fiestas,* pp. 125–126.

7. Baumann, "Matanzas," p. 90.

8. Kamen, *Philip,* p. 131.

9. Rodríguez de Ardila y Esquivias, "Historia," p. 110.

10. Brisset, *Fiestas,* pp. 74–77.

11. Gómez García, "Mala," p. 136.

12. Linares Palma, "Fiesta," p. 177; Gómez García, "Mala," p. 125.

13. Gómez García, "Mala," p. 140.

14. *Válor,* p. 39.

15. Gómez García, "Mala," p. 142.

16. The letter was transcribed and published by Alenda y Mira, *Relaciones,* pp. 82–83. There is some confusion as to whether Per Afan III died in 1571 or 1572. It is possible that the progress from Alcalá to Tarifa honored Fernando alone, but the letter refers to *"los Excelentísimos Duques,"* and it is more natural to read the plural "dukes" in reference to both Per Afan and Fernando than to Fernando and his eldest son, then six years old, or to Fernando and Juana. For biographical data on Per Afan, Fernando, Juana, and the Enríquez de Ribera family in general, see González Moreno, *Don Fernando,* pp. 33–36, 186–187; Ramos Romero, *Alcalá,* pp. 234–236; Corzo Sánchez, *Tarifa,* pp. 78–81; and Martínez, *Hernán Cortés,* pp. 525–527. For the earlier liberation of the area from Moorish occupation, see Ramos Romero, *Alcalá,* p. 186; Corzo Sánchez, *Tarifa,* pp. 58–60; and Hillgarth, *Spanish Kingdoms,* 1: 59, 327–328, 341–342.

17. Ahmad R'honi, *Historia,* pp. 39, 84.

18. Brisset, *Fiestas,* pp. 94–95, also speaks, without further explanation, of the mock battle on the shore being "linked" to the earlier capture of Motecuzoma. He suggests that the author of the festivities may have been the young Juan de la Cueva, twenty-one years old at the time, whose strong interest in Mexico was soon to take him there for three years (1574–1577). On his return, de la Cueva wrote plays under the patronage of the Enríquez family and dedicated his *Exemplar poético* (1609) to Fernando's grandson, also called Fernando Enríquez de Ribera.

19. Warman, *Danza,* p. 40.

CHAPTER 23. CHANGING TASTES
(DAROCA TO VALENCIA, 1585–1586)

1. For a record of the journey, see Cock, *Relación.* For a summary in English, see Kamen, *Philip,* pp. 257–262.

2. Cock, *Relación,* pp. 17, 23–28; Beltrán, *Historia,* pp. 60–73; Sánchez, *Guía,* p. 90.

3. Cock, *Relación*, pp. 34–79.
4. Ibid., pp. 120–121.
5. Ibid., pp. 128–145.
6. Bouza, *Cartas*, p. 94; Cock, *Relación*, p. 146.
7. Cock, *Relación*, pp. 184–201.
8. Ibid., pp. 222–224.
9. Cock, *Relación*, pp. 227–233; Carreres Zacarés, *Ensayo*, 1: 143–164, 2: 322–325; Marsden, "Entrées," p. 398; Varey, "Spectacles," p. 624.
10. Cock, *Relación*, pp. 252–253.
11. Warman, *Danza*, pp. 46–47; Gallop, *Portugal*, pp. xii–xiv.
12. Mansanet Ribes, *Fiesta*, pp. 50–59, 82–83.
13. For an earlier and more detailed account of the fiestas in Villena and nearby Castalla, see my "Muhammed."
14. Foster, *Culture*, p. 224.
15. See also Bernabeu Rico, *Significados*, p. 74.

CHAPTER 24. GILDED INDIANS (1521–1600)

1. Shergold, *History*, p. 242; Alenda y Mira, *Relaciones*, p. 77.
2. Brooks, *Dances*, p. 365.
3. For compendia of citations concerning the European *matachines*, see Cotarelo y Mori, *Colección*, 1: cccviii–cccxiv; Caro Baroja, *Estío*, pp. 139–145; Forrest, *Morris*, pp. 34–41; and Esses, *Dance*, 1: 677–681.
4. For a brief overview of the distribution of the American *matachines*, see Kurath, "Moriscas," pp. 90–94. For more detailed studies of the New Mexican *matachines*, see Champe, *Matachines*, and Rodríguez, *Matachines*.
5. Robb, "Matachines," pp. 89–91; Forrest, *Morris*, p. 43.
6. Champe, *Matachines*, p. xii; Kurath, "Moriscas," p. 100; see also Rodríguez, *Matachines*, pp. 6–7.
7. Meketa, *Legacy*, p. 76.
8. Treviño and Gilles, "History," pp. 117–119.
9. Martire d'Anghiera, *Orbe*, 2: 195, 202–204 (decade 5, bk. 10).
10. Cline, "Hernando," pp. 82–86.
11. Brooks, *Dances*, p. 187.
12. Kurath, "Moriscas," p. 97. I know of only one scholar who claims to have uncovered a specific reference to European *matachines* before 1530. Bragaglia, *Danze*, p. 18, mentions a "fifteenth-century" collection of poetry, preserved in Milan's Biblioteca Ambrosiana, in which there is a *Balland mattazzin dennanz all'eccelsa Paolina Visconti*. Toschi, *Origini*, p. 498, cites Bragaglia, but comments, "One could wish for more precise bibliographical data." I have been unable to identify Bragaglia's source. Since the first verifiable references to *mattaccini*, which I discuss below, both come from mid-sixteenth-century examples of genres that were at their height in the fifteenth century, it is possible that Bragaglia's date is misleading. In any case, Bragaglia's uncertain reference is far too flimsy a foundation for a theory of medieval *mattaccini*.
13. Singleton, *Canti*, pp. 346–348. The Florentine origin of the song is suggested by the provenance of the *canti carnascialeschi* in general, the nearby location of the town (Volterra) from which the author comes, and the prevalence of old Tuscan words, such as *barbachéppo*

(fool), and forms, such as *dreto* for *dietro* (behind). Although in his notes, pp. 476–480, Singleton does not assign a specific date of composition to the song, he does place it late in his collection, among those *canti* that can be dated between 1530 and 1550, rather than among those from earlier in the century.

14. For views on the etymology of *matachines*, see Champe, *Matachines*, pp. 1–2; Forrest, *Morris*, pp. 34–35; and Rodríguez, *Matachines*, p. 6. The options appear to be Italian, as a diminutive form of *matto* (fool); Arabic, from *mutawajjihin* (maskers), although Forrest claims that this word, purportedly derived from *tawajjaha* (to assume a mask), "does not occur in literature"; Nahuatl, from *matlatzincayotl* or some other related word; and Spanish, from *matar* (to kill) and *chinos* (Chinese), by analogy with *matamoros* (killer of Moors), but since no version of the dance makes reference to Chinese opponents, this would appear the least likely.

15. Banfi, *Sacre*, p. 799; Rossi, *Quattrocento*, p. 460; Newbigin, personal communication, 28 August 1997.

16. Cited in Forrest, *Morris*, pp. 35, 40, and Battaglia, *Dizionario*, 9: 946–947.

17. Rabelais, *Oeuvres*, pp. 1488, 1499; Rabelais, *Works*, pp. 790, 800.

18. Arbeau, *Orchesography*, pp. 182–195. Having watched my videotape of the Sant Feliu de Pallerols *ball de cavallets* (see above, Chapter 5), Ingrid Brainard told me (personal communication, 10 May 1999) that one of the accompanying melodies is a variant of Arbeau's "tune of the buffens or mattachins."

19. Heartz, "Divertissement," pp. 333–336.

20. Quoted in Cotarelo y Mori, *Colección*, 1: cccix.

21. Díaz, *Historia*, p. 170 (ch. 91). Champe, *Matachines*, p. 1, unfortunately introduces her chapter on "the historical background" of the dance—in which she concludes that "all evidence provides such a solid foundation for the European origin of the name Matachines that the assumption of a Nahuatl origin may be disregarded"—with a late-eighteenth-century mistranslation of Díaz's remark as "some danced like those in Italy called by us Matachines." The original makes no mention of "Italy" or "us." Champe then compounds the problem by implying that Díaz wrote these words in Tenochtitlan in 1519.

22. For these and other English uses of the term, see Forrest, *Morris*, pp. 37–38.

23. Brooks, *Dances*, p. 237. For the Toledo performance, see above, Chapter 18.

24. Alenda y Mira, *Relaciones*, p. 77; Marsden, "Entrées," pp. 400–401. Marsden mistakenly gives the date as 1571.

25. Cotarelo y Mori, *Colección*, 1: clxxiii–clxxiv; Marsden, "Entrées," p. 392.

26. Brooks, *Dances*, pp. 159–160, 163, 365–375.

27. Ibid., pp. 163, 186–187.

28. Cotarelo y Mori, *Colección*, 1: cccix–cccxiv; Esses, *Dance*, 1: 677–681.

29. Esses, *Dance*, 1: 678–679.

CHAPTER 25. DANCING WITH MALINCHE (NEW MEXICO AND OAXACA, 1993–1994)

1. More detailed accounts of these dances may be found in my "Return."

2. Gillmor, "Dance," pp. 18–24; Cordry, *Mexican*, p. 34; Champe, *Matachines*, p. 12; Leyenaar, "Some," p. 203; Gutiérrez, "Politics," p. 58. Rodríguez, "Taos," p. 247, admits that "the upper Rio Grande Malinche resembles Cortés's famous Indian mistress . . . in name only." Ichon, *Religion*, pp. 347, 351, and Lamadrid, "Querencia," p. 5, are equally hesitant. Treviño and Gilles, "History," pp. 121–122, are the only previous scholars to have clearly

distinguished the Malinche of the dance and the Malinche of the conquest narratives. Without their patient help and many personal communications, I could not have begun to understand. For a general discussion of the role of Malinche in Mesoamerican dance, see my "Moctezuma." For a fine summary of the historical and "various mythic strands" of La Malinche, see "Malinche" in Read and González, *Handbook.*

3. Gillmor, "Dance," p. 18; Augur, *Zapotec,* p. 71.

4. Gillespie, *Aztec,* pp. 17–22, 166–201.

5. Treviño and Gilles, "Dance," p. 4.

6. Bricker, *Indian,* pp. 60, 73.

7. Starr, *Indian,* p. 250; Zúñiga, *Rápido,* p. 7, as translated by Johnson, "Opata," p. 182.

8. Juarros, *Compendio,* pp. 398–400.

9. Gregg, *Commerce,* pp. 188–189; see also Weigle and White, *Lore,* pp. 70–73, and Parmentier, "Mythological," p. 619.

10. Applegate, *Indian,* pp. 171–176.

11. Dumarest, *Notes,* pp. 229–230; Benedict, *Tales,* pp. 191–192; VanEtten, *Ways,* pp. 53–60.

12. Kloeppel, "Matachines," p. 7; Champe, *Matachines,* p. 84; Rodríguez, *Matachines,* pp. 43–63, 101–111, 115–131; Sinclair, *New Mexico,* pp. 62–66.

13. Treviño and Gilles, "Dance," p. 15.

14. Rodríguez, *Matachines,* pp. 36–40, 54–61.

15. Kloeppel, "Matachines."

16. Champe, *Matachines,* p. 84.

17. Dumarest, *Notes,* p. 86.

18. Treviño and Gilles, "Dance," p. 13.

19. Treviño and Gilles, "Dance," pp. 12–14. Kay Read, personal communication, 8 February 1998, writes, "The role of deceased-but-still-to-come Messiahs strikes me as very pre-Conquest. History simply did not mean the same thing for pre-Conquest folks as it does for us. Time not only marched forward in our historical sense, but also simultaneously cycled back to pick up particular moments in the past, thereby joining them to the present and marking the future. . . . This means that deceased-but-still-potent past historical figures like Motecuzoma I could continue lending their powers to the present in order to shape the future. The recouping of these powers by the living was done by means of ritual, the passing on of potent names . . . , and the inevitability of returning time in a kind of complex spiraling motion of reincarnation. . . . 'Ghost' . . . is a bad term to use because these revived powers were not ghostlike in our sense of the word. The past ancestor was not revived entirely because people did not have single souls to revive in the same way that our ghosts do. . . . Rather, messianic leaders, like everything else, were a composite of many powers and forces that scattered at their death. Only a couple of those powers were reclaimed by their heirs, messianic or otherwise."

20. Rodríguez, *Matachines,* p. 31.

21. Sweet, *Dances,* p. 42; see also Parsons, *Social,* pp. 179–185.

22. Starr, "Popular," p. 167; Toor, "Glimpse," pp. 5–6.

23. Starr, "Popular," p. 166; Cohen, "Danza," pp. 152–153.

24. Gillmor, "Symbolic," p. 104.

25. Gillmor, "Symbolic," pp. 104–105, citing Loubat, "Letra"; Parsons, *Mitla,* p. 256; Cohen, "Danza," p. 150.

26. For a plan of the dance floor, see my "Return," p. 115. For the introduction of European dance bands to Mexican folk life, see Thomson, "Ceremonial." Teotitlán's orchestra has long had a reputation as one of the best (see Thomson, p. 337).

27. Starr, *Indian,* p. 30.
28. Markman and Markman, *Masks,* p. 123.
29. Parsons, *Mitla,* p. 255.
30. Ibid., p. 256.
31. Cohen, "Danza," p. 150.

BIBLIOGRAPHY

Abun-Nasr, Jamil M. *A History of the Maghrib*. Cambridge: Cambridge University Press, 1971.

Acosta Saignes, Miguel. *Tlacaxipeualiztli: un complejo mesoamericano entre los caribes*. Caracas, Venezuela: Universidad Central, 1950.

Actas de cabildo de la ciudad de México. 1st ser., 1524–1722. 54 vols. Ed. Ignacio Bejerano. Mexico City: Municipio Libre, 1889–1913.

Ahmad R'honi, Sidi. *Historia de Tetuán*. Trans. Mohammed Ibn Azzuz Haquim. Tetuán: Editora Marroqui, 1953.

Aiton, Arthur Scott. *Antonio de Mendoza, First Viceroy of New Spain*. Durham: Duke University Press, 1927.

Alenda y Mira, Jenaro. *Relaciones de solemnidades y fiestas públicas de España*. Madrid: Rivadeneyra, 1903.

Alford, Violet. *The Hobby Horse and Other Animal Masks*. London: Merlin Press, 1978.

———. *Pyrenean Festivals*. London: Chatto and Windus, 1937.

———. *The Singing of the Travels*. London: Max Parrish, 1956.

———. *Sword Dance and Drama*. London: Merlin Press, 1962.

Alva Ixtlilxochitl, Fernando de. *Obras históricas*. 2 vols. Ed. Edmundo O'Gorman. Mexico City: Universidad Nacional Autónoma de México, 1975.

Alvarado Tezozómoc, Hernando. *Crónica mexicana*. [1598]. Mexico City: Leyenda, 1944.

Alvarez, Vicente. *Relation du beau voyage que fit aux pays-bas, en 1548, le prince Philippe d'Espagne . . . .* Trans. M.-T. Dovillée. Brussels: Presses Académiques Européennes, 1964.

Amades, Joan. *Costumari Català: El curs de l'any*. 5 vols. Barcelona: Salvat Editores, 1950–1956.

———. *Las danzas de moros y cristianos*. Valencia: Institución Alfonso el Magnánimo, 1966.

———. *Folklore de Catalunya*. 3 vols. Barcelona: Selecta, 1950–1969.

———. *Gegants, nans i altres entremesos*. Barcelona: Pujol i Casademont, 1934.

Ametller y Viñas, José. *Alfonso V de Aragón en Italia*. 3 vols. Vols. 1 and 2, Gerona: P. Torres, and Vol. 3, San Feliu de Guixols: Octavio Viader, 1903–1928.

Applegate, Frank. *Indian Stories from the Pueblos*. Philadelphia: J. B. Lippincott, 1929.

Arbeau, Thoinot. *Orchesography*. [1589]. Trans. Mary Stewart Evans. New York: Dover, 1967.

Arco, Ricardo del. *Zaragoza histórica*. Madrid: Viuda de Justo Martínez, 1928.

Armengou, Josep. *La Patum de Berga*. [1968]. Barcelona: Columna, 1994.

Arróniz, Othón. *Teatro de evangelización en Nueva España*. Mexico City: Universidad Nacional Autónoma de México, 1979.

Aubrun, Charles-V. "La Chronique de Miguel Lucas de Iranzo." *Bulletin Hispanique* 44 (1942): 40–60.

———. "Sur les débuts du théâtre en Espagne." In *Hommage à Ernest Martinenche: Etudes hispaniques et américaines*, ed. Mário Cardozo, pp. 293–314. Paris: Editions d'Artrey, 1939.

Augur, Helen. *Zapotec*. Garden City, N.Y.: Doubleday, 1954.

Austin, Mary. "A Drama Played on Horseback." *The Mentor*, September 1928, pp. 38–39.

Autenboer, E. van. "Ommegangen in het Noorden van het oude Hertogdom Brabant." *Taxandria*, n.s., 35 (1963): 109–128.

Axton, Richard. *European Drama of the Early Middle Ages*. London: Hutchinson, 1974.

Bagnyon, Jehan. *L'Histoire de Charlemagne: Parfois dite Roman de Fierabras*. [1478]. Ed. Hans-Erich Keller. Geneva: Librairie Droz, 1992.

———. *Historia del Emperador Carlo Magno*. [1498]. Trans. Nicolás de Piamonte. Barcelona: A. Berdeguer, 1840.

———. *The lyf of the noble and Crysten prynce, Charles the Grete*. [1484]. Trans. William Caxton. 2 vols. London: Oxford University Press, 1934.

Bakhtin, Mikhail. *Speech Genres and Other Late Essays*. Trans. Vern W. McGee, ed. Caryl Emerson and Michael Holquist. Austin: University of Texas Press, 1986.

Balaguer, Andréu. "De las antiguas representaciones dramáticas y en especial dels entremesos catalans." *Calendari Català*, 22 Sept. 1871. Reprinted in Manuel Milá y Fontanals, *Obras completas*, 6: 362–373. Barcelona: Álvaro Verdaguer, 1895.

Balaguer, Víctor. *Historia de Cataluña y de la corona de Aragon*. 5 vols. Barcelona: Salvador Manero, 1860–1863.

Banfi, Luigi, ed. *Sacre rappresentazioni del quattrocento*. Turin: Unione Tipografico-Editrice Torinese, 1968.

Barber, Richard, and Juliet Barker. *Tournaments: Jousts, Chivalry, and Pageants in the Middle Ages*. New York: Weidenfeld and Nicolson, 1989.

Barker, Ruth Laughlin. *Caballeros*. New York: Appleton-Century, 1931.

Bartrina, Enric. *El castell de Guardiola*. Guardiola de Berguedà: Ambit de Recerques de Berguedà, 1985.

Battaglia, Salvatore. *Grande dizionario della lingua italiano*. 18 vols. to date. Turin: UTET, 1975–.

Baumann, Roland. "Matanzas en las fiestas: La rebelión de la Alpujarra y las fiestas de moros y cristianos." *Demófilo* 18 (1996): 81–92.

———. "Tlaxcalan Expression of Autonomy and Religious Drama in the Sixteenth Century." *Journal of Latin American Lore* 13 (1987): 139–153.

Beccadelli, Antonio. *Dels fets e dits del gran rey Alfonso*. Trans. Jordi de Centelles. [1715]. Ed. Eulalia Duran, Mariàngela Vilallonga, and Joan Ruiz i Calonja. Barcelona: Editorial Barcino, 1990.

Beeching, Jack. *The Galleys at Lepanto*. London: Hutchinson, 1982.

Beltrán, José. *Historia de Daroca*. Zaragoza: Heraldo de Aragón, 1954.

Benedict, Ruth. *Tales of the Cochiti Indians*. Bureau of American Ethnology Bulletin 98. Washington, D.C.: U.S. Government Printing Office, 1931.

Bermúdez de Pedraza, Francisco. *Historia eclesiástica de Granada*. [1638]. Granada: Editorial Don Quijote, 1988.

Bernabeu Rico, José Luis. *Significados sociales de las fiestas de moros y cristianos*. Alicante: Publicaciones de la Universidad Nacional de Educación a Distancia—Centro Regional de Elche, 1981.

Bertoldi, Massimo. "Spettacoli e musiche nei secoli XV e XVI." In *Musica e società nella storia trentina*, ed. Rossana Dalmonte. Trent: Edizioni U.C.T., 1994.

Besozzi, Cerbonio. *Crónica*. Ed. and trans. Cesare Malfatti. Barcelona: N.p., 1967.

Bierhorst, John. *Cantares Mexicanos: Songs of the Aztecs*. Stanford: Stanford University Press, 1985.

———. *Codex Chimalpopoca: The Text in Nahuatl with a Glossary and Grammatical Notes*. Tucson: University of Arizona Press, 1992.

———. *History and Mythology of the Aztecs: The Codex Chimalpopoca*. Tucson: University of Arizona Press, 1992.

Bigongiari, Dino. "Were There Theaters in the Twelfth and Thirteenth Centuries?" *Romanic Review* 37 (1946): 201–224.

Biringucci, Vannoccio. *The Pirotechnia of Vannocio Biringuccio*. Trans. Cyril Stanley Smith and Martha Teach Gnudi. New York: American Institute of Mining and Metallurgical Engineers, 1942.

Bisson, T. N. *The Medieval Crown of Aragon*. Oxford: Clarendon Press, 1986.

Boudignon-Hamon, Michèle, and Jacqueline Demoinet. *Fêtes en France*. Paris: Chêne, 1977.

Boudot-Lamotte, Antoine. *Contribution á l'étude de l'archerie musulmane*. Damascus: Institut Français de Damas, 1968.

Bouza Alvarez, Fernando J., ed. *Cartas de Felipe II a sus hijas*. Madrid: Turner, 1988.

Bové, Francesc de P. *El Penedès: Folklore dels balls, danses i comparses populars*. Vilafranca del Penedès: Joan Solé i Bordes, 1990.

Bragaglia, Anton Giulio. *Danze popolari italiane*. Rome: ENAL, 1950.

Braudel, Fernand. *The Mediterranean and the Mediterranean World in the Age of Philip II*. Trans. Siân Reynolds. 2 vols. New York: Harper & Row, 1973.

Bricker, Victoria Reifler. *The Indian Christ, the Indian King: The Historical Substrata of Maya Myth and Ritual*. Austin: University of Texas Press, 1981.

Brisset, Demetrio. *Fiestas de moros y cristianos en Granada*. Granada: Diputación Provincial de Granada, 1988.

Brock, Alan St. H. *A History of Fireworks*. London: Harrap, 1949.

Broda de las Casas, Johanna. "Templo Mayor as Ritual Space." In Johanna Broda, Davíd Carrasco, and Eduardo Matos Moctezuma, *The Great Temple of Tenochtitlan: Center and Periphery in the Aztec World*, pp. 61–123. Berkeley: University of California Press, 1987.

———. "Tlacaxipeualiztli: A Reconstruction of an Aztec Calendar Festival from Sixteenth-Century Sources." *Revista Española de Antropología Americana* 5 (1970): 197–273.

Brooks, Lynn Matluck. *The Dances of the Processions of Seville in Spain's Golden Age*. Kassel: Reichenberger, 1988.

Brotherston, Gordon. "Huitzilopochtli and What Was Made of Him." In *Mesoamerican Archaeology: New Approaches*, ed. Norman Hammond, pp. 155–166. Austin: University of Texas Press, 1974.

Brown, Betty Ann. "Ochpaniztli in Historical Perspective." In *Ritual Human Sacrifice in Mesoamerica*, ed. Elizabeth H. Boone, pp. 195–210. Washington, D.C.: Dumbarton Oaks, 1984.

Brown, Lorin W., with Charles L. Briggs and Marta Weigle. *Hispano Folklife of New Mexico*. Albuquerque: University of New Mexico Press, 1978.

Broyles González, Yolanda. "Native Dialectics and Cultural Subversion: The Santa Barbara Pastorela." *Gestos* 11 (1991): 127–133.

Brundage, Burr Cartwright. *The Fifth Sun: Aztec Gods, Aztec World*. Austin: University of Texas Press, 1979.

Burkhart, Louise M. *Holy Wednesday: A Nahua Drama from Early Colonial Mexico*. Philadelphia: University of Pennsylvania Press, 1996.

Butterworth, Philip. *Theatre of Fire: Special Effects in Early English and Scottish Theatre*. London: Society for Theatre Research, 1998.

Cabestany, Joan-F. "Alfons el Cast." In Percy E. Schramm, Joan-F. Cabestany, and Enric Bagué, *Els Primers Comtes-Reis*, vol. 4 of *Biografies Catalanes*, pp. 53–99. Barcelona: Editorial Teide, 1960.

Cabeza de Vaca, Alvar Núñez. *Naufragios*. Ed. Juan Francisco Maura. Madrid: Cátedra, 1989.

Cala y López, Ramón, and Miguel Flores González-Grano de Oro. *La fiesta de Moros y Cristianos en la Villa de Carboneras*. [1918]. Ed. Juan A. Grima Cervantes. Almería: Instituto de Estudios Almerienses, 1993.

Calvete de Estrella, Juan Cristóbal. *El felicísimo viaje del alto y muy poderoso príncipe don Felipe*. [1552]. 2 vols. Madrid: Sociedad de Bibliófilos Españoles, 1930.

Campa, Arthur L. *Hispanic Culture in the Southwest*. Norman: University of Oklahoma Press, 1979.

———, ed. *Los Comanches: A New Mexican Folk Drama*. University of New Mexico Bulletin, no. 376. Albuquerque: University of New Mexico Press, 1942.

Canto-Lugo, Ramiro Fernando. "La danza de moros y cristianos en México (con una edición de cuatro morismas)." Ph.D. diss., University of California, Davis, 1991.

Capmany, Aurelio. "El baile y la danza." In Vol. 2 of *Folklore y costumbres de España*, pp. 167–418. 3 vols. Ed. F. Carreras y Candi. Barcelona: Alberto Martín, 1944.

———. *Los enramades del Corpus de la ciutat de Barcelona*. Barcelona: Dalmau i Jover, 1953.

Carey, F. M. "Translation of a Letter from the Archbishop of Cosenza to Petrus de Acosta." *Hispanic American Historical Review* 9 (1929): 361–363.

Caro Baroja, Julio. *El estío festivo*. Madrid: Taurus, 1984.

———. *Los moriscos del reino de Granada*. Madrid: Instituto de Estudios Políticos, 1957.

Carrasco, Davíd. "Give Me Some Skin: The Charisma of the Aztec Warrior." *History of Religions* 35 (1995): 1–26.

———. "Myth, Cosmic Terror, and the Templo Mayor." In Johanna Broda, Davíd Carrasco, and Eduardo Matos Moctezuma, *The Great Temple of Tenochtitlan: Center and Periphery in the Aztec World*, pp. 124–162. Berkeley: University of California Press, 1987.

Carrasco Urgoiti, María Soledad. "Aspectos folclóricos y literarios de la fiesta de moros y cristianos en España." *PMLA* 78 (1963): 476–491.

———. *El moro retador y el moro amigo*. Granada: Universidad de Granada, 1996.

Carreres Zacarés, Salvador. *Ensayo de una bibliografía de libros de fiestas celebradas en Valencia y su antiguo reino precedido de una introducción*. 2 vols. Valencia: Vives Mora, 1925–1926.

Carriazo, Juan de Mata, ed. *Hechos del condestable Don Miguel Lucas de Iranzo (Crónica del siglo XV)*. Vol. 3 of *Colección de Crónicas Españolas*. Madrid: Espasa-Calpe, 1940.

Casademont i Donay, Miquel. "Cavallets, gegants i mulassa, o la fantasia esdevinguda tradició." Sant Feliu de Pallerols, Gerona: Typescript, 1985.

Caso, Alfonso. *The Aztecs: People of the Sun*. Trans. Lowell Dunham. Norman: University of Oklahoma Press, 1958.

Castellá y Raich, Gabriel. "Estudi sobre la Patera d'Igualada." *Catalana* 6 (1923): 140–141, 166, 191–192, 243–244, 269–271, 292–293, 339–340.

———. "Igualada: Comparsas o Balls Populars." *Revista Música Catalana* 2 (1905): 155–157, 171–173, 191–193.

Castellanos, Basilio Sebastián de. "Costumbres españolas: De las romerías y verbenas de la Virgen del Carmen y de Santiago Apóstol. . . ." *Museo de las Familias* 6 (1848): 164–167.

Castro de la Rosa, María Guadalupe. "Voladores and Hua-Huas: Two Ritual Dances of the Region of Papantla." *UCLA Journal of Dance Ethnology* 9 (1985): 47–64.

Chambers, E. K. *The Mediaeval Stage*. 2 vols. London: Oxford University Press, 1903.

Champe, Flavia Waters. *The Matachines Dance of the Upper Rio Grande*. Lincoln: University of Nebraska Press, 1983.

Chimalpahin Cuauhtlehuanitzin, Francisco de San Antón Muñón. *Relaciones originales de Chalco Amaquemecan*. Trans. Silvia Rendón. Mexico City: Fondo de Cultura Económica, 1965.

Ciudad Real, Antonio de. *Tratado curioso y docto de las grandezas de la Nueva España.* 2 vols. Ed. Josefina García Quintana and Víctor M. Castillo Farreras. Mexico City: Universidad Nacional Autónoma de México, 1993.

Clavijero, Francisco Javier. *Historia antigua de México.* 4 vols. Ed. Mariano Cuevas. Mexico City: Porrúa, 1945.

————. *The History of Mexico.* Trans. Charles Cullen. 2 vols. [1787]. New York: Garland, 1979.

Clendinnen, Inga. *Ambivalent Conquests.* Cambridge: Cambridge University Press, 1987.

————. *Aztecs: An Interpretation.* Cambridge: Cambridge University Press, 1991.

————. "Ways to the Sacred: Reconstructing 'Religion' in Sixteenth-Century Mexico." *History and Anthropology* 5 (1990): 105–141.

Cline, Howard F. "Hernando Cortés and the Aztec Indians in Spain." *Quarterly Journal of the Library of Congress* 26 (1969): 70–90.

Cock, Enrique. *Relación del viaje hecho por Felipe II en 1585.* Madrid: Aribau, 1876.

Codex Borbonicus: Bibliothèque de l'Assemblée National, Paris (Y120). Faksimile. Ausgabe de Codex im original format. Ed. Karl Nowotny. Graz: Akademische Druck-u. Verlagsanstalt, 1974.

Códice Chimalpopoca: Anales de Cuauhtitlán y Leyenda de los Soles. Trans. Primo Feliciano Velázquez. [1945]. 3rd ed. Mexico City: Universidad Nacional Autónoma de México, 1992.

Cohen, Jeffrey H. "Danza de la Pluma: Symbols of Submission and Separation in a Mexican Fiesta." *Anthropological Quarterly* 66 (1993): 149–158.

Colección de documentos inéditos relativos al descubrimiento, conquista y organización de las antiguas posesiones españolas de América y Oceania. . . . Ed. Joaquín F. Pacheco, Francisco de Cárdenas, and Luis Torres de Mendoza. 42 vols. Madrid: Imprenta del Hospicio, 1864–1884.

Collon-Gevaert, Suzanne. "L'art précolombien et le palais des princes-évêques de Liège." *Bulletin de la Société d'art et d'histoire du diocèse de Liège* 41 (1959): 73–95.

Cordry, Donald. *Mexican Masks.* Austin: University of Texas Press, 1980.

Corrsin, Stephen D. *Sword Dancing in Europe: A History.* London: Hisarlik Press, 1997.

Cortés Peña, Antonio Luis, and Bernard Vincent. *Historia de Granada.* Vol. 3, *La época moderna: Siglos XVI, XVII y XVIII.* Granada: Editorial Don Quijote, 1986.

Corzo Sánchez, Ramón. *Tarifa.* Cádiz: Diputación de Cádiz, 1984.

Cotarelo y Mori, Emilio, ed. *Colección de entremeses, loas, bailes, jácaras y mojigangas desde fines del siglo XVI á mediados del XVIII.* 2 vols. Madrid: Bailly, 1911.

Croce, Benedetto. *La Spagna nella vita italiana durante la Rinascenza.* 2nd ed. Bari: Laterza, 1922.

Cuche, Denys. *Pérou Nègre.* Paris: Editions L'Harmattan, 1981.

————. *Poder blanco y resistencia negra en el Perú.* Lima: Instituto Nacional de Cultura, 1975.

Curcio, Linda Ann. "Saints, Sovereignty, and Spectacle in Colonial Mexico." Ph.D. diss., Tulane University, 1993.

Curet, Francesc. *Visions Barcelonines, 1760–1860: Costums, Festes i Solemnitates.* Barcelona: Dalmau i Jover, 1957.

Dal Prà, Laura, ed. *I Madruzzo e l'Europa.* Milan: Charta, 1993.

Davidson, David M. "Negro Slave Control and Resistance in Colonial Mexico, 1519–1650." *Hispanic American Historical Review* 46 (1966): 235–253.

Davies, Nigel. *The Aztecs: A History.* London: Macmillan, 1973.

Delangre, A. *Le théâtre et l'art dramatique à Tournai.* Tournai: Vasseur-Delmée, 1905.

Denis, Ferdinand. *Une fête brésilienne célébrée à Rouen en 1550.* Paris: Techener, 1859.

De Roos, Marjoke. "Battles and Bottles: Shrovetide Performances in the Low Countries

(c. 1350–c. 1550)." In *Festive Drama*, ed. Meg Twycross, pp. 167–179. Cambridge: D. S. Brewer, 1996.

De Spenis, Geronimo. "Breve cronica dai 2 giugno 1543 a 25 maggio 1547." Ed. Bartolomeo Capasso. *Archivio storico per le provincie napoletane* 2 (1877): 511–531.

Devoto, Daniel. "Folklore et politique au Château Ténébreux." In Vol. 2 of *Les Fêtes de la Renaissance,* ed. Jean Jacquot, pp. 311–328. 3 vols. Paris: Centre National de la Recherche Scientifique, 1960–1975.

d'Haenens, Albert, ed. *Folklore de Belgique.* Brussels: Diféedit, 1974.

Díaz del Castillo, Bernal. *Historia verdadera de la conquista de la Nueva España.* Ed. Joaquín Ramírez Cabañas. 15th ed. Mexico City: Porrúa, 1992.

———. *The True History of the Conquest of New Spain.* Trans. Alfred Percival Maudslay. 5 vols. London: Hakluyt Society, 1908–1916.

Díaz Roig, Mercedes. "La danza de la conquista." *Nueva Revista de Filología Hispánica* 32 (1983): 176–195.

Dibble, Charles E., ed. and trans. *Historia de la nación mexicana Códice de 1576 (Códice Aubin).* Madrid: José Porrúa Turanzas, 1963.

Documentos inéditos para la historia de Colombia. Ed. Juan Friede. 10 vols. Bogotá: Academia Colombiana de Historia, 1955–1960.

Dotor, Angel. *Hernán Cortés.* Madrid: Gran Capitán, 1948.

Dumarest, Noël. *Notes on Cochiti, New Mexico.* Trans. and ed. Elsie Clews Parsons. Memoirs of the American Anthropological Association 6, pp. 137–236. Lancaster, Pa.: American Anthropological Association, 1919.

Dumont, Louis. *La Tarasque.* 2nd ed. Paris: Gallimard, 1987.

Durán, Diego. *Book of the Gods and Rites, and the Ancient Calendar.* Trans. Fernando Horcasitas and Doris Heyden. Norman: University of Oklahoma Press, 1971.

———. *Historia de las Indias de Nueva España e Islas de la Tierra Firme.* [1967]. 2 vols. 2nd ed. Ed. Angel Ma. Garibay K. Mexico City: Porrúa, 1984.

———. *The History of the Indies of New Spain.* Trans. Doris Heyden. Norman: University of Oklahoma Press, 1994.

Duran i Sanpere, A., and Josep Sanabre. *Llibre de les Solemnitats de Barcelona.* 2 vols. Barcelona: Patxot, 1930–1947.

Durán y Sanpere, A. [Duran i Sanpere, A.] *La Fiesta del Corpus.* Barcelona: Ediciones Aymá, 1963.

Durant, Will, and Ariel Durant. *The Story of Civilization.* 11 vols. New York: Simon and Schuster, 1935–1975.

Dürer, Albrecht. *Records of Journeys to Venice and the Low Countries.* Ed. Roger Fry, trans. Rudolph Tombo. Boston: Merrymount Press, 1913.

Eccles, Mark, ed. *The Macro Plays.* Early English Text Society 262. London: Oxford University Press, 1969.

Enciclopedia Universal Ilustrada Europeo Americana. 70 vols. Barcelona: Espasa-Calpe, n.d.

Enders, Jody. "Medieval Snuff Drama." *Exemplaria* 10 (1998): 171–206.

Epton, Nina. *Spanish Fiestas.* London: Cassell, 1968.

Erdmann, Louis Otto. "Theatrical Performances within Sixteenth-Century Festivals." *Ohio State University Theatre Collection Bulletin* 14 (1967): 12–23.

Espinosa, Aurelio M., ed. *Los Comanches.* University of New Mexico Bulletin, no. 45. Albuquerque: University of New Mexico Press, 1907.

Espinosa, Gilberto, trans. "Los Comanches." *New Mexico Quarterly* 1 (1931): 133–144.

Espinosa de Luján, Josie. *Los Moros y Cristianos: A Spectacular Historical Drama.* Chimayo, N.Mex.: Josie Luján, 1992.

―――. "Los Moros y Cristianos." *New Mexico Magazine* 55, no. 6 (June 1977): 34–35.

Espinosa Maeso, Ricardo. "Ensayo biográfico del maestro Lucas Fernández (1474–1542?)." *Boletín de la Real Academia Española* 10 (1923): 567–603.

Esser, Janet Brody. "Those Who Are Not from Here: Blackman Dances of Michoacán." In *Behind the Mask in Mexico,* ed. Janet Brody Esser, pp. 106–141. Santa Fe: Museum of New Mexico Press, 1988.

―――, ed. *Behind the Mask in Mexico.* Santa Fe: Museum of New Mexico Press, 1988.

Esses, Maurice. *Dance and Instrumental Diferencias in Spain during the Seventeenth and Early Eighteenth Centuries.* 3 vols. Stuyvesant, N.J.: Pendragon Press, 1992.

Faber, Frédéric. *Histoire du théatre français en Belgique depuis son origine jusqu'à nos jours: D'aprés des documents inedits reposant aux Archives Generales du Royaume.* 5 vols. Brussels: Olivier, 1878–1880.

Farràs, Jaume. *La Patum de Berga.* Barcelona: Labor, 1992.

Fergusson, Erna. *Dancing Gods.* Albuquerque: University of New Mexico Press, 1931.

Florencia, Francisco de. *La Estrella del norte de México: Historia de la milagrosa de María Stma. de Guadalupe.* . . . [1688]. Guadalajara: J. Cabrera, 1895.

Flores, Richard. "History, 'Los Pastores,' and the Shifting Poetics of Dislocation." *Journal of Historical Sociology* 6 (1993): 164–185.

Flores Solís, Miguel. *Morismas de Pánuco.* Zacatecas: N.p., 1995.

Foreman, Carolyn Thomas. *Indians Abroad: 1493–1938.* Norman: University of Oklahoma Press, 1943.

Forrest, John. *Morris and Matachin: A Study in Comparative Choreography.* Sheffield: Centre for English Cultural Tradition and Language, 1984.

Foster, George M. *Culture and Conquest: America's Spanish Heritage.* Chicago: Quadrangle Books, 1960.

Froissart, Jean. *Chronicles.* Trans. Geoffrey Brereton. Harmondsworth: Penguin, 1968.

Fruth, Mary Ann. "The American Indian as a Motif in the Triumphal Entry of the Sixteenth Century." *Ohio State University Theatre Collection Bulletin* 14 (1967): 24–29.

Fuentes, Manuel A. *Estadística general de Lima.* Lima: M. N. Corpancho, 1858.

―――. *Lima: Apuntes históricos, descriptivos, estadísticos y de costumbres.* Paris: Firmin Didot, 1867.

Fuentes y Guzmán, Francisco Antonio de. *Recordación Florida.* [1882]. Guatemala: Tipografía Nacional, 1932.

Gage, Thomas. *Travels in the New World.* Ed. J. Eric S. Thompson. Norman: University of Oklahoma Press, 1958.

Gallop, Rodney. *Portugal: A Book of Folk-Ways.* [1936]. Cambridge: Cambridge University Press, 1961.

Gallop, Rodney, and Violet Alford. *The Traditional Dance.* London: Methuen, 1935.

García Icazbalceta, Joaquín. *Colección de documentos para la historia de México.* Mexico City: Porrúa, 1971.

―――. *Don Fray Juan de Zumárraga.* 4 vols. Colección de Escritores Mexicanos, nos. 41–44. Mexico City: Porrúa, 1947.

García Rodero, Cristina, and J. M. Caballero Bonald. *Festivals and Rituals of Spain.* Trans. Wayne Finke. New York: Harry N. Abrams, 1994.

Garibay K., Angel Mª. *Poesía Náhuatl.* 3 vols. 2nd ed. Mexico City: Universidad Nacional Autónoma de México, 1993.

Gayangos, Pascual de. *Relación de los fechos del mui magnifico é mas virtuoso señor el Señor Don Miguel Lucas,* . . . Vol. 7 of *Memorial histórico español: Colección de documentos, opúsculos y antigüedades,* . . . Madrid: J. Martín Alegría, 1855.

Gibson, Charles. *Tlaxcala in the Sixteenth Century.* 2nd ed. Stanford: Stanford University Press, 1967.

Gillespie, Susan D. *The Aztec Kings.* Tucson: University of Arizona Press, 1989.

Gillmor, Frances. "The Dance Dramas of Mexican Villages." *University of Arizona Bulletin* 14, no. 2, 1943.

———. "Symbolic Representation in Mexican Combat Plays." In *The Power of Symbols,* ed. N. Ross Crumrine and Marjorie Halpin, pp. 102–110. Vancouver: University of British Columbia Press, 1983.

Glotz, Samuël. *Le carnaval de Binche.* Gembloux: J. Duculot, 1975.

Gómez de Orozco, Federico, ed. "Costumbres, fiestas, enterramientos y diversas formas de proceder de los indios de Nueva España." *Tlalocan* 2 (1945): 37–63.

Gómez García, Pedro. "La mala conciencia del conquistador: Dramas de moros y cristianos en Granada." *Demófilo* 18 (1996): 125–146.

González Casarrubios, Consolación. *Fiestas populares en Castilla-La Mancha.* Ciudad Real: Junta de Comunidades de Castilla-La Mancha, 1985.

González Moreno, Joaquín. *Don Fernando Enríquez de Ribera, Tercer Duque de Alcalá de los Gazules (1583–1637).* Seville: Ayuntamiento de Sevilla, 1969.

González Torres, Yólotl. *El culto a los astros entre los mexicas.* Mexico: SepSetentas, 1975.

Gradie, Charlotte M. "Discovering the Chichimecas." *The Americas* 51 (1994): 67–88.

Gran enciclopedia Rialp. 25 vols. Madrid: Rialp, 1975.

Grau, Jan. "Cavallets, cavallins, cavalls cotoners, cotonines." *Gegants* 31 (1995): 4–5.

Graulich, Michel. *Myths of Ancient Mexico.* Trans. Bernard R. and Thelma Ortiz de Montellano. Norman: University of Oklahoma Press, 1997.

Gregg, Josiah. *Commerce of the Prairies.* [1844]. Ed. Max L. Moorhead. Norman: University of Oklahoma Press, 1954.

Gutiérrez, Ramón. "The Politics of Theater in Colonial New Mexico: Drama and the Rhetoric of Conquest." In *Reconstructing a Chicano/a Literary Heritage,* ed. María Herrera-Sobek, pp. 49–67. Tucson: University of Arizona Press, 1993.

Hammond, George P., and Agapito Rey, eds. and trans. *Don Juan de Oñate: Colonizer of New Mexico, 1596–1598.* Albuquerque: University of New Mexico Press, 1953.

Harris, Max. "The Arrival of the Europeans: Folk Dramatizations of Conquest and Conversion in New Mexico." *Comparative Drama* 28 (1994): 141–165.

———. "A Catalan Corpus Christi Play: The Martyrdom of Saint Sebastian with the Hobby Horses and the Turks." *Comparative Drama* 31 (1997): 224–247.

———. *The Dialogical Theatre: Dramatizations of the Conquest of Mexico and the Question of the Other.* London: Macmillan, 1993.

———. "The Dramatic Testimony of Antonio de Ciudad Real: Indigenous Theatre in Sixteenth-Century New Spain." *Colonial Latin American Review* 5 (1996): 237–251.

———. "Fireworks, Turks, and Long-Necked Mules: Pyrotechnic Theatre in Germany and Catalonia." *Comparative Drama* 32 (1998): 362–388.

———. "Moctezuma's Daughter: The Role of La Malinche in Mesoamerican Dance." *Journal of American Folklore* 109 (1996): 149–177.

———. "Muhammed and the Virgin: Folk Dramatizations of Battles between Moors and Christians in Modern Spain." *The Drama Review* 38, no. 1 (1994): 45–61.

———. "The Return of Moctezuma: Oaxaca's *danza de la pluma* and New Mexico's *danza de los matachines.*" *The Drama Review* 41, no. 1 (1996): 106–134.

Hassig, Ross. *Aztec Warfare: Imperial Expansion and Political Control.* Norman: University of Oklahoma Press, 1988.

————. *War and Society in Ancient Mesoamerica.* Berkeley: University of California Press, 1992.

Heartz, Daniel. "Un divertissement de palais pour Charles Quint à Binche." In Vol. 2 of *Les Fêtes de la Renaissance*, ed. Jean Jacquot, pp. 329–342. 3 vols. Paris: Centre National de la Recherche Scientifique, 1960–1975.

Hernández, Francisco. *Antigüedades de la Nueva España.* Trans. Luis García Pimentel, ed. Ascensión H. de León-Portilla. Madrid: Historia 16, 1986.

Herrera-Sobek, María. "The Mexican/Chicano Pastorela." In *Feasts and Celebrations in North American Ethnic Communities*, ed. Ramón A. Gutiérrez and Geneviève Fabre, pp. 47–56. Albuquerque: University of New Mexico Press, 1995.

Heth, Charlotte. "American Indian Dance: A Celebration of Survival and Adaptation." In *Native American Dance: Ceremonies and Social Traditions*, ed. Charlotte Heth. Washington, D.C.: Smithsonian Institution, 1992.

Hicks, Frederic. "'Flowery War' in Aztec History." *American Ethnologist* 6 (1979): 87–92.

Hillgarth, J. N. *The Spanish Kingdoms, 1250–1516.* 2 vols. Oxford: Clarendon Press, 1976–1978.

Hoenerbach, W. *Studien zum «Mauren und Christen»: Festspiel in Andalusien.* Waldorf-Hessen: Verlag für Orientkunde Dr. H. Vorndran, 1976.

Honour, Hugh. *The European Vision of America.* Cleveland, Ohio: Cleveland Museum of Art, 1975.

Horcasitas, Fernando. *El teatro náhuatl.* Mexico City: Universidad Nacional Autónoma de México, 1974.

Ichon, Alain. *La Religion des Totonaques de la Sierra.* Paris: Editions du Centre National de la Recherche Scientifique, 1969.

Irving, Washington. *History of the Life and Voyages of Christopher Columbus.* 2 vols. Philadelphia: Lea and Blanchard, 1841.

Jacquot, Jean, ed. *Les Fêtes de la Renaissance.* 3 vols. Paris: Centre National de la Recherche Scientifique, 1960–1975.

Jaramillo, Cleofas M. *Shadows of the Past.* Santa Fe, N.Mex.: Seton Village Press, 1941.

Jedin, Hubert, *A History of the Council of Trent.* Trans. Ernest Graf. 2 vols. London: Nelson, 1961.

Johnson, Harvey Leroy, ed. *An Edition of Triunfo de los santos with a Consideration of Jesuit School Plays in Mexico before 1650.* Philadelphia: University of Pennsylvania Press, 1941.

Johnson, Jean B. "The Opata: An Inland Tribe of Sonora." In *The North Mexican Frontier: Readings in Archaeology, Ethnohistory, and Ethnography*, ed. Basil C. Hedrick, J. Charles Kelley, and Carroll L. Riley, pp. 169–199. Carbondale: Southern Illinois University Press, 1971.

Jonckbloet, W. J. A. *Geschiedenis der middennederlandische dichtkunst.* 3 vols. Amsterdam: P. N. Van Kampen, 1851–1854.

Juarros, Domingo. *Compendio de la historia del reino de Guatemala, 1500–1800.* [1818]. Guatemala: Piedra Santa, 1981.

Julien, Charles-André. *Histoire de l'Algérie contemporaine.* 2 vols. Paris: Presses Universitaires de France, 1964–1979.

Junco, Alfonso. *Un radical problema guadalupano.* 3rd ed. Mexico City: Jus, 1971.

Kamen, Henry. *Philip of Spain.* New Haven: Yale University Press, 1997.

Kandell, Jonathan. *La Capital: The Biography of Mexico City.* New York: Henry Holt, 1988.

Karasch, Mary. "Commentary One." In Monica Schuler et al., "Afro-American Slave Culture," pp. 139–141. *Historical Reflections/Réflexions historiques* 6 (1979): 121–155.

Kelly, John Eoghan. *Pedro de Alvarado, Conquistador.* [1932]. Port Washington, N.Y.: Kennikat Press, 1971.

Kenner, Charles L. *A History of New Mexican–Plains Indians Relations.* Norman: University of Oklahoma Press, 1969.

Keyes, Frances Parkinson. *The Grace of Guadalupe.* New York: Julian Messner, 1941.

King, Pamela M. "The *Festa D'Elx:* Civic Devotion, Display, and Identity." In *Festive Drama,* ed. Meg Twycross, pp. 95–109. Cambridge, England: D. S. Brewer, 1996.

———. "Morality Plays." In *The Cambridge Companion to Medieval English Theatre,* ed. Richard Beadle, pp. 240–264. Cambridge: Cambridge University Press, 1994.

Kloeppel, Richard Joseph. "Los Matachines: A Dance Drama for San Lorenzo." Bernalillo, N.Mex.: Mimeograph.

Kolve, V. A. *The Play Called Corpus Christi.* Stanford: Stanford University Press, 1966.

Kurath, Gertrude Prokosch. "Mexican Moriscas: A Problem in Dance Acculturation." *Journal of American Folklore* 62 (1949): 87–106.

Lafaye, Jacques. *Quetzalcoatl and Guadalupe: The Formation of Mexican National Consciousness, 1531–1813.* Trans. Benjamin Keen. Chicago: University of Chicago Press, 1976.

Lamadrid, Enrique R. "La Querencia: Moctezuma and the Landscape of Desire." *Blue Mesa Review* 7 (1995): 3–8.

Langdon-Davies, John. *Gatherings from Catalonia.* London: Cassell, 1953.

Larsen, Helga. "Notes on the Volador and Its Associated Ceremonies and Superstitions." *Ethnos* 2 (1937): 179–192.

Las Casas, Bartolomé de. *Apologética historia sumaria.* Ed. Edmundo O'Gorman. 2 vols. Mexico City: Universidad Nacional Autónoma de México, 1967.

———. *Historia de las Indias.* Ed. Agustín Millares Carlo. 3 vols. Mexico City: Fondo de Cultura Económica, 1951.

———. *History of the Indies.* Ed. and trans. Andrée Collard. New York: Harper & Row, 1971.

Lea, Henry Charles. *The Moriscos of Spain.* [1901]. Westport, Conn.: Greenwood Press, 1968.

Leal, Luis. "Los Voladores: From Ritual to Game." *New Scholar* 8 (1982): 129–142.

Ledesma Rubio, María Luisa, and María Isabel Falcón Pérez. *Zaragoza en la baja edad media.* Zaragoza: Librería General, 1977.

León-Portilla, Miguel. *Aztec Thought and Culture.* Trans. Jack Emory Davis. Norman: University of Oklahoma Press, 1963.

———. *Pre-Columbian Literatures of Mexico.* Norman: University of Oklahoma Press, 1969.

Leyenaar, Ted. "Some Dances of the Nahuas and Otomies of the Sierra Norte de Puebla." In *Behind the Mask in Mexico,* ed. Janet Brody Esser, pp. 190–213. Santa Fe: Museum of New Mexico Press, 1988.

Linares Palma, J. "La fiesta de moros y cristianos es un hecho histórico perfectamente unido a la fiesta religiosa de los pueblos." In Vol. 1 of *I Congreso Nacional de Fiestas de Moros y Cristianos (Villena 1974),* pp. 175–188. Alicante: Caja de Ahorros de Alicante, 1976.

Livermore, Harold. "El caballero salvaje: Ensayo de identificación de un juglar." *Revista de Filología Española* 34 (1950): 166–183.

———. *A History of Spain.* 2nd ed. London: George Allen and Unwin, 1966.

Lladonosa y Pujol, Josep. *Història de Lleida.* 2 vols. Tàrrega: F. Camps Calmet, 1972.

Llompart, Gabriel. "La fiesta del 'Corpus Christi' y representaciones religiosas en Barcelona y Mallorca (siglos XIV–XVIII)." *Analecta Sacra Tarraconensia* 39 (1966): 25–45.

Lockhart, James. "Care, Ingenuity, and Irresponsibility: The Bierhorst Edition of the *Cantares Mexicanos.*" *Reviews in Anthropology* 16 (1991): 119–132.

———. *The Nahuas after the Conquest.* Stanford: Stanford University Press, 1992.

Loomis, Laura H. "Secular Dramatics in the Royal Palace, Paris, 1378, 1389, and Chaucer's 'Tregetoures.'" [1958]. In *Medieval English Drama,* ed. Jerome Taylor and Alan H. Nelson, pp. 98–115. Chicago: University of Chicago Press, 1972.

Lopes Don, Patricia. "Carnivals, Triumphs, and Rain Gods in the New World: A Civic Festival in the City of México-Tenochtitlan in 1539." *Colonial Latin American Review* 6 (1997): 18–40.

López Austin, Alfredo. *Juegos rituales aztecas.* Mexico City: Universidad Nacional Autónoma de México, 1967.

López Cantos, Angel. *Fiestas y juegos en Puerto Rico (siglo XVIII).* San Juan, P.R.: Centro de Estudios Avanzados de Puerto Rico y el Caribe, 1990.

López de Gómara, Francisco. *La conquista de México.* Ed. José de Rojas. Madrid: Historia 16, 1987.

———. *Cortés: The Life of the Conqueror by His Secretary.* Ed. and trans. Lesley Byrd Simpson. Berkeley: University of California Press, 1964.

Lotz, Arthur. *Das Feuerwerk.* [1941]. Zurich: Olms, 1978.

Loubat, Joseph Florimond. "La letra de la danza de la pluma." In *Congrès International des Americanistes* (Twelfth Session, Paris, 1900), pp. 221–261. Paris: Ernest Laroux, 1902.

Louis, Maurice A.-L. *Le folklore et la danse.* Paris: Maisonneuve et Larose, 1963.

Lucero-White Lea, Aurora. *Literary Folklore of the Hispanic Southwest.* San Antonio: Naylor, 1953.

Lynch, John. *Spain under the Hapsburgs.* 2 vols. Oxford: Basil Blackwell, 1964–1969.

McDowell, Bart. "The Aztecs." *National Geographic* 158 (1980): 714–751.

McGowan, Margaret. "Form and Themes in Henri II's Entry into Rouen." *Renaissance Drama,* n.s., 1 (1968): 199–251.

Madariaga, Salvador de. *Hernán Cortés.* New York: Macmillan, 1941.

Madurell, Josep M. "Les noces de l'infant Joan amb Matha d'Armanyac." *Estudis Universitaris Catalans* 19 (1934): 1–57.

Mandach, André de. "The Evolution of the Matter of Fierabras: Present State of Research." In *Romance Epic: Essays on a Medieval Literary Genre,* ed. Hans-Erich Keller. Kalamazoo, Mich.: Medieval Institute Publications, 1987.

———. *Naissance et développement de la chanson de geste en Europe.* Vol. 5, *La Geste de Fierabras.* Geneva: Droz, 1987.

Mansanet Ribes, José Luis. *La fiesta de Moros y Cristianos de Alcoy y sus instituciones.* 2nd ed. Alcoy: Mansanet Ribes, 1981.

María y Campos, Armando de. *Guía de representaciones teatrales en la Nueva España.* Mexico City: B. Costa-Amic, 1959.

Markman, Roberta H., and Peter T. Markman. *The Flayed God: The Mesoamerican Mythological Tradition.* San Francisco: Harper, 1992.

———. *Masks of the Spirit: Image and Metaphor in Mesoamerica.* Berkeley: University of California Press, 1989.

Marsden, C. A. "Entrées et fêtes espagnoles au XVIe siècle." In Vol. 2 of *Les Fêtes de la Renaissance,* ed. Jean Jacquot, pp. 389–411. 3 vols. Paris: Centre National de la Recherche Scientifique, 1960–1975.

Martí, Samuel, and Gertrude Prokosch Kurath. *Dances of Anáhuac.* Chicago: Aldine, 1964.

Martin, Ernst, ed. *Freiburger passionspiele des 16. Jahrhunderts.* Offprint from *Zeitschrift der historischen Gesellschaft zu Freiburg,* 3: 1. Freiburg: Franz Josef Scheuble, 1872.

Martín Arrúe, Francisco. *Historia del Alcázar de Toledo.* Madrid: Imprenta de Infantería de Marina, 1889.

Martínez, José Luis. *Hernán Cortés*. Mexico City: Universidad Nacional Autónoma de México, 1990.

Martínez de Campos y Serrano, Carlos. *España bélica: El siglo XVI*. 2 vols. Madrid: Aguilar, 1966.

Martínez Ferrando, J. E. "Jaume II." In *Els Descendents de Pere el Gran*, vol. 6 of *Biografies Catalanes*, pp. 55–145. Barcelona: Editorial Teide, 1954.

Martire d'Anghiera, Pietro. *De Orbe Novo*. Trans. Francis Augustus MacNutt. 2 vols. New York: Putnam, 1912.

Massa, J.-M. "Le Monde Luso-Brésilien dans la joyeuse entrée de Rouen." In Vol. 3 of *Les Fêtes de la Renaissance*, ed. Jean Jacquot, pp. 105–116. 3 vols. Paris: Centre National de la Recherche Scientifique, 1960–1975.

Massip, Francesc. "Continuïtat i vigència del teatre de la tradició." *Revista de Catalunya* 63 (1992): 91–105.

———. "El rei i la festa: Del ritu a la propaganda." *Revista de Catalunya* 84 (1994): 63–83.

Matos Moctezuma, Eduardo. *Life and Death in the Templo Mayor*. Trans. Bernard R. Ortiz de Montellano and Thelma Ortiz de Montellano. Niwot: University Press of Colorado, 1995.

———. "The Templo Mayor of Tenochtitlan: History and Interpretation." Trans. John G. Copeland. In Johanna Broda, Davíd Carrasco, and Eduardo Matos Moctezuma, *The Great Temple of Tenochtitlan: Center and Periphery in the Aztec World*, pp. 15–60. Berkeley: University of California Press, 1987.

Meketa, Jacqueline Dorgan, ed. *Legacy of Honor: The Life of Rafael Chacón, a Nineteenth-Century New Mexican*. Albuquerque: University of New Mexico Press, 1986.

Mendieta, Gerónimo de. *Historia Ecclesiástica Indiana*. 4 vols. Mexico City: Salvador Chávez Hayhoe, 1945.

Meurant, René. *Géants processionels et de cortège en Europe, en Belgique, en Wallonie*. Tielt: Editions Veys, 1979.

Michel, Edouard. "Un tableau colonial de Jan Mostaert." *Revue Belge d'Archéologie et l'histoire d'art* 1 (1931): 133–141.

Milá y Fontanals, Manuel. *De los trovadores en España*. [1861]. Barcelona: Consejo Superior de Investigaciones Científicas, 1966.

———. *Obras completas*. 6 vols. Barcelona: Alvaro Verdaguer, 1889–1895.

Mills, Leonard R., ed. *Le Mystère de Saint Sébastien*. Geneva: Librairie Droz, 1965.

Monroe, James T. "Prolegomena to the Study of Ibn Quzman: The Poet as Jongleur." In *El romancero hoy: Historia, comparatismo, bibliografía crítica*, ed. Samuel G. Armistead, Antonio Sánchez Romeralo, and Diego Catalán, pp. 77–129. Madrid: Editorial Gredos, 1979.

Montoya, Matilde. *Estudio sobre el baile de la conquista*. Guatemala: Editorial Universitaria, 1970.

Moriarty, James Robert. "Ritual Combat: A Comparison of the Aztec 'War of Flowers' and the Medieval 'Mêlée.'" Miscellaneous Series, no. 9. Greeley: Museum of Anthropology, Colorado State College, 1969.

Motolinía, Toribio de. *Historia de los indios de la Nueva España*. Ed. Edmundo O'Gorman. [1969]. 5th ed. Mexico City: Porrúa, 1990. [References in the notes are to this edition unless otherwise stated.]

———. *Historia de los indios de la Nueva España*. Ed. Georges Baudot. Madrid: Clásicos Castalia, 1985.

———. *History of the Indians of New Spain*. Ed. and trans. Francis Borgia Steck. Washington, D.C.: Academy of American Franciscan History, 1951.

————. *Memoriales.* Ed. Edmundo O'Gorman. Mexico City: Universidad Nacional Autónoma de México, 1971.

Mullaney, Steven. "Strange Things, Gross Terms, Curious Customs: The Rehearsal of Cultures in the Late Renaissance." In *Representing the English Renaissance,* ed. Stephen Greenblatt, pp. 65–92. Berkeley: University of California Press, 1988.

Muntaner, Ramón. *Crónica.* Ed. Joan Francesc Vidal-Jové. 2 vols. Barcelona: Editorial Selecta, 1973.

Muñoz Renedo, Carmen. *La representación de "moros y cristianos" de Zujar.* Madrid: Consejo Superior de Investigaciones Científicas, 1972.

Murlà i Giralt, Josep. *Gegants i altres entremesos de la Garrotxa.* Olot: Patronat d'Estudis Històrics d'Olot i Comarca, 1984.

Nájera-Ramírez, Olga. *La Fiesta de los Tastoanes: Critical Encounters in Mexican Festival Performance.* Albuquerque: University of New Mexico Press, 1997.

Navagero, Andrés. "Viaje por España del magnífico Micer Andrés Navagero" and "Cartas de Micer Andrés Navagero a M. Juan Bautista Ramusio." In Vol. 1 of *Viajes de extranjeros por España y Portugal desde los tiempos más remotos hasta fines del siglo XVI,* pp. 839–892. 3 vols. Ed. J. García Mercadal. Madrid: Aguilar, 1952–1962.

Nebel, Richard. *Santa María Tonantzin Virgen de Guadalupe: Continuidad y transformación religiosa en México.* Trans. Carlos Warnholtz Bustillos and Irma Ochoa de Nebel. Mexico City: Fondo de Cultura Económica, 1995.

New Encyclopaedia Britannica. 15th ed. Chicago: Encyclopaedia Britannica, 1974.

Nirenberg, David. *Communities of Violence: Persecution of Minorities in the Middle Ages.* Princeton: Princeton University Press, 1996.

Noguera i Canal, Josep. *Visió històrica de la Patum de Berga.* Barcelona: Rafael Dalmau, 1992.

Noyes, Dorothy Pettit. "The Mule and the Giants: Struggling for the Body Social in a Catalan Corpus Christi Festival." Ph.D. diss., University of Pennsylvania, 1992.

Oxford Classical Dictionary. 2nd ed. Ed. N. G. L. Hammond and H. H. Scullard. Oxford: Clarendon Press, 1970.

Pagden, Anthony. *The Fall of Natural Man.* Cambridge: Cambridge University Press, 1982.

Palau y Dulcet, Antonio. *Manual del librero hispanoamericano.* 28 vols. 2nd ed. Revised by Agustín Palau. Barcelona: Antonio Palau y Dulcet, 1970.

Palm, Erwin Walter. "Tenochtitlan y la ciudad ideal de Dürer." *Journal de la Société des Americanistes,* n.s., 40 (1951): 59–66.

Palmer, Colin A. *Slaves of the White God: Blacks in Mexico, 1570–1650.* Cambridge: Harvard University Press, 1976.

Palomera, Esteban J. *Fray Diego Valadés.* Mexico City: Editorial Jus, 1962.

Parise, Frank, ed. *The Book of Calendars.* New York: Facts on File, 1982.

Parkes, Henry Bamford. *A History of Mexico.* Boston: Houghton Mifflin, 1938.

Parmentier, Richard J. "The Mythological Triangle: Poseyemu, Montezuma, and Jesus in the Pueblos." In Vol. 9 of *Handbook of North American Indians,* ed. Alfonso Ortiz, pp. 609–622. Washington, D.C.: Smithsonian Institution Press, 1979.

Parsons, Elsie Clews. *Mitla, Town of the Souls, and Other Zapateco-Speaking Pueblos of Oaxaca, Mexico.* Chicago: University of Chicago Press, 1936.

————. *The Pueblo of Jemez.* New Haven: Yale University Press, 1925.

————. *The Social Organization of the Tewa in New Mexico.* Memoirs of the American Anthropological Association 36. Menasha, Wisc.: American Anthropological Association, 1929.

Partington, J. R. *A History of Greek Fire and Gunpowder.* Cambridge, England: Heffer, 1960.

Paso y Troncoso, Francisco del, ed. *Epistolario de Nueva España, 1505–1818.* 16 vols. Mexico City: Robredo, 1939–1942.

Pearce, T. M. "Los Moros y Los Cristianos: Early American Play." *New Mexico Folklore Record* 2 (1947–1948): 58–65.

Pereyra, Carlos. *Hernán Cortés.* Madrid: Aguilar, 1931.

Pérez de Ribas, Andrés. *Historia de los triunfos de nuestra santa fe entre gentes las más bárbaras. . . .* [1645]. 3 vols. Mexico City: Editorial Layac, 1944.

———. *My Life among the Savage Nations of New Spain.* Trans. Tomás Antonio Robertson. Los Angeles: Ward Ritchie Press, 1968.

Phelan, John Liddy. *The Millennial Kingdom of the Franciscans in the New World.* 2nd ed. Berkeley: University of California Press, 1970.

Pierce, Donna L. "Identification of the Warriors in the Frescoes of Ixmiquilpan." *Research Center for the Arts Review* 4, no. 4 (1981): 1–8.

Plá Cargol, Joaquín. *Gerona popular.* 2nd ed. Gerona: Dalmáu Carles, 1944.

Pomar, Juan Bautista. "Relación de Tezcoco." [1582]. In *Relaciones de Texcoco y de la Nueva España,* ed. Joaquín García Icazbalceta, pp. 1–64. [1891]. Mexico City: Salvador Chávez Hayhoe, 1941.

Poole, Stafford. *Our Lady of Guadalupe: The Origins and Sources of a Mexican National Symbol, 1531–1797.* Tucson: University of Arizona Press, 1995.

Popham, A. E. "The Authorship of the Drawings of Binche." *Journal of the Warburg and Courtauld Institutes* 3 (1939): 55–57.

Potter, Robert A. "Abraham and Human Sacrifice: The Exfoliation of Medieval Drama in Aztec Mexico." *New Theatre Quarterly* 2 (1986): 306–312.

———. "The Illegal Immigration of Medieval Drama to California." *Comparative Drama* 27: 140–158.

Powell, Philip Wayne. *Mexico's Miguel Caldera.* Tucson: University of Arizona Press, 1977.

———. *Soldiers, Indians, and Silver.* Berkeley: University of California Press, 1969.

Pradier-Fodéré, Camille. *Lima et ses environs.* Paris: A. Pedone, 1897.

Prescott, William H. *History of the Conquest of Mexico and History of the Conquest of Peru.* New York: Modern Library, n.d.

Pujades, Gerónimo. *Crónica universal del principado de Cataluña escrita a principios del siglo XVII.* 8 vols. Barcelona: José Torner, 1829–1832.

Puthussery, Joly. "Chavittun;amatakam: A Music-Drama of Kerala Christians." *The Early Drama, Art, and Music Review* 19 (1997): 93–104.

———. "Chavittun;amatakam: An Appendix." *The Early Drama, Art, and Music Review* 20 (1997): 27–33.

Rabelais, François. *Complete Works.* Trans. Donald M. Frame. Berkeley: University of California Press, 1991.

———. *Oeuvres complètes.* Ed. Guy Demerson. Paris: Seuil, 1995.

Ramos Romero, Marcos. *Alcalá de los Gazules.* Cádiz: Diputación de Cádiz, 1983.

Rangel, Nicolás. *Historia del toreo en México.* Mexico City: Manuel León Sánchez, 1924.

Raven, Susan. *Rome in Africa.* 3rd ed. London: Routledge, 1993.

Ravicz, Marilyn Ekdahl. *Early Colonial Religious Drama in Mexico.* Washington, D.C.: Catholic University of America Press, 1970.

Read, Kay Almere. *Time and Sacrifice in the Aztec Cosmos.* Bloomington: Indiana University Press, 1998.

Read, Kay Almere, and Jason J. González. *Handbook on Mesoamerican Mythology.* Santa Barbara, Calif.: ABC-CLIO Press, forthcoming.

Recinos, Adrian. *Pedro de Alvarado.* Mexico City: Fondo de Cultura Económica, 1952.

Reilly, Bernard F. *The Contest of Christian and Muslim Spain, 1031–1157.* Oxford: Blackwell, 1992.

Resende, Garcia de. *Vida e feitos d'el Rey Dom João Segundo.* In *Livro das obras de Garcia de Resende,* ed. Evelina Verdelho, pp. 147–456. Lisbon: Fundação Calouste Gulbenkian, 1994.

Ricard, Robert. "Contribution á l'étude des fêtes de 'moros y cristianos' au Mexique." *Journal de la Société des Américanistes,* n.s., 24 (1932): 51–84.

———. *Etudes et documents pour l'histoire missionnaire de l'Espagne et du Portugal.* Louvain: A.U.C.A.M., 1931.

———. "Une fiche supplémentaire sur les fêtes de 'moros y cristianos.'" *Bulletin Hispanique* 61 (1959): 288–289.

———. *The Spiritual Conquest of Mexico.* Trans. Lesley Byrd Simpson. Berkeley: University of California Press, 1966.

Rivera, Luis N. *A Violent Evangelism.* Louisville, Ky.: Westminster/John Knox Press, 1992.

Roach, Joseph. *Cities of the Dead: Circum-Atlantic Performance.* New York: Columbia University Press, 1966.

Robb, J. D. "The Matachines Dance: A Ritual Folk Dance." *Western Folklore* 20 (1961): 87–101.

Robe, Stanley L. *Coloquios de pastores from Jalisco, Mexico.* Berkeley: University of California Press, 1954.

Rodríguez, Sylvia. *The Matachines Dance: Ritual Symbolism and Interethnic Relations in the Upper Río Grande Valley.* Albuquerque: University of New Mexico Press, 1996.

———. "The Taos Pueblo Matachines: Ritual Symbolism and Interethnic Relations." *American Ethnologist* 18 (1991): 234–256.

Rodríguez de Ardila y Esquivias, Gabriel. "Historia de los condes de Tendilla." Ed. R. Foulché-Delbosc. *Revue Hispanique* 31 (1914): 63–131.

Rodríguez Becerra, Salvador, ed. *Guía de fiestas populares de Andalucía.* Seville: Consejería de Cultura Junta de Andalucía, 1982.

Roeder, Beatrice A. "Los Comanches: A Bicentennial Folk Play." *Bilingual Review/Revista Bilingüe* 3 (1976): 213–220.

Romero de Terreros, Manuel. *Bocetos de la vida social en la Nueva España.* Mexico City: Porrúa, 1944.

———, ed. *Torneos, mascaradas y fiestas reales en la Nueva España.* Mexico City: Cultura, 1918.

Rossi, Vittorio. *Il quattrocento.* [1933]. Padua: Piccin Nuova Libraria, 1992.

Ruiz, Teofilo F. "Elite and Popular Culture in Late Fifteenth-Century Castilian Festivals: The Case of Jaén." In *City and Spectacle in Medieval Europe,* ed. Barbara A. Hanawalt and Kathryn L. Reyerson, pp. 296–318. Minneapolis: University of Minnesota Press, 1994.

Ryder, Alan. *Alfonso the Magnanimous.* Oxford: Clarendon Press, 1990.

Sahagún, Bernardino de. *Florentine Codex: General History of the Things of New Spain.* Ed. and trans. Arthur J. O. Anderson and Charles E. Dibble. 12 books in 13 vols. Salt Lake City: University of Utah Press, 1950–1982.

———. *Historia general de las cosas de Nueva España.* Ed. Angel Mª. Garibay K. 8th ed. Mexico City: Porrúa, 1992.

———. "Relación breve de las fiestas de los dioses." Ed. Angel Mª. Garibay K. *Tlalocan* 2 (1948): 289–320.

Sánchez, María Angeles. *Guía de fiestas populares.* 2nd ed. Madrid: Viajar, 1982.

Sánchez, Miguel. "Imagen de la Virgen María Madre de Dios de Guadalupe (1648)." In

Testimonios históricos guadalupanos, ed. Ernesto de la Torre and Ramiro Navarro de Anda, pp. 152–281. Mexico City: Fondo de Cultura Económica, 1982.

Sando, Joe S. *Pueblo Nations: Eight Centuries of Pueblo Indian History*. Santa Fe, N.Mex.: Clear Light, 1992.

Schaub, Owen W. "Pleasure Fires: Fireworks in the Court Festivals in Italy, Germany, and Austria during the Baroque." Ph.D. diss., Kent State University, 1978.

Schmitt, Jean-Claude. "'Jeunes' et danse des chevaux de bois: Le folklore méridionel dans la littérature des 'exempla' (XIIIe–XIVe siècles)." *Cahiers de Fanjeaux* 11 (1976): 127–158.

Schramm, Percy E. "Ramon Berenguer IV." In Percy E. Schramm, Joan-F. Cabestany, and Enric Bagué, *Els Primers Comtes-Reis*, vol. 4 of *Biografies Catalanes*, pp. 7–51. Barcelona: Editorial Teide, 1960.

Scott, James C. *Domination and the Arts of Resistance: Hidden Transcripts*. New Haven: Yale University Press, 1990.

Segura i Vila, Joan. *Historia d'Igualada*. 2 vols. [1907]. Igualada: Ateneu Igualadí, 1978.

Seler, Eduard. *Collected Works in Mesoamerican Linguistics and Archaeology*. Trans. Charles P. Bowditch, ed. Frank E. Comparato. 5 vols. Culver City, Calif.: Labyrinthos, 1990.

———. *Comentarios al Códice Borgia*. [1904]. 3 vols. Trans. Mariana Frenk. Mexico City: Fondo de Cultura Económica, 1963.

Shergold, N. D. *A History of the Spanish Stage from Medieval Times to the End of the Seventeenth Century*. Oxford: Clarendon Press, 1967.

Sinclair, John L. *New Mexico: The Shining Land*. Albuquerque: University of New Mexico Press, 1980.

Singleton, Charles S., ed. *Canti carnascialeschi del Rinascimento*. Bari: Laterza, 1936.

Smith, Colin, ed. *Poema de mio Cid*. Oxford: Clarendon Press, 1972.

Smith, John Holland. *Constantine the Great*. New York: Scribner's, 1977.

Snyder, James. "Jan Mostaert's West Indies Landscape." In *First Images of America: The Impact of the New World on the Old*. 2 vols. Ed. Fredi Chiappelli, 1: 495–502. Berkeley: University of California Press, 1976.

Soriano Fuertes, Mariano. *Historia de la música española desde la venida de los fenicios hasta el año de 1850*. 2 vols. Madrid: Bernabé Carrafa, 1855.

Southern, Richard. *The Medieval Theatre in the Round*. [1957]. 2nd rev. ed. London: Faber, 1975.

Starr, Frederick. *In Indian Mexico*. Chicago: Forbes, 1908.

———. *Notes upon the Ethnography of Southern Mexico*. Davenport, Iowa: Putnam Memorial Publication Fund, 1902.

———. "Popular Celebrations in Mexico." *Journal of American Folklore* 9 (1896): 161–169.

Sten, María. *Ponte a bailar, tú que reinas: Antropología de la danza prehispánica*. Mexico City: Joaquín Mortiz, 1990.

———. *Vida y muerte del teatro náhuatl*. Mexico City: SepSetentas, 1974.

Stern, Charlotte. *The Medieval Theater in Castile*. Binghamton, N.Y.: Medieval & Renaissance Texts and Studies, 1996.

Strong, Roy. *Art and Power: Renaissance Festivals, 1450–1650*. Berkeley: University of California Press, 1984.

Sturtevant, William C. "First Visual Images of Native America." In *First Images of America: The Impact of the New World on the Old*. 2 vols. Ed. Fredi Chiappelli, 1: 417–454. Berkeley: University of California Press, 1976.

Suárez de Peralta, Juan. *La conjuración de Martín Cortés*. Ed. Agustino Yáñez. 2nd ed. Mexico City: Universidad Nacional Autónoma de México, 1994.

Surtz, Ronald E. *The Birth of a Theater: Dramatic Convention in the Spanish Theater from Juan del Encina to Lope de Vega.* Madrid: Castalia, 1979.

————. "Spain: Catalan and Castilian Drama." In *The Theatre of Medieval Europe,* ed. Eckehard Simon, pp. 189–206. Cambridge: Cambridge University Press, 1991.

————. "A Spanish Play (1519) on the Imperial Election of Charles V." In *Formes teatrals de la tradició medieval,* ed. Francesc Massip. Barcelona: Institut del Teatre, 1996.

Sweet, Jill D. *Dances of the Tewa Pueblo Indians.* Santa Fe, N.Mex.: School of American Research Press, 1985.

Teixidor y Barceló, José. *Discurso sobre la historia universal de la música.* Vol. 2. MS [1804] reportedly in possession of the author's heirs.

Thomas, Hugh. *Conquest: Montezuma, Cortés, and the Fall of Old Mexico.* London: Hutchinson, 1993.

Thomson, Guy P. C. "The Ceremonial and Political Roles of Village Bands, 1846–1974." In *Rituals of Rule, Rituals of Resistance: Public Celebrations and Popular Culture in Mexico,* ed. William H. Beezley, Cheryl English Martin, and William E. French, pp. 307–342. Wilmington, Del.: SR Books, 1994.

Toor, Frances. "A Glimpse of Oaxaca." *Mexican Folkways* 6 (1926): 5–8.

————. *A Treasury of Mexican Folkways.* New York: Crown, 1947.

Toral Peñarada, Enrique. *Estudios sobre Jaén y el condestable Miguel Lucas de Iranzo.* Jaén: Instituto de Estudios Giennenses, 1987.

Toro, Alfonso. "The Morismas." *Mexican Folkways* 1, no. 2 (1925): 8–10.

Toschi, Paolo. *Le origini del teatro italiano.* Turin: Edizioni Scientifiche Einaudi, 1955.

Torquemada, Juan de. *Monarquía indiana.* 3 vols. Ed. Miguel León-Portilla. Mexico City: Universidad Nacional Autónoma de México, 1976.

Torras i Serra, Marc. *Manresa: Festes i tradicions.* Manresa: Ajuntament de Manresa, 1989.

Tovar, Juan de. *Relación del origen de los indios que habitan esta Nueva España, según sus historias.* [1878]. Reprinted as *Origen de los mexicanos,* ed. Germán Vázquez. Madrid: Historia 16, 1987.

Treviño, Adrian, and Barbara Gilles. "The Dance of Montezuma: Some Remarks on the Origins and History of the Matachines Dance in Northern New Mexico." Manuscript, 1991.

————. "A History of the Matachines Dance." *New Mexico Historical Review* 69 (1994): 105–125.

Trexler, Richard C. "We Think, They Act: Clerical Readings of Missionary Theatre in Sixteenth-Century New Spain." In *Understanding Popular Culture: Europe from the Middle Ages to the Nineteenth Century,* ed. Steven L. Kaplan, pp. 189–227. Berlin: Mouton, 1984.

Turrent, Lourdes. *La conquista musical de México.* Mexico City: Fondo de Cultura Económica, 1993.

Tydeman, William. *The Theatre in the Middle Ages.* Cambridge: Cambridge University Press, 1978.

Uhagón, Francisco R. de, ed. *Relaciones históricas de los siglos XVI y XVII.* Madrid: Sociedad de Bibliófilos Españoles, 1896.

Válor: Festejos de moros y cristianos. Válor: N.p., 1972.

VanEtten, Teresa. *Ways of Indian Magic.* Santa Fe, N.Mex.: Sunstone Press, 1985.

Van de Put, Albert. "Two Drawings of the Fêtes at Binche for Charles V and Philip (II) 1549." *Journal of the Warburg and Courtauld Institutes* 3 (1939): 49–55.

Varey, J. E. "Les spectacles pyrotechniques en Espagne (XVIe–XVIIe siècles)." In Vol. 3 of *Les Fêtes de la Renaissance,* ed. Jean Jacquot, pp. 619–633. 3 vols. Paris: Centre National de la Recherche Scientifique, 1960–1975.

Versényi, Adam. *Theatre in Latin America.* Cambridge: Cambridge University Press, 1993.

Very, Francis George. *The Spanish Corpus Christi Procession: A Literary and Folkloric Study.* Valencia: N.p., 1962.

Villagrá, Gaspar Pérez de. *Historia de la Nueva México, 1610.* Trans. and ed. Miguel Encinias, Alfred Rodríguez, and Joseph P. Sánchez. Albuquerque: University of New Mexico Press, 1992.

Wachtel, Nathan. *The Vision of the Vanquished.* Trans. Ben and Siân Reynolds. New York: Barnes and Noble, 1977.

Walsh, John K. "Performance in the *Poema de mio Cid.*" *Romance Philology* 44 (1990): 1–25.

Warman Gryj, Arturo. *La danza de moros y cristianos.* Mexico City: Secretaría de Educación Pública, 1972.

Weiditz, Christoph. *Das Trachtenbuch des Christoph Weiditz.* Ed. Theodor Hampe. Berlin: Walter de Gruyter, 1927. Reprinted as *Authentic Everyday Dress of the Renaissance,* New York: Dover, 1994.

Weigle, Marta, and Peter White. *The Lore of New Mexico.* Albuquerque: University of New Mexico Press, 1988.

Wellens, Robert. "Un compte relatif aux fêtes de Binche et de Mariemont en 1549." *Bulletin de la Commission Royale d'Histoire* 124 (1959): 275–297.

West, Delno C. "Medieval Ideas of Apocalyptic Mission and the Early Franciscans in Mexico." *The Americas* 45 (1989): 293–313.

White, Leslie A. "The Impersonation of the Saints among the Pueblos." *Papers of the Michigan Academy of Arts and Sciences* 27 (1942): 559–564.

———. *The Pueblo of Santa Ana, New Mexico.* Memoirs of the American Anthropological Association 60. [1942]. Reprint. New York: Kraus, 1969.

———. *The Pueblo of Santo Domingo, New Mexico.* Memoirs of the American Anthropological Association 43. Menasha, Wisc.: American Anthropological Association, 1935.

Williams, Jerry M. "El teatro de evangelización en México durante el siglo XVI: Reseña histórico-literaria." Ph.D. diss., Yale University, 1980.

———. *El teatro del México colonial: Epoca misionera.* New York: Peter Lang, 1992.

Williams, Stephen. *Diocletian and the Roman Recovery.* London: B. T. Batsford, 1985.

Wright, John, trans. *The Play of Antichrist.* Toronto: Pontifical Institute of Mediaeval Studies, 1967.

Young, Karl. *The Drama of the Medieval Church.* 2 vols. Oxford: Clarendon Press, 1933.

Zaragoza, Edward C. *St. James in the Streets: The Religious Processions of Loíza Aldea, Puerto Rico.* Lanham, Md.: Scarecrow Press, 1995.

Zúñiga, Ignacio. *Rápido ojeada al estado de Sonora, dirigida y dedicada al supremo gobierno de la nación.* Mexico City: Juan Ojeda, 1835.

INDEX

audience, 4, 8–9, 13, 34–35, 38–39, 55,
58, 69, 72–73, 77, 83, 94–95, 99, 106,
113, 117, 126–127, 130, 132, 147, 164,
181–182, 192–193, 202, 217–218, 222,
228, 230, 233, 242, 246–248
Austria, Anne of, 178, 227, 231
Austria, John of, 3, 6, 8, 12–14, 148, 209–
210, 212
authorship, 145–146
auto-da-fé, 217
Avila, Alonso de (father), 124
Avila, Alonso de (son), 148
Axayacatl (ruler of the Mexica), 69–71,
107–108
Azcapotzalco, 86

Bagnon, Jehan, 251n2
Bakhtin, Mikhail, 76
Balaguer, siege of, 40–42, 191
ball game, Mexica, 176, 178, 231
Bances y Candamo, Francisco, 233
baptism, 14, 39, 58, 126, 134, 144–146,
161–162, 165, 225–226, 237
Barber, Richard, and Juliet Barker, 60
barbones (bearded ones), 5, 9, 12–14
Barcelona (Catalonia), 31, 32, 43–50, 61,
63, 94, 174, 179, 191, 193–195, 197,
217–218, 223
Barriga Dulce (Sugar Belly), 164
Bartholomew, Saint, 49
Battle of the Wild Men and the Blacks, 128–
131, 136, 138, 150
Baudot, Georges, 137, 145
Baumann, Roland, 137–138, 209
beards, false, 5, 9, 44–45, 56, 166, 168, 199,
271n24, 271n28
Beccadelli, Antonio, 47–48
beheading, 4, 7–8, 10–12, 14, 68, 78, 85,
101, 198; of geese, 212
Beheading of Saint John the Baptist, 4, 8–9
Benamaurel (Granada), 39
Benavente, Count of (Antonio Pimentel),
136, 140–141
Berga (Barcelona), 19, 44, 51–53, 191–194
Bergen-op-Zoom (Netherlands), 196
Berlin (Germany), 194
Bernal Díaz. See Díaz del Castillo, Bernal
Bernalillo (New Mexico), 39, 162, 239–241
Bernardo (New Mexico), 162

Besozzi, Cerbonio, 184
Bierhorst, John, 106, 108, 113, 241, 262n5
Binche (Belgium), 179, 182, 198–202, 230
Biringucci, Vannoccio, 191
blacks, 59, 128–131, 136, 151, 153, 162,
178, 231–232. See also Battle of the Wild
Men and the Blacks; negrillos/negritos
Blasting, Ralph, 255n10
Bologna (Italy), 184
Bourke, John G., 155–156
Bracho, Morismas of, 3–17, 18–21, 24, 39,
80, 95, 143, 148, 250
Bragadino, Marcantonio, 68
Brainard, Ingrid, 277n18
Braudel, Fernand, 206
Brazil, 173, 178, 179, 203–205
Broda, Johanna, 74, 78, 98–99
Brooks, Lynn, 228, 232
Brown, Betty Ann, 76–78, 82
Brown, Lorin, 164
Bruges (Belgium), 33
Brussels (Belgium), 173, 198, 218
bullfights/running of bulls, 121, 124, 127,
163, 179, 214, 216
Buñol (Valencia), 37
Bureddan, Muhammed (governor of Te-
touan), 214–215
Burgos (Castile-León), 176, 178, 227, 231
Burkhart, Louise, 94

Cabeza de Vaca, Alvar Nuñez, 121–122
Calcutta (India), 173
calendar, Mexica, 11, 19, 74, 113
Calvete de Estrella, Cristóbal, 184–185,
272n1
Campa, Arthur, 164
Cantares mexicanos, 106–111, 152, 175
Capture of Motecuzoma, 213–215
Carboneras (Almería), 95, 211
Caribbean Islands, 117, 136, 140–141, 174–
175. See also Loíza
carnival, 55, 59, 74, 125, 202, 217, 223–224,
228–229, 231
Caro, Annibal, 230
Carrasco, Davíd, 74, 98, 103
Carrasco Urgoiti, María Soledad, 173
Castellón de la Plana (Valencia), 219
castle/castillo. See scenic units
Castle of Perseverance, 40

Tlacochalca, 68–69
Tlacotepec, 107
Tlajomulco (Jalisco), 154–156
Tlaloc, 4, 128
Tlatelolco, 110
Tlaxcala, city of (Tlaxcala), 39, 123–124,
    132–147, 154, 159–160, 176
Tlaxcalteca 69, 98, 107, 108, 111, 117, 124,
    132, 134, 137–139, 143–145, 159–160,
    161, 213
Tliliuhquitepec, 70
Toci, 76–84, 85, 93, 238
Toledo (Castile-La Mancha), 31, 176, 178,
    179–182, 231, 233
Toluca (México), 107
Toor, Frances, 21, 243
Torquemada, Juan de, 77, 81, 113, 151
Torrer, Joan, 49
Tortosa (Tarragona), 34, 36, 218–220
Totonacs, 174–175
Totoquiuaztli (ruler of the Tepaneca), 110
tototecti, 99. See also xipeme
Tournai (Belgium), 68, 198
tournament, 19, 31, 35, 38, 41, 56, 60–62,
    68, 71–72, 217. See also juego de cañas;
    mêlée
Tovar, Juan de, 112
Toxcatl (Festival of Dryness), 117
transcripts, public and hidden, 21, 23–27,
    62, 67, 75, 78, 89, 98, 103, 108, 114,
    122, 127, 131, 136, 138, 141, 145, 150,
    156, 166, 181, 237, 239, 247, 250
Trent, Council of, 184
Trent (Italy, formerly Germany), 179, 182,
    184–191, 195–197
Trevelez (Granada), 18, 211
Treviño, Adrian, and Barbara Gilles, 106,
    108, 227–228, 234, 241–242, 277n2
Treviso (Italy), 39
Trexler, Richard, 21, 156, 158–159
triumphal arch, 118, 132, 146, 188, 198,
    215, 219
triumphal entry, 32, 47–48, 57, 62, 118,
    179–183, 188, 194, 203–204, 215
Tula (Hidalgo), 85
Tunis, 123, 180. See also al-Hasan
Tupinamba, 173, 204
Turtle Dance, 242

Twelve Peers of France, 3, 5–8, 12, 18,
    251n2

Ulm (Germany), 198
ibn Umaiya, Mahomet, 210
Urban IV (pope), 47
Urgel, Jaume of, 40–41

Valadés, Diego, 176
Valdellop (Barcelona), 46, 50
Valencia, city of (Valencia), 31, 34, 37, 41,
    49, 60, 195, 219–220
Valeriano, Antonio, 119
Valladolid (Castile-León), 61, 174, 176, 184
Valois, Elizabeth of, 176, 231
Válor (Granada), 211
VanEtten, Teresa, 239
Varengeville (France), 174
Vélez de la Gomera, 219
vices, 40, 147
viejos. See abuelos/viejos
Vienna (Austria), 123, 194
Vilafranca del Penedès (Barcelona), 44, 195
Villagrá, Gaspar Pérez de, 161–163
Villena (Alicante), 221–226
Virgin Mary, 4, 20, 39, 42, 43, 54–55, 134,
    154, 198, 233; Our Lady of the Assump-
    tion, 132–133, 178, 231; Our Lady of
    the Pillar, 37, 217; Our Lady of the Vir-
    tues, 222–226; Virgen de la Preladita, 4,
    6; Virgen of Guadalupe, 119–121; Vir-
    gin of the Snows, 211
virtues, 40, 48–49
Viseu (Portugal), 173
Visitador (Zacatecas), 10
voladores. See danza de los voladores
Volterra, Piero da, 229, 231

Wachtel, Nathan, 26
Walsh, John, 34–35
Warman, Arturo, 118, 215, 220
weapons in mock battles: alcancía, 77, 143,
    148; arquebus, 3, 5–9, 12–14, 18, 108,
    126, 150, 158, 163–164, 187, 190, 194,
    201–202, 206–207, 210, 220–226; ar-
    tillery, 6, 108, 141, 163, 179, 181, 183,
    184–186, 198, 200–202, 207, 213, 217,
    219; ax, 5, 9, 14; ball, 100, 143; bladder,